Outcome-Driven Business Architecture

Outcome-Driven Business Architecture

Synergizing Strategies and Intelligence with Architecture

Amit Tiwary and Bhuvan Unhelkar

CRC Press
Taylor & Francis Group
Boca Raton London New York

CRC Press is an imprint of the
Taylor & Francis Group, an **informa** business

AN AUERBACH BOOK

CRC Press
Taylor & Francis Group
6000 Broken Sound Parkway NW, Suite 300
Boca Raton, FL 33487-2742

International Standard Book Number-13: 978-1-4987-2429-6 (Hardback)

Renu, Aneesh, Ayesha, Ayush and Ayansh (AT)

Asha, Pratima, Nivedita and Chinar (BU)

Contents

SECTION B PRACTICE AND TOOLS

SECTION C   CASE STUDIES

List of Figures

List of Tables

Acknowledgments

Abbass Ghanbary	Colleen Berish	Monica Lenko
Abhay Saxena	Faizan Ali	Nikhil Tandon
Ajey Tiwary	Girish Nair	Poonam Mehra
Akash Trivedi	Haydar Jawad	Phil Mizzi
Alka Trivedi	James Curran	Ram Govindu
Alpana Tiwari	Javed Matin	S.D. Pradhan
Amar Trivedi	Joe Askren	San Murugesan
Andy Lyman	Jyoti Bhatacharjee	Sanjeev Sharma
Ankit Pandey	Keith Sherringham	Steve Blais
Anurag Agarwal	Kelvin Mcbride	Sunita Lodwig
Archana Shukla	Krishna Patil	Thomas Santos
Arun Gupta	Larry Bobbitt	Tushar Hazra
Asim Chauhan	M.N. Sharif	Vivek Eshwarappa
Aurilla Aurelie Arntzen	Masa K. Maeda	Walied Askarzai
Bhargav Bhatt	Milind Barve	Warren Adkins
Ciaran Loughlin	Mohammed Maharmeh	Yi-Chen Lan

Family:

(AT) Thanks to my, grandparents and parents who installed in me the desire to look for simple solutions to any complex problems. Thanks to my family for their support in editing, reviewing, and formulating ideas and constant good wishes: Renu (wife), Ayesha (daughter), Ayush (son-in-law) and Aneesh (son), and our grandson Ayansh.

(BU) Thanks to my family for their support and good wishes: Asha (wife), Sonki (daughter), Keshav (son), and Chinar (sister-in-law), and our dog Benji.

The following figures in this book are based on APQC framework:

Figure 1.6: The Business Architecture Map
Figure 3.1: Further details of the Business Architecture Map

Foreword

Repeat customer satisfaction surveys tells businesses and organizations of all sizes and types that the best experience a customer has is when the interaction with the business is seamless. There are few things more frustrating to customers than needing detailed knowledge of internal business operations and moving across silos or business areas in order to achieve their objectives. Within many organizations, and especially in project management, working across the disparate siloes can be a challenge. A collective governance, a common approach to management, a shared vocabulary, integrated end-to-end processes, and assurance of hand-off across operations are all sought by customers and those within organizations (from executive management, to service team managers, to project managers) alike.

Buildings are architected to conform with building codes and standards to ensure safety, fitness of purpose, and suitability for use of the building. A common understanding of how buildings are constructed, managed, and operated is also achieved through building architecture. The globally recognized Object Management Group have applied the same approach to business operations and have identified the need for frameworks, standards, and codes within businesses for effective governance structures, business processes, and business information sharing. Like a building code, a Business Architecture (BA) enables a common understanding of an organization and can also be used in aligning strategic objectives with tactical demands.

BA is a common set of standards, governance, frameworks, and processes (best practice) for the design, operation, and management of a business (of any size and type of organization) and its products and services. The need for BA arises because all businesses have common processes and operations within and between businesses with a need to share and align these interactions to lower costs, improve services, and to better the offerings to customers. Like the use of building architecture to manage risk with buildings, BA is used for the management of risk within business, e.g., operational risk in financial services.

Just as an architecture for an 80-story building in a major global city applies and is different to that of a small farm shed, similarly, BA is not a one size fits all arbitrary standard that is fixed in time. BA applies to all businesses (organizations) of differing types, sizes, offerings, and customers—and similar to changes in a building code, BA is pragmatically implemented according to needs of the business that is changing over time. BA is a framework to keep what works within a business and replace that which does not work in an ongoing approach based on changes in markets, legislation, customers, and costs.

Now this is where this book comes in. Taking a pragmatic cross-disciplinary and cross-silo approach to BA, this book explains BA to a diverse audience, shows how to use BA, illustrates practical examples, and outlines benefits from BA.

Consider one area of business, the increased provision of services from the cloud. Transformation of a business around cloud services is a strategic business transformation initiative starting at the board with its strategy and strategic risk management. The business integration of services from the cloud like Audit as a Service, Project Management as a Service, and Testing as a Service are all transforming business operations. The provision of Software as a Service from the cloud transforms ICT operations and changes the vendor dependency risk. The increased use of Analytics as a Service with real-time decision-making and automation of knowledge workers further increases the need for effective information sharing, common processes, and shared governance, i.e. the need for a BA.

For an undergraduate entering the workforce in a few years' time, BA will be a prerequisite. For the post graduate study of business management, the importance of BA is increasing. Whether consulting on strategy, or service improvement, or mergers and acquisitions, or ICT, knowledge of an organization's BA will be necessary for the future management consultant. BA will become a requisite of project handover and ICT Enterprise Architecture (EA) is set to become part of the overall organizational BA. This book will provide the necessary background and understanding for any reader striving to align their activities in an organization with its desired outcomes by developing and utilizing an "outcome-driven" BA.

Keith Sherringham
FACS, Australia

Preface

A business' competitive advantage is driven by how effectively it utilizes its limited resources and capabilities to result in excellence and value to its customers—as compared with the competitors. Strategies, outcomes, architectures, actions, and projects make up the repertoire for an organization to direct its efforts in generating value.

Simply put, if there is no close link between a project and the corresponding desired outcome, the business is likely to fall into a trap of commencing major yet meaningless projects. Accordingly, projects need to be closely aligned to the business strategy, and any difference between the two is minimized.

While this is a simple thing to write, the actual process of managing organizational resources is a perpetual challenge for executive management. The effective use of organizational resources requires an understanding of how the business is organized, how they initiate projects, and the purpose of these projects. While the literature is replete with case studies of project failures, what is even more interesting is when even successfully executed projects fail to deliver value to business. This is so because a project's successful output does not always equal to achievement of desired business outcomes.

BA is the glue that binds the organization's projects with the business's desired outcomes. A well-constructed and well-maintained BA changes the dynamics of projects in a business. For example, it can highlight if a project is not likely to provide business value even if successfully executed and, therefore, question its continuation. Reducing or eliminating such projects not only results in significant savings for businesses, but can also render it lean and agile—the key requirements of almost all business organizations of today.

A lean organization works on a minimum number of well-directed and executed projects that help it achieve its business outcomes. Due to its lean processes, the organization is also able to update its business strategies to correspond to the changing business environment. As a result, the direction of a business is influenced as certain outcomes are brought to light by the BA that may have been overlooked or not fully considered by the direction-setters. A good BA thus provides the organization with the ability to change directions quickly and with minimal risks—another way of describing Business Agility.

Architectural frameworks can be utilized to undertake an enterprise-wide assessment of business capabilities and their alignment with business strategies. This requires assessment of the gaps between the current and the desired state of these business capabilities. These capability frameworks are developed through consultation at all levels of the organization, resulting in a consensus at both at a divisional and enterprise level on which gaps need to be prioritized.

This book is in direct response to the need to discuss in detail BA as a basis for aligning efforts with outcomes. While the erstwhile technically intense EA provides an overall view of the myriad technologies and systems supporting an enterprise, the BA focuses on the *value* of those technologies and associated projects to business. This book views BA as complementary to EA—wherein the focus of technological initiatives and inventories is to understand and improve business organization, business direction, and business decision-making.

Business and technologies are closely intertwined in most modern business processes. This closeness requires further inspection to ensure that the EA is robust and agile—that is, it holds strong in the face of rapid change and, at the same time, enables the business to change, to respond to changing external and internal circumstances. Thus, the mapping of EA to business is considered equally important in the context of the BA–EA nexus.

This book aims to provide a practical, long-term view on BA. Based on our consulting experience and industrial research, we believe the material in this book will be a valuable addition to the repertoire of thought processes around BA and EA. The lead author has direct and practical experience with three large clients within Australia in applying APQC capability framework for undertaking multiple enterprise-wide capability assessments.

This book brings together our thoughts and practical experiences to fruition. We believe this book will be a very good addition to a consultant's repository.

Amit Tiwary
Bhuvan Unhelkar

About This Book

This book is suited to a wide audience of readers in business, government, and academia including:

a. Business Decision-makers/Directors seeking to improve business operations requiring a framework for revised business operations.
b. Project and Program Managers within business and ICT that are managing projects and deliverable into business as usual that can leverage BA.
c. Business Analysts, Business Architects, Enterprise Architects, and Solution Architects tasked with operational design, service assurance, and business transformation.
d. Those developing, establishing, and managing Business Intelligence that seek a greater appreciation of the role BA play in service assurance and service maturity.
e. Higher degree students (including MBA, MSc, and MIT students) who seek opportunities in Business and Enterprise Architecture and Business Intelligence with its related services.
f. Higher researchers (PhDs) in areas of Business Management and Information Technologies, including the role of BA in business transformation and emerging technology markets.
g. Lecturers and Professors responsible for teaching skills related to BA,EA, and Business Intelligence.

This book provides:

■ Value to businesses seeking to realize returns from the adoption of BA in operational design and management including business alignment of EA.

- Ways to achieve tangible outcomes from Capability Mapping (gap analysis) across both BA and EA.
- Understanding on the pragmatic and tactical use of Key Performance Indicators (KPI) within BA and EA for improved operations.
- Assistance in the Strategic Alignment of Collaborative Capabilities within an organization through Business Intelligence and Collaborative Intelligence within service delivery.
- Opportunities for aligning the domains of BA, EA, and Collaborative Intelligence to deliver better information management services.
- A practitioner's view on BA aligning with EAs for better utilization of infrastructure and resources.
- Take away real life and practical examples to serve as models for adoption and integration within business.

This book is well suited for use within Masters Programs at University levels in the business, technology, and joint courses. Each chapter includes an abstract, key points, detailed descriptions, figures and focused literature review of relevant books, articles, and websites. The workshop and discussion topics work best in a moderated environment while the exercises can be completed individually or in groups to consolidate the learnings. This combination of information is ideal for final year students considering a Masters, full time and part time students undertaking a Masters, and those creating and managing courses.

Mapping Book to a 2-Day Workshop

Here is a potential mapping of the book to the workshop
Day 1

Session	Presentation and Discussion Workshop Topic	Relevant Chapters	Comments
8:30–10:00	What is business capabilities	1	Covers the definition of business capabilities in organizational context
10:30–12:00	What is BA	1, 2	Define outcome-driven business architecture and how it is useful in current environment where disruptive technology
1:30–3:00	Business capability frameworks	3	Defines options to adopt a business capability framework
3:30–5:00	Business capability framework alignment with capability dimensions	4	Define the capability dimensions and alignment with IT, financial and people skills dimensions

Day 2

Session	Presentation & Discussion Workshop Topic	Relevant Chapters	Comments
8:30–10:00	Developing BA roadmaps	5	How to adopt BA in an organization—discuss various options and also team discussions
10:30–12:00	Develop architecture practice using maturity models and governance frameworks	6–9	An intensive session developing the BA practices
1:30–3:00	Case study 1	10	Developing strategies for a production company using Chapter 12 as basis
3:30–5:00	Case study 2 and what next in 30, 60, 90 days	11, 12	Dividing in group and going through another case study based on utility/government sector

Key Terms & Acronyms

Terms and Acronyms	Description
Adaptive strategy	Strategy that responds incrementally to change in the external environment
APQC	American Productivity Quality Center
Architecture	Fundamental concepts or properties of a system in its environment embodied in its elements, relationships, and in the principles of its design and evolution. A distinctive collection of relational contracts. The benefits of architecture typically rest in the development of organizational knowledge, flexibility in response and information exchange within or between organizations a primary distinctive capability
Architecture Description (AD)	Work product used to express an architecture
Architecture description language (ADL)	Any form of expression for use in architecture descriptions
Architecture Framework	Conventions, principles, and practices for the description of architectures established within a specific domain of application and/or community of stakeholders

(Continued)

Architecture View	Work product expressing the architecture of a system from the perspective of specific system concerns
Architecture Viewpoint	Work product establishing the conventions for the construction, interpretation, and use of architecture views to frame specific system concerns
BA	Business Architecture
BC	Business Capability
BCM	Business Capability Model
BI	Business Intelligence
BOM	Board of Management
BS	Business Strategy
Business level strategy	The stream of decisions that establishes the competitive position of a particular business or business unit within its chosen market(s)
CEMS	Carbon Emissions Management System
Chaos, chaotic systems	A system of nonlinear differential equations which has the property that its evolution may be very sensitive to small changes in its initial conditions
CI	Collaborative Intelligence
CIA	Confidentiality, Integrity, and Availability
CIO	Chief Information Officer
CMM	Capability Maturity Model
Cognitive map	The set of templates or mental models that individuals use to help them interpret and make sense of the world in which they live
Competitive advantage	The ability of the organization to add more value than another organization in the same market
Competitive environment (stable or unstable)	A competitive environment is stable if firm sacrifice short-term competitive gains in the expectation of large returns from reciprocal behavior by the competitors. It is an unstable competitive market, where firms engage in short-run profit maximization
Contingent strategy	Strategy which is distinctive both to the organization and to its economic environment
Core business	The set of markets in which the firm's distinctive capability is likely to yield competitive advantage
Corporate level strategy	The steam of decisions that establishes the degree of diversification that characterizes a corporation and how that diversity will be managed

(*Continued*)

EA	Enterprise Architecture
EADA	Enterprise Architecture Design Authority
EC	Executive Command
EIM	Enterprise Information Model
EPMO	Enterprise Program Management Office
ERM	Enterprise Risk Management
ESB	Enterprise Service Bus
eTOM	Business Process Framework
GLB	Global Line of Business
GRC	Governance, Risk Management and Compliance
HA	High Availability
ICT	Information and Communication Technologies
ICT	Information and Communication Technology
IM	Information Management
IMS	Information Management System
IMSSD	Information Management Standards and Security
IoT	Internet of Things (also has variations Personal IoT; and Industrial IoT)
IT	Information Technology
ITO	Inputs – Transformation – Outputs
KPIs	Key Performance Indicators
LOB	Lines of Business
Meta model	A model that defines the components of a conceptual model, process, or system
ML	Machine Learning
NFR	Non Functional Requirements
ODBA	Outcome-Driven Business Architecture
PCF	Process classification Framework
PCF	Process Classification Framework
PIR	Post Implementation Review
PMO	Project Management Office

(Continued)

PRM	Performance Reference Model
R&D	Research and Development
RFP	Request for Proposal
SLA	Service Level Agreement
SOA	Service Oriented Architecture
SOX	Sarbane Oxley
SWOT	Strengths, weaknesses, opportunities, threats
TCO	Total Cost of Ownership
TMT	Top Management Team
TOGAF	The Open Group Architecture Framework
TRM	Technology Reference Model
TSV	Total Sustainability Value

Authors

Amit Tiwary has over three decades' experience in developing pragmatic, implementable EA solutions for customer base ranging from manufacturing, utilities, government, and financial sector. Amit recently implemented an EA and BA framework for a large organization which has proven to be an extremely valuable communication device and has been further developed with subsequent EA initiatives. He is currently working with a government organization to establish an EA framework with business-oriented architectural principles and governance processes. Amit has also delivered multiple workshops and lunch time sessions on various management and information technology topics. In the past, he has also been a sessional lecture for postgraduate courses at RMIT, specializing in EA.

- Author *Driving Efficiency in Local Government Using a Collaborative Enterprise Architecture Framework*, IGI Global 2017.
- Co-author, "Transitioning business processes to a collaborative business environment with mobility," A chapter in *Handbook of Research in Mobile Business, Second Edition: Technical, Methodological and Social Perspectives* published in Feb 2009.
- Presented a seminar on "Organisational Culture and Success of Enterprise architecture."
- Unhelkar, B., and Tiwary, A., 2010, *Cutter IT Journal* (Dave Higgins, Guest Editor),
- Tiwary, Amit. "Collaborative intelligence." Alinement Network, 10 May 2010 (http://alinement.net/component/content/article/50?Itemid=34).
- Goel, A., Tiwary, A., and Schmidt, H. (2010). "Green ICT and architectural frameworks". In B. Unhelkar (Ed.), *Handbook of Research on Green ICT: Technical, Methodological and Social Perspectives*, IGI Global, Hershey, PA.
- Goel, A., Tiwary, A., and Schmidt, H. (2010). "Approaches and initiatives to green IT strategy in business". In B. Unhelkar (Ed.), *Handbook of Research on Green ICT: Technical, Methodological and Social Perspectives*, IGI Global, Hershey, PA.
- Usability of metrics collection system on November 1997 at Australian Software Metrics Association's "Better Business Through Metrics" conference in Canberra.
- "Metrics collection and implementation: An integrated and extensible approach" in World Multi-conference on Systemics, Cybernetics and Informatics (SCI 97) at Caracas, Venezuela in July 1997.

Dr Bhuvan Unhelkar (BE, MDBA, MSc, PhD; FACS; PSM-I; CBAP®) has extensive strategic and hands-on professional experience in the Information and Communication Technologies (ICT) industry. He is a professor of IT (lead faculty) at the University of South Florida Sarasota-Manatee (USFSM), and is the founder and Consultant at *MethodScience*. Areas of expertise include:

- Big Data Strategies (*BDFAB* – emphasis on application of Big Data technologies and analytics to generate business value)
- Agile Processes (*CAMS* – practical application of composite Agile to real-life business challenges not limited to software projects)
- Business Analysis and Requirements Modeling (Use Cases, BPMN, BABOK; helping organizations up-skill and apply skills in practice)
- Software Engineering (UML, Object Modeling; includes undertaking large-scale software modeling exercises for solutions development)
- Corporate Agile Development (Up-skilling Teams and applying Agile techniques to real-life Projects in Practice)
- Quality Assurance and Testing (with focus on prevention rather than detection)
- Collaborative Web Services (SOA, Cloud; upgrading EAs based on services including developing Analytics-as-a-Service)
- Mobile Business; Green IT (with the goal of creating and maintaining sustainable business operations)

His industry experience includes banking, finance, insurance, government, and telecommunications where he develops and applies Industry-Specific Process Maps, Business Transformation Approaches, Capability Enhancement and Quality Strategies.

Dr. Unhelkar has authored numerous executive reports, journal articles, and 20 books with internationally reputed publishers, including *Big Data Strategies for Agile Business* (Taylor and Francis/CRC Press, 2017). Recent *Cutter* executive reports (Boston) include *Psychology of Agile* (two parts), *Agile Business Analysis* (two parts), *Collaborative Business & Enterprise Agility, Avoiding Method Friction* and *Agile in Practice-a Composite Approach.* He is also passionate about coaching senior executives, training, re-skilling, and mentoring IT professionals, forming centers of excellence and creating assessment frameworks (SFIA-based) to support corporate change initiatives. Dr. Unhelkar is an engaging presenter delivering keynotes, training seminars and workshops that combine real-life examples based on his experience, with audience participation and Q&A sessions. As a result, these industrial training courses, seminars, and workshops add significant value to the participants and their sponsoring organizations as the training is based on practical experience, a hands-on approach and accompanied by ROI metrics. Consistently ranked high by participants, the seminars and workshops have been delivered globally to business executives and IT professionals notably in Australia, USA, Canada, UK, China, India, Sri Lanka, New Zealand, and Singapore. Dr. Unhelkar is the winner of the Computerworld Object Developer Award (1995), Consensus IT Professional Award (2006), and IT Writer Award (2010). He also chaired the *Business Analysis Specialism Group* of the Australian Computer Society.

Dr. Unhelkar earned his PhD in the area of "object orientation" from the University of Technology, Sydney. His teaching career spans teaching at both undergraduate and masters level wherein he has designed and delivered courses, including *Global Information Systems, Agile Method*

Engineering, Object Oriented Analysis and Design, Business Process Reengineering, New Technology Alignment in Australia, USA, China and India. Many courses have been designed and delivered online for Australian Computer Society's distance education program, the M.S. University of Baroda (India) masters program, and, currently, *Program Design with the UML* and *Mobile App Development* at the University of South Florida Sarasota-Manatee. Earlier, at the Western Sydney University, he supervised seven successful PhD candidates and published research papers and case studies. His current industrial research interests include *Big Data and business value* and *Business Analysis in the context of Agile.* Dr. Unhelkar holds a Certificate-IV in TAA and TAE and is a Certified Business Analysis Professional® (CBAP of the IIBA).

Professional affiliations include:

- Fellow of the Australian Computer Society (elected to this prestigious membership grade in 2002 for distinguished contribution to the field of information and communications technology), Australia
- Life member of the Computer Society of India (CSI), India
- Life member of Baroda Management Association (BMA), India
- Member of Society for Design and Process Science (SDPS), USA
- IEEE Senior Member
- Rotarian (President) at Sarasota Sunrise Club, USA; Past President Rotary Club in St. Ives, Sydney (Paul Harris Fellow; AG), Australia
- Discovery volunteer at NSW Parks and Wildlife, Australia
- Previous TiE Mentor, Australia

CONCEPTS AND ODBA FRAMEWORK

Chapter 1

Business Strategies and Outcome-Driven Business Architecture

KEY POINTS

- Defining Business Capabilities, Business Outcomes, and Business Architecture (BA)
- Understanding Outcome-Driven Business Architecture (ODBA) from a Business perspective
- Establishing ODBA's relationship to Business strategies and Business planning
- Overcoming challenges in developing Business strategies using ODBA
- Aligning Business Strategies, Enterprise Architecture (EA), and BA
- Positioning Business and Technology Stakeholders in ODBA
- Following an iterative and incremental approach to ODBA

This chapter discusses Outcome-Driven Business Architecture (ODBA) and its application to business strategy and operational improvement. The elements comprising ODBA include Business Capabilities, Business Outcomes, and Business Architecture (BA). Aligning capabilities, especially IT with business outcomes, is an important part of this discussion. This chapter explains the elements that make up a BA and the various associated terms. The alignment of Enterprise Architecture (EA) and BA is discussed, keeping business needs in mind.

Introduction

Architectures and Outcomes

Business Architecture (BA) describes the organization from a business viewpoint. BA explicitly provides a common mechanism to understand the organization in order to align strategic objectives with capabilities. An Outcome-Driven Business Architecture (ODBA) extends a BA further to ensure continuous alignment of the organizational capabilities with the dynamically changing business outcomes. Thus, an ODBA is a BA approach with specific focus on alignment and outcomes. This is different from business process reengineering (BPR) [1] where processes are changed in a big way before the organization benefits from the change.

The desired business outcomes, in turn, are inputs to the BA. Desired outcomes enable an understanding of what the organization is looking for. Thus, the outcomes and the architecture influence each other in an iterative and incremental manner. An in-depth and strategic approach to handling business outcomes and aligning them with BA is necessary. A strategic approach provides the basis for patterns in decisions made within the organization and establishes the long-term direction of the organization. Business strategies result in actions, which are eventually carried out through projects. Projects are thus a means to fulfilling the desired outcomes of the business. Executing the projects, however, requires significant resources. Different projects (or initiatives) are continuously vying for organizational resources. Therefore, developing the strategies requires careful attention to the perpetually scarce resources that are required when those strategies are implemented through projects. Clarity of the desired business outcomes provides the mechanism going forward in resource allocation.

ODBA enforces clarity of the desired outcomes. Thus, with ODBA, the leadership of an organization ensures all projects within the organization exist for a purpose. This purpose is to contribute directly to the business outcomes. Projects that do not contribute to the business outcomes are critically evaluated. There is a significant elapsed time between the formulation of a strategy and its eventual realization through projects. Therefore, what is strategic today may not be so tomorrow. As a result, organizations may be investing in projects that, even if successful, don't contribute to the strategic outcomes. ODBA aims to redress this situation by identifying these projects. Once identified, these projects are stopped as they are a waste of scarce resources. A good BA provides the fundamental building block to obtain value from the organization's resources. The ODBA, through its continuous alignment emphasis, goes a step further to ensure the initiatives to enhance organizational capabilities are highly streamlined with the outcomes. In order to achieve that aim, ODBA provides significant impetus to Enterprise Architecture (EA) which encompasses a full understanding of the technologies and systems of the organization. This understanding reduces the friction amongst the various technologies, systems, and applications. ODBA is the basis for a strategic approach to the application of EA in practice. Business strategies direct the organization's long-term plans of key products and services, as well as partnerships and collaborations. This includes analysis of competitors and collaborators, and the social, political, and legal environment in which the organization operates. The mission and vision of the organization are also a part of business strategies. The desired objectives of a business strategy translate to achievable and realistic goals. The organizational level goals are further decomposed into divisional and departmental goals. Strategic plans are implemented through the initiatives at division and department levels.

Organizational strategies are not set in concrete. Often a strategy document requires revision based on various factors such as a dynamically changing market, innovations from within and legislative requirements. Competitors can come up with new products, or governments can change rules and regulations and suddenly, there is a disruption in the market. A business responds to a situation by overcoming or sidestepping it. In either case, there is a regular realignment of its business strategy. Therefore, organizational strategies are best developed in an iterative and incremental manner. Strategies take continuous feedback from the market, staff, and partners in terms of how the environment in which the organization operates is changing. Incorporating that feedback in the strategies is important for the organization to remain competitive.

Strategies, outcomes, architectures, actions, and projects make up the repertoire an organization uses to direct its efforts.

Strategies and Capabilities

Strategies, Actions, and Projects

The business strategy defines program goals and projects. A business strategy comprises a set of decisions that affect the long-term competitive position of the organization. Such strategy heavily depends on the context within a particular market or industry. Consider, for example, the retail grocery industry; the strategy for such an organization includes decisions related to store location, store refurbishment, advertising, promotions, and investments in staff development. The current social, legal, and political climate, and their patterns are inputs in this long-term decision-making. These decisions impact the organization's ability to develop capabilities. The vision and aspirations of the organization are tied to its products and services. Business strategy enables an organization to compete and, even more importantly, ensures its products and services do not end up competing with each other.

The business strategy includes the marketing and sales approach, and provides direction to optimize operational areas. Business strategy outlines how stakeholder value is delivered. Metrics to monitor the strategy execution (e.g., satisfaction, loyalty, and costs) help in its control and continuous alignment with projects. The strategy execution plan keeps the customer, infrastructure, and resources in continuous alignment. Strategies continuously align the capabilities to achieve business outcomes.

The strategy of an organization is created and maintained in a formal manner. Initially, senior executive teams spend time identifying and defining organizational strategies. This ritual is repeated across the organization structure depending upon the size of the organization. There are risks associated with this ritual. For example, individual personalities may come into play in strategy development. Stronger personalities can sway the formulation of strategies. Senior-most decision makers may influence strategies based on popular journal articles. The alternative to this approach follows a more consultative and objective approach to developing organizational strategies. Any approach that is based on visibility, collaboration, discussions, and objective reality of the environment in which the business operates is beneficial in strategy development. For example, Composite Agile Management System (CAMS) [2]-based approach allows cross-functional teams at the business, corporate, and departmental levels to iteratively define and manage these strategies without the defined timeframe. Each strategy outcome is mapped to the business capabilities and the desired business outcomes.

Organizational Strategies: Components

A strategy has three components: a vision defining the organizational aspirations, goals defining outcomes, and an implementation plan to achieve both. Strategies are measured, defined, and visible. The vision and goals provide the basis for outcomes. Outcomes can be defined, measured, and implemented. Organizations define an enterprise vision, but the actions are assigned to the individual divisions and departments. At the department level, strategies cascade down to projects with corresponding implementation plans. Departments develop plans to achieve Key Performance Indicators (KPIs) and related measures of success. An important criterion of success for projects is how closely the project aligns to outcomes.

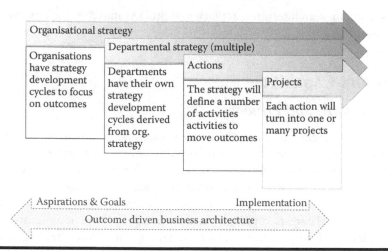

Figure 1.1   Relating organizational and departmental strategy to actions and projects.

Implementation deals with actions needed to achieve goals and a method to manage these actions. Strategic risk associated with the implementation is managed.

Figure 1.1 shows the organizational strategy. The departmental strategies shown in Figure 1.1 are effectively the strategy implementation plan of an organization and the relationship to each other. The multiple departmental implementation strategies are accompanied by actions through projects. While the strategies deal with aspirations and goals of the organization, the actions and projects enable goals implementation. However, success of a project is not a guarantee of the organization's success. The time difference between strategies and corresponding implementation projects causes friction. This is mainly because of the rapidly changing business context. Strategies need to be continuously aligned to the context in order to reduce the friction and for the business to succeed.

Business Capability

A business capability is a combination of skills, tools, processes, and resources. A business capability is a generic term grouping management practices, resourcing, intelligence, and processes that coordinate and allocate tasks. Business capabilities can also be thought of as a collection or container of people, process, and technology addressed for a specific purpose. A business capability brings together multiple dimensions of the organization to enable quality response to the organization's core functions.

The business capability definition varies for different organizations. Following are some key aspects of business capabilities to be considered:

■ Business capability is a combination of multiple attributes. These attributes, or dimensions, are customized based on the organization but the definition of the capability is the same across the organization. Each attribute has multiple perspectives depending on the context.
■ Business capabilities provide an excellent way of understanding the organization's technical priorities. Assessing current performance levels (including gaps, risks, inefficiencies, and opportunities) against required performance provides an understanding of where technical investment is required.

- Capability management is applied by organizations in order to align strategic intents and outcomes with capability-building initiatives.
- Capability management provides a resource allocation to meet various competitive dimension[*] *"such as **speed** to respond quickly, **consistency** to produce a product unfailingly to customers' expectations, **acuity** ability to see the competitive environment clearly, **agility** to adapt simultaneously to many different business environments, and **innovativeness** to generate new ideas and combine existing elements to create new sources of value."*
- Projects enhance or develop new business capabilities. The key requirement is a capability-based governance of organizational resource allocation and an enterprise-wide prioritization of the resource allocation.
- Business capabilities help the organization achieve its objectives in a pragmatic and timely manner. The mindset of the organization changes from a technical, solutions-oriented one to business outcome-driven approach.
- Capabilities help the organization move away from disparate and disjoint recommendations from external stakeholders. Furthermore, independent projects across different divisions and departments are stopped and a big picture approach is instituted to build business capabilities.

One of the most challenging aspects of this exercise is defining the capabilities using the same definition across the whole organization. It can be defined from scratch, but the effort requires a great deal of time commitment and resources. When the organization is just embarking on a journey to change itself, it is prudent to look for options that are easy to implement. It can use existing processes or policy frameworks to define the business capabilities. As process is a dimension of capabilities, and the processes are well understood within the organization, the transition is easier. In some cases, maturity assessment is in place as well, making it a step up to add the capabilities to it.

There are a number of standard frameworks in use. The American Productivity Quality Center (APQC) Capability Model[†] is used by a large number of organizations for process frameworks. The APQC model is a hierarchical and internationally recognized model tailored on industries processes such as utilities, local governments, manufacturing, and financial sector as well as cross-industry frameworks. The proposed framework for understanding and assessing capabilities is based on APQC. The APQC framework is used across the world for standardizing business capabilities. This framework offers APQC-developed business taxonomy and a globally recognized business process model that defines activities and processes across 12 enterprise-level operating and management categories.

The APQC Process Control Framework (PCF©) predominantly defines the process layers but is usable for the capability layer definitions based on the five levels of the APQC PCF framework. Figure 1.2 shows the five levels as business capability categories. The first two levels of business capability definition (which are business category and business process groups) provide goals of immediate interest to the organization. These business capability categories are defined irrespective of the organizational structure. For example, business capabilities that develop vision and strategy are required at organizational, divisional, and departmental levels irrespective of the organizational structure. The next three layers are process, activity, and tasks. Together the five layers are a comprehensive definition of a business capability.

---

[*] Hammer and Champy *Op Cit.*
[†] American Productivity & Quality Centre (APQC).

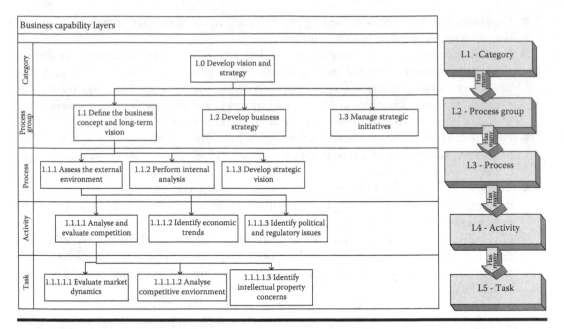

Figure 1.2 Business capability layers.

Each of the business capability categories have many process groups. For example, as shown in Figure 1.2, the "Develop vision and strategy" category has process groups such as "Define the business concept and long-term vision." The process groups are further refined in more detailed processes, activities, and tasks.

This multilayered capability framework provides summarized capabilities definitions for the senior executives, whereas more detailed activity and task-based definitions are for the implementation teams. The APQC capability framework provides numbering of systems for each layer of the definition.

Organizational Strategies: Goals and Outcomes

Goals and outcomes are mentioned earlier in this discussion as part of organizational strategies. Table 1.1 shows an example of a strategic goal and, the actions and projects required to realize that goal. Each goal requires corresponding actions that translate into projects.

Organizational Strategies: Actions and Projects

Actions define the organization's plan to achieve the required business outcome. Actions are carried out as activities of each division or department. Actions are assigned an owner. For example, as shown in Table 1.1 *A concerted effort towards establishing alternative distribution modes (go direct, own shop, on-line)* action is owned by the head of sales and marketing division. Actions are further divided into tasks and sub-tasks. For example, tasks are assigned the distribution modes of *Go direct, own shop, on-line.*

A project is a planned approach to complete an action or task. Projects have a defined scope, resources (e.g., budgets and people) and timeframe. People work within the project roles and have defined skills to complete the action.

Table 1.1 Sample Business Strategy, Action and Projects

Strategy (leading to a desired goal or outcome)	Actions (Figure 1.2)	Projects (Figure 1.2)
Develop profitable future growth platforms Identify and invest in profitable and sustainable new growth platforms aligned to the vision; Seek new business opportunities to reach the stated goals of ROIC (Return on Investment component) and an increase in revenue.	A concerted effort toward establishing alternative distribution models (Go direct, own shop, online).	Implement Go direct project (may be owned by the marketing department) Implement own shop project (infrastructure department) Implement online project (IT).
	Invest in new product trends.	Assess market for new product (marketing department) Create analytics reports for customer's needs (IT).

Iterations and Increments (Agility) in Projects

A new and important approach to project execution is through Agile Framework. Agility in projects is based on rapid iterations, increments, and visibility. Agility at an organizational level implies iterations and increments from strategies and actions through to project implementation [2].

Figure 1.3 shows iterative cycles in an Agile-based project and how they relate to strategies and actions.

Each strategic cycle has a number of actions and projects. Strategy changes result from changes in the external environment. Such changes during project execution cause misalignment of outcomes with projects. The challenges and risks associated with these changes cannot be entirely eliminated. They can be reduced with the help of a good BA and an iterative and incremental approach to projects. The iterations are key to keeping the strategies aligned with the external environment of the organization and the corresponding internal actions.

Positioning BA

ARCHITECTURE

From a systems' viewpoint, architecture is an abstraction of many software and systems in an organization. An architecture provides the basis to handle complexity of the systems. Some of the most well-known architectural categories, methods, and models are: enterprise, data, application, systems, infrastructure, information, business, network, security, model-driven architecture (MDA), and service-oriented architecture (SOA). Corresponding well-known architectural frameworks include Zachman* and The Open Group Architectural Framework (TOGAF).† A brief description of the four well-known frameworks is as follows [3]:

---

* https://www.zachman.com/about-the-zachman-framework.
† http://pubs.opengroup.org/architecture/togaf9-doc/arch/.

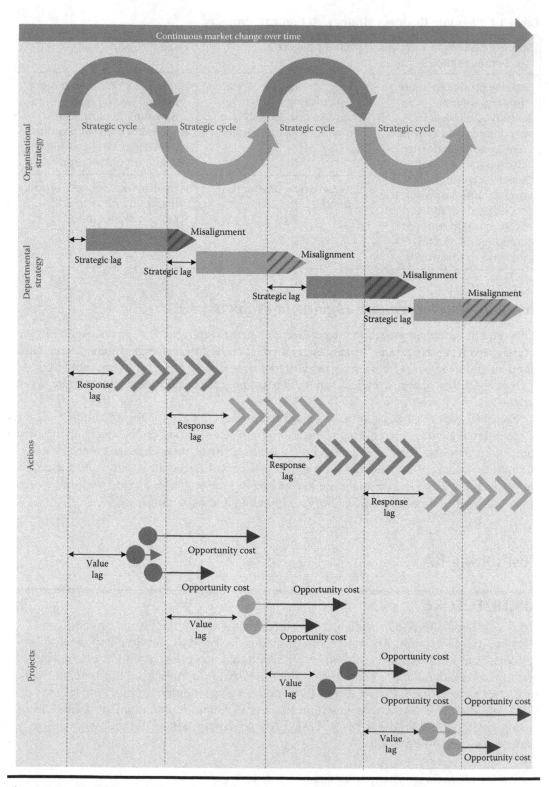

Figure 1.3 Iterative cycles and details of relating strategies to actions and projects.

The Zachman Framework for EAs—Although self-described as a *framework*, it is more accurately defined as a *taxonomy*.

TOGAF—Named a *framework*, is defined more as a *process*.

The Federal EA—Can be viewed as either an *implemented EA* or a *prescriptive methodology* for creating an EA.

The Gartner Methodology—Can be best described as an *enterprise architectural practice*.

These architectural frameworks carry a lot of whole theoretical and practical knowledge.

Architecture also provides a basis for communication amongst stakeholders, analysis of problems, and decision-making.

Business strategies are developed with a presumption that the organization is capable of implementation. The failure rate of strategy implementations paints a different picture. In a dynamic business environment, organizations often refine business strategies in the middle of implementation. This results in a major disconnect between project completion and desired, strategic outcomes. The reasons are a lack of preparedness in strategy implementation and inadequate business capabilities to implement strategies.

BA enables decision makers to make, design, and prioritize choices as well as understand their impact. Associated with these choices are corresponding costs and benefits. A BA supports strategic investment decisions across the organization within its constraints and fiscal realities. A BA Framework enhances management of information technology (IT) and its alignment to organizational strategy. The strategy is flexible enough to respond quickly to changes in the internal and external organizational environment. BA is the foundation to develop and achieve strategic intents. BA identifies core business processes critical to the success of the organization and matures them to a level required to achieve organizational goals.

Architecture provides the basis for stability; a well-designed business is stable and capable of withstanding external and internal changes. A strategy, on the other hand, provides the basis for outcomes and future growth. A strategy provides the blueprint for controlled change for the business. Given the key differences in the way architectures and strategies provide business value, it is vital that both are kept in close alignment.

BA connects strategies with implementation activities. Absence of such an architecture results in a mismatch of effort and, worst case, complete loss of desired outcomes. For example, an organization with merger and acquisition as a strategy for growth but with a major mismatch between desired outcomes and capabilities, results in destroying, rather than increasing, the acquiring organization's value. The merger and acquisition planning are mostly done as a senior executive level activity supported by many legal and strategic functions. The assessment performed by these functions focuses only on the financial aspects of merger and acquisition. As a result, other aspects such as people skills, knowledge management, information management, or application of resources that add value to the organization's bottom-line are missed.

BA as a discipline provides holistic input from all organizational dimensions. These include people, processes, technologies, information, and knowledge management. BA also highlights any duplication of capabilities or gaps. BA provides a framework to understand, develop, and manage business capabilities. Thus, BA is an important input in implementing projects that build business capabilities. For example, when considering organizational consolidation of business units, the BA provides collective input for the business processes, data, and systems capabilities.

Business values are occasionally created by one dimension of business capability that is far more advanced than its competitors. For example, organizations with a highly skilled workforce may compensate for inadequate processes and information management. In case of the aforementioned merger example, BA provides the input to keep the right people skills within the merged organization. In its absence, organizations let go critical people skills or retire efficient systems. BA indicates which people skills and systems to retain and which to let go. BA framework informs organization redesign teams the strength of the workforce so that adequate measures are taken to retain skilled staff.

Following is the value-add resulting from a good BA:

- BA helps manage the entire organization holistically rather than limiting the projects to a division or department silo. Most business operations and corresponding capability improvement initiatives (projects) are launched in siloes. The assumption is that if each silo works the whole will somehow work, which is not true.
- A major contribution of BA is handling shifts in the business environment. The dynamicity of the business environment may not be sufficiently factored in the development of strategies. A BA improves understanding of the organizational structure and the way it operates within the overall business environment.
- BA enables an understanding across multiple siloes in an organization and, as a result, provides cross-functional inputs in projects. BA prevents the inability of a single individual to reach out across the multiple siloes of an organization. This is a typical management and organizational challenge wherein that lynchpin role, usually undertaken by the CEO, is not effective.

Capabilities, Outcomes, and Architectures

The challenges in building business capabilities come from increasing business complexities and changing technologies. With the advent of Big Data, Social and Mobile media, and Cloud computing this challenge is further exacerbated—as these technologies impact existing organizational systems such as Enterprise Resource Planning (ERP), Supply Chain Management (SCM), and Customer Relationship Management (CRM). These systems are closely intertwined with business functions and processes of the organization. Having a framework to guide building and aligning business capabilities with the desired business outcomes becomes imperative. This imperative is the starting point for a BA.

The ODBA provides a focused approach to assess the business capabilities required to achieve the desired strategic outcomes. ODBA also aligns business processes and operations with the IT capabilities of an organization to meet business expectations. ODBA further helps align an organization's desired outcomes with its business functions and its ability to deliver outcomes. Consider, for example, an organization planning to make inroads in the retail business. The organization faces stiff competition from existing retailers. The organization is a major supplier of the goods internationally. The organizational business capabilities are strong in supply chain but missing customer life cycle management capabilities. BA identifies gaps between current business capabilities and the level of business capabilities required to compete for this organization.

Consider some common business functions such as production, marketing, finance, and human resources (HR). These functions are served by corresponding business capabilities. People, processes, technology, and financial resources make up these capabilities. Business initiatives (i.e., projects) develop the business capabilities which, in turn, serve these business functions. These capabilities are understood, documented, refined, modified, and enhanced to support the needs of the business functions, which then equip the organization to achieve its desired outcomes.

Arguments for ODBA

Developing business capabilities is important but only one aspect of business success. To sustain a business, functions and capabilities are carefully and continuously aligned with the desired business outcomes. These desired outcomes are a function of the changing context and environment of the business. This situation is where architecture plays a crucial role. Business processes and operations are architected to function end-to-end, cut across siloes and eliminate duplication.

The alignment of outcomes with processes and functions of the organization requires a holistic examination of all these functions in an organization, their relationship with each other, and contribution to the business outcomes. Traditionally, such examinations focus on the key attributes of an organization: people, processes, and technologies. At times, these assessments are limited to departments and divisions of the organization. As a result, the organizational functions are most likely examined and assessed in isolation. ODBA, however, strives to provide a holistic view of the organization's capabilities and functions in order to continuously align with the outcomes.

Attempting to improve business capabilities without the benefit of a BA results in localized efforts at the departmental or divisonal level. Such localized initiatives focus on the *outputs* from that business area rather than overall business *outcomes*. Outputs are the successful completion of an activity or project. Outputs are not concerned with relevance to business and successful project-based ouputs do not equate to business relevance. Furthermore, outputs can also conflict with each other, or duplicated and therefore, redundant (e.g., duplication of request management systems across different business areas).

A well-thoughtout architecture encompassing the entire business is the way to redress potential conflicts, duplicate activities, escalating costs, and improved customer outcomes. A BA enables the business to synchorize and synergize its projects (initiatives) so they align with the desired business outcomes.

Since the overarching focus of BA in this book is *Outcomes,* this architecture is called *ODBA.* Project completion is not the main goal of ODBA. Instead, ODBA focuses on how well the solutions and initiatives within the organization align with each other. ODBA aspires to bring together various, disparate elements of a business synergestically in order to achieve business outcomes, hence the name *ODBA.*

Outcomes are dictated by the core values of the business. For example, a bank may consider customer service one of its core values. This translates into value-based outcomes. In order to achieve the outcome of excellence in customer service, a bank needs to consider various initiatives (projects) where outputs align with the desired outcomes. The bank aspires to create online portals, secured access to those portals, train and place people behind the online access, and complement online access with physical access to tellers and officers. Customer service excellence is achieved through a combination of multiple initiatives within the bank—each of these initiatives is a unique project.

A typical bank can have hundreds of projects running simultaneously. With ODBA, each of these projects is studied not only for what their outputs produce but also how well each project *aligns* with the desired outcomes. In this example, creating a successful online portal for customers to log-in to the bank is an important element but this access in itself is no guarantee of a great customer service and experience. For example, if staff remains unskilled and untrained in these initiatives, even if the online portal is a success, the desired outcome of providing great customer service and experience is not achieved.

Balancing Act of ODBA

Lack of a holistic, outcome-driven architectural viewpoint is a common cause for failed strategies. This is because without an architecture that is outcome-driven, there is a mismatch between organizational resources and the desired business outcomes. This mismatch results in either conflict between the various elements (e.g., online access and staff skills in the bank example) or an unbalanced growth of the organization. For example, a concentrated effort in redefining and reengineering business processes yields a highly optimized suite of business processes, but the organization may lack in technology investments. Alternatively, the up-skilling of people to support the technologies and processes may get neglected, resulting in an imbalance.

As an example, there can be a wide gap between the skills and motivation of the people and corresponding optimization of processes. The best skills in an organization may not be sufficient to remove the gap of unoptimized processes. On the other hand, highly optimized processes do not work if the people operating within those processes do not have the skills or the motivation to perform their tasks.

The technologies and systems of the organization provide yet another possibility of gaps or shortcomings within the organization. Legacy systems are unable to change to reflect the rapidly changing business situations. Existing ERP and CRM systems can not absorb disruptive technologies (e.g., IoT and Big Data) without upgrades. Similarly, knowledge management and knowledge sharing need strategies to be continously upgraded. The inability to balance resources with desired outcomes results in strategy failures.

Unless the various functions of an organizaton are in balance, they do not easily align with the strategic goals of the business. As an analogy, consider completing only one side of a Rubik's Cube: while that one completed side shows the same color, the other sides remain mismatched and the cube is incomplete. Surveys conducted by various consultancy organizations [4] report that most strategies defined and set by the organizations are not fully realized. A business can be good at setting goals, describing the final outcomes, and even identifying what tasks are required to achieve their established goals; however, the actual goals fulfilled is less than 10% [5].

ODBA is a framework that achieves the necessary balance and proper alignment of the business capabilities of an organization, resulting in efficient and effective business.

Optimization of Resources with ODBA

An architecture is a mechanism to understand, assimilate, and align the various elements of an organization. ODBA enforces a mechanism for effective communication right from the beginning—by using the same language as that used by the business. ODBA (as with most BA efforts) defines the various terms used across the organization. It is common for the same term to mean different things to different people. For example, *customer* has a different meaning to the marketing and sales team than to the billing and support part of the organization. One of the primary roles of the ODBA is to articulate and gain consensus on the use of business terminologies across all business units. This consensus helps improve communications and reduces confusion. ODBA is thus a mechanism to develop, maintain, and assess the business capabilities of an organization, their interrelationships with each other, and impact on business functions and ensuing business outcomes (see Figure 1.4).

An ODBA also helps build an outcome-driven roadmap for the organization. Such a roadmap duly considers all parameters that impact the strategies of the organization. Eventually, the capabilities required to achieve the outcomes in an ODBA provide the foundation for projects.

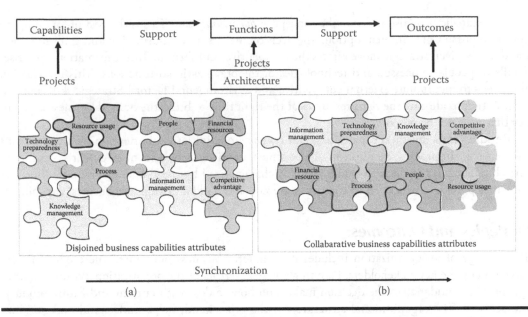

Figure 1.4 ODBA optimizes organizational resources and enables their collaboration. a) Disjointed business capabilities, b) collaborative business capabilities.

Well-aligned outcomes, business functions and capabilities are essential to create and execute successful projects. Thus, ODBA is invaluable in driving efficiency of the overall suite of projects in an organization. This, in turn, reduces costs and improves the quality of projects.

Strategic Planning in Business

The close relationship between ODBA and business strategies is evident in the discussion thus far. Each impacts the other. A strategy is a deliberate plan of action that develops a business's competitive advantage [6]. *Strategic* planning is the iterative process that begins with an assessment of the current state of maturity of an organization's business capabilities.

The basic elements of a strategy are determined by the desired outcomes of the organization and balanced by available technologies and resources. This invariably results in a trade-off between outcomes and resources. Strategy formulation is the balancing act of trade-offs, achieved iteratively. Since business occurs in a dynamically changing ecosystem, the strategic plan needs to be continuously monitored. The plan may need to undergo major changes, or simply need finetuning depending on the changing business context.

Consider the two key desired outcomes of a typical business strategy: reducing costs or increasing sales. Technology-based solutions are used to facilitate these outcomes. However, without an underlying architectural framework, implementing technology solutions may not produce results. This is because, when treated in isolation, technology solutions can cause friction and conflict with other functions, and vice versa. For example, a successful strategy may result from dedicated employees. This may cover up inefficient technology solutions and also inefficient business processes. Isolated technology solutions tend to hide capability gaps in the area of processes. In this example, the gaps become evident only when the dedicated employees are absent.

The strategic plan also includes the concept of *opportunity cost*. This is the cost of forgoing one option in pursuit of a different option. The decision makers need information and skills to understand how a given strategic move affects the competitive equilibrium. This information comprises details of people, processes, and technologies of the organizational functions. This information also needs to incorporate external competitive and environmental factors. Strategic skills use this information to allocate the right resources at the right time to build the desired business capabilities that provide the outcomes.

Building these business capabilities requires sustained initiatives in developing new products and services, improving monitoring of investments and returns, and managing risks. This, in turn, builds agility in decision-making that is characterized by speed and accuracy [7]. Business outcomes provide justification to commit resources, and build and align the business capabilities.

Strategies and Outcomes

The strategy of an organization includes its long-term business outcomes. These outcomes are agreed on by the key stakeholders. Planning and goal setting of the organization, within the strategy, provides guidance to the decision makers on how to deal with current and future products and services. The organizational structure, on the other hand, helps understand and optimize the operating environment. Thus, strategies can provide support and guidance even in the daily operations of a business keeping the futuristic viewpoint in mind. External relationships of an organization help define its products, services, pricing, customer management, and regulatory and compliance requirements. Bringing together these disparate internal and external elements of an organization is accomplished through a strategy. Developing and implementing a strategy involves committing significant resources of the organization. Judicious utilization of these resources requires consideration of the following questions:

- What are the key desired outcomes of the organization?
- How are the key business functions of an organization defined?
- What are the strengths and weaknesses of these key business functions of the organization?
- How well do these key business functions relate to each other (support or resist)?
- What is the competitive advantage of the organization in terms of its products and services?
- What are the existing key business capabilities of the organization?
- How do the organization's key capabilities relate to its desired business outcomes?
- What is the organization's value proposition to customers and to investors?
- What makes it sustainable from within—based on its optimized operations?
- Why might related diversification be better than unrelated diversification?*
- How quickly is the organization able to respond to stimuli (measure of its agility)?
- What products and services can this organization offer effectively and optimally to its users?
- What is an optimal structure of organization to provide the best value for money?
- What products and services overlap with each other, with departments and agencies (conflicts)?

---

* Related diversification can be defined as diversification in same value chain. For example, a food company also buying a retail chain is classified as related diversification. In unrelated diversification could be a shoe manufacturing company buying a phone company. As the industry are not related and there is minimum opportunity to streamline the value chain.

Business Strategy Implementation

Strategy Planning and Risks

A well-defined strategic plan helps an organization achieve its desired goals and outcomes by effective utilization of resources. The components of this strategic plan are its vision (direction) and alignment with available resources. An assessment of the current and required resources provides key input to formulate the strategic plan.

Table 1.2 lists the organizational factors in terms of importance and risk in developing business strategy. The strategic importance of organizational factors is also shown in Table 1.2. For example, products and services offered are the main contributor of revenue and profits. This factor has a risk of excessive inventory and product failures.

The BA highlights the business capabilities gaps in an organization with reference to a product or service being developed. For example, the location between a production facility and customer

Table 1.2 Organizational Factors; Strategic Importance and Business Risks

Organizational Factors	Strategic Importance of Factors	Risks if not considered Strategically	Importance in BAs
Products and services offered	Revenue and profit to organization over time.	Unable to sell to the market resulting in product failure.	Understanding core capabilities to optimize resources. This offers a competitive product to the customers and assists in realization of the business goals.
Customers	Understand customer needs to provide the right product at the right cost and time.	Competitors encroach upon the existing share of market— particularly with electronic outreach.	Managing the design, production and fulfilment of customer requirements holistically—starting with understanding the dynamically changing needs of the customer (using electronic media).
Nature of competition	The price that could be charged to customer, also share of customer base.	Revenue and also cost of doing business (marketing and managing competition).	Provide visibility to the capabilities, gaps, and expected level of maturity to compete in the market.
Resources and availability	Optimal and profitable utilization of resources and skills.	The cost of production or services is high and quality of service deteriorates.	Provide options to utilize the resources optimally by understanding capabilities that are required within organization and other support capabilities that could be outsourced.

impacts the cost of transportation. In case of perishable consumables, the distance between production lines and consumer location impacts the cost and durability of the product.

There are many market differentiators that enable achievement of business outcomes. These outcomes eventually dictate why customers engage with the organization. This engagement is a function of product quality, brand values, and cost. In order to succeed in a particular market-space, organizations need to excel in at least one of three following disciplines (based on Wiersema [8]):

a. Operational excellence
b. Customer intimacy
c. Product leadership

These disciplines are all related to business outcomes, which in turn, are closely related to strategy elements. Out of the three types of business outcomes, organizations focus on the one that provides the most value while remaining aware of the other two outcomes. For example, if the organization goes for product leadership, it still needs to be aware of good customer service and maintain operational excellence. By keeping the focus on one discipline, the organization increases its chances of success.

Operational Excellence and Business Outcomes

Choosing operational excellence as the area to excel requires the company to have a desirable product at the lowest cost in the market. This means that all the costs associated with building and delivering the product, including any re-work through a lapse in any process, are as low as possible. As there is a base cost associated with manufacturing of the product, the cost of additional work and re-work needs to be minimal. This means the operational processes are at maximum efficiency.

The organization also collaborates with partners to reduce costs. For example, a manufacturer keeps inventory at a minimum, requesting suppliers to deliver products in a short turn around time. Thus, the organization can offset the costs of maintaining a huge inventory by collaborating with its suppliers.

The organization chooses the changing market segment based on how it can respond most efficiently and profitably to its customers. The market segment decision is also based on internal resources (people, technology, and processes). BA provides an assessment of the capabilities and resources required to save that market segment. Timely information on products and customers to all departments and channels helps create and serve market segments irrespective of the channel the customer chooses. The call center needs the most up-to-date information on order status for customer inquiries. Sales, marketing, production, and order fulfillment functions need this information in real time for excellence in service. Inventory and delivery information from partners is also required in real time.

Thus, operational excellence implies organizational processes operate with maximum efficiency and minimum cost. Seamlessness, from order placement to fulfillment, is imperative for operational excellence. Similarly all supply chain processes are vital for operational excellence.

Differentiation capabilities or the areas of expertise of the organization also play an important role in operational excellence. BA provides the required insight in the core differentiating capabilities of the organization and uses it to achieve profitable business outcomes. Understanding the differentiating capabilities and utilization requires technologies and systems. Assessment of the capabilities and resource allocation for these technologies is provided by BA. Consider, for example, an organizational differentiating capability called *strategy execution* [9]. Strategy execution highlights the IT capabilities of Amazon and Facebook, and the supply chain capabilities of Walmart and Dell.

Customer Intimacy and Business Outcomes

Customer-centric organizations go beyond merely sales and service and enter the area of customer value. These organizations are keen to see their clients succeed. This shifts the focus from just being a supplier to an organization that is part of the customers' journey. This approach is a win-win situation for both organization and customer. This requires detailed knowledge of customer needs, buying habits, and operating style. This knowledge is easy for small local business owners, who deal with customers face to face. The digital world offers this information from various sources like social media, mobile, and IoT. With this information, relevant products and advice are offered. For example, a bank lets its small business customers have access to aggregated information on the demographics of the customers in its operating local area. Once the hobbies, interests and lifestyle of the local neighborhood are available, the local businesses can tailor products to suit the customer community.

Loyalty cards are another option to know, understand, and shape customer needs. Such a card accumulates points ending in some type of reward. At the same time, the use of the card lets the company know the customer preferences such as buying pattern, timing, and specific items, for example, bulk buying to save money, special dietary products, and a preference to shop on Saturday mornings. The customer and product analytics driven from customer loyalty cards is used in scheduling resources, managing inventory, and providing specialized services in some store locations based on customer demographics. Tesco in United Kingdom and Coles in Australia are some examples of the supermarkets that are reaping benefits from this option [10].

In the context of this discussion, BA is a key enabler of customer intimacy. Personalized knowledge of the customer requires technologies and systems. Assessment of the capabilities and resource allocation for these technologies is provided by BA. For example, many banks are modeling the customer experience "from cradle to grave" as a life cycle. This requires information management and analytical capabilities to understand the products and services required at different stages of a customer's life. Customer analytics is also aligned with sales and marketing capabilities. The customer is proactively engaged in creating options for products and services. The technologies and systems are geared toward sharing real-time information of customer communications to cross-sell or upsell the products. Thus, customer intimacy is an important business outcome.

Product Leadership and Business Outcomes

Organizations differentiate themselves by having a product that is a 'must have' for the customer. The branding of the product entices the customer to buy irrespective of cost. For example, certain shoes and clothes retailers are preferred brands over similar quality and possibly cheaper alternatives.

Kano* defined a product by categorizing its features by perceived customer value. Below are three features of a product that need to be considered carefully in order to achieve product leadership.

---

* Noriaki Kano is an educator, lecturer, writer and consultant in the field of quality management. He is the developer of a customer satisfaction model (now known as the Kano model).

- **Essentials**—product features that customers consider essential for purchasing;
- **Linear**—product features that are linearly valuable, i.e., those where doubling an element of the feature is perceived as being twice as desirable;
- **Delighters**—product features that delight a customer, usually only a small number is necessary.

The opportunity window to create and sell a new and niche product in the digital world is very short. Leaders in product development move fast to make the most of this short window. Such organizations are business agile. They have a succinct business strategy, hire the best people, and promote a culture of excellence and innovation. Decisions are taken quickly with clear and straight forward guidelines. Agile teams are encouraged to try new and unique ideas and come up with pioneering products on a continuous basis.

Figure 1.5 depicts the product and service development life cycle. Figure 1.5 further shows the business capabilities required to achieve outcomes. The competitive advantage enjoyed by

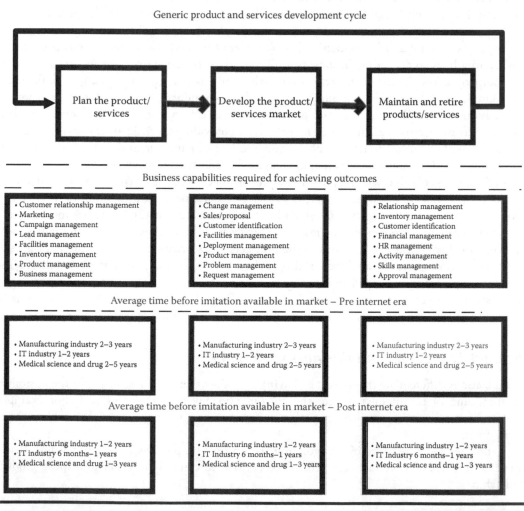

Generic product and services development cycle

| Plan the product/ services | → | Develop the product/ services market | → | Maintain and retire products/services |

Business capabilities required for achieving outcomes

- Customer relationship management
- Marketing
- Campaign management
- Lead management
- Facilities management
- Inventory management
- Product management
- Business management

- Change management
- Sales/proposal
- Customer identification
- Facilities management
- Deployment management
- Product management
- Problem management
- Request management

- Relationship management
- Inventory management
- Customer identification
- Financial management
- HR management
- Activity management
- Skills management
- Approval management

Average time before imitation available in market – Pre internet era

- Manufacturing industry 2–3 years
- IT industry 1–2 years
- Medical science and drug 2–5 years

- Manufacturing industry 2–3 years
- IT industry 1–2 years
- Medical science and drug 2–5 years

- Manufacturing industry 2–3 years
- IT industry 1–2 years
- Medical science and drug 2–5 years

Average time before imitation available in market – Post internet era

- Manufacturing industry 1–2 years
- IT industry 6 months–1 years
- Medical science and drug 1–3 years

- Manufacturing industry 1–2 years
- IT Industry 6 months–1 years
- Medical science and drug 1–3 years

- Manufacturing industry 1–2 years
- IT Industry 6 months–1 years
- Medical science and drug 1–3 years

Figure 1.5   The ever-shrinking cycle of opportunity in product development and corresponding business capabilities.

some organizations before the Internet era has improved dramatically. Innovative ideas provide first movers advantage depending upon the industry. In the case of manufacturing industries, organizations have a 2 to 3-year first mover advantage before their products are imitated in the market. This provides organizations time to benefit from the innovations. This time is now reduced and the innovation advantage lasts a shorter time. In many cases, the imitation also has some additional features that the original design may not have. Figure 1.5 also shows a comparison of pre- and post-Internet era in terms of advantages to organizations in product leadership.

Comparison between the Three Disciplines of Product Leadership, Operational Excellence, and Customer Intimacy

Table 1.3 compares the three types of business outcomes with respect to business characteristics. This comparison is helpful in developing corresponding business strategies. For example, the strategic outcomes for the product leadership is to innovate the product and requires investment in research and development capabilities, whereas operational excellence organizations focus on optimizing the processes. Customer intimacy organizations are required to develop better customer relationship capabilities.

Table 1.3 Characteristics and Comparison between the Three Disciplines of Product Leadership, Operational Excellence, and Customer Intimacy

Characteristics	Product Leadership	Operational Excellence	Customer Intimacy
Vision and strategy	Seek to differentiate by product; leadership characterized by a leading-edge "must-have."	Has the minimum cost of product as compared to the competitors. This cost includes all manufacturing and process slip-up costs.	Defined by not just providing goods or services, but also partnering with clients for success.
Expected customer experience	Brands are well recognized. For example, the car industry has established brands such as Mercedes and BMW that are known for the engineering excellence and other Japanese brands such as Toyota and Honda are known for the operational efficiencies.	The services are excellent and low cost.	Products are long life and maintenance is low.

(Continued)

Table 1.3 (*Continued***) Characteristics and Comparison between the Three Disciplines of Product Leadership, Operational Excellence, and Customer Intimacy**

Characteristics	Product Leadership	Operational Excellence	Customer Intimacy
Culture	Competitive and intense. For example, the organizations such as Walmart and Dell are known its competitive culture developed over a number of years and is not imitable outside these organizations [17].	Very efficient processes with minimal missteps. Processes are very lean and tight. Partners are expected to do the same. Flexible capacity to create new demand during-slack periods.	Detailed knowledge of customer needs and buying habits. A mind shift from supplier to partner is a core component in organizational philosophy.
Structure	Highly fluid and dynamic internal structure, with overlapping, self-organizing teams, and low importance on job titles. They have differing teams competing internally to produce products that surpass existing products.	Departments are based on the processes' maturity. Reporting is quite hierarchical.	Based on customer services model (type of customer categorization or services). Departmental segregation is boundary-less.
Staff	They hire the best people and provide the freedom to innovate—not only for new products but also to enhance these products.	The employees are assigned the roles matching the specific skills demanded by the roles. For example, assigning the knowledgeable and empathic employees to the customer services roles.	Two categories of staff are required: one that quickly interacts with the customers and attend to their requests (customer-centric), the other has expertise on cross-products to help customers select the most suitable product.
Required organisation collaboration	Product designers drive the organizational initiatives.	Supply chain organization is a driving force.	Sales and marketing drives the work.

(Continued)

Table 1.3 (*Continued*) Characteristics and Comparison between the Three Disciplines of Product Leadership, Operational Excellence, and Customer Intimacy

Characteristics	Product Leadership	Operational Excellence	Customer Intimacy
Required data and information	Product information.	Supply chain information.	Consumer information about buying patterns.
Required technology	Product/Asset-centric CRM.	Supply chain-centric CRM.	Customer-centric CRM.
Metrics	Product excellence, product life span, cost to maintain.	Operational excellence, cost to serve, cost to produce.	Brand value and sales volumes.
Example	Companies that fall into this category are Apple (hi-tech hardware), Nike (sportswear), and Sony (electronic devices).	Dell, for example, keeps just two hours' inventory at its factories.	TESCO, Coles.

Identifying the Business Outcomes

Which outcomes are relevant to an organization? How does an organization select one? Identifying and selecting outcomes is part of developing an appropriate business strategy. The current position, desired competitive advantage, and availability of resources dictate the outcomes to a certain extent. Outcomes are broken down into goals for large, multinational organizations. For small to medium organizations, there is not much difference between outcomes and goals. Following are examples of typically desired organization outcomes that become the goals.

- **Growing market share**—Increase the current market share of the organization. This outcome is based on organizational capabilities to increase the volume of current product and services or add new products and services. Optimized manufacturing adds new products quickly and easily. Similarly, optimized services (e.g., postal service adding parcel services), can expand offerings with ease. Optimized processes are the key to growing market share.
- **Providing solutions**—Business capabilities can scale vertically or horizontally resulting in a complete solution provider based on the value stream. Based on a single vendor, this results in a "one stop shop" for a customer—providing convenience to acquire the product or service, an increased comfort level and legal protection. The business also sends signals to the market that it has a strong commitment to provide complete business solutions. Acquiring or merging with another complementary/supplementary business where in-house capabilities are inadequate is part of this strategy. The acquisition or merger makes customers feel more comfortable and confident in engaging with a re-branded organization.
- **Optimizing knowledge resources**—The planned structure (or restructure) as a capability needs to generate growth opportunities for employees with business and functional skill sets

and also provide opportunities to the current staff to upskill and grow into other organizational future employment needs. The understanding of these knowledge capabilities aid in achieving organizational strategy.

■ **Utilizing disruptive innovations**—The organization utilizes IT as an enabler of the business [11]. This may require the organization to innovate in a way that it impacts customers, competitors, investors, and society positively, and starts differentiating the company from others. Knowledge that IT gathers during product development helps in speeding up implementations. This assists in changing the current perception IT having long delays in package implementation. Quick implementation also assists in growth of CRM and ERP sales. This requires business capabilities that provide the advantage of either products, costs, price, or market innovations when entering new markets.

■ **Focusing on business**—The products and services are conceptualized and designed based on the core capabilities of the organization. Strategies keep business as a constant focus; they are dynamic and adaptable as the business context shifts. The business capability-based architecture provides the organization with a better business focus. Capabilities are uplifted to keep pace with the changing needs of customers. The capabilities facilitate changing needs from product design to those suitable for the future needs of customers and providing required solutions customized for customer growth needs.

■ **Ensuring flattened organizational structure**—Current organization structures could be based on processes, products, and services. In order to move quickly in the business market, this requires an organizational structure change from the products and services siloes to the capability providers and service builders. This reduces duplication of skills and optimizes the organizational resources.

■ **Using capability metrics**—Changes from current product-based metrics to capability-based metrics. The performance management system is realigned with business metrics. The marketing and sales focus on total product solutions. Marketing strategies are realigned with the strategic positioning and based on advantage capabilities. Marketing as a capability is transferable within the organization.

■ **Innovation with technology**—Innovation in technology is adopted on the basis of suitability to solutions and customer's requirements that could *reduce* total cost of ownership.

■ **Maintaining a low cost of capital**—Organizations can leverage the infrastructure of multiple development and production centers to extend product development activities. These centers are well resourced with capabilities for software development and training. Low-cost capital required for product development assists in reducing the package solution costs and grow the market adoption of these packages.

Business Strategy Failures

Michael Hammer [12], the father of process management and operational innovation, estimates that only about 10% of enterprises successfully execute their strategy. Dr. David Norton, noted management consultant and father of the Balanced Scorecard methodology, reiterates in "Strategy Execution: A Competency that Creates Competitive Advantage," [13] that 85%–90% of organizations fail to execute on their strategy. Bossidy et al in "Execution: The Discipline of Getting Things Done," [14] state that "execution is the missing link between strategy and results." Jamie Dimon CEO of JPMorgan Chase even commented "I'd rather have a first-rate execution and second-rate strategy any time than a brilliant idea and mediocre management" [15].

Risks of Faulty Strategy: The 'Cardinal Sins'

The gaps in business strategies are its risks that lead to implementation failures. Strategies satisfy organizational goals. Strategy planning includes estimations of resources. Faulty strategy leads to either over/under-estimation of resources and business capabilities. This wrong estimation leads organizations to envision outcomes with inadequate supporting capabilities. For example, in early 2000, large numbers of organizations jumped on the e-business bandwagon without assessing the core capabilities required for the e-business, and failed miserably. Some management experts have compared these strategy risks originating from the equivalent of the biblical seven sins [16].

Table 1.4 describes the failures of business strategy by using the analogy of the cardinal sins. It defines the reasons for the failure. This table also shows how BA can help reduce the risks of failures. A scenario is depicted in the Table 1.4, where organizations plan the expansion or mergers without adequately comparing business infrastructure, culture, and products and services. BA assists organizations in assessing business capabilities or merged organizations on its own and after the merger. This provides information where duplicated business capabilities exist and can be optimized. It also shows capability gaps in other areas. The effective use of BA provides the right level of synergies between the merged organizations and optimizes its resources.

Table 1.4 Flaws "Cardinal Sins" in Strategy Designs and Corresponding Impacts on BA

Cardinal Sin Driving Business Goals	Missing Business Context in the Strategy	Missing BA Context
Lust where the desire is extreme to gain from any dimension of the business without proper justification	In business terms, the main purpose of planned expansions of the organizations is being seen as powerful.	Organizations expand without considering the business capabilities and end up with disparate capabilities across the organization.
Glutonny is where organizations are involved in wasting of resources due to being overzealous or oversupplied with resources.	Businesses are oversubscribing to a particular strategy or plan and ignoring others.	Some capabilities are allocated more resources at the cost of others. A BA framework identifies these excesses and highlights them to the executive teams.
Greed is where an excessive focus is on any dimension due to a justifiable competitive issue.	Business strategy planned with expansion in mind, without considering the synergies that need to exist in the planned expansion strategy.	BA could identify the gaps in business capabilities and could provide how these expansions may increase the gaps resulting in failure of expansion.
Sloth is where the organizations are comfortable with the current growth.	The organizational horizon planning is limited and is not factoring in disruptive forces either in technology or in business environments.	BA can identify the maturity of core capabilities to handle any disruptive forces and could create a plan to prepare the organization with a new set of capabilities that assist in expansion or when the business environment changes.

(Continued)

Table 1.4 (*Continued*) Flaws "Cardinal Sins" in Strategy Designs and Corresponding Impacts on BA

Cardinal Sin Driving Business Goals	Missing Business Context in the Strategy	Missing BA Context
Wrath is where organizations get into competative spirit and start playing Chicken Game (game theory) for dare to death.	The organization might initiate or participate in price or product number war just to meet or do better than competitors. This may overconsume resources.	BA could assist in choosing the right fight based on winnable capabilities.
Envy is where organizations are following new products or services just for the Competition without understanding the market dynamics.	The organization may invest in areas without having adequate business expertise and can fail. Internet boom and burst of early 2000 was because of a number of business entering in the Internet market without having a well-thoughtout strategy.	BA assists in planning and assessing the capability gaps before embarking on new products or services.
Pride is identified as believing that one is essentially better than others.	Many organizations may offer services at a high cost and reduced margin just for the business pride. This might bleed organization and resources not be used optimally.	BA can assist in identifying the capabilities that are receiving extra attention at the cost of other capabilities (overinvestment in some capabilities). This assists in allocating resources optimally.

Mismatched Decision-Making

Agility, as mentioned earlier, is excellence in decision-making. Strategy implementations should enhance business agility. The decision-making process benefits from analytics support, decentralization of organizational structure, and governance. Strategic initiatives need to be subjected to rigorous decision-making processes. Intuition occassionally slips in to override the rationale in strategic decisions.

The rationality of the decision-making process is compromised when intuition and biases influence selection of projects. Over time, this results in a culture of similar decisions. Lack of vigor and governance in decision-making justifies wrong projects.

The common reasons for the mismatch in strategy and decision-making are organizations unable to define and or execute a pragmatic strategy. Strategy-related failures stem from the inability to articulate the strategy by senior management where the understanding of the organizational capabilities is not analyzed or the market disruptors are not understood correctly. An example is the Kodak company that missed out on the digital revolution and lagged behind competitors.

In many cases, the lack of communication to all stakeholders and, perhaps, due to a lack of common language creates confusion among departmental leaders, creating activities to be seen as implementing strategic outcomes. These projects are initiated without understanding the strategic goals, and focus on short-term results which are more tactical and visible rather than strategic outcomes. In many cases, the execution of the strategy is assigned to multiple leaders and there is no accountability of the business outcomes resulting from strategy.

In some cases, strategy development is planned without senior management involvement (i.e., only an external consulting expert develops the strategy). The senior executives or only a handful of executives assist the consulting expert in formulating the strategy. The defined strategy has a limited buy-in from senior management and creates conflicting strategies (organizational versus departmental) that pull resources in different directions or a static strategy stuck in time (i.e., the business context has moved on).

Another reason for failure of strategic outcomes is the lack of progress measurement (KPI are not connected to strategic goals or the strategic goal that can not be quantified). The actions generated from the strategic outcomes are normally assigned to departmental heads for execution. Lack of current capability assessment by these departmental heads results in inaccurate strategy implementation planning. In many cases, lack of understanding of the capabilities of the business results in over or underdeveloping the core capabilities required to achieve the business outcomes with corresponding over or under-spending on IT implementation. Projects end up implementing the business requirements rather than business capabilities required (e.g., developing a business capability for the efficient demand management rather than a specific project to manage the scheduling of resources). The elapsed time between strategy definition and actual project initiation results in project resources not having a good understanding of the strategic intent of that investment. The current state of systems, applications, and infrastructure are not carefully assessed but rather assumed. Hence, there is a heightened risk of that project not delivering the intended outcomes. Lack of enterprise-wide project management contributes to strategic execution failures. This results in assigning actions and projects to multiple departments which adopt a silo approach of developing the same capabilities in different areas, wasting precious resources. The resulting actions and projects conflict with each other and reduce available resources.

The siloed allocation of the strategic actions results in inefficient management of individual projects. Communication of roles and responsibilities may not be correctly communicated to the implementers. The lack of effective leadership and lack of communications leads to widening of gaps. This, if not assisted by positive and dynamic culture, does not support agility, introspection, and results. The disconnect between strategic, operational realities, and management styles results in delayed projects. The organization is unable to justify building capabilities based on cost and benefit of one individual project. The mindset of managers needs to change to one of building the foundational capabilities as a priority and a required base for other forthcoming development. This requires multiple projects that are part of the foundation program of work, to be scheduled. The overall benefits of a project need to be calculated based on whole program of work and not on an individual project, especially as the cost of the first few projects are higher when creating a foundation on which the capabilities can be built. The strategic projects align with business strategies and objectives for the next 3–5 years.

IT as a Capability

IT Utilization

IT is a vital business capability. Business strategies depend on IT and its widespread effects on the organization, often providing opportunities for new products and services. Products are often IT-based and services are IT-enabled. Organizations that provide traditional products and services also rely on IT systems for marketing, sales, customer service, and administrative support. IT is thus integral to implementing a strategy.

Business strategy based on outcomes needs to carefully plan and utilize IT. The IT function is required to produce, or source, appropriate technologies and assist the organization in implementing the changes. However, IT includes rapidly changing and emerging technologies (e.g., Big Data, IoT, Cloud). These changes put pressure on the IT function. Effective utilization of IT depends on understanding its dynamically changing nature. IT specialists need to continuously monitor this changing nature of IT. Furthermore, IT specialists need to incorporate change management and innovation in effective utilization of IT. Change is often difficult for people and organizations. Soft issues add to the mix of challenges. For example, IT specialists are early adopters of technology. They view technology as the solution to business and social problems; it is an engineering worldview that is not shared by other organizational stakeholders. Failure in technology utilization is attributed to making decisions on the basis of technical cost-benefit analyses, often failing to consider the economic, social, and political aspects of the decision. For example, the potential misunderstanding between the technical specialists and business stakeholders arises with the interpretation of the word *implementation*. When business talks about *implementation* it means getting people to use the system to achieve business results (outcomes). IT implementation, is delivery of a system (output).

In addition to these differences in worldview and language, IT specialists do much of their work via project organizational structures. This is because IT specialists are very familiar with projects and project management, whereas other people in the organization may not be. For example, an ERP system implementation project can be led by business. Yet many times an outsider experienced with IT project management is hired.

Project teams are often formed with representatives of various functional areas or divisions. But interviews from companies undertaking reengineering projects show that the represented units often do not feel represented. In one case, the representatives were relabeled 'IT specialists' within days of their joining the reengineering project team [6].

Finally, the risks of failure in utilizing technology increase with project length. One reason is that the longer the project, the greater the likelihood of change in the situation that the project was designed to solve. The problem can go away or change in nature. The organization changes, too. As a result, a delay in delivering project results can mean that the solution is no longer needed. Another reason is that managerial priorities—and, indeed, the managers themselves—can change during a project. Management changes lead to stop and start of projects. Experience suggests that a project that does not appear to complete within a year of its start should be seriously reviewed for viability.

Further to Business Capability Gaps

The strategic outcomes expect a level of business capability maturity. However, many organizations lack an understanding of their business capability maturity. Often, it is assumed that the business capabilities are matured—and that the organization can implement the strategies it is developing. The gap in business capabilities and their corresponding, expected maturity is important to understand how to successfully implement strategic outcomes. For example, Table 1.5 defines the business information management gaps and the desired outcome that impacts the strategies. Strategies fail due to inefficient information management and information technologies. The primary reason for this inefficiency is the wide gap between the desired business outcomes and the capabilities delivered by the project. The BA practice highlights the gaps in capabilities and initiates the actions to achieve the level of business capability maturity required before implementing strategic outcomes.

Table 1.5   Gaps in Business Capabilities and Impact of Strategy Failures

Gaps in Business Capabilities and Desired Outcomes in Business Capabilities	*Description of the Gap*	*Impact on Business Strategies*
Ability to manage information is at a low level.	Information cannot be repeatable and there is no platform to control it. Governance, tools, business processes, and systems have limited capabilities.	Decisions are not following any processes, and their governance is also not defined. This results in poor decisions, and information could be unusable or lacking quality. There are no set of defined rules and each department is creating its own. Makes it difficult to integrate all systems.
Limited capabilities to achieve strategic goals	Projects for improved control and management of the information are not at a matured level organization.	Information management maturity reflects the existing capability of the organization. There must be a commitment from senior management to develop Information Management capability.
Unmanaged and unrepeatable business processes	Unable to be supported by managed information flows.	Technology does not have standards in processes and projects are not delivered efficiently.
Fragmented organizational structures	Ownership of information, processes, and business capabilities not defined.	Management often lacks clear guidance and confusion of roles and direction might end up in duplication or diversion from goals of capabilities.

BA Roadmap Supporting IT Capabilities

A BA roadmap provides the basis to implement business strategies. Such a roadmap provides stakeholders with a common understanding of the activities and steps. A BA changes the perception of IT from that of a service to an enabler of business outcomes. This is a major change from that of IT being a service project with outputs. BA also provides opportunities to promote innovation by revealing otherwise hidden business capabilities within the organization.

BA provides the foundation to use technology as an enabler to build vital business capabilities. This change is difficult for many organizations because investment measure is based on a limited number of parameters (e.g., financial or people). The organizational mindset should focus on building a wide-range of business capabilities that are required for current and future strategies. Traditionally, performance management is carried out in a single dimension. Current profits and other accounting assessments (e.g., asset to profit ratios) form the basis of traditional performance management. This poses a major problem to organizations when disruptive technological or environmental events occurs. The absence of understanding business capabilites and what capabilties are required as a result of new environmental demands leaves organizations vulnerable.

BA also cuts across the capability requirements of multiple business functions. This ensures investments of time, resources, and money are made in a way that best supports the business strategy and maximizes the transformational opportunities for the organization. The BA discovers opportunities across different business units and functional areas to drive efficiencies, reduce costs, and provide a reference point for governance (discussed in Chapter 7).

BA Map

Figure 1.6 shows an example of a BA map based on APQC PCF Framework©. The APQC framework defines the business capabilities based on business activities rather than on organizational structure. These business capabilities are defined at multiple levels, and each capability can have multiple dimensions.

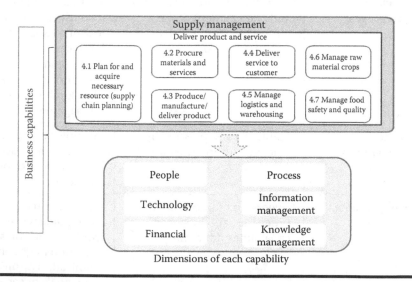

Figure 1.6   BA map (based on the APQC process framework).

Capabilities and Management

Capability Management understands and manages the capabilities of the organization. Organizational capabilities are aligned to strategic outcomes. As a result, a consensus on the desired outcomes and business capability requirements is generated.

The senior executives define the business outcomes and the internal units agree on the roadmap to achieve those outcomes. Capability management produces a commonly acceptable definition of the capability and skills. Standard capability definitions are available from various industry-specialist vendors. They are defined for individual industries or cross-industries; an example is the APQC©.* These definitions are used to define organization specific capabilities. When various capability dimensions are mapped onto the foundation of business, capability management is useful in highlighting the key areas for growth and investment. This creates a guideline for the enterprise-wide governance to build core capabilities.

Capability management also includes capability assessments that safeguard the investments of time, resources, money, and helps maximize transformational opportunities. The assessment indicates collaborative opportunities across business units and functional areas to drive efficiency and optimize costs in current and future business capabilities.

Capability Heat Maps

BA provides a method to develop a capability heat map for the organization that represents the levels and importance of various business capabilities. The heat map relates the capabilities to the desired outcomes. Once the organization accepts the map of capabilities, additional information is overlaid. The most valuable information is the 'gap' (current versus required) in business capabilities required to deliver the strategy.

As the initial maps are supplemented by additional information, the richness of the BA grows. Just as a geographic map includes the physical features of a particular region or country and is more useful when transportation infrastructure, population centers or service station locations are superimposed, the heat map becomes more useful as more information about the organization is layered on top of the base capability map. For example, financial metrics, IT, and organizational risks are presented as layers on top of the underlying map. This capability heat map is the basis for communicating capabilities and their continous alignment.

Annotating Capability Heat Maps

BA defines multiple levels of resources on heat maps. A heat map illustrates resources and the level of attention required for each. Heat maps are based on effectiveness and efficiency scores and the gap between targeted and actual performance. The map can use colors such as red, indicating 'high attention' required, orange, representing medium attention, and green, suggesting that capabilities are 'at par' with desired outcomes. This color-based ranking helps determine the importance of an investment. For example, business advantage capabilities with high heat (red) move to the highest priority, followed by essential business capabilities that optimize scope and streamline operations for efficient resource use.

For example, supply management can have a level 1 capability and some at levels 2 and 3. Each of these capabilities contains dimensions that include people skills, processes, technology,

---

* APQC https://www.apqc.org/about.

information management, financial investment, and knowledge management. The overall BA map is a combination of all the above dimensions based on business rules.

Capability Categorization

A business capability defines the mechanisms and expertise required to produce desired business outcomes. A capability is a combination of people, process, technology, resources (financial, intellectual property, skills), maturity of information, and knowledge management. For example, a capability to deploy a team from point A to point B is determined by what resources are required in the context of deployment.

The capability categorization, shown in Figure 1.7 can be divided into the following major areas:

- **Business advantage capabilities** directly contribute to the customer value proposition and have a high impact on company financials. Value contribution is assured when performance is among the best in peer organizations at an acceptable cost. For example, the business advantage capability for the Dell and Walmart may be managing logistics and warehousing, whereas Apple's business advantage capability is designing innovative and customer-friendly products.
- **Business support capabilities** have high contribution in direct support of advantage capabilities. Value contribution is assured when they are performed above industry parity at competitive cost. IT in many organizations is categorized as business support capabilities. However, in many organizations IT capability is now becoming a business advantage capability as well.
- **Business basic capabilities** may not be visible to the customer but contribute to a company's business focus and have a big impact on the bottom line. They focus on efficiency improvement; especially in high-volume work. Value contribution is assured when they are performed at industry parity performance below competitors' cost. In case of a production industry, supply chain management capabilities can be categorized as business basic capability.
- **Business needs capabilities** are capabilities (e.g., efficent customer management) that provide value contribution when performed at industry parity performance below competitors' cost. These capabilities can be candidates for alternate sourcing. The human resource management and financial planning services are categorized as business need capabilities.

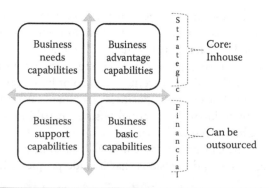

Figure 1.7   Capability categorization.

Making Use of BA in Practice

Effective BA modernizes organizational technologies, systems, culture, behaviour, and partnership. An enterprise that is unable to align its resources to strategy and vision faces hidden risks. Customers do not see nor care about internal organizational structures. Inefficiencies in processes are exposed to the customer, for example, by the number of handovers during a single call to customer service. The concept of a single customer view (SCV) in many organizations is not realized due to lack of systems integration. In most of the organizations, systems are embedded within the departments. However, SCV requires multiple business functions to work together. A well-organized BA ensures organizational structure is based on business capabilities. This results in alignment of organizational structure with customer intent and orchestrates a seamless customer experience. The desired outcomes build customer-centric understanding within the enterprise, resulting in cross-departmental incentives instead of siloed investments.

BA roadmaps help create, maintain, and deploy correct, complete, consistent, and up-to-date customer information. Analytics based on such integrated data provide insights in decision-making. Strong customer information management strategies optimize customer interactions and deliver consistent customer experiences. Determining which information and insights are needed is an important contribution of BA. BA can assist organizations by using information as a dimension of the capabilities. This assigns business owners with correct information and the needed business capability. A BA determines the needs for different types of customer information and required insight at different stages of the customer life cycle. BA also assists by identifying the most relevant type of analysis, and the frequency of its availability. This also helps secure business ownership of the customer information strategy, data governance, and data stewardship processes.

BA ensures high-quality, accurate, and complete customer data by setting up data ownership, governance, and quality management structures and processes based on business capability. Business capability based on integrated data assists in creating, maintaining, and leveraging complementary single views of the customer for analytical purposes. BA guides the development of the right set of capabilities that utilize customer information and build insights. These insights enable delivery of desired customer experiences, drive cross-selling/upselling, and enable retention.

The culture of the company along with the skills and competencies of the workforce play a crucial part in the eventual success of strategy of the company. A skilled and motivated workforce provides the business with differentiators in product and services. Differences between IT and business focus (solution focus instead of outcome based) could create internal conflict within the organization and could affect the motivation and productivity of workforce.

Discussion Points

1. Describe the differences between Business Capabilities, Business Outcomes, and BA. What value does each provide to business strategy? Provide specific examples.
2. What is an ODBA? What is the relationship of ODBA to Business strategies? How does ODBA benefit organizations?
3. Why is it important to relate strategies to actions and projects?
4. What is the role of iterations and increments in projects?

5. How important is it to accurately identify and select outcomes? What can go wrong if outcomes are not identified correctly? How can an organization make corrections if outcomes are incorrectly identified?
6. Describe how ODBA helps organizations excel in each of the three market differentiator disciplines. Use specific examples.
7. What are the ways in which understanding of Outcomes influence development and implementation of business strategies? Outline scenarios where strategies are developed without the benefit of Outcomes consideration.
8. What is the role of Business and Technology Stakeholders in developing and implementing ODBA?
9. How is of ODBA related to creating, supporting, and promoting Business Planning and Business Strategies?
10. What is the impact of strategy failures? Can ODBA help organizations prevent strategy failures?
11. What are the business strategy failures by gap identification and approaches to avoiding them?
12. What are the challenges of business strategy formulation and using ODBA to handle those challenges?
13. What is the importance of a single-page heat map in directing capability enhancement work? How can such a heat map help an organization save money and time?

References

1. Hammer, M. and Champy, J. (1993). *Reengineering the Corporation: A Manifesto for Business Revolution*, HarperBusiness, New York.
2. Unhelkar, B. (2013). *The Art of Agile Practice: A Composite Approach for Projects and Organizations*, CRC Press, Boca Raton, FL.
3. Sessions, R. (2007). *A Comparison of the Top Four Enterprise-Architecture Methodologies*, Microsoft Press (O'Reilly) Sebastopol CA.
4. Schmitt, B.H. (2007). *Big Think Strategy: How to Leverage Bold Ideas and Leave Small Thinking Behind*, Harvard Business School, Boston, MA.
5. Orr, L.M. and Orr, D.J. (2014). *Eliminating Waste in Business: Run Lean, Boost Profitability*, Apress, New York.
6. Watkins, M.D. Demystifying Strategy: The What, Who, How, and Why, *Harvard Business Online*, September 10, 2007.
7. Bente, S. and Bombosch, U. (2012). *Collaborative Enterprise Architecture: Enriching EA with Lean, Agile, and Enterprise 2.0 practices*, Morgan Kaufmann, Massachusetts.
8. Treacy, M. and Wiersma, F. (1997). *The Discipline of Market Leaders*, Addison-Wesley, Boston, MA.
9. Guillén, M.F. and García-Canal, E. (2012). Execution as Strategy, Harvard Business Review, October 2012.
10. Kaplan, R.S. (2008). Tesco's Approach to Strategy Communication, *Harvard Business Review*, September 02, 2008.
11. Heisterberg, R. and Verma, A. (2014). *Creating Business Agility: How Convergence of Cloud, Social, Mobile, Video, and Big Data Enables Competitive Advantage*, John Wiley & Sons, Hoboken, NJ.
12. Michael, S. (2007). The Upside of Falling Flat, *Harvard Business Review*, April 2007.
13. Naroff, J.L. and Scherer, R. (2014). *Big Picture Economics: How to Navigate the New Global Economy*, John Wiley & Sons, Hoboken, NJ.

14. Bossidy, L., Charan, R. and Buck, C. (2002). *Execution: The Discipline of Getting Things Done*, Crown Business, New York.
15. Martin, R.L. (2010), The Execution Trap, *Harvard Business Review*, July–August 2010.
16. Birkinshaw, J. (2012). The Seven Deadly Sins of Management, *Harvard Business Review*, August 16, 2012.
17. Stewart Louise O'Brien, T.A. (2005). Execution without Excuses, *Harvard Business Review*, March 2005.

Chapter 2

Developing Business Architecture I—Capabilities and Challenges

KEY POINTS

- Examining strategies, actions, and projects in the context of architecture
- Interpreting contemporary Business Architecture (BA) and relating it to Enterprise Architecture (EA)
- Outlining the framework for Outcome-Driven Business architecture (ODBA)
- Recognizing the Value proposition of ODBA in business organizations
- Aligning ODBA with the organizational strategy development cycle
- Identifying the Key Elements of ODBA and their practical use
- Understanding Business Capabilities in further details and relating them to the ODBA
- Introducing the APQC framework and its three phases
- Introducing a case study in developing ODBA

The close relationship between business outcomes and business architectures (BAs) is the premise of Outcome-Driven Business Architecture (ODBA). This chapter discusses the development of such a BA. This chapter also outlines the capabilities needed by an organization to produce such an ODBA. The key elements of ODBA are explained in detail together with the challenges of developing an ODBA. Since there is an overlap between BA and Enterprise Architecture (EA), that comparison is undertaken here.

Introduction

As mentioned in the previous chapter, Outcome-Driven Business Architecture (ODBA) extends the business architecture (BA) to focus on business outcomes. Outcomes are supported by business capabilities. Therefore, an ODBA is an integral part of a business strategy that is based on business capabilities. Figure 2.1 shows elements of a capability-based strategic approach by business. As seen in the figure, the BA is the common glue for the three aspects of the capability-based strategic approach by a business.

Figure 2.1 depicts these three important aspects of such an architecture:

■ Business goals are directly based on the organization's desired outcomes. The strategies and visions set by decision makers guide the formation of outcomes and goals. Organizations aware of their business capabilities define realistic and achievable goals. For example, an organization aiming to develop a global product needs to specify outcomes and produce goals that deal with development and deployment of the product on a global scale. One goal for such an organization is creating a multi-cultural workforce that is capable of producing and selling globally.

■ Business capabilities provide the ability and the intelligence in business decision-making. Business capabilities are put into actions to achieve business outcomes. The business capability framework links strategy and outcomes with actions. Capability assessments are undertaken by organizations at regular intervals to ensure they are current. New opportunities are mapped against existing business capabilities. A roadmap is created to build the missing capabilities in order to achieve the outcomes.

■ Projects are initiatives to implement the business capabilities. The business capabilities prioritization and assessment help in deciding the investment areas within the business strategy. The projects are prioritized based on business capabilities required to achieve business goals and strategies. The key success indicators of these projects are an uplift in capabilities. The BA links projects with the capabilities. BA also helps avoid duplicate actions taken by different departments for the same strategic actions. The project office maintains the list of projects and functionality being developed aligns project activities. The project outputs are directly and continuously related to capabilities being developed. If the project output does not uplift the capability (perhaps due to change in strategic direction) then that project is discontinued.

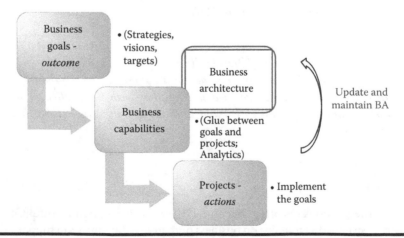

Figure 2.1 ODBA capability-based strategic approach.

Business Capabilities Drive Business Outcomes

Goals, capabilities, and actions work together in the organization's effort to achieve its outcomes. An example of a strategy goal to *develop profitable future growth platforms* is shown in Table 2.1. A number of actions mapped to the business capabilities, also listed in Table 2.1, help achieve this strategy goal. In this example, a combination of the following actions can drive the aforementioned strategy:

■ Understanding the current and alternative market by the sales people
■ Innovative product or service created by the designers
■ Delivery to customer at a price and provides necessary advantage over the competitors by faster and cost-effective delivery

Table 2.1 also shows how these capabilities mature with the help of a maturity indicator. The current organizational assessment shows a gap between the existing and required business capability maturity. This gap is an indicator that the strategic goal may not be achieved in the expected timeframe.

BA: Positioning

BA plays a key role in understanding business capabilities, their maturity, and ongoing alignment with outcomes. The difference between a BA and an EA is the former includes non-technical aspects of business such as people, processes, and financials. Acedemic discussion on where EA is part of BA or vice versa is not the focus of this topic. The organizational maturity may consider the EA and BA either way. A matured BA works in close collaboration with EA by providing a robust

Table 2.1 Example of Business Strategy and Maturity Gaps in Business Capabilities: "Develop Profitable Future Growth Platforms"

Strategy	Required Actions	Business Capabilities Required	Current Maturity	Required Maturity	Gap
Develop profitable future growth platforms Identify and invest in profitable and sustainable new growth platforms aligned to the vision. Seek new business opportunities to reach the stated goals of 14% ROIC, 10% increase in revenue.	A concerted effort toward establishing alternative distribution modes. (Go direct, own shop, online)	Define and manage channel strategy	2.83	4.35	1.53
	Invest in new product trends.	Develop business strategy	3.04	4.09	1.05
		Design product and services	3.45	4.54	1.10

foundation for EA. Traditionally, EA focuses on the information technology (IT) capabilities, but increasingly EA is seen as dealing with enterprise-wide capabilities. Thus, EA can make good use of BA rather than being limited to technologies and systems.

BA is an organizational framework to define business outcomes, investment priorities, and activities required to achieve the strategic goals. BA transcends projects and delves substantially into business outcomes. BA provides a robust starting point to develop and document business processes, capabilities, and relevant information flows. When a BA is outcome driven, it assists the organization in achieving the following goals:

■ Enables the organization to focus on high market value adding activities and capabilities. BA assists the organization in allocating resources to build or acquire capabilities to effectively and efficiently achieve the business outcomes and goals.

■ Ensures that investments of time, resources, and money are made in a way that best supports the organizational strategy. BA assists in understanding the investment needs and priorities and provides pragmatic roadmaps. The organizational strategic intent uses this framework to set the direction. The business capability framework assists in maximizing transformational opportunities while creating the base level capability. This is achieved when an organization has visibility of strengths and weakness across its divisions.

■ Creates standardized architecture and processes to ensure collaboration within the organization and with external partners. The business capability-based architecture provides a common vision for the partners and the organization. The standard processes and framework assist in seamless integration with external and internal service providers. This requires organizations share their business capability framework so partners can align with organizational priorities and assist in achieving required business outcomes and goals.

■ Sources and adopts reference models and artifacts from industry-specialist vendors based on the organizational capabilities demands. This reduces the reactive approach adopted by organizations when external economic or technological forces pose a disruption and necessitate a need for quick uplift or change.

■ Establishes architecture practice partners and develops deep relationships by understanding each other's key capability requirements while utilizing the partner's core competency to achieve its business outcomes.

■ Establishes architecture capability by understanding the organizational requirements and sourcing the best capabilities. This helps organizations adopt new technology faster and pass the competitor.

■ Leverages the business strategic strengths to understand the business outcomes required. The BA provides the roadmap to achieve these outcomes efficiently and effectively.

■ Develops BA progressively and pragmatically in phases. Organizational culture is used to decide on the style in BA development. For example, the first phase outlines the high-level business capabilities framework. The use of high-level framework assists in prioritizing the capabilities that are developed first. The subsequent phases develop more detailed capability maps for prioritized capabilities. The approach depends on the size of organization, culture, workforce skill set, and financial resources available for framework development.

■ Understands and practically documents business drivers and keeps documents up-to-date. As organizational or departmental strategies change, the activities initiated by previous strategies might no longer provide the outcomes the changed organizational direction needs. BA and capability framework provide this input to strategy owners and assists in managing the initiatives based on organizational priorities.

■ Discovers harmonization opportunities that cross-organizational and functional areas to drive efficiency and reduced costs. It also helps to understand the implications of cost optimization efforts on current and future business capabilities.

■ Provides the reference point for governance. The framework maintains the appropriate level of analysis and governance and reduces over analysis by focusing the right resources on required capabilities. This also assists with governance. For example, assessment of projects changes as requirements get modified or when strategies change. Governance helps control the projects.

■ Establishes a metrics regime to monitor and improve business value by anchoring business capabilities framework driving the projects and action governance. As discussed later in Chapter 7, governance, risk assessment, and compliance (GRC) provides enterprise-wide metrics measuring holistic capabilities. These are multidimension measurements such as process efficiency, people skills, technological alignment, efficient information, and knowledge management. The change from using current Key Performance Indicators (KPIs) that measure outcomes of projects to measuring the business capability assessments provides a better indicator of the resource utilization in achieving business outcomes.

BA: Key Elements

BA comprises a number of key elements. Figure 2.2 shows the key elements of an outcome-driven BA. These key elements start with Business Vision, Business Strategy, and Business Prioritization. These key elements are followed by the Business Capabilities dimensions such as people, process,

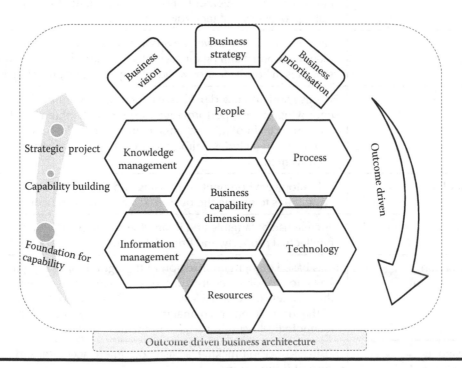

Figure 2.2   Key elements of a BA: outcome focus.

technology, resources, information management (IM), and knowledge management. These elements are defined in the organizational context and based on the outcomes desired (Table 2.2).

BA and EA

BA is a specialized discipline in organizations. At times, the BA of an organization is handled by the EA teams. As far as technologies are concerned, there is a link between EA and BA. The scope of BA is foundational to business as compared to EA, which encompasses both technologies and business. BA matures over the years and requires more business focus skills such as understanding organizational strategy from people, finance, and change management. Business architects with predominant technical skills and limited business experience may not be able to provide the required business value.

Table 2.2   The Outcome Focus of Key Elements of BA

Key Elements of BA	Outcome Focus
Business vision	Business vision is required to accurately define business capabilities. The BA articulates the vision in implementable steps and associates capability building.
Business strategy	Business strategies based on business vision drive the capability assessment and building activities.
Business prioritization	Business prioritization results in allocation and governance of the resources. It defines the skills and outcomes required for the performance management of other components such as people skills, processes, and technology alignments.
People	Providing innovation-driven environment to the organization. Identifying and planning for current and future skills and how to fill skill gaps in both scenarios while managing the change effectively.
Process	Effective and optimized processes; focus is on continually improving process performance through both incremental and innovative technological change management. Process management includes deliberate process optimization/ improvement.
Technology	Technology environment supporting and equipping business capabilities to enable the business to achieve its outcomes.
Resources	Optimal use of tangible and intangible resources like brand, intellectual property, and financial standing.
Information management	IM is based on right information to the right people at right time. The information is secured and only provided in the context of the business activities. BA assists in defining the right owners of the information and managing the currency to avoid the technological issues discussed in the next section.
Knowledge management	Business decision-making is based on timely, accurate, and current information.

BA is the link between the business strategy (outcomes) and the corresponding capabilities and technology assets of the organization. EA is a model of an organization's technical (IT) architecture, systems, contents (databases), interfaces, applications, networks, and solutions. BA is a specific focus on the outcomes desired by the business.

BA results in the *alignment* of the aforementioned enterprise elements with the corresponding business strategies, objectives, and vision. While an EA is across the enterprise, BA takes a business view of the enterprise. BA includes long term and strategic input into the business decision-making process of an organization. BA also bridges any disconnect between a business need and an enterprise architectural constraint.

For example, an organization develops a suite of mobile applications (apps) to provide personalized services to a user. Simply providing these apps to individual users is not enough. There is a need to explore the capabilities of the organization (through its BA and EA) to ascertain the *value* that such apps provide to the end-user. The exploration of business capabilities goes beyond a single application and a single technology. Instead, it explores an array of technologies (highlighted by EA) and their corresponding value to a user or a group of users, through the BA.

Table 2.3 identifies key differences within the EA and BA. This difference is based on management of technology, business, finances, knowledge, information, management, and project governance.

Benefits and Challenges of Business Capability-Based Strategic Implementation

Success with business capabilities requires resources that develop, implement, and socialize the various business capabilities across the organization. The suite of business capabilities is identified and prioritized based on the outcomes desired. This prioritization is a collaborative process with senior executives participating in an Agile format to ascertain which capabilities should be developed first and so on. The challenges and benefits of implementing business capabilities are summarized in Table 2.4.

Impact of Misaligned and Immature Capabilities on Business Outcomes

A business strategy provides the basis for future growth. A business strategy is the blueprint for controlled change whereas the BA provides stability to the organization. Thus, strategies are forward-looking expressing the future state of an organization in time and form the basis of a roadmap to achieve that state. BA, on the other hand, ensures the strategies are not implemented in a haphazard manner. Instead, a BA ensures the changes resulting from strategies are based on robust architectural principles and practices. Given the key differences in the way architectures and strategies provide business value, it is vital to keep both closely aligned with each other. In the absence of such alignment, the following challenges are most likely faced by organizations:

■ Incorrect assumptions about the level of capabilities. Under- or overestimation of existing capabilities makes some future movements prohibitive. For example, an organization that plans to use their online website as a primary contact point for the customer, requires IT systems capable of processing large volumes of data with speed and integration of all systems with their online data collection. In most organizations, integration of new technology with the existing systems is not seamless. This may make the project costs prohibitive.

Table 2.3 BA versus EA

Organizational Factors	EA	BA
Technology management	EA is focused on the use of technology across the enterprise. Dimensions include data, information, communication, and governance of projects. The key drivers for the EA are business technology strategies that utilize technology to achieve the organizational goals.	Based on business capabilities of the organization. Assists in consolidating similar functionality applications. The business foundation provided here helps in directing technology investments and ascertaining risks.
Business management	The architecture is driven from the business requirements. Success of technological projects is measured by their provision of agility and enablement of business strategy.	The architecture is driven by business capabilities and outcome needs. The scope of the BA could be extended to other dimensions such people skills, processes, IMs as a whole (including technology and non-technical IM).
Financial management	EA provides guidance in developing reusable capabilities. This reduces duplication and proliferation of solutions. The scope of EA is sometimes limited to technology under the IT departments and may not be governing the shadow IT activities taken by divisions and departments on their own initiatives.	Projects are developed for building priority business capabilities. The focus is on refining the outcomes and ensuring they are financially achievable.
Knowledge management	Information is used for the functional intelligence reporting and performance management of the organizational activities.	Information is used for capabilities and meeting the strategic needs of the organization.
IM	Information domain definitions may be departmental or functional.	Information domains based on capabilities that can be shared across and inter-organization.
People management	Role and responsibilities are functionality based.	Roles and responsibilities are capability based.
Project governance	Projects are governed individually and prioritized on cost and benefit analysis.	Projects are driven by capability and outcome that is aligned to strategy.

Table 2.4 Benefits and Challenges of Business Capability-Based Strategic Implementation

Benefits	Challenges
Articulate and gain consensus on business capability requirements for each business unit.	The business capability approach requires effort across the organization to agree on the capability definitions. This is a difficult task if departments are unable to come to a consensus, resulting in multiple definitions of the business capabilities. Business capabilities encompass a number of dimensions such as financial, people skills, and technology. In many organizations, maturity measurement framework for all or any of these dimensions is not agreed upon, making it difficult to assess overall business capabilities.
Ensure the enterprise is prepared for growth & profitability.	An initial assessment of the enterprise results in decisions to manage and govern resource allocations. This may be undermined by the executives or departments with their own agenda and interpretation of growth and priorities. The governance model requires senior management enforce governance across the organization and any exceptions or exemptions are based on predefined business rules. The governance model and framework are understood by all decision makers so it is not undermined because of authority level or influence of the person or position within the organization.
Ensure investments of time, resources, and money are made in a way that best support the business strategy.	Understanding of the strategic goals across the organization is difficult. Different interpretations made by various divisions and departments could allocate resources to projects that are not aligned with strategic goals. The decisions also need to be aligned with the business capabilities priorities. This is a major change in organizational processes and requires authority to be given to the governance body.
Maximizing transformational opportunities.	The siloed activities and projects may undermine the transformational opportunities. In some cases, the timing of the various projects demands that tactical or duplicate solutions are put in place. In some cases, multiple strategies are in place and may undermine any transformational opportunities.

(Continued)

Table 2.4 (*Continued*)   Benefits and Challenges of Business Capability-based Strategic Implementation

Benefits	Challenges
Discover harmonization opportunities that cross business units and functional areas to drive efficiency and reduced costs. Understand the implications of cost optimization efforts on current and future business capabilities.	The business units may not cooperate for fear of losing control over the functionality and dividing costs may become a contentious issue. The timing, priorities, and speed of the implementation may be different across functional units and the consensus process may delay the implementation of projects.
Provides the reference point for the governance framework that is socialized and implemented across the organization.	Governance frameworks without an underlying industry-accepted standard can create confusion— especially when multiple organizations merge and bring with them their own governance frameworks.

- Undertaking projects without considering the capabilities required results in developing the same capabilities (such as customer contact point channels) in different ways by different divisions. As a consequence, the organization finds varying ways to engage with the customers, leading to inconsistent customer experiences depending on the chosen channel.
- Activities to enable strategies are missing. For example, if there is no governance on how the program work is completed, the subprojects, due to their short-term nature, puts employees' long-term happiness, safety, and growth at risk. This makes employees less effective in the long run.
- Not knowing the gaps in the capabilities that are the foundation for the strategic implementation or success of the strategy.

Controlled Change with ODBA

Organizations need to constantly adjust direction and priorities based on market dynamics to sustain competitive advantage and market share. This requires constant redesign and adjustment of strategies. In turn, the BA is also constantly aligning to the changing strategies. With increasing outcome focus, the BA identifies the changes to be brought about. The BA also indicates how the changes can be brought about systematically. Developing capabilities to handle the gaps is based on the following six-step process:

1. Define and structure the challenges and business capability gaps that need attention to achieve the business goals.
2. Identify the business capability assessment criteria against which project alternatives are evaluated (in many cases, strategic decisions may include multiple objectives).
3. Determine the weights assigned to each criterion to assess business capabilities.
4. Identify the possible alternative courses of action to uplift the prioritized business capabilities.
5. Evaluate each project alternative against the business capabilities assessment criteria—and assess uncertainties in the projects.
6. Compute the optimal decision and actions required to uplift the desired business capabilities (usually defined in terms of the alternative with the highest expected value).

Developing Business Capabilities: An Iterative Approach

Multiple Levels of Strategies Lead to Chaos

Figure 2.3 depicts a traditional strategy development cycle. Strategies are developed at corporate, departmental, and organizational levels, and refined on a yearly basis. This results in implementing projects with potentially conflicting capabilities. In many cases, projects may be implementing capabilities that were required by discontinued strategies. Figure 2.3 further depicts the situation where a number of strategies at various levels within the organization are in play. These are strategies at the organizational level which cascade down to departments where they take the shape of a business implementation plan. With these multiple levels of strategies and implementation, there is strong potential for confusion and conflict.

An approach to building these business capabilities with more clarity is to develop them in an iterative and incremental manner. The ODBA prevents individual divisions and departments from building their own capabilities. The ODBA provides a basis to build capabilities in an iterative and incremental way while keeping the business outcomes in mind. Outcomes decompose into actions and projects that build capabilities. This building to capabilities is an iterative process that is constantly managed. Figure 2.4 presents an iterative process for developing business capabilities. The following steps are a modification of the six steps mentioned earlier and are required to avoid multiple strategic and orphan activity traps:

1. Define the end state or business outcomes and capabilities required to support the business strategy. For example, if the goals are to *Develop Profitable Future Growth Platforms*, then the expected maturity of the capability of defining channel strategy is documented.

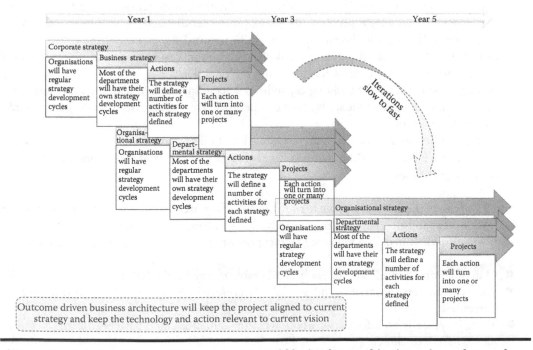

Figure 2.3   At a given time multiple strategies could be in play resulting in projects that are been implemented for old or discontinued strategy. This results in implementing orphan projects.

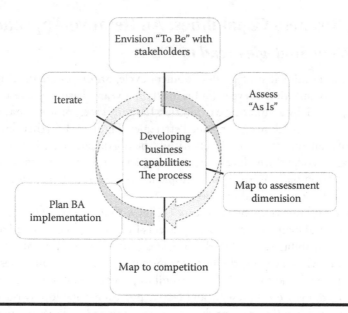

Figure 2.4 Basis of an iterative process of developing business capabilities.

This assessment is based on a predefined framework. This is an iterative process and each iteration refines the measurement of maturity of "to be" state capabilities.

2. Once the end state of capabilities is defined, a quick assessment of current state is completed using the same assessment framework.
3. The gaps identified in business capabilities are classified in dimensions used for the assessment such as technology, people skills, process, or other dimensions used in the framework assessment. The gap dimension directs the initiative and the owners of the initiatives. For example, if the gap identified is people skills, the Human Resources division is the owner of the initiative. The gap owners decide on the plan of action.
4. A pragmatic roadmap for building capabilities is recommended to map the skill gaps of the organization along with the skills of the competitors. This reduces overspending of resources to build capability.
5. The capability owners use an iterative approach to build required capabilities.
6. The process is iterated at the change of the strategies or any external factors that affect the business outcomes.

Figure 2.5 defines the major components for ODBA. This architecture defines the strategies to build business capabilities. Number of gaps in business processes, mismatch between actions and strategy are also identified. The following factors present challenges in developing capabilities:

■ Outcomes are delayed and not easily attributable to any particular action.
■ The environment is variable and so there is noise which makes it hard to interpret the outcomes.
■ There is typically no information about what the outcome could have been if another alternative had been chosen.
■ Most important decisions are unique and provide little opportunity for learning.

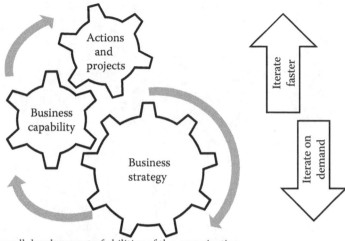

Capabilities are overall development of abilities of the organization. Capabilities for a soccer game does not deal with a specific game; Its an overall development of capabilities.

Figure 2.5   ODBA implementation builds (and is based on) business capability: Resulting in projects and actions.

BA Alignment and Decision-Making

There are two major categories of decision-making—external and internal. Strategic decisions can be external to the organization—such as positioning the business (products and services) in the market. The opportunities and threats of a SWOT analysis are usually facing the external market. Strategic decisions also deal with the internal organization of the business, its capabilities to handle the desired outcomes, and provisioning the supporting technologies and infrastructure. ODBA provides the necessary relationship and binding among all other architectural aspects of an organization. As a result, BA helps in decision-making based on business values and supporting strategies, keeping their advantages and challenges in mind. Following are the advantages of BA alignment:

- Provides a suite of parameters enabling smoother and consistent decision-making that keeps outcomes in mind.
- Enables a long-term approach to setting business directions based on desired outcomes.
- Provides the basis for future products and services that do not conflict with each other.
- Reduces focus on operational and tactical decisions.
- Makes use of static, analytical data, and associated trends.

The alignment of various elements of business capabilities with the strategy is required to achieve excellence in decision-making. Lack of alignment results in a fragmented view of the organization. Figure 2.6 shows a sketch of the proverbial elephant and the story of five blind men. The number of key elements is considered when assessing and developing business capabilities are shown in Figure 2.6. This alignment balances the overspending in some elements and underspending in others.

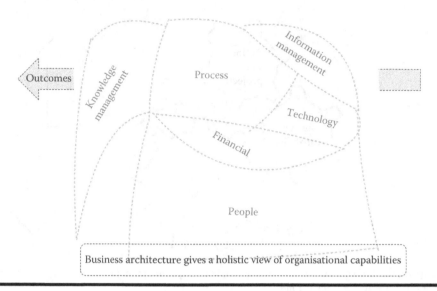

Figure 2.6 Alignment of various elements of a BA (holistic view) crucial for a holistic strategy.

*"The story of the **blind men and an elephant** is popular in explaining the need for a holistic approach to BA. It is a story of a group of blind men (or men in the dark) who touch an elephant to learn what it is like. Each one feels a different part, but only one part, such as the side or the tusk. They then compare notes and learn that they are in complete disagreement"*[*]

The strategy formulation and implementation need to be linked with the business goals and outcomes. The definition and implementation of an effective strategic position utilizes the available internal capabilities. An effective strategic implementation supports the strategic position. A holistic view of the organization, as against the fragmented view, provides the following advantages:

■ Assists in achieving sustainable, superior returns from execution of the strategies. This is based on the assumption the defined strategy is *fit for purpose* of the organizational goals and outcomes required. This should avoid the cardinal sins discussed in Chapter 1 while designing the strategy.
■ Defines the relationship between organizational differences and performance measurements.
■ Defines the policies and practices for a manager to organize and motivate staff to pursue a strategic goal.
■ Optimizes the resources (people, structure, systems, culture) to support a given strategy and ensure the resources are optimized, protected, and developed.
■ Facilitates development and implementation of seamless change strategies to support the business outcomes.

---

[*] https://en.wikipedia.org/wiki/Blind_men_and_an_elephant.

ODBA REDUCES THE NUMBER OF PROJECTS

Consider a medium-to-large size manufacturing organization with a problem of unmanageable IT projects. The PMO is struggling with the sheer volume of initiatives. On initial analysis, this organization had more than 300 projects on the to-do project list. IT Project managers, business analysts, and architects are spending a majority of their time and resources evaluating initiatives. The high number of projects in assessment means they have less time to spend on enhancing the capabilities to help the organization move forward. A new way of thinking is required to prioritize the projects for the benefit of the enterprise as a whole.

Initial assessment of projects highlighted a deficiency in overall governance—there was no thread linking the organizational direction and strategy with the business plans and actions. This absence of linkage and guidance delayed and created confusion in project prioritization. This did not help the total outcome for the organization.

A proposal is put forward to the executives to use the ODBA. The basis of this architecture is to analyze the current standing of the organization and its capabilities and the lag between current and future state of these attributes. The study provides a list of critical skills required to meet the organization's strategic goals. The projects in the list are assessed for the skills and the outcome they bring to the organization. Only those contributing to the required critical success factors were shortlisted and progressed into a to-do list. The result of this assessment reduces the number of projects from 300 to around 20, making it more manageable with IT resources and budgets.

BA and IM

IM enables understanding of the information needed to support business capabilities. IM also deals with how and when the information is used by the organization; who owns the information; where it is stored and the preferred format; defines security classification; and who can access it. An enterprise-wide data platform efficiently controls and manages information. Otherwise, each division within a large organization has its own approach to IM. The end result is overlapping and conflicting data structures and usage. This results in inconsistent investment decision planning and ad hoc technology investments. For example, while the marketing division is focused on collecting and analyzing the Net Promoter Score (NPS) data, the products division is deeply involved with the upcoming regulatory changes. The IM dimension of the business capabilities is used to align the projects and activities with the business outcomes. For example, if the business outcome is to increase customer intimacy, the information collected for the business capabilities provides the gap capabilities. A need for a formal set of structures, policies, procedures, processes, employee roles, and controls (effective GRC) cannot be overemphasized.

Data entry into information systems involves significant overhead when there is repeated data entry or poor controls over data entry, resulting in degraded data quality. As a result, the opportunities to exploit the organization's information for strategic use are not optimized. ODBA assists in ascertaining the value of information based on needs of corresponding business capabilities. ODBA supports constant organizational strategic revision based on the competitive market. The goals and opportunities change based on competitor actions either by realigning their own strategies or responding to their competitor's actions. ODBA works holistically across multiple capabilities and dimensions of the organization.

The IM landscape is changing because large volumes of data are analyzed and shared across organizations, and with partners. The business capabilities using this information to make decisions are restricted by timely access to information as a result of network infrastructure and performance. A lack of storage capacity planning and slow reaction to technology shifts significantly hampers IM abilities of the organization.

With big data and analytics, infrastructure solutions require a careful strategic approach to capitalize on the Cloud-based storage and analytical opportunities [1]. Understanding data risks and the impact of change across the data platforms requires a good architecture in the background. Decisions based on inadequate analysis of data or misinformation are costly to remedy. The ODBA assists in developing the business capabilities to utilize the information available for the strategic outcomes by classifying the information and nominating business owners of information based on business capability owners.

Business processes are supported by IM: data, applications, and tools. However, business processes themselves may not be sufficiently modeled and audited—resulting in inconsistence use. In particular, new and upcoming technology such as mobile-based business processes in the banking sector need rigorous modeling and quality checks. This is a major challenge in rapid decision-making because analytics-based decision-making requires the ability to change the business process pathways to reflect the needs of the customer at different times and places. Lack of standards in business processes adds to this challenge of modeling processes. BA assists with the changes in the business processes. This is done by providing standards for modeling, a common language for communications and a target outcome supported by the process.

Business Intelligence, Collaborative Intelligence, and ODBA

Business Intelligence (BI) is the use of data together with analytics to provide insights for decision-making. Traditional BI is information systems based. ODBA, however, also shifts the focus of BI to outcomes. Thus, instead of simply providing analytical insights for specific problems, ODBA encourages BI analytics to enhance macro-level decision-making. BI extends beyond the organization and into the collaborative space. The impact of one decision at one point in time on many other aspects of the business requires analysis and insights provided by BI. This, in turn, requires BI to consider more wide-ranging business factors in undertaking analytics and providing insights. For example, an ODBA-based BI algorithm for marketing a product considers not only the market situation but also incorporate data from sources, such as weather, political events, traffic conditions, and so on to improve the accuracy and timeliness of that market situation.

Figure 2.7 shows an organization's BI journey based on ODBA. BI is analytics based and uses collective information from within and outside the organization to optimize its business performance, enhance customer service, and provide an overall competitive advantage and sustainability. BI is also understood as the creative use of data and information within the organization in a way that results in new bodies of knowledge that are applied in practice. This BI journey in an organization starts with an understanding of the problem space and continues through to decision-making. The solution space creates and presents analytical results. These results, seen within the context of a problem, result in improved and agile decision-making. Agility in decision-making is understood as increase in accuracy and reduction in time to make decisions [2].

BI, implemented in a holistic manner, also provides the insights in organizational capabilities and bridges the gap between the vision of the organization and its execution strategies. The progress of Agile decision-making is the transition from an output focus to an outcome focus. Output

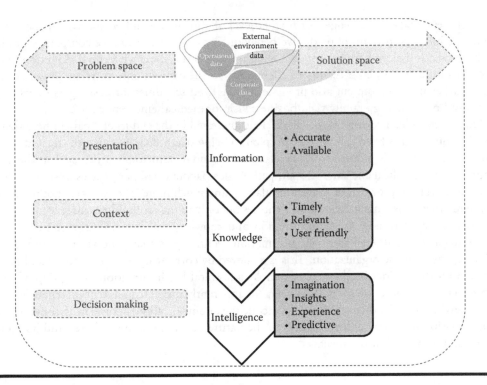

Figure 2.7   An organizational BI journey based on BA.

is achieved with significant efficiency; however, it may not have the necessary effect on what the business wants. The outcome is related to effectiveness—which, in turn, relates to decision-making in an agile manner. This is the value of BI to business. BA makes it possible for BI to focus on outcomes rather than inputs.

Increasing sophistication of communication technologies extends the concept of BI in a collaborative manner to a group of organizations, by sharing and reusing data, information, processes, and knowledge. As a result, businesses collaborate with each other along multiple axes. These include vertical business functions (e.g., sales and marketing) and horizontally across technological platforms.

This concept is referred to as collaborative intelligence (CI) [3,4]. In CI, multiple organizations share their BI for a win-win outcome without compromising their own market position. Developing and formalizing the CI capabilities provide collaborating organizations with the necessary capabilities to develop market differentiators—particularly an enhanced customer experience. CI ensures the organizational intelligence that is not part of organizational differentiation capabilities is shared with other organizations and reduces duplicating capabilities for each collaborating organization. There are incremental complexities and levels of collaboration—from data to information, process, knowledge, and finally intelligence.

Knowledge and Intelligence

Knowledge, which comes from correlating information, provides insights to the users who can then apply that understanding in making decisions.

Intelligence takes knowledge to a further level of abstraction and, at the same time, provides actionable insights in terms of predictive behavior. For example, insurance companies can correlate hospital admissions with patient demographics and bring about a potential reduction in insurance costs for a certain cross-section of clients. An airline can not only correlate passenger traffic with weather information, but also produce personalized schedules for passengers depending on their travel purpose (e.g., family visit, business visit, or medical emergency).

Finally, consider a patient in a hospital. He is interested in the end-to-end patient flow that handles his requirements from entering the hospital to being diagnosed, investigated, treated, and discharged. Such a holistic process requires collaboration among numerous entities, such as the hospital administration, medical and surgical staff, pathological laboratories, pharmacies, insurance companies, transportation providers (e.g., the ambulance), and much more. The patient is not interested in the interconnections among these various entities but only in the result. These three scenarios depict creative and dynamic uses of data, information, and knowledge taken from varied sources.

Intelligence is gathered through information technologies that generate new and dynamic knowledge within the organization. This is achieved by correlating seemingly unrelated pieces of information that resides in silos. For example, a hospital has information on a group of patients who suffer from a particular type of cancer. An apparently unrelated piece of information hidden away elsewhere may be their residential postcode (i.e., home location). Correlating these two kinds of information may provide an insight into the nature of that geographical area and its potential relationship to the cause of cancer.

Organizational Levers and BA

The organization exists to maximize the returns to its owners or shareholders. In simple terms, as depicted in Figure 2.8, business growth options are to reduce the operational cost and thus increase the profit margin or have a larger share of market by increasing the revenue. The organizational growth has a number of levers to achieve the main business outcome—that of maximizing the returns on investments.

Increase Revenue

As depicted in Figure 2.8, the increase in revenue requires the products or services of the organization demand high prices as they are the leaders in the industry and desired by the customers. This is achieved by higher product quality or increasing product sales. The better quality and branded products demand higher prices than other similar products in the market and thus makes more profit for the organization. Business capabilities of customer management, understanding demand, and providing trusted and quality products come into play here.

The increase in the sales volume requires optimized supply chain capabilities. The demand management capability of the organization is able to predict the right demand and provides the product and services to consumers at a price acceptable. The market leaders, up to a limit, are able to increase the price of products and services and if acceptable to market, consumers still buy the products.

Improved Product Branding

This requires organization processes, IM, and analytic knowledge management that are dynamic and adoptable. The BA assesses and maintains these capabilities so they are compatible to strategic

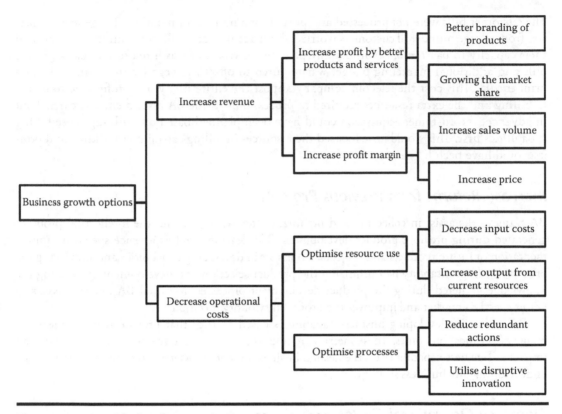

Figure 2.8 Considering the organizational levers within BA.

demands. The focus ensures the advantage capabilities are in sales and marketing and provides a roadmap to utilize these capabilities. The BA assists in dynamic customer assessments. This assists organizations in achieving business outcomes by meeting customer needs and developing capabilities required to remain competitive.

Expanding Markets and Increasing Sales

The development and marketing of the products is based on the organization core competencies. BA assists in developing 'marketing' as a capability by identifying and articulating the strengths of the business in marketing campaigns. The BA develops transferable capabilities within the organization irrespective of the type of products that are marketed.

A well-developed BA helps develop capabilities that assist in growing market shares. This focuses the resource allocation in the areas where there are gaps in capabilities required for the market growth or making better use of advantage capabilities. For example, if the market growth is based on increasing the customer base, then the core capabilities of holistic customer management should be assessed. Gaps in capabilities need to be fixed before acquiring new customers.

For example, a telecommunication company wanting to enter a new market in another country has to address some shortcomings in its billing capabilities. They market the customer services first while fixing the billing capabilities in parallel. This approach is based on assumptions that billing capabilities are available by the time of the first billing cycle. The customer growth is more than expected and this, in turn, multiplies the billing woes of the organizations.

The customer bills were not processed and posted for a number of months. This generated queries from a large number of customers worried about accumulated bills for a number of years and their capacity to pay the bills without any penalties. Extra staff was hired to manually process bills and additional marketing budget was required to offset the negative image in social and print media. This cost the telecom company almost the entire first year's profits due to delays in billing and the extra resources required to process bills. If the BA assessment was carried out in advance, the customer acquisition could have been planned based on building these billing capabilities first. This would have focused the resources in billing capabilities building and profits would have been higher.

Increase Returns from Previous Projects

BA frameworks assist in collecting and organizing the experience and the intellectual property generated during previous product development. This learning and experience speeds up implementation of future products and projects. BA assists in developing capabilities and improving the processes and profitability by optimizing the product selection and development cycle using the knowledge gathered during the product development processes. Matured BA practice assists in better speed to market and improves the profitability of organizations.

BA assists in developing business capabilities-based metrics that provide realistic measurements of business outcomes. These metrics are important to measure the existence, maturity, and impact of business capabilities on the desired business outcomes. Metrics are thus an integral part of developing any business strategy.

Decrease Operational Costs

Organizational outcomes of growth are also achieved by decreasing the operations costs. Operational excellence was discussed previously. For example, Walmart [5] provides cost-effective products at a lower price than competitors. The operational costs are reduced by providing complete solutions and better resource utilization.

Decrease Input Costs

BA assists in developing capabilities that assist the organization in becoming a complete solution provider based on the value stream. This results in compatible capabilities with other service providers and also assists in selecting the right service providers for the strategic alignments. Proactively assessing and developing the business capabilities results in market efficiency and decreased input costs.

Optimize Resource Utilization

BA assists in highlighting the current resources capabilities including the skills available within the workforce. This assists in planning and utilizing the right resources in changing circumstances when exploring new markets or developing new products and services. In times of economic downturn, one manufacturing company realized the capability of its workforce in designing new products. The organization decided to expand into new products and started the process of new sites development. The workforce was given the choice of transferring into new products and new sites. This reduced the organizational retrenchment budget and was instead used in training and developing new products. Once the market picked up, the organization had a better market share in new products. The capabilities assessment and alignment with business strategies provides opportunities with these resources. The BA assists organizations in planning for right resources in growth and recession cycles. The organization, without understanding the key resources required for the business capabilities acquire or retrench the wrong resources. In a growth cycle, wrong decisions may be overlooked, but in a recession cycle this affects the operations of the organization. BA used effectively provides the capabilities and skills required for both growth and recession times.

Reduce Redundant Actions

BA identifies the core capabilities required in a "go to market" approach. The assessment of the capabilities identifies the timing and products that can be developed to provide a market advantage to the company. BA is also used to identify other supporting products that could be offered by the organization and the next wave of innovative products. In most of the cases, BA framework provides a realistic assessment of organizational capabilities and resources and how it can make the best use of these resources.

BA is used to assess organizational capabilities in the current market and future designed products. BA assists in identifying core capabilities that are required for the business strategic goals and assists in developing these capabilities. BA also assists in identifying and acquiring support capabilities to optimize costs.

Utilizing Disruptive Innovations

The BA assists in achieving market differentiation by assessing and creating a deep understanding of the organizational capabilities. In a time of disruptive innovations, organizations who understand their strength capabilities can develop plans to adopt these innovations. For example, when the Internet became another channel for customer interactions, organizations with streamlined supply chains were successful in growing their business. BA assists in developing innovation capabilities in such a way that it facilitates customers, competitors, investors, and society positively, and starts differentiating the company from others.

Refining Organizational Structure

The organizational structure over time develops inefficiencies and duplication. BA can assist organizations in structure redesign based on the business capability-based skills set. This is different from the previous process re-engineering approach that most of the organizations went through in 1990s. The capability-based organization structure provides a platform to insource or outsource skills depending on the outcomes.

Achieving Better Technology Utilization

BA provides capabilities mapped with the processes and applications. The BA provides organizations with optimization of the IT resources. Furthermore, BA also changes the project mindset to that of a capability-building mindset. BA also enables improved anticipation of new and disruptive technologies and, thereby, prepares the organization to incorporate those technologies within its existing systems and processes.

Establishing ODBA

ODBA offers an enterprise-wide approach to achieve business outcomes. ODBA starts by assessing current organizational resource allocation and their gaps. This assessment is useful in creating initiatives to fill in capabilities gaps to ensure successful business outcomes.

The ODBA helps continuously align the resources to fit in with the operational and strategic goals. This provides organizations the ability to redistribute its resources in areas that are important to achieve its goals. A successful ODBA program is a business capabilities-based approach for the organizational resource allocations.

For most businesses, the demand for IT service exceeds the supply capacity. Complicating this demand is information as an enterprise resource and is shared across business units. The management of information, unfortunately, evolves in many cases through individual department business initiatives which work in siloes. The challenge is to find a way to normalize the demand across the customer base to ensure that the enterprise is deriving the most value from its IM capabilities.

ODBA helps in enterprise-wide assessment of business capabilities and effective alignment with business strategies. ODBA uses a variety of techniques including surveys, interviews, and workshops to measure capability gaps across the business (including People, Process, Technology and Information issues, risks, and requirements). This build is a consensus at both divisional and enterprise level in terms of prioritization of capability gaps that need to be addressed most urgently.

The ODBA implementation in any organization as depicted in Figure 2.9 requires capabilities development in one or more dimensions. The ODBA implementation is triggered by the business-defined goals and visions. The business capabilities dimensions such as process, technology, and people skills need to work in coordination as depicted in Figure 2.9 to achieve target goals. As

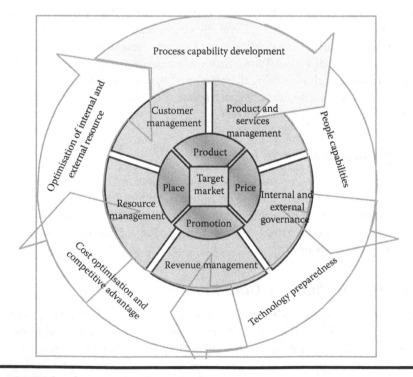

Figure 2.9 ODBA implementation framework.

depicted in the Figure 2.9, to achieve the vision of "Target Market" entry, understanding products required, customer base, product pricing, and how it is branded need to be established. The definition of the products and price defines the business capabilities such as customer management, resources management required. The BA framework provides the assessment, gaps, and initiatives required for the dimensions of the business capabilities such as process, people skills, technology, and financial resources as depicted in Figure 2.9

A BA roadmap is established and executed to achieve required business capabilities—which in turn helps achieve desired business outcomes. BA results in a program of work and/or as center of excellence (discussed in Chapter 8). Establishing ODBA is divided into three distinct phases:

- Establish BA based on outcomes
- Assessment of Business Capabilities to support the business strategy
- Roadmap to build capabilities to support the business strategy

Positioning Business Capability Frameworks within ODBA

The business capability framework development starts with a common taxonomy of the organizational capabilities. For example, basic terms like "Customer" mean different things to different departments. In case of sales and marketing, Customer is the person who pays for the product and services. In case of maintenance or order fulfillment, the customer depends on the use of the product and service. This creates difficulty in getting one capability definition across the organization. Organizations can develop in-house or adopt an industry standard capabilities definition. A hybrid approach is also possible where industry standards are adopted as per organizational needs. The hybrid option may need constant maintenance to keep up changes to industry standards.

Extending and Applying American Productivity Quality Center Framework

The American Productivity Quality Center (APQC) framework organizes operating and management processes into 12 enterprise-level categories, including process groups and over 1,000 processes and associated activities. Architecture and Planning group defines application portfolio for logical and contextual grouping of the application and business activities.

Each process element is referred to by two numbers: a number used to locate the content within that particular framework (in the format 1.2.3.4)* and a number used to uniquely identify the process element across the various Open Standards Benchmarking frameworks (beginning with 10000).

The Process Classification Framework (PCF) is organized as follows:

- Category: The highest level within the PCF is indicated by whole numbers (e.g., 8.0 and 9.0) (http://bmc-eu.com/rokdownloads/Framework/12_pharmaceutical.pdf).
- Process Group: Items with one decimal numbering (e.g., 8.1 and 9.1) are considered a process group.

---

* http://bmc-eu.com/rokdownloads/Framework/12_pharmaceutical.pdf.

- Process: Items with two decimal numberings (e.g., 8.1.1 and 9.1.2) are considered processes.
- Activity: Items with three decimal numbering (e.g., 8.3.1.1 and 9.1.1.1) are considered activities within a process.

The ODBA informs organizations of the state of their current and targeted business capabilities. The current state of business capabilities articulates their role in achieving current business outcomes. An understanding of the current state of business capabilities enables the business to calculate its probablity of achieving those outcomes. An understanding of the target state of business capabilities indicates an idea of the investments required to achieve capabilities target state.

The ODBA framework presents the results of the business capabilities assessment on a single page [6]. Such a summarized picture provides valuable information on where the business should invest in terms of uplifing the capabilities. Figure 2.10 is an example of a business capability heat map. Such a heat map is used to layer information for each important capability of the business. It is important for the heat map to be based on risks and issues, capability maturity index, overlays of applications, and duplication of actions. Figure 2.10 depicts the following:

- A capability gap assessment is portrayed in a heat map. This heat map is a visualization of the capabilities of the business that require attention and that will require an initiative.
- A heat index is calculated using effectiveness and efficiency scores and the gap between targeted and actual performance. The heat indexes are visually differentiated through colors mostly using traffic light colors where red and orange defines that the business capabilities need attention and are not sufficiently matured to achieve the business outcomes. whereas green means the organizational capabilities are matured enough to achieve the required business outcomes.
- Capability value contribution helps stack and rank investments, for example, advantage capabilities with high heat move to the top of the agenda, followed by business essential capabilities with large inefficiencies.

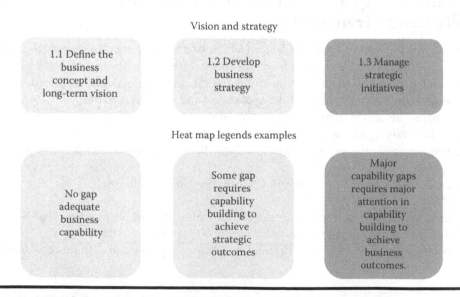

Figure 2.10 Sample heat map of capabilities (depicted in color in practice).

Case Study Outline

This section describes a case study for developing business capabilities in the context of ODBA. This section further describes the methodological approach and deliverables that are used in achieving results discussed in the case study. The business capability assessment project is divided into three distinct phases.

- Phase I establishes Business Architecture Framework, where the capability map is built and socialized with all the departmental heads and their direct reports for the consensus on capability definitions and attributes.
- Phase II maps business capabilities to support the current strategy and assesses them for desired ratings to identify the gaps. In the meantime, the executive team works on a refined strategy.
- Phase III, realigns the capabilities with the new strategies (as capability data is still considered valid and correct). This realignment provides a roadmap required to implement the organization's new strategy and any current capability gaps.

A significant amount of the reusable capability and intellectual property is created during the *establishment* phase of the project. The subsequent phases leveraged (and iterated upon) this framework. However, the use and value of "Business Architecture Framework" extended way beyond its initial use in Phases II and III of the project.

Phase I: Establish BA Framework

A BA framework establishes a 'Capability Reference' model that defines the business capabilities. The APQC© Capability Model, was already in use by the EA team. This hierarchical model is an internationally recognized design tailored to manufacturing-type organizations. Therefore, this APQC© model is adopted as the Business Capabilities Reference model.

At this stage, a process is developed to assess capabilities. This process determines the initial capabilities required to deliver the strategy. Those capabilities are identified by mapping the strategic initiatives of the Corporate Strategy to APQC capabilities at 'Level II' of the capability map. It develops a questionnaire that evaluates those capabilities only. The questionnaire consists of three pieces of information.

- The current maturity state of a capability (based on a Capability Maturity Model (CMM) where '1' represented low maturity and '5' represented best-in-class)
- The desired level of maturity required to achieve the goal
- The importance to the business of this capability

This stage develops the "Business on a Page" model representing the critical capabilities of the organization on a single page. Essentially this is the "base map" upon which various layers of information are overlaid in order to present the developed and uncovered information during the BA and capability sessions. The "Business on a Page" model represents the business capabilities at their assessed level, and the Capability Assessment Heat map (depicted throughout this document) is layered on top of this. The heat map depicted the status of a capability gap at CMM levels.

- *Red*: The capability is more than 1.5 level below what is required.
- *Orange:* The capability is less than 1.5 level below but more than .5 level above the maturity required.

■ *Green:* The gap of assessed and required capability is less than .6. This was considered as at the required level.

For the diverse manufacturing organization in this case study, a divisional perspective is employed and there is an enterprise-wide evaluation of business capabilities. The organization agreed to provide the means to analyze the data in this manner. It is proposed to carry out the survey and interview upwards of 60+ people. A database is created to house the information collected in this manner. The database initially designed in this phase had to go through many design iterations to accommodate additional requirements.

A challenge of the project is to try and gain some organizational consensus around the priority of capabilities. A process is developed in this phase to enable everyone to come to an agreement. Putting all these pieces together, the project methodology is depicted in the project set out to achieve a "Bottom Up" assessment of the organization's business capabilities to support the business strategy. In addition to this harmonization, workshops are designed to gain consensus on capabilities that need focus in immediate and mid-term future.

Phase II: Vogue Business Capability Assessment

The project is kicked off with the Board of Management's (BOM) approval to conduct the surveys and individual interviews of all division's Executive General Managers (EGMs) and their direct reports. The survey is sent to all the EGMs and their direct reports. The response is positive, and a significant number of responses were received. Most of the respondents of the survey, including the executive general managers, are interviewed in detail to understand their issues and in particular the following:

■ Details of their divisional strategy
■ Review survey area where capability gap is >2
■ Identify risks/challenges
■ Alignment with other divisions

Each department conducted a harmonization workshop and the top-five capabilities are prioritized for short- and long-term plans. The findings of these workshops are documented at the divisional level and distributed to all the participants of the workshop. The report included recommendations on how to address the closure of the capability gaps. Based on the divisional priorities, a compiled enterprise view of organization's priorities is developed and presented to the executive team.

It is at this stage the Managing director requests Phase III of the BA project to align the BA with the new strategy which is nearing completion.

Phase III: Alignment with Updated Strategy

The focus of Phase III establishes a board of management (BOM) consensus on priority business capability gaps to achieve the new strategy. The new strategy had three horizons:

■ Focus on profitability
■ Embrace new products and services
■ Invest in new products and services

In order to expedite realignment with the new strategy, it is assumed the current assessment of capabilities for the first two phases are mostly valid. The third phase requires a comprehensive evaluation of the capabilities needed to achieve that strategy.

Actions needed to achieve the first two phases are documented and required capabilities (using existing research from Phase I) are mapped to see what is needed to achieve the goal of the enterprise. Phase III also identifies additional capabilities that are not noted for the current strategy. A revised divisional heat map is drawn up which highlights all the capabilities required for achieving the updated strategy.

This heat map is used to determine the divisional priorities for the new strategy and adjustments are made to the previous list of priorities to reflect the new strategies. The consolidated list of divisional priorities then is presented and co-organized with the BOM as enterprise-wide priorities. Recommendations to bring up the skills of the business to achieve the goals of the organization are submitted in a report.

This project stops short of working with the divisions to establish divisional priorities taking into account the new divisional strategy and the recommendations that are adopted to close capability gaps at an enterprise level.

Discussion Points

1. Describe the relationship between ODBA and a capability-based business strategy. Use specific examples in your discussion.
2. Why is it important to identify maturity gaps in business capabilities?
3. What types of goals do ODBA-assisted organizations achieve?
4. Explain the key elements of ODBA. Using current business, provide examples of each.
5. What are the key differences between ODBA and EA? How does one support or conflict with the other?
6. Why is it important to keep business strategies and architectures aligned? What can happen when the two are not aligned?
7. What are the benefits to developing business capabilities iteratively? What are the challenges in the iterative process?
8. How does ODBA impact decision-making and IT?
9. Explain, with examples, some key organization levers that need to be considered within BA.
10. What are the three components of a strategy? How are they interrelated? Answer with specific examples.
11. What is a heat map? Why is developing a heat map important in aligning outcomes and capabilities? Provide specific examples in your answer.
12. How does gap analysis help achieve business outcomes?

References

1. Rittinghouse, J.W. and Ransome, J.F. (2010). *Cloud Computing: Implementation, Management and Security*, CRC Press, Boca Raton, FL.
2. Unhelkar, B. (2017). *Big Data Strategies for Agile Business*, CRC Press, Boca Raton, FL.
3. Tiwary, A. and Unhelkar, B. (2011). Chapter 6: Extending and Applying Business Intelligence and Customer Strategies for Green ICT, p. 83, B. Unhelkar (ed.), in *Handbook of Research in Green ICT: Technical, Business and Social Perspectives*, IGI Global, Hershey, PA.

4. Unhelkar, B., Ghanbary, A. and Younessi, H. (2009). *Collaborative Business Process Engineering and Global Organizations: Frameworks for Service Integration*, IGI Global, Hershey, PA.
5. Porter, M.E. and Ramirez-Vallejo Walmart, J. Navigating a Changing Retail Landscape Case Study, *Harvard Business Review*, March 07, 2017.
6. Tjan, A.K. Strategy on One Page, *Harvard Business Review*, June 01, 2011.

Chapter 3

Developing Business Architecture—II

KEY POINTS

- Understand organizational Change Management and its relationship to Business Architecture (BA) and Business Capabilities
- Utilize the Outcome-Driven Business Architecture (ODBA) within organizations in practice
- Identify the Key Artifacts of ODBA
- Further the role of business capabilities in ODBA
- Develop the BA program to measure the success of ODBA
- Promote knowledge sharing with ODBA

This chapter discusses development and utilization of Outcome-Driven Business Architecture (ODBA). This discussion starts with an understanding of the business architecture (BA) challenges. ODBA is a BA but with specific focus on business outcomes of the organization. This outcome focus is accompanied with capability enhancement as its guiding force. The development and use of ODBA necessitates change and measuring the effect of that change. Therefore, Change Management becomes an important part of the discussions in this chapter. Metrics and measurements for change are also introduced.

Business Architecture Challenges

Outcome-Driven Business Architecture (ODBA) provides a clear and precise overview of an organization's Information Technology (IT) system assets, directions for innovations, prioritization of IT-related investments, and an approach to align these elements with business for improved performance. ODBA provides a means to support the definition of policy, needs, and goals—which drives organization priorities and builds services that results in an increasingly mature organization. As a result, there is efficiency and effectiveness in the organization providing long-term sustainability of the organization.

A well-defined ODBA is a measure of the total sustainability value (TSV) [1] of internal and external organizational IT assets. Successful implementation of a value-based ODBA model has a positive impact on a company's overall sustainability. The benefits of its IT investments are reflected in increased profits, reduced costs through improved operational efficiency, and enhanced competitive advantages.

Developing and using BA in an organization has its own suite of challenges. It is important to understand and address these challenges in order to develop and maintain a good ODBA. These challenges, which include those related to development and implementation are outlined next.

Lack of Use of Standards

Perhaps the most important of all challenges in building BA is when an organziation builds it from scratch. Building from scratch requires organization-wide consultation and agreement on the capability definition. This option requires time and patience, and enough resources to achieve the acceptable definition within the enterprise. In many cases, it becomes an academic discussion. The purpose of this book is to provide pragmatic and ODBA frameworks and methods to establish. Recommendations are to adopt an industry-wide standard from dimensions of the capability such as process definitions. Development of BA is ideally undertaken by the use of a base standard.* This standardized framework for BA is then extended to suit the organization. In the absence of using a known standard, BA loses the benefit of a good and robust starting point. Furthermore, lack of standard results also means it is not transportable and, therefore, not understood by another organization (with whom, typically, the organization developing the BA wants to communicate).

Consolidation without Understanding the Outcomes

Initiatives to consolidate operations result in multiple projects that bring together various systems and processes for cohesive functioning. Without such optimization, demand on resources continues to increase disproportionately to the actual needs of the organization. For example, larger servers, additional infrastructure, and people are required to handle the complexity of processes, all trying to work together for a common outcome. The consolidation towards a single tool or platform becomes the bottleneck of operations. Streamlining operations and using a single solution requires detailed understanding of the outcomes and an information flow to a centralized infrastructure.

Treating Architecture as a 'Solution' to a Problem Rather than a Basis for Handling Multiple Problems

Architecture is not a solution. Nor is it meant to solve a specific problem with technologies. Understanding the complexity of a problem and its associated infrastructure across the enterprise is facilitated by BA. If the focus of architecture is a solution, then it becomes piecemeal. This piecemeal architecture leads to challenges such as a number of projects building redundant capabilities. Developing solutions in silos, where the efforts of one department is undermined by another department in the same value chain, results in potententially conflicting activities.

---

* TOGAF, Zachman are the standard Enterprise architecture frameworks.

Focus on the immediate need contributes to misuse of resources and is not a good architectural practice. More often than not, resources are consumed in fixing symptoms rather than the root cause of the problem. This, in turn, results in process inefficiencies and waste.

Architecture without Process Management

Architecture provides greater value in re-engineering processes rather than automating them. Lack of re-engineering and suboptimal architectures lead to process inefficiencies automation. This adds to the complexity of organizational processes and systems. Undocumented, out of date and redundant processes with justifications such as "we have always done it this way" are a major BA challenge.

Non-standard and complex processes are difficult to integrate and manage effectively especially without a good architecture. The resulting solutions do not align to the needs of the organization, demand excessive management overhead and result in unplanned costs. These legacy assets impede the organizations ability to change and increase exponentially and drain resources to maintain operations. Consider, for example, a critical legacy system for billing. This out of date process takes up key resources such as servers and subject matter experts to maintain its operations. The time consumed by subject matter experts in running the systems leaves no time to develop new systems. A large part of the information techology budget is also allocated to the legacy systems operations. Hence, investment in newer, hoslistic systems is not planned.

Lack of Good Governance in Projects

Governance models do not go beyond the usual economic or operational benefits to look holistically at what business value is offered by the project as an outcome. In many organizations, governance criteria are limited to either economic or operational benefits that are difficult to measure. For example, a project based on reducing processing time may only provide the metrics for the "in scope" process, however, overall process complexity, including "out of scope" processes may not be considered. On the surface, the project meets the business case requirements but the organization is worse off.

Poor Communication across the Organization

Good architectures are built on good communications across the organization. Even more importantly, they enable good communication. Inadequate and inaccurate communication across the organization leads to a poor architecture. An example is when the same capabilities are implemented through multiple projects. Lack of communication results in inconsistent approaches to architecture which results in standalone solutions.

Lack of Leadership in the Organization

Lack of leadership results in significant expenditure with minimal realization of organizational benefit. The business is disillusioned with the implementation and management of increasingly complex technology. IT departments are seen as unable to produce value-added deliverables. This is exacerbated by a growing change imperative, driven by audit recommendations, legacy, and emerging trends impacting demands on business outcomes.

Lack of Trust among Key Stakeholders

When business units and their owners lack trust and confidence in each other, the result is poor architecture. Lack of trust results from inadequate controls on measurements, lack of scope and clear communication issues, wasted resources, and duplicate efforts. As a result, many business units develop their own strategy and architectures. These shadow architectures happen without knowledge and participation from centralized IT departments.

Applying BA to Projects

Once the organization understands the challenges in developing a good BA, the same challenges are converted into action points to overcome them. Applying a unified standard in developing BA provides many advantages. For example, unified BA provides a strong rationale to develop a structured enterprise-level approach to projects that is also disciplined. BA enables the organization to look beyond individual projects within departments and assess the impact of change on the organization resulting from the projects.

Role of IT in ODBA

IT remains integral to Enterprise and Business architectures. ODBA ensures solutions are developed and implemented with consideration to broader organizational impacts. The following factors impact ODBA:

- **Business**—Desired goals and outcomes enable alignment of projects with the business strategy. This provides value in undertaking projects and realizing their potential benefits.
- **Information**—Understanding of how information is collected, what is collected, what is required, and how it is retrieved is vital in developing ODBA. Limited understanding results in missing key requirements.
- **Applications**—Embedded in business processes or workflows improve processes, data sourcing, and integration of information to enable knowledge sharing and decision-making.
- **Technology**—Detailed assessment of available technological options with respect to the external and internal environment and with due consideration to sustainability, flexibility for future growth, and changes to requirements.
- **Costs and Risks**—Without the ability to accurately understand and assess the costs and risks associated with change, investments continue to be disproportionate to the value provided. This contributes to ongoing financial pressures and further damage to the credibility of the organization when it comes to responsible solution procurement, implementation, and delivery.

In the absence of an enterprise-wide view of current processes and practices senior management cannot understand and evaluate the potential impact of change across the business environment. Table 3.1 shows the IT-specific organizational challenges. This table also shows expected business actions to meet the organizational challenges.

Improving Organizational Readiness

Organizational readiness is a strategic initiative. Undertaking projects (that build capabilities) while keeping the ODBA in the background is the best way to improve organizational readiness.

Table 3.1 IT Specific Challenges and Key Outcomes from a BA Framework

Key Challenges	Actions to Meet the Challenges
IT projects are siloes and may be delivering outdated solutions	Ensure information and technology management and initiatives are aligned to strategy and resources are allocated to the actions and projects that contribute to the strategic goals and outcomes.
Unable to identify the core processes and owners	BA framework identifies the processes for each capability and the process owners. Identify core business processes critical to the success of the organization, assess the maturity of processes, and create actions and projects to remove identified gaps.
Information management is in silos and owners of information are not identified	The BA framework identifies the information required for each capability and defines a corporate data model to assign the information owners. The framework also determines key information required to support core business processes, identifies the gaps, and initiates actions to remove identified gaps.
Core processes are not documented, mapped or shared. Processes and systems may be duplicated and interdependence is unknown	The BA framework lists and document the core processes. Core process owners are identified/assigned. The process owners are responsible for the maintenance of processes based on organizational goals. Identify which core business processes require technology enablement; initiate projects to build capabilities. Document the interdependencies of business processes and systems (both internally and with partner agencies).
Systems are overlapping in functionality Infrastructure is legacy and not scalable	BA maps the systems for each of the capabilities and shows where system redundancy and overlap exist. Examine how complexity in infrastructure is simplified. The projects use the roadmaps for the legacy systems replacement, plan for and determine costs to refresh the infrastructure.
Cost of projects and business is not known Resource allocation decisions are ad-hoc and not governable	Establish the true cost of enabling the business through information and technology management; make informed decisions and investments based on the outcomes and benefit to organization.

Planning the development of business capabilities requires a portfolio-based approach to change. The change is anchored by activities and projects to build capabilities that advance the strategic goals and result in better revenue. The ODBA establishes and presents clear and pragmatic outcomes. Business capabilities consolidate and act as a reference for the strategic business outcomes that guide detailed IT strategies and plans.

The change in organizational approach from tactical response to any business challenge to organizational readiness enables consistent decision-making, supports processes with systems and guides organization-wide governance on IT. This reduces the complexity and duration of projects undertaken by or on behalf of IT departments.

Developing and implementing an effective ODBA improves the manageability, effectiveness, efficiency, and agility of an organization, and ensures investment decisions are supported and informed. Changes considered through BA typically include:

- Optimized and efficient use of information management resources including systems, processes, and workflow.
- Integration and/or standardization of business processes.
- Improving the quality and timeliness of business information.
- Assessing the impact of organizational change.

ODBA, in particular, enables better understanding of customer needs and wants. This provides the business capability of developing better customer interaction strategies. BA-driven strategies assist organizations in developing differentiating products by developing better customer engagement capabilities. Thus, a customer can differentiate products and services based on organizational capabilities for example serviceability, product quality management, or customer service management.

The ODBA Framework

The architectural view of an organization is its holistic, long-term view. Such a view transcends immediate, short-term, solution-based views. When the architecture of an organization is built based on its desired outcomes, it is called ODBA. ODBA acknowledges the need for a single source of information in an organization. Additionally, ODBA also understands that not all activities within an organization (well-meaning or otherwise) are directed toward its outcomes. Inadequate assessment of options results in inadequate planning, demand management, and impact assessment. ODBA of an organization helps set proper direction, reduce duplication, and enable the much needed alignment with desired business outcomes.

The ODBA framework provides the following:

- Business Capability maps that enable identification of capabilities for desired outcomes
- IT system assets map to business capabilities
- Prioritization of business capabilities and related investments to uplift them
- Targeting business outcomes for improved performance
- Directing innovations and optimization of resources
- Managing organizational and IT risks

Importance and Value of ODBA

The importance and value of ODBA is discussed in greater detail next:

- Directs enterprise-wide governance and provides a structure to allocate resources for strategic and tactical projects or actions. The governance and decision-making are done on multiple dimensions and provide a comprehensive measurement of the benefits to the organization. The outcomes include tangible and intangible benefits. For example, customer and employee satisfaction are included along with the financial benefits of any actions.

- IT leadership and management use the ODBA framework for planning and developing IT roadmaps and future investments in new technologies. ODBA framework defines the application, infrastructure, and system consolidation opportunities. It assists in identifying and mitigating organizational and IT-related risks. The framework has risk as a dimension, where at any given time senior executives are informed about the organizational and IT-related risks, and possible impact on future strategies.
- Prioritizes changes in product and service management, skill development, and any action that helps embrace environmental changes such as new competitors, new or updated legislation, and tax changes. ODBA Framework assists in creating an ideal business environment where changes are assessed using the capabilities framework. The framework dynamically assesses the impact of change and presents options to handle the change.
- IT investments are based on business goals. IT uses the ODBA framework to plan, schedule, prioritize, and implement the actions.
- Scope of projects/innovations and their prioritization are based on business capabilities development. All projects either meet the governance criteria of improved business capabilities or are required due to legislative or operational demands.
- Vendor engagement and procurement based on ODBA frameworks assist in developing organizational strategic capabilities or supporting capabilities. The vendors collaborate business outcome implementation.
- Articulate and gain consensus on business capability requirements for each business unit. This requires senior executive sponsorship. The consensus assists in developing and maturing ODBA across the organization. This is an important step for the organization to move from tactical to strategic with investment decisions. The outcome of the consensus is uniform and enterprise-wide governance framework follows. Resource allocation is optimized based on organization-wide requirements. This business outcome-driven maturity of ODBA takes time, but mapping of business capabilities to various IT domain assists in making right decisions on application suites, infrastructure investments, and enterprise-wide information management. ODBA Framework does not fix everything but streamlines the decision-making process for resource allocation.
- Ensure the enterprise is prepared for growth and profitability by allocating the right mix of resource experience required to achieve the business outcomes. The strategies designed are pragmatic and provide internal direction for new challenges facing the organization. The organization plans for growth in areas where its internal business capabilities support requirements for expansion and profitability of the enterprise; for example, mergers and acquisitions.
- Ensures that investments of time, resources, and money are made in a way that best supports the business strategy. ODBA defines the roadmaps for the business strategies and highlights organizational risks and mitigation plans. ODBA defines the activities and projects to achieve strategic goals. It is dynamic and integrates new or changed activities when there is a change in strategic goals.
- Maximizes transformational opportunities. It enables investments that are of use to the entire organization. Opportunities to harmonize processes that are repeated in different business units and functional areas are found and prioritized in the Framework which reduces costs and drives efficiency. It defines key components required to support specific business objectives for the next 3–5 years and is a roadmap defining initiatives supporting multiple priorities. Implications of cost optimization efforts on current and future business capabilities are included in project plans, and provide a reference point for governance.

Establishing ODBA

The ODBA is a part of the organizational strategy, playing a critical role in supporting management and governance practices. ODBA ensures information and technology decisions and investments are optimized with organizational outcomes and goals. ODBA provides guidance, direction, and approval of investments in people, process, and technology. An ODBA aligns to and supports the strategy of the organization. In doing so, it also identifies and supports the needs of all aspects of strategy and implementation plan. The ODBA is pragmatic and based on corporate culture and feasibility.

The ODBA has the following objectives:

- Establish end-to-end views of the business capabilities and operations of the organization
- Align return on business and IT investments with the desired business outcomes of the organization
- Identify and prioritize business capabilities to consolidate and reduce costs with projects
- Simplify executive decision-making and provide agility to the process
- Increase realization of benefits from innovation within the organization
- Assess change impact on organizational processes due to strategy implementation
- Manage and socialize business transformation activities

Developing the ODBA needs a planned and phased approach. The foundation of ODBA is an organization-wide accepted business architecture framework. Developing an ODBA has three phases detailed in Table 3.2.

Table 3.2 Establishing an ODBA

Activity	Rationale
Establish ODBA Framework	Provide a structure to manage outcomes and the key capabilities required to support the organization's decision-making process. The ODBA is pragmatic and serves the goals of the organization. Developing this framework is an iterative process. The outcome from the business architecture framework enables strategic investment and resource allocation activities. The framework considers the culture of the company and the flexibility required for future changes. Senior executives communicate this framework across the organization.
Populate the ODBA Framework with relevant content	Provide a single source of truth for architectural information with an appropriate governance plan and ensure decisions are based on accurate and appropriate information. The information mapped to the BA framework includes applications, systems, processes, policies, organizational risks, and information exchanges. The framework is agile to support any other dimensions such as costs of maintaining the capabilities as a whole.
Use the ODBA as a Business As Usual' tool	All relevant and available facts are considered for decision-making. Access to the right information promotes easy decision-making and increased understanding of the impact on the organization's operations. Solutions are compliant and aligned with the vision, principles and standards defined.

Table 3.3   Elements of BA That Are Extended and Applied to ODBA

Elements	ODBA Focus
Scope	ODBA focuses on the entire business for its outcomes and IT functions, and not just on the IT components.
Direction	Organization centers on strategic planning (i.e., business transformation, strategic change programs) and not on tactical operational change.
Timeline	Planning considers the long-term view of future scenarios rather than a short-term view of the current state. BA focuses on a roadmap of changes to an organization's capabilities.
Value chain	BA focuses on the enterprise organization as a whole and the value chain it offers, and not just on the scope of one delivery project.
Stakeholders	Needs and concerns of the executive management team for the entire organization as well as at a divisional/departmental level are considered and become stakeholders in BA planning and implementation.

Business capabilities are the foundation for BA. The capabilities are layered based on the organizational appetite for the capability-based framework. The capability-based framework implementation is a well-defined program of work with key dimesions. Two examples of dimensions are the scope of the program that is defined to achieve the organizational strategies and projects linkages; and the selection and prioritization of the business capabilities are based on the organizational value chain analysis. Table 3.3 defines the elements of BA:

Business Capabilities and ODBA

The BA helps define the capabilities map. The definition of business capabilities within an organization is a difficult and time-consuming activity. For example, as shown in Figure 3.1, to define "plan for and acquire resource" capability requires consultation and agreement across the organization. A well-accepted industry-wide definition speeds up the adoption of ODBA. Figure 3.1 depicts the business capability map using APQC process classification framework (PCF©). The APQC PCF is useful to obtain organizational-wide definitions. The map defines the business capabilities. Each business capability is then layered with organizational dimensions such as people, process, technology, financial resources, or information and knowledge management. The ODBA map depicted in Figure 3.1 is layered with information about each dimension. The layering of the map with dimensions is used to depict heat maps, risks, or opportunities.

ODBA incorporates an organization's operational capability map. This map defines capabilities required across the organization for effective and efficient operations. This map enables the business to understand how its capabilities map to the desired outcomes. The capability map represents an understanding of the business needs, its existing capabilities, and represents those needs to the cross-functional community of business users and developers of solutions.

Business units comprise the users with different contexts of business capabilities based on their roles; and the architects collaborate with the project managers to enable them to develop capabilities needed by the users. The ODBA ensures both Business and Enterprise Architecture decisions are made in alignment and consideration of Business Unit (BU)-specific capability needs and

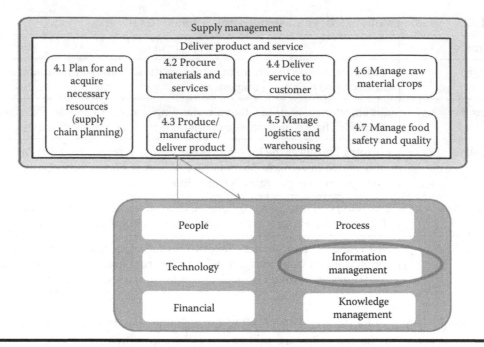

Figure 3.1   Further details of the BA Map (based on the APQC process framework).

enterprise standards. The BA program guides and influences IT Strategy initiatives within the BU and has adequate representation of BU in all relevant forums to shape the initiatives during the assess and select phase, and influences solutions and program architects during development and execution phases.

Capabilities are understood in multiple ways—such as core or supporting; and strategic or tactical. Mostly, however, the focus of ODBA is to develop the core, strategic capabilities that directly enable the organization to achieve its key outcomes.

To categorize a capability as core depends on organizational priorities and size. The categorization is aligned with the strategies and outcomes. For example, if the organizational strategy is to merge and acquire new companies then it is important to understand the core capabilities of all the potential merged organizations. This understanding assists in deciding which organization is strong in a particular capability and which capabilities need to be further developed in order to achieve the overall outcomes. After such an assessment, duplicate (redundant) capabilities are also discovered which can be removed. Maturity of the capabilities is another important dimension to keep in mind when organizations are merging. Another example is use of outsourcing as a strategic direction. In this case, the outsourcing model needs to consider which capabilities are in-house and which other capabilities need to be developed through the outsourcing partners. A possible option is to outsource the supporting capabilities (rather than the core capabilities) for outsourced development. The capability categorization is divided into two major areas:

- **Business advantage capabilities** are strategic and directly contribute to the customer's value proposition and have a high impact on company financials. Value contribution is assured when performance is among the best in peer organizations and at an acceptable cost.
- **Business support capabilities** directly support advantage capabilities. Value contribution is assured when performance is above industry parity at a competitive cost.

Advantage capabilities are the organization's core differentiators in achieving market or product leadership. For example, if an organization is dealing with goods (such as phones, laptops, and other electronic personal computing devices) then its strategic capabilities are related directly to effective supply chain management. The organization develops and nurtures these capabilities in order to be competitive. In some cases, these capabilities are valuable and rare, making an organization's position unique and difficult to mimic by the competitors.

Support capabilities support the core capabilities. The organization can outsource these capabilities to optimize its processes and resource utilization. In many industries, IT, and human resources are considered support capabilities and can be outsourced.

Yet another way of looking at the capabilities is:

- **Business basic capabilities** may be invisible to the customer but are a major contributor to a company's core business and have a huge impact on its bottom line. These capabilities focus on efficiency improvments, especially in high-volume work. When processes are performed at industry level parity and the performance is above the competitors then business capability value contribution increases.
- **Business needs capabilities** as value contribution is assured when performed at industry parity performance below competitors' cost. These can be candidates for alternate sourcing.

Business capabilities are defined clearly across the organization and shared with business partners when providing or requesting services. Business capabilities are defined in the organizational language for all operational functions. It adapts to various dimensions such as process, people skills, and information and knowledge management. A capability management framework that defines a complete picture of the capabilities is the enterprise capability model. It is a blueprint for the business, connotated in terms of the necessary capabilities for execution of strategy including delivery of services.

Business Capability Layers

The multiple levels and types of business capabilities are summarized in Figure 3.2. The business capability definition, in many organizations, follows the layering of their process development frameworks such as eTOM* or APQC.

The layers of the capability definition provide enough detail at each layer to measure organizational outcomes and aggregate to a higher level. The definition at any layer provides clarity to the organization and assigns an owner of the capability or sub-capability. The definition is not tailored to fit in the current organization roles and responsibilities. Roles are assigned based on fit and re-assigned when the organizational structure changes.

In many cases, the business capability definition at level 1 facilitates agreement in the organization to prioritize organization level goals and outcomes. The mapping of the business capabilities to organizational systems, risks, and activities in most cases results in all the project and activities mapped to a large number of business capabilities. The recommended approach is to take prioritized business capabilities and define level 2 as sub-capabilities, level 3 as activities and level 4 as tasks to map projects, application, and systems more granular and provide single owners of the activities, tasks, and projects.

---

* https://en.wikipedia.org/wiki/Business_Process_Framework_(eTOM).

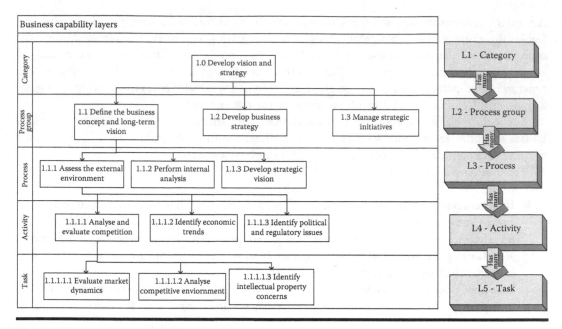

Figure 3.2   Business capability layers.

For example, Figure 3.2 depicts APQC© defined PCF. This framework defines a five-layered approach where level 1 is the category of the business capabilities such as "1.0 Develop vision and strategy." Layer 2 defines the process group "1.3 Manage strategic initiatives." The organization, based on its available resources, adopts a standard framework or develops its own.

Vision and Strategy for Business Capability

Capabilities define what to use but not how to use them. For example, faxing and emailing are not capabilities because they describe 'how' a capability is fulfilled. Similarly, mailing a report is not a capability. ***Develop vision and strategy*** is a capability because it describes what is being done. In most organizations, every department has their own vision and strategy. This isolated approach creates competing strategy and conflicts with other departmental vision and strategies. The purpose of the business capabilities is to build a framework that is useable and repeatable across the organization. A capability-based outcome ensures an event has a high level of information integrity at all times. Lower level capabilities have related outcomes that are more specific in their outcome to their parent.

As shown in Figure 3.3, the framework identifies capabilities across various layers and is adaptable across the organization. For example, *understand market and customer* defines a capability to understand the market and customers to provide products the customer needs or wants. To determine the capability, the key activity includes understanding the customer's requirements. The definition includes the expected outcome at the end of the activity. The *understand market and customer* or *develop vision and strategy* defines outcomes required from the capabilities along with the measurement and governance associated with the outcomes. The *develop vision and strategy* capability specifies the direction of the organization and subsequent financial rewards. The outcome of the capability is a vision for the organizational future direction. The organization's

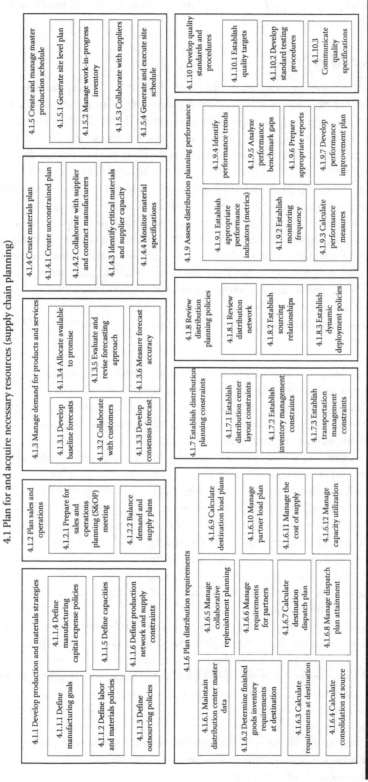

Figure 3.3 Developing vision and strategy in the business capability. Note: Using on APQC capability PCF.

capability of *develop vision and strategy* measures financial gains and profit margin, for example, by embracing the new vision.

Capabilities and Processes

A clear distinction between a capability map and process is that **capability** defines what to do and **process** defines how to do it. Sometimes companies wrongly exchange process definition with capability definition. In the last two decades, most organizations concentrated on processes as the backbone of the organizational structure. Processes define the dynamics of achieving the outcomes. In many cases, initial implementation of business capabilities imitates the structure of a process, but it is important to make it a dimension of the capability and defining only the what of organizational activities. Capabilities are purely business views of the organization.

Before embarking on the development of capabilities, senior management agrees on the capability definition and structure. The expected outcomes from this initiative are a holistic definition of the organization's capabilities that are used across various departments and business units.

The number of capabilities depends on the size of the organization and level of complexity between organizational departments. The organization takes small steps and starts with some common definitions. The level 1 hierarchy defines the organization's model of activities and does not imitate the organizational structure.

Some of the well-known business capabilities used across the many processes of an organization are as follows:

- **Define market and customer:** An organization needs to understand the market and customers to provide products based on customer needs or wants. A key activity for this capability includes determining customer requirements. This is the driving capability for the rest of the organization and is a short-term focus based on market dynamics. Examples are threats from the competitors and first-mover advantage.
- **Develop vision and strategy:** Most organizations have different departments creating their own vision and strategy. Disparate visions prevent the organization from moving forward as one entity. A single shared vision across the enterprise ensures each department is focused on activities that contribute to the achievement of the goal and organization success.
- **Design products and services:** Every commercial organization exists to sell some product and/or service. The organizational vision, strategy, and understanding of the market determine the design of products and services. When an organization's structure is defined in siloes, the design and services may be duplicated for each product offered by the organization. Because this impacts total sustainability, the product and services definition has to be uniform across the enterprise.
- **Market and sell product and services:** Similar to product and services, sales and marketing functions are separate departments. It is not uncommon for an organization to have conflicting marketing engagements where one area of the organization promotes green products and may adopt some green policies, and another department overuses the resources. For example, marketing could implement programs to reduce their carbon footprints via new channel of self-serve, but it might have an impact of increasing manual workload or actually increasing the paperwork in another department. The total impact of these activities on the organization should be thought through by considering the whole organization.
- **Maintain and support products and services:** In any organization, resources are devoted to maintaining and supporting product and services.

- **Retire products and services:** Organizations usually ignore this capability and do not give it enough thought. Product disposition is planned after its life validity is expired. Although these capabilities are often considered to be of least importance when designing the products, they could have a huge effect on the environment. For examples, garbage tips across the world are overflowing with the previous models of PC, laptops, printers, and printer cartridges from the computing industry. Retirement of products requires a strategy and is aligned with the product design, development, and marketing to maximize the resource usage.
- **Management support processes:** This function requires optimizing resources used by the organization during the total life cycle of the products and services. Financial management, skills management, human resource, and vendor management activities all contribute to either optimizing or wasting resources due to duplication varying or uncoordinated demands on resources.

Process to Define Capabilities

While capabilities support business processes, there is a need for a step-by-step approach to develop capabilities. Applying business capability management aligns organizations to strategic intent and accelerates results. The following is the process to define capabilities:

- Identify clearly defined business outcomes, and ensure Business Architecture (BA) is positioned to achieve those outcomes. The BA framework provides the glue between the business strategy and IT projects. The business architecture framework uses business capabilities and governance to shape projects holistically. The outcome of projects is based on business capability building rather than traditional business requirements.
- Ensure that risk-adjusted value is part of the criteria for designing BA governance. The BA defines the holistic risk-based framework. The risk is assessed based on the business capabilities and the projects are carried out to alleviate these risks. For example, an organization strategy changing from a purely product-based organization to a products and services-based organization requires a transition to a reactive organization, where products are designed based on customer requirements, to more a dynamic organization. Organizations may lack capabilities to manage customer expectations, thus, creating a new risk. The reason for the risk could be limitations and scalability of information management systems to manage a large volume of information from the current product-based information.
- Match BA governance decision-making and assurance to organizational culture, maturity, and approach to BA. The BA framework is based on organizational trichotomy maturity in processes and culture across the organization and within divisions. The success of the governance depends upon the whole organization abiding by the capability-based governance. If the organizational culture encourages individual success over holistic capability building activity, governance fails. For example, if an activity or project can be implemented tactically in shorter time than a capability-building initiative, then a tactical path would be more popular. This, when repeated across the organization nullifies any benefit of business architecture framework and governance. This requires an integrated BA governance with other processes such as project portfolio management, application portfolio management, and investment decision processes to maximize business outcomes for the organization.

Embedding Business Capabilities in ODBA

Business capability maps help in aligning the capabilities to outcomes. This is an important part of ODBA. The capabilities maps represent layers of IT systems assets, information management requirements, processes, policies, and information owners that need to be aligned to outcomes. ODBA provides direction for innovation and optimization of resources by dynamically managing the organizational information and technology risks. Thus, the capability maps provide important information and flexibility to adapt and plan for the challenging IT landscape.

The business capabilities become the base of the ODBA, similar to the geographical maps, where a number of layers are overlaid with different attributes. In the case of the BA, business capability maps are overlaid with the maturity of the overall capability, information management maturity, and gaps in organizational capabilities to meet business outcomes.

The ODBA based on business capabilities provides agile analysis, design, and governance to manage dynamic and ever-changing market expectations and business demands. For example, when an organization is planning or implementing mergers and acquisitions, the BA framework uses the business capabilities map and layers the maturity of each organization in the capabilities. This assists in deciding if the merger should consolidate capabilities or choose between two similar capabilities where maturity is more advanced.

The other use of the BA identifies common business capabilities in organizations or some immature capabilities that exist across the organization. The business capability map is overlaid with multiple dimensions such as processes across capabilities, systems and information needs. This assists in proper consolidation of the systems across organizations.

BA Context and Outcomes

BA provides valuable context at the solution or project level. However, it has a significant value in the strategic decision-making process across the organization. Organizational leadership is supported by ODBA as the decisions are based on facts and knowledge base (BA repository) delivered by the BA function. The decision-making process is compromised unless there is an end-to-end and inter-departmental view of the organization. BA enables informed, effective, and controlled changes in a planned and efficient manner, and provides:

■ Views based on change context to understand and guide appropriate decision-making
■ The capability that promotes the monitoring of coherence and completeness of the enterprise and its strategic change agenda/portfolio
■ The opportunity to manage an increasingly complex technology landscape
■ Ensure that information/data provided is contextually appropriate
■ Format, determine, and regulate decision-making associated with change
■ Understand the impact of decisions and transformation on organizational operations

Table 3.4 depicts the ODBA benefits to the organization. The BA-based prioritization of projects and investment provides a path to transparent and objective investment decisions, avoiding any favorite project mentality. Table 3.4 depicts the business outcomes that are achieved by a matured BA.

Measuring BA maturity is done annually and utilizes the industry standard maturity model. The maturity methods are discussed in Chapter 6 in more detail. This evaluation enables the organization to review rates of progress, determine the achievability of target rates and modify organizational plans to facilitate further improvement.

Table 3.4 The Context Provided by BA in Business Outcomes

Outcomes	BA Context
Establishing and aligning initiative prioritization.	BA provides various layers identifying organizational priorities for building capabilities. To prioritize initiatives, the maturity an initiative brings to a capability is considered. The governance is streamlined and prioritization criteria is defined for business understanding.
Comparing options to validate ideas and solutions.	The business capability maturity is achieved from selecting the projects that maximizes business outcomes. This assists in identifying projects that do not add capability enhancement or building capabilities not in current prioritization of organization.
Assessing and prioritizing possible solutions. Providing structure to support appropriate assessment, comparison and decisions.	A set of predefined criteria adopted across the organization assists in prioritizing the possible solutions. The BA, when matured in an organization with the framework embedded assists in reducing IT project demands from the business units. The IT project is defined on the basis of strategic results when strategy is defined.
Presenting complex information to targeted stakeholder groups. Enabling impact and scenario analysis.	The outcome of the projects on its own becomes difficult to articulate and communicate. A BA provides outcomes in business language. The building of capabilities and risks mitigated layers overlaid on business capability maps communicates complex information to the stakeholders.
Guiding technology selection.	Outcomes form the basis of selecting technology and vendors. Assessing concepts. Assessing capacity for change guiding vendor selection and assessment.
Supporting financial management (investment and benefit) of the portfolio.	BA consolidates projects and invests in technologies at an organizational level, reducing proliferating tactical solutions for capabilities. The project selection and investment management framework include business capabilities-based investment processes and procedures.
Informing release planning and optimization of release of change portfolio.	BA provides optimized information and knowledge management dimensions to the business capabilities. The reporting, information release, and information planning is anchored by the business capabilities and key performance indicators are managed by the information collection and planning. The business capability-based GRC provides an information exchange framework based on context-based information sharing using business capabilities.

Approach to Developing ODBA

Since ODBA impacts decision-making in an organization, its development is necessarily consensus based. ODBA also supports strategic investment decisions across the organization within the constraints of the fiscal realities of organization. This requires involving multiple non-technical disciplines of the organization.

ODBA development starts with workshops with subject matter experts about goals, visions, and objectives from the requirements of BA. The workshops explore the strengths and weaknesses of the organization. The following results come out of a workshop:

■ Understand which business capabilities are at risk by defining and assessing current capabilities and assessing maturity level and their mapping to business outcomes
■ Undertake a gap analysis (both qualitative and quantitative) to evaluate and prioritize which business capabilities require investment. This requires an understanding of the organization's current state and its desired future state.
■ Align new IT initiatives to business capabilities
■ Highlight gaps, overlaps, and interdependencies within planned projects
■ Establish roadmap (with 5 years rolling investment plan) and an annual prioritized investment plan for information management and technology

Key Artifacts of ODBA

ODBA comprises a hierarchy of products (commonly called artifacts) as outlined in Table 3.5. These are the key artifacts required to establish business architecture practice in any organization.

Table 3.5 Overview of Artifact Types, Focus and Brief Description

Artifact Type	Focus	Description
Principles	What are the beliefs and values that guide the organization to achieve its vision?	These embody the core beliefs and values of the organization in relation to the management of information and technologies. The concepts influence decisions about various resource and initiative portfolios across the sector.
Strategy	What general direction is appropriate for the organization.	Strategies are brief high-level documents intended to achieve principle agreement from senior executives to a general course of action. The course of action achieves an agreed upon desired future state or goal in support of organization's vision in the form of ambitions and priorities. Strategies establish a baseline of the current environment; identify the drivers that lead change needs to a particular environment; articulate the future desired environment; and propose a series of actions to realize that future desired state.
Standards and policy	What are the specific directions, constraints, and requirements which achieve organizational strategies?	Clear and specific statements of direction based on general principles which support achieving long-term strategies or provide a response to issues. They include detailed constraints and compliance requirements and in doing so they provide business units, and organizations with an indication of the level of discretion available when making decisions.

(Continued)

Table 3.5 (*Continued*)   **Overview of Artifact Types, Focus and Brief Description**

Artifact Type	Focus	Description
Goals	Where does organization wish to be?	A noticeable and assessable end result having one or more objectives to be achieved within a specific timeframe.
Objectives	What are the key mileposts that should be achieved to meet the defined goals?	A specific result that a person or system aims to achieve within a timeframe and with available resources. In general, objectives are more specific and easier to measure than goals. Objectives are basic tools that underlie all planning and strategic activities. They serve as the basis for creating policy and evaluating performance [2].
Measures	How well is organization performing against internal and external targets?	A number or quantity that measures a directly observable value or performance [3].
Models	Targeted views of individual facets of organization. Models facilitate navigation through the BA and the search and identification of key areas of interest.	A visual or textual representation or simplified version of a concept, phenomenon, relationship, structure, system, or an aspect of organization. The objectives of a model include to: • Facilitate understanding by eliminating unnecessary components; • Assist in decision-making by mimicking 'what if' scenarios; • Explain, control, and predict events on the basis of past observations. A model contains only those features from the phenomenon that are of primary importance to the purpose, as events are usually quite complex and have multiple interconnections.

These artifacts use existing organizational documentation style guides for artifacts, templates, and table of contents. The key artifacts are endorsed by the executive team and a communication plan is developed to socialize these artifacts across the organization.

ODBA Requirements: High-Level

Developing the BA framework and practice is treated as a program of work that adopts project management methodologies. As an aid to shaping the ODBA Framework, requirements are gathered from organization representatives who form the Project Reference Group, relating to what is needed from BA. The outcome-driven business outcomes require a clear definition of business outcomes and maturity calibrations. For example, roles and responsibilities of each artifact owner are required throughout the BA framework.

Table 3.6 High-Level ODBA Requirements

High-Level Requirement	BA Framework Focus
Roles and responsibilities for the 'owners' of every artifact within the BA are to be defined.	All artifacts have an owner of the document. These documents by nature are living documents and as such without a responsible owner: document life cycle is not maintained.
Decision support (supporting agility and 'Time to Market')	BA provides the capabilities and key success indicators for the decision support systems by prioritizing business capabilities and governance of investment based on prioritized capabilities.
Establish relationship between application, interface, data service, security (level), and between function, process, projects, and technology	Provides holistic view of the IT capability dimensions such as applications, interfaces, and infrastructure.
Support making technical forecasts (sunset, goals, future)	Technology roadmaps for the current and future technology. Business capabilities-based technology roadmap defines the technology capabilities in applications, infrastructure, information, and knowledge management. For example, many organizations are struggling with additional infrastructure demand to accommodate "Big Data" initiatives. Business capabilities-based technology investment provides the future states for the technology and information management. The future state is used in defining the life cycle management of the current investment, deploying new technology and framework to migrate current technological capabilities to target state technologies.

Table 3.6 provides a sample of requirements related to BA framework. The business requirements in relation with the framework developed at the start of the BA implementation project are maintained during the life of the BA implementation.

Details of the ODBA Framework

The ODBA framework adopts and extends existing management and enterprise architecture frameworks. ODBA forms the basis for development of future frameworks. ODBA is developed iteratively to enable:

- Agility in organization faster and more accurate decisions than before
- Sharing business capabilities across the organization to provide for efficiency
- Lower change management costs
- Flexible workforce that is equipped for decentralized decision-making by understanding the people skills required for the business capabilities and providing right skills to the workforce
- Improved business productivity resulting from leanness and agility of organizational structure

The conceptual model (a conceptual description of the business model) provides a high-level overview of the Framework. It is supported by a meta-model, which contains the detailed elements of the Framework, including definitions of key artifacts. ODBA provides clear and precise details of the following aspects of an organization:

- Business Capabilities maps that are used to identify missing or weak capabilities
- IT systems assets that are in use currently and that enable provisioning of capabilities
- Prioritization of IT related investments in order to build capabilities
- Approach to deliver targeted business outcomes for improved performance
- Directions for innovations within the organization

Conceptual Sub-Framework for Business Capabilities

The conceptual view (a sub-framework) for business capabilities serves multiple purposes. To start with, it provides an understandable structure of business capabilities mapped to ODBA. This becomes a good communication tool across the organization. Table 3.7 describes components of the business capabilities framework. These business capability components are defined as part of the conceptual phase of the implementation.

Business Capability Model

The Business Capability Model (BCM) facilitates a holistic functional view of the organization's Lines of Business (LoB), independent of the organizational units, thus providing a clear view of

Table 3.7   Description of the Business Capabilities Framework Components

Model	Description
Business capability model	Provides a functional view of the business, independent of the organizational units performing them thus providing a clear view of what organization does.
Business service model	Provides a functional model of the business, classifying services according to how they support business and their performance objective.
Process reference model	Provides detail of cross-functional business processes, providing the ability to identify and analyze processes of interest to the organization.
Enterprise information model	This model is driven by the functions and activities carried out by the organization, and define the set of information entities.
Performance reference model	Used to develop and manage standard measures that support the efficiency of business processes, and effective realization of outcomes.
Application overlay model	Defines the applications that support the various capabilities and functions of the organization.
Technology reference model	Used to categorize and catalog the standards and technologies that support and enable the organization. It provides a foundation to advance the re-usability and standardization of technology.

what an organization does. The capabilities are structured into a tiered hierarchy as agreed by the business areas at the top level, broken down into lines of business composed of a selection of business capabilities at the bottom level of functionality in the BCM.

APQC PCF© is used extensively to demonstrate how to use business capability models. The PCF model has multiple verticals. There are multiple ways to define business capability models, and each organization decides on its own definition. The business capability models are adapted to organizational needs. There may be a summarized version or "one pager" with level 1 capabilities for the senior executives, and a detailed model for departments. A large number of organizations invest in developing models and each organization decides to create one from scratch or adopt a standard model. In this book, APQC PCF is used for illustration purposes.*

Business Capability-Based Gap Analysis

The business capability-based assessment requires understanding the business capability categories within the organization. Business capabilities are categorized into strategic and support categories. This categorization is useful after assessing gaps when building roadmaps and initiatives. The categorization of the business capabilities requires consensus to support strategic outcomes of the entire organization rather than individual departments. A quick assessment based on an organization's value proposition to its shareholders and market position provides a capability categorization overlay on the business capability model. Figure 3.4 is a sample representation using APQC PCF.

The business capability gap assessment is the next step in understanding organizational capabilities. The outcome of the gap assessment is an organizational business capability gap heat map. This comprises a representation of the **capabilities** of the business and an enterprise-wide assessment of the **current state** of maturity of business capabilities and desired **future state** of these capabilities to achieve strategy. A number of capability map views are generated to present the current state of capabilities, gaps and also the future state of the capabilities required as shown in Figure 3.5 and is applied to align organizations to strategic intent and accelerate results. Gap analysis and heat maps are used to provide organizations with the focus areas for investment and action. The gap analysis lists the capabilities gaps that impact on achieving strategic outcomes.

A typical heat map, as shown in Figure 3.5 represents the business capabilities required to run the business. The business capability map is enhanced with additional layers of information such as organizational risks on business capabilities and information requirements. Similar to a geographic map that represents the physical features of a particular region, this Business Capabilities heat map includes technical, operational, security, and organizational information on top of the underlying cap abilities. For example, in an organization dealing with a state policing function, this Heat Map became more useful when the transport infrastructure is superimposed, or population centers or locations of service stations were included. The overlaid traffic information and weather data was correlated in the Big Data environment to offer multiple, additional opportunities for the client to provide service.

---

* With permission from APQC to use the terminology, the maps are defined by authors and can be drawn as per organization's presentation styles.

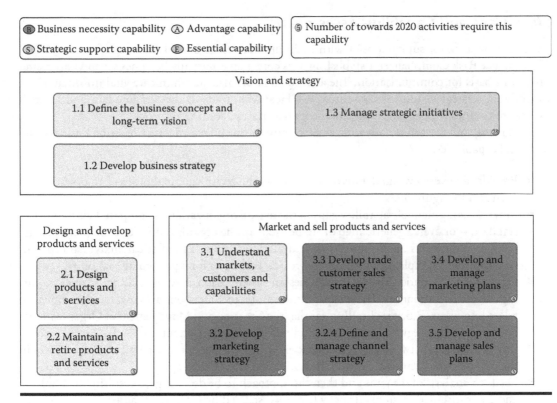

Figure 3.4   Capability category assessment.

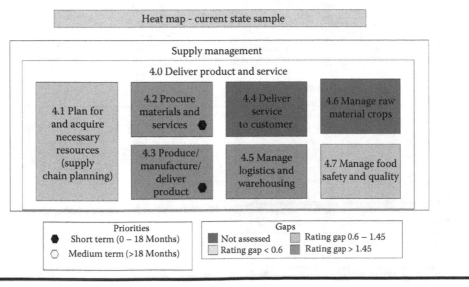

Figure 3.5   Capability current state assessment.

Heat Maps and Capability Assessments

Thus, the basic Map, superimposed with additional layers, is a vital element of overall GRC. (Governance Risk Compliance). Establishing this core map eventually becomes second nature and provides a basis for communication. The additional layers also communicate vital information on capabilities, strategies, and risks. Eventually, a Heat Map leads to the development and use of a rich set of common vocabulary that enhances organization communication.

Following are the typical advantages of creating a multilayered Heat Map of business and technical capabilities:

■ Provides an overview and details of the business and technical capabilities of an organization as shown in Figure 3.7.
■ Provides assessment of capability gaps in the overall organization as compared with industry standard—or even a generic map of "to be" state of the organization. For example, a generic Heat map indicates the need to have both Hadoop as well as statistical analytical capabilities. Another example, as shown in Figure 3.5, is the gap for a particular capability.
■ Draws visual attention to the capabilities an organization may be lacking or ones requiring immediate attention. These capabilities can be technical but also legal and compliance related. In Figure 3.6, it is visually clear that the Creation and Management of Organizational Performance Strategy has major gaps and needs immediate attention.
■ Presents the gap between targeted and actual performance of those particular capabilities in the organization. This is a live and dynamic indicator of the gaps.
■ Leads to analysis of the gaps and then the approach to bridge the gaps resulting in a holistic and enterprise-wide systems strategy (e.g., as discussed by Cruz-Cunha [4]).

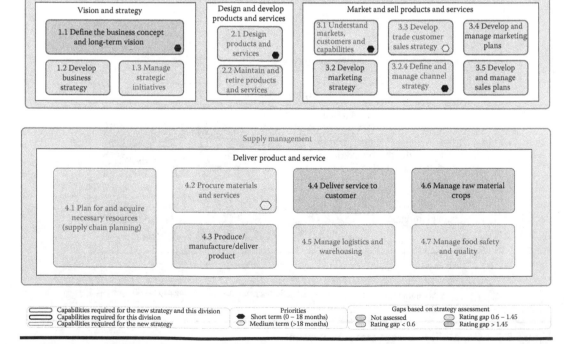

Figure 3.6 Assessing business capabilities.

A heat map also documents the capabilities that work and those that do not. This comparison is used to eliminate redundant or negative capabilities. For example, having capabilities to write Key-Value pairs in Big Data space may not be relevant if the organization is a small and medium enterprise (SME); a more rewarding effort is plugging into Cloud-Analytics.

A Heat Map is a visualization of capabilities requiring attention. Capability value contribution assembles and ranks investments. For example, advantage capabilities with high heat move to the top of the program, followed by business essential capabilities with large inefficiencies. The assessment is based on:

- What questions need to be answered?
- What business capabilities are needed to enable strategy goals?
- What maturity level(s) is required for these capabilities?
- What are the differences between current capabilities and the desired maturity level?
- How much alignment and integration are needed for planned growth?

Incorporating Business Capabilities in Business Development

The business capabilities maps are used in growth plans over time by either acquiring or developing specific assets, investing in new projects, or buying or merging other firms. The business capability assessment provides a prioritization of required business capabilities. The shortlisted capabilities are mapped with the growth approach. When essential capabilities are not strong, the organization could decide to grow by developing new areas from scratch to add to their existing portfolio of activities or through mergers and acquisitions. The importance of corporate acquisitions to a firm's overall corporate strategy is driven from the capabilities desired to meet the strategies. In technology sectors, acquisition by technology giants is in areas where organizational capabilities are complementary.

The business capability mapping is done from both grassroots and top management levels to provide a realistic picture of the organizational view. Figures 3.7 and 3.8 show an organizational gap map with different views—overall organizational assessment of gaps and how the senior executives assess the business capability gaps.

Figure 3.7 depicts the organization-wide assessment where a number of business capabilities are highlighted that require immediate investment. This contrasts with the assessment by the senior executives as shown in Figure 3.8. A capability gap assessment as shown in Figure 3.8 is depicted in a heat map version of the assessment by the senior executive. This results in senior executive unawareness of ground realities and in many cases the investment is directed toward initiatives that do not result in the expected outcomes. In some cases, investments are required to first build a level of maturity to support capabilities to achieve the business outcomes.

The change in focus from business requirement-based implementation to business capability-based outcome is required. Figure 3.9 depicts IT complexity mapped on business capabilities. The IT investment is based on capabilities that need to be built. The assessment of capabilities before and after implementation provides a better measurement of the success of the projects.

The business capability framework is a critical success factor in capturing business value from the IT function and from the organization's IT investments. It is the link between business strategy, IT infrastructures and systems, and organizational performance outcomes. The

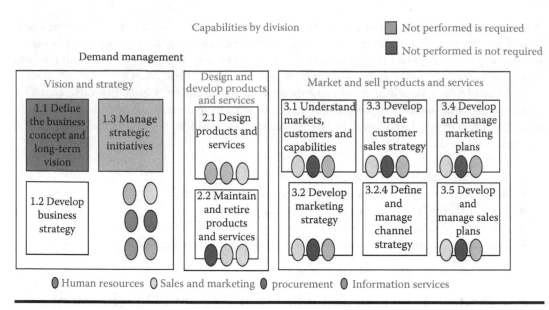

Figure 3.7 Capabilities by divisions.

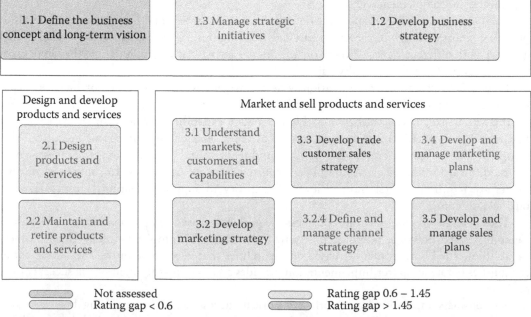

Figure 3.8 Capability assessment by senior executives.

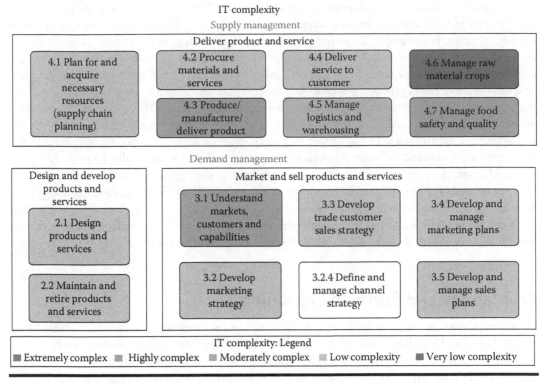

Figure 3.9 Capability assessment showing IT complexity.

capability-based anchor also assists in organizational change management. The following are benefits of the capability-based changes:

- Re-engineering business processes, as the benefit is measurable if used with business capability as foundation for the process changes.
- Implementing enterprise resource planning systems to achieve the business capability for adopting new organizational models.
- Transforming the IT function (which is periodically required when deploying new ITs and tackling new strategic business challenges). Enhancing Business capability to assist in a more efficient IT design and operations.

Organizational Change for Efficiency

At a strategic, macro-level, organizations change by mergers, acquisitions, divestments, and restructures. Such changes can lead to duplications in processes, information, and systems. The incompatability between business operations can increase costs and risks, and lead to a loss of intellectual property. It takes time, resources, and funds to bring merged enitites together and consolidate operations, or to separate entities while assuring service delivery. This generates unbalanced demand on IT resources and makes it difficult to consolidate and optimize. For example, without application capabilities consolidation, any virtualization of servers would only provide minimal improvement in resource usage.

The study of business capabilities in the context of ODBA is the starting point for many changes in the organization. These changes include changes to the operations and functions of the organization. For example, an insurance organization includes the functions related to clients, underwriting, premiums, policies, actuary, investments, and claims. Each of these functions has processes like provide a quote, issue a policy, calculate premium, and settle claims. With every year in operation, the organization accrues a number of business systems, processes, and associated management practices that no longer serve the original purpose. ODBA starts creating change within the above-mentioned functions and processes. This change occurs because the functions and operations are aligned with the desired business outcomes; and if they don't align properly they are upgraded, optimized, or removed. As a result, people and technologies also have to change.

In addition, the current business environment invariably changes so much that the existing systems are incapable of providing effective support. Organizational inefficiencies start impacting business operations if these systems and processes are outdated, unsustainable, or ineffective. Being able to change these systems and processes starts with an overall view of the operations end-to-end. This overall view goes beyond the technologies and systems and into the realms of people and processes.

Profitability and Business Capabilities

IT is accepted as an essential business capability of any organization but the value added of IT is not clear. The IT industry has evolved in the last 50 years from being a simple automation of manual processes capability to a strategic capability for the decision-making. The industry has not matured to the level of other industries such as production or construction industry. The success of one IT project does not guarantee future IT project successes compared to other matured industries. The IT processes of development are not repeatable within or inter-organizations. The failure and success parameters are sometimes not fully understood and thus not repeatable. One of the reasons for this state of confidence in IT is because of its focus on building based on business requirements. The organizations are dynamic and business requirements could change from the time of inception of project to completion.

Business capabilities are the way in which enterprises combine resources, competencies, information, processes, and their environment to deliver consistent value to their customers. They are used to describe what the business does, and how it needs to change in response to strategic challenges and opportunities (Balasubramanian, et al. [5]). Examples of Big Data-based capabilities include Analytical capabilities (e.g., Predictive, Net Promoter Score—NPS), unstructured databases, networks and security infrastructures and business agility.

Thinking in terms of business capabilities is one of the ways enterprises understand and express how they combine technologies and processes to deliver value. This is the dynamic value to the customers. What makes business capability modeling unique is the focus on what the business does and what it needs to do in differently to counter the strategic challenges arising from Big Data technologies and the ensuing opportunities.

A capability gap assessment, as shown in Figure 3.9, is portrayed in a heat map. The visualized gaps are enhanced with the GRC framework, identify the organizational risks and prioritize the capabilities. These prioritizations focus on enterprise-wide efforts to develop a prioritized list of capabilities and the approach to implement. For example, this prioritization considers capabilities needed, existing capabilities with maturity level, the gaps between the two, and efforts needed to align, integrate, and ensure uniformity in capability-building activities. This in a way is governance around GRC based on White et al. [6].

Discussion Points

1. Describe the challenges of implementing a BA in an organization? Answer with specific examples.
2. What is the importance of processes when it comes to implementing ODBA?
3. What the benefits of a BA? How are these benefits different to the benefits from technologies?
4. How does a BA help move an organization from tactical decision-making to strategic decision-making? Discuss with tactical and strategic examples.
5. What is the importance of IT to ODBA? Explain why IT is integral to ODBA
6. What are the key activities in ODBA development? Provide examples of activities within each stage (hint: Table 3.2)
7. Name the dimensions of ODBA. Why is it important to consider these dimensions of the ODBA?
8. What does the organization achieve by developing an ODBA? What would happen to an organization in the absence of an ODBA? Discuss specifically in the context of communications within the organization.
9. Why is change management so important when an organization implements ODBA?
10. What is the definition of Business Capability and what is considered when analyzing business capabilities?
11. How does business capability enhance IT design and operations?
12. Describe the key differences between BA and business capabilities, with examples.

References

1. Tiwary, A. and Unhelkar, B. (2015). Enhancing the Governance, Risks and Control (GRC) Framework with Business Capabilities to Enable Strategic Technology Investments, *SDPSnet Conference* (1–5 Nov, 2015. Dallas, TX). 2015 Society for Design and Process Science. (www.sdpsnet.org).
2. What Is an Objective? Definition and Meaning (n.d.). Retrieved from http://www. businessdictionary.com/definition/objective.html.
3. Appendix A: Business Architecture Glossary. (n.d.). Retrieved from https://c.ymcdn.com/sites/businessarchitectureguild.site-ym.com/resource/resmgr/.
4. Cruz-Cunha, M.M. (2010). *Enterprise Information Systems for Business Integration in SMEs: Technological, Organizational, and Social Dimensions*, IGI Global, Hershey, PA.
5. Balasubramanian, P, Kulatilaka, N. and Storck, J. (1998). *Managing Information Technology Investments Using a Real-Options Approach*, School of Management, Boston University, Boston, MA.
6. White et al. (2015). *Andrew White, Debra Logan, Governing the Information Governance*, Gartner Inc. Stamford, CT.

Chapter 4

Building and Assessing Business Capabilities—I

KEY POINTS

- Identifying gaps in business capabilities as basis for actions
- Developing realistic and timely capabilities that are aligned to business outcomes
- Describing the roles, tasks, and deliverables associated with business capabilities
- Targeting projects to build and enhance necessary business capabilities
- Planning for business strategy implementation
- Prioritizing enterprise-wide business capabilities to support outcomes
- Changing mindset from technical solutions to business-oriented, outcome-driven activities
- Identifying the Return on Investment for capability building
- Ascertaining IT Risks—application, information, infrastructure, and security in capabilities

This chapter further describes the business capabilities identified in the previous chapter as (basis for actions). Since outcome-driven business architecture (ODBA) aligns business capabilities with the outcomes, such alignment forms the basis for identification of gaps in the organization's capabilities. Projects are identified and scoped to build precisely those business capabilities that support the desired business outcomes. Sensible prioritization of business capabilities is possible only when they are viewed across the enterprise. This chapter contains valuable advice to define, enhance, and apply business capabilities within the context of ODBA.

Aligning Business Capabilities

Business capabilities form the building blocks of a contemporary organization. These capabilities provide the basis for an agile (non-hierarchical) structure of the organization. This is because capabilities support business processes as against a hierarchy of roles.

Business capability alignment facilitates management of strategic initiatives of an organization in a much better way than the hierarchical division and department-based management.

ODBA provides a mechanism for assessing and analyzing various options by prioritizing and implementing those capabilities. For example, designing new products requires the business capabilities of market research and production. If capabilities are not carefully studied and implemented, then the market can be misunderstood and a different product line may be implemented. Such production, even if it is highly efficient, may not be effective in generating the desired outcomes for the organization. Alternatively, incompatible products may be produced with higher costs and longer timelines than if those products were aligned with the marketing outcomes. The business capabilities alignment provides opportunities for better product designs as well as improved planning and implementation of product capabilities of the organization. As a result, capabilities provide an opportunity for the business to optimize its efforts toward achieving desired outcomes.

Business capability is built through an overall program of work. The program is planned in phases and adequate allocation of resources is required. Capability modeling is approved by senior executives. This executive level approval also gains necessary participation and commitment from the key stakeholders. A Business Technology Roadmap is developed in collaboration with capability development. This provides a business technology reference framework supporting the long-term strategies, priorities and business goals of the organization while also supporting the relevant standards and operational performance against agreed business capabilities. The roadmap for such a program of work is discussed in Chapter 5 in more detail.

The business vision of an organization forms the basis of desired outcomes. Once these outcomes are prioritized, they influence the business strategy. A study of the outcomes results in refinement of the organizational vision. This iterative approach to vision, prioritization, and strategy forms the basis for action as shown in Figure 4.1. The business strategy life cycle shown in Figure 4.1 generates corresponding actions and projects. Since most business organizations operate in a highly volatile digital space, their strategies also need to keep pace with that changing environment. Although there is an expectation that strategies should not change, senior executives

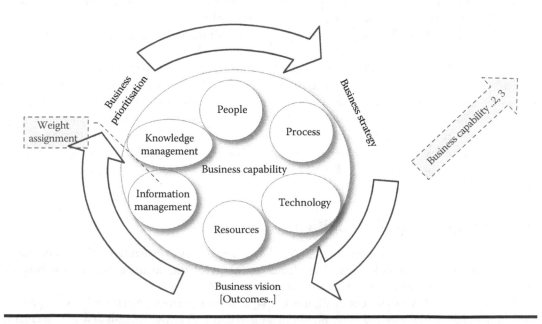

Figure 4.1 Business strategy components and their alignment.

need to ensure the direction of the organization is relevant to its environment. Strategies provide stability but not at the cost of direction. For example, strategies cater to the digital transformations and, as a result they change. This change in strategies, in turn, results in some parts of the strategy becoming obsolete. Obsolete strategies create orphan projects and futile actions. The strategic alignment supported by ODBA identifies these obsolete strategies, activities, and projects in the organization. As a result, senior leadership of the organization can take appropriate measures to either reassign the direction of the projects that are building the capabilities or, in extreme cases, close the projects.

Business capabilities are orthogonal to vision, strategy, and prioritization. This is because all three aspects (vision, strategy, and prioritization) come into play in development of business capabilities. As shown in Figure 4.1, a business capability comprises people, process, technology (mostly information technology—IT), resources, information management (IM), and knowledge management.

As more disruptive technologies come into the market, they create demands for corresponding new capabilities from the business. Consider, for example, the rapid advent of Big Data along with its volume, variety, and velocity. The business needs to develop analytics as a capability. Such capability allows the business to capitalize on the predictive abilities of analytics and provide an impetus for enhanced decision-making. Analytics help the business improve its financial performance by understanding the estimates for revenues and associated costs. Thus, the business is in a better position to understand its investment in people skills, processes, and technologies. Another example is of the upcoming Internet-of-Things (IoT) disruption. Envisioning a futuristic digital enterprise is impossible without giving due consideration to IoT—as every customer and staff of this digital enterprise is bound to carry multiple personal IoT devices. Capabilities that help connect the business with its customers and users through IoT is becoming a necessity rather than an option.

Apart from the factors that go into each business capability (Figure 4.1), additional capability dimensions of an organization need to be understood. For example, resource management, financial management, critical asset management, IM, and knowledge management—are not only feeding into the individual business capabilities but they also operate at the organizational level.

The dimensions that enhance the capabilities of the organization are not all uniform. An important organization-specific function is assigning weight to each dimension of a business capability (mentioned in Figure 4.1). For example, organizations led by information allocate higher weighting to IM, knowledge management, and technology. In other cases, where design of the products, branding, or people skills are the key components for success, higher weight is assigned to resources or people dimensions. The need for flexibility in the dimensions and their corresponding weighting is equally important because of the changes in the digital environment in which the organization operates.

Resources and Business Capabilities

A crucial aspect of any capability in the organization is its resources such as intellectual property, people skills, processes, or financial resources. For example, if a research capability is known to only one scientist, then the firm is vulnerable. That person can claim all the benefits that he creates. In such a case, the benefits associated with the research capability may be in-appropriable by the firm. As a result, the bargaining power of only one person with research knowledge is a significant risk for the firm. The capability is embedded firmly within the organization.

Resource management starts with a clear understanding of supply and demand of resources. The management of supply and demand requires multiple corporate business capabilities such as customer engagement and operational management working together. If any of these capabilities are not adequate, resource allocation suffers. For example, for a given customer engagement, if the tasking and coordination systems are not integrated with human resource management systems, resource allocation is manual. Such resource allocation is duplicated and results in multiple handling of the customer queries. Resources and their impact on business capabilities are classified according to the extent to which they are:

■ **Valuable**. Such resources/capabilities contribute to an activity directly or indirectly linked to a paying customer. Customer needs are at the forefront of all strategic analysis. The resources directly or indirectly contribute to the business outcome expected and add to the "bottom line" or the profit of the organization.

■ **Rare**. Rare resources or capabilities are given priority as these give the company a competitive advantage. Valuable common resources are equally important, but on their own only achieve parity with its competition. The company work force, culture, or branding could be a rare resource developed by the employee skills, processes, and products.

■ **Unique**. These resources are not easily acquired or imitated by the competition. To have a competitive advantage, companies usually have some research capability to make its product unique and/or improve processes, so that costs are reduced. At the same time, the organizations have to protect this uniqueness so they can continue this advantage and sustain profits for a longer period. Eventually, competition catches up, but profitability is sustained in the duration period of the advantage. The unique advantage of organizations is reduced over time as available information from the Internet revolution has changed the differentiation time of any product from years, to months or weeks.

■ **Cultural**. In most of the organizations, culture is a hidden component of its capabilities. Culture is a fundamental component in organizational performance and is included in the organizational assessment. Corporate culture defines the organizational capabilities and employees' skills and effectiveness. The sidebar provides the impact of cultural factors on capabilities.

IMPACT OF CULTURAL FACTORS ON CAPABILITIES

The cultural dimension provides an insight in the organizational capabilities and capacity-building process. Therefore, incentives and rewards are defined by the culture of the organization. A capability-based assessment of the organization is a trigger to potential culture changes required to achieve the desired outcomes.

Measurement practices define work habits and are useful in planning realistic outcomes. Criteria for employee selection for a project or a piece of work determine preferred behavior.

The business capabilities are dependent on the people skills dimension. The people skills are reflected in the organizational performance and overall collective team performance. Performance of teams: cultural differences in communication styles of a team or within teams can create conflict. Some teams/team members might be clear and concise but **indirect or unspoken**. Some might have a differing style of simple and **clear verbal exchange** of information. In some cases, team members believe in value of time being more polychromic where as other team members value time as money. This creates conflicts and adds time and cost to projects (e.g., when meetings do not start on time, or it is extended without prior notice).

Hierarchical organizational culture is where the power is based on the role and position of the person. As a result, decisions are made by 'higher-ups' in the hierarchy. Wrong decisions are not challenged by junior staff. In these types of societal organizations (where fitting in with the team is more important than having independent thinking), the decision of a group is accepted by all to avoid any exclusion (although the decision may be wrong).

People and Business Capabilities

Sourcing people (recruiting) and maintaining skill levels is another important dimension of capability building in an organization. This process of sourcing people and skills is based on the actual needs or on traditional organizational views. This is adjusted for new industry demands of selective hiring, extensive training, reduced status, and wage distinctions. There may be a strong need to change the structure of the organization to facilitate and nurture innovations. A high percentage of teams need to have an environment of collaboration and innovation, where team members are empowered to take quick and innovative decisions and provide high-quality services.

The need to upgrade these aforementioned capabilities requires honest introspection and assessment. The outcome of the capability assessment is documented and it defines the need to reorganize in style, structure, culture, skills, or staff to build an ambidextrous organization to achieve the targeted business outcome. The change from traditional to a digitally transformed organization reflects a flexible and agile structure that changes according to the changing needs of the environment in which the business operates. Leadership becomes crucial in these situations. The need to provide an environment of innovation and empowerment where individual staff members are encouraged to contribute becomes the responsibility of leadership. Upskilling people is not a singular activity—it is made up of sourcing new people and training existing people that results in a workable mix of business, technology, and functional capabilities.

Recruiting in such scenarios is a judicious mix of business, functional, and domain experts based on the priority of capabilities and corresponding demands on skills. The team structure and the corresponding remuneration structures also undergo change that result in proper incentives and progression plans. Creating appropriate job titles and pathways harnesses the capabilities of the organization. Capabilities in both hard, technical skills and soft behavioral skills are enhanced during the resource management process.

A transformational leadership style is outcome-oriented. This style keeps the change process on track while using relationship building to motivate and create an exciting environment for the employees.

The culture shift of the organization to 'risk taking' from 'risk averse' involves a number of structural, social, and individual changes. This requires an environment of freedom to try new approaches and accept mistakes as long as there are lessons learned. The reward system includes soft skill contributions of the team members (e.g., managing team spirit, developing processes, resilience and stress management in critical and stressful requirements, able to communicate thoughts without offending, handling unrealistic demands). The reporting structure is changed from task oriented to a resource management system, where resource managers are responsible for the overall capability building of the employees.

IT and Business Capabilities

A large part of current business capability is invested in IT. Senior executives in private and government sectors, and consultants, watch and embrace the disruptive technological revolution. The challenge is to realize the potential business benefits promised by IT-based innovations. Most established companies have decades of investment in IT capabilities. Over that time, the role of technology has shifted from automating non-core routine tasks to becoming the core enabler of business. Many companies have changed the way they do business because of technology enablement. For example, oil and gas exploration is far more about the sophisticated analysis of seismic data than it is about the physical process of making test drills. Or an investment broker offers ease of access and tools for customers to construct their investment portfolios, at a minimal cost, which were unavailable to the most sophisticated of stockbrokers of the 1980s.

Business capabilities in the area of IT provide:

- **I&T vision:** Sets IT vision for the organization to achieve its business outcomes. In general, the IT strategies are driven from the technology aspect, but a change in developing I&T vision and strategy may be required to align with the organizational goals and business outcomes expected. IM is defined as an organizational capability and is developed across the organization, not just in IT.
- **I&T principles:** Defines a set of principles to guide behavior of IT investments. The organizational structure could be centralized or distributed IT capabilities. It is important that all IT initiatives, irrespective of how they are kicked off, follow the same principles. "Shadow IT" is a common term used to highlight IT-related initiatives by individuals or departments without centralized consent. "Shadow IT" exists because of a poor delivery track record of centralized IT and when departmental priorities not aligned with the overall IT priorities. In some cases, the delivered projects from centralized IT might not be meeting the expectations or outcomes expected from the project implementation. This causes duplication of capabilities. Once the business capability matures and applications are mapped to the business capabilities, organizational governance can develop IT vision of consolidating duplicate applications for the same capability. This requires senior management commitment to address instances of shadow IT and bring these capabilities within the centralized IT.
- **Strategic themes and drivers:** Strategic drivers represent the priorities for IT investment and management. The drivers are grouped into strategic themes or portfolios based on business capabilities prioritization.
- **Strategic objectives:** Activity enabling implementation of projects that achieve the strategic goals.

Perception of the IT Capabilities in Organizations

Business capability dimension of IT is an integral service to the organization. In the current disruptive technology environment, IT as a cost center or supporter of services needs to change as part of business capabilities building. For example, if the business capability is to "manage strategic initiatives," the IT dimension is essential in developing a strategic enterprise program management office (EPMO) to manage the strategic initiative proactively. In many organizations, the perception of IT dimensions is different based on the traditional and historic investment in IT.

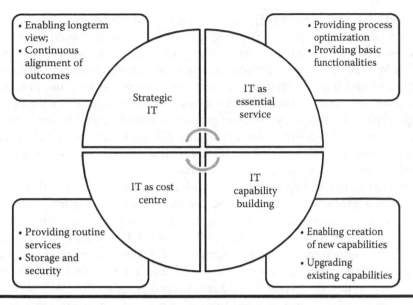

Figure 4.2 IT Functions and perceptions in an organization.

It is important to understand how IT investment is perceived to make it an enabler of the business capabilities. Following are IT perceptions (also summarized in Figure 4.2):

■ IT as Cost Service—this mindset treats IT similar to HR and finance. ITs purpose is to automate organizational processes. This creates an issue with positioning IT as a department. Also, because of its technical nature, experts provide this service. This results in IT being treated as a black box service where only data is considered rather than a holistic view of the service. New technology may not provide the business benefits projected. IT initiatives run the risk of being hype. IT does not always work toward building organizational capabilities. IT can block strategic initiatives because of its inability to deliver.

■ IT as essential services—in this case, IT works with the organizational goals and creates business capabilities. It provides analytics and information to better utilize organizational resources and focuses the resources in the right direction.

■ IT as capability building—IT capabilities are used in either product building, organizational capabilities, or customer intimacy. For example, IT assists companies such as Walmart, Dell, and Amazon in optimization of supply chain processes. IT becomes the "Information Led" organizational capability and provides an environment of steadily building them up.

■ Strategic IT—where IT leads the organization in building capabilities and identifies the new capabilities required to compete and advance in the marketplace. Many telecommunication and banking organizations have used IT as a capability-building dimension.

IM, Intelligence and Business Capability

IM is shown in Figure 4.1 as one of the key dimensions of a business capability. IM is concerned with organized and creative use of data and information within the organization. Excellence in IM results in well-organized data that is secured, accessible, and managed formally in the organization. Business Intelligence (BI) is the extension of IM further in the realms of improving business outcomes. BI is the process of using collective information within the organization. This collective information results in establishing correlations between otherwise separated information siloes. BI results in improved identification and alignment of business outcomes. BI also helps optimize business performance, enhance customer service, and provide an overall competitive advantage and sustainability to the business. As a result of the organization entering the digital space, BI capabilities of an organization extend further beyond into a group of organizations—resulting in collaborative intelligence (CI) [1]. CI is when multiple organizations or in some cases, multiple divisions within a large, multinational organization, share BI for a win-win outcome without compromising their own market position.

CI takes BI to the next level by synergizing knowledge within and across multiple organizations to produce actionable value to the collaborators. The use of BI and CI requires a robust underlying business architecture. This architecture includes business, enterprise, and solution level architectures. ODBA provides the mechanism to utilize BI and CI. CI provides a mechanism to develop business capabilities across departments and partners. For example, the marketing capability developed in one organization is shared across partners, reducing the need for each partner to develop this capability. Decision-making is enhanced due to the collaborative effort. Although BI can mean the use of technical and analytical intelligence decision-making, it also represents the tools, technologies, and platforms that enable creating and utilizing knowledge within the organization.

Business Strategy Alignment

Figure 4.3 depicts aligning strategic outcomes with the required business capabilities. For example, if the organizational goal is to utilize technology as a key driver of growth, the strategic direction is improving resource utilization by better management of skills and resources. A number of strategic directions are available and each requires different business capabilities. For example, if the strategic direction selected by the organization is to "improve capabilities through workforce reform and technology," the corporate services, tasking, and coordinating business capability maturity is required. The organization assesses these capabilities, and plans activities to mature these capabilities at the level required to achieve the business outcomes.

Business strategy is based on the business outcomes required by the organization. These include factors that make the organization more competitive, and thus more profitable, than others in the market. For example, Amazon's business strategy is to provide a better customer interaction by optimizing the supply chain capabilities. The first mover advantage Amazon had in the online ordering business is now replicated in traditional fast-moving consumer goods, and the range of products offered is based on replicating optimized supply chain business capabilities. Strategies also protect the innovative aspects of an organization from being mimicked by the competition. Thus, development of sound business strategies is vital in the process of aligning capabilities with outcomes. There is a need to define and agree upon the principles to achieve the optimal business strategy. Table 4.1 lists the principles to achieve strategies that enable alignment of outcomes and business capabilities.

Business Strategy Implementation Plan

The organizational structures, processes, and resources are optimized to achieve its business goals. The business strategy implementation plan provides a detailed roadmap to achieve the business outcomes. It serves as a critical role in supporting administration and governance practices to

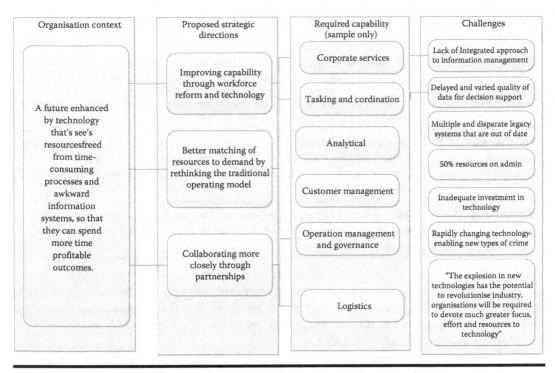

Figure 4.3   Aligning outcomes to the strategic goals.

Table 4.1   Principles to Develop Business Capabilities Alignment with Strategies

Effective	The business capabilities are used to improve accessibility, timeliness, agility, and effectiveness of information and services. This demands a pragmatic approach for the definition of business capabilities and details.
Efficient	Business capabilities shape functions, solutions, and priorities to maximize value for money. The governance model is based on business capabilities prioritization and is adopted across the organization. One of the benefits of the business capabilities-based assessment is the harmonization of business activities across various departments and divisions.
Relevant	The business capability meets the needs of the organization. The ODBA is pertinent to the current state.
Business-driven	The enterprise-wide needs, solutions, and priorities are identified and driven by the business, with clear ownership of capabilities and solutions, and an enterprise-wide commitment to priorities.
Interoperable	Business capabilities continuously improve information flows and exchanges with all stakeholders.

(Continued)

Table 4.1 (*Continued*)   Principles to Develop Business Capabilities Alignment with Strategies

Secure	The business outcomes and solutions shaped by information context needs to enable necessary security requirements to be met.
Sustainable	The strategies, plans, and practices meet the needs of the present while providing a platform for the future.
Flexible and adaptive	The capabilities deployed enable the organization to respond promptly to the evolving needs of customers and partners. The systems supporting the capabilities are sufficiently flexible to enable such changes.
Deliverable	Solutions are pragmatic, realistic, and achievable, and delivered in a way that enables stakeholder confidence in organizations' systems and information.

ensure strategy implementation decisions and investments are optimized by the organizational strategy and goals. These decisions are anchored using a predefined assessment criteria. The business strategy implementation plan is owned by a senior executive responsible for the strategy implementation. This is usually the CEO.

The business strategy implementation bridges the gap between business priorities and investment decisions. It enables cohesive, consistent, and efficient prioritization of investment for maximum benefits. The key objectives of the business capability enhancement or enablement are as follows:

- In most organizations, starting the business capability-based journey does not have an organization structure where all dimensions of the business capabilities are managed by one group. The gaps in people skills, organizational structure, and other resource areas must be allocated to respective organizational groups or divisions specializing in these areas such as human resources departments.
- Define key principles to guides behaviors of key stakeholders, in making consistent investment decisions.
- Define strategic drivers to direct innovation and investment decisions.

The implementation plan is designed to enable safe changes in business strategies. This plan enables recalibration of the implementation when a significant event impacts strategic direction, or when new plans are set by the organization. The components of business strategy implementation plan depicted in Figure 4.4 are:

- **Trends:** Identifies the key trends impacting the organization. The trends include both market environment changes of the organization and technology trends to facilitate organizational goals. The pattern analysis process is built on standard criteria and avoids implementing new technology without assessing against business strategy outcomes. The change in trends is evaluated against the business capabilities required to meet the market challenges. This assists in developing capabilities and also prioritizing initiatives.
- **Foundations of organization:** Core strategies of the organization, and in some case of the departments, are inputs in defining the business strategy implementation and capability-building roadmap.

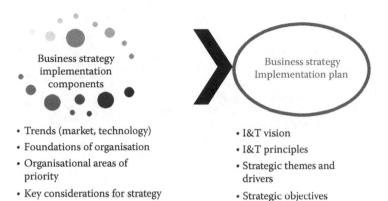

Business strategy implementation components

• Trends (market, technology)
• Foundations of organisation
• Organisational areas of priority
• Key considerations for strategy
• Technology current state
• Capability assessment and gaps

Business strategy Implementation plan

• I&T vision
• I&T principles
• Strategic themes and drivers
• Strategic objectives
• Alignments with IT components

Figure 4.4   Components of business strategy implementation plan.

■ **Organizational areas of priority:** The priority sectors identified by outcomes required and company reports, strategies, and information, collected from the executive leadership teams.
■ **Key considerations:** Considers the constraints that may impact strategy realization. For example, the resource constraints, such as people skills require some lead time to develop these capabilities.

Business Capability Building and Alignment Roadmap

The objective of a business strategy roadmap is to establish the direction and priorities for all investments and governance. It also sets a strategic roadmap for information and technology for both 5- and 10-year horizons. This business strategy is intended to provide direction for governance and decision-making required to manage the strategic outcomes. The organization needs to define enterprise-level initiative assessment aligned investment plan based on the prioritized business capabilities. The business capabilities-based governance assesses business capabilities before and after the investment to validate the business capabilities-building projects deliver the business outcomes.

Figure 4.5 depicts the business strategy alignment with the capabilities as a continuous and iterative process. The assessment of business capabilities provides a structured program of work to boost capabilities. The upliftment of the capabilities in an area may highlight gaps in other capabilities and thus the cycle continues. For example, if the first assessment highlighted capability gaps in *customer management*, boosting the capability may highlight gaps in *billing capabilities* or *managing supplier* capabilities. The assessment strategy business capabilities are used to assess the current state of business capabilities to achieve the desired strategy and required rating for implementation of the strategy. Success implementation of business strategies comes from a combination of defining and implementing business capabilities. The implementation of business capabilities uses the following steps:

■ Identify the business capabilities that are required to each of the strategy items
■ Assess required rating of the capabilities to achieve targeted strategy

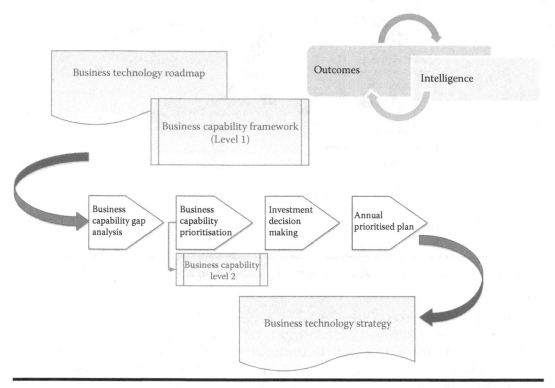

Figure 4.5   Business capability building and alignment roadmap.

- Assess current rating of the capabilities
- Create a roadmap to fill in the capability gap
- Implement the strategy using upgraded capabilities

Business Capability Building—Tasks and Artifacts

The business capability building needs to be planned as an iterative program of work with clearly defined artifacts and project tasks. The outcome of the key tasks completed as part of development, mapping, assessment, and prioritization is managed as project and is reported to senior executives. Some artifacts are defined before embarking upon the business capability assessment initiatives.

Developing Business Capabilities: Tasks, Roles, and Deliverables

The business capability building necessitates involving senior executives of the business and their direct reports to participate actively in developing business capabilities. The organization has this commitment from their executives and is sponsored by the board of management or the chief executive office of the organization. The business capabilities are mapped and socialized within the organization. The capabilities mapping also define the owners for the business capabilities.

To implement and maintain a satisfactory solution for business capability management, there is a clearly defined 'owner' who is held accountable to lead the strategic alignment, coordination, development, and direction of their allocated capability. Business capabilities incorporate policy, finance, process, information, application, and people, and, as such, the capability owner is expected to fully collaborate within those areas to ensure a smooth delivery of services.

- Create Business Capability Framework: The business capabilities mapping to the owners, is based on the decision makers of divisions or departments. The owners are the highest authority of the division. As they do not have the time to manage day-to-day activities for the information, a custodian and capability manager is defined and notified within the organization.
- Target Information Owner: Each capability utilizes, creates, or modifies information domains. Each information domain owner is defined in a similar structure as the capability owner. The details of these roles are described in Chapter 8.
- Policy to Capability Map: Defines organizational policies and what capabilities they are serving. This mapping assists in redesigning policies when any change in business capability is implemented. In some cases, assessment and use of the policies results in optimizing the processes and policies.
- Application to Capability Map: Defines how an application is used across the organization. In most cases, applications serve more than one capability.
- Organization Survey results for maturity, organizational risks, IT risks to Capability Map: An interval study may be necessary when assessing capabilities. In most cases, surveys answers are associated with more than one capability. This mapping is required for the capability assessment. The details are discussed in Chapter 8.
- Organization Risk to Capability Map: Required for the prioritization of the projects that reduces organizational risks.
- IT Risk to Capability Map: Assists in investing resources to IT projects building priority capabilities. Harmonies and Prioritization Communications package for target owners are well planned to maximize the assessment outcomes. In most of the organizations, multiple surveys, evaluations, and reorganizations are always in play. Sometimes this fatigues employees. In capability assessment, it is important to have a realistic and truthful assessment of these capabilities. The communication pack articulates the objectives clearly to get better capability results of evaluation.
- Roles and responsibilities for capability and sub-capability owners are defined: In most of the organizations, these roles and responsibilities may not exist and need careful planning to assign them.

Roles

Each business capability is created and supported by a number of roles. These roles include: target capability owner, target capability sub-owner, policy owner, information owner, system owner, application owner, and infrastructure owner.

Each target capability and target sub-capability has owner roles and responsibilities. These roles and responsibilities are agreed upon and finalized with the nominated owners, are position based and assigned to position owners. From time to time, changes to the organizational structure results in changes to the owners.

Target Capability Owner

The capability owner is a senior executive who is accountable for ensuring that matters relating to their allocated capabilities meet the organization's needs and requirements. This includes:

■ Ensuring the capabilities have an assigned sub-capability owner and identified owners for other layers of the capability map definitions within organization
■ Ensuring that owners meet their responsibilities
■ Providing advice and direction to information, application, policy, and process owners as required
■ Approving capability change or IT investment decisions or signing-off on advice
■ Handing over the Capability Owner's role to the person that occupies their position during leave or other extended periods of absence.

Target Sub-Capability Owner

Sub-capability owners are department or division heads responsible for undertaking or coordinating the day-to-day business of their areas. This includes:

■ Providing input into policy, process, and application advice on the subject, including legislative changes.
■ Initiating reviews on issues relating to their subject, in consultation with various departments. Reviews may be in response to general monitoring of the sub-capability, risk assessments, internal or external reviews, or continuous improvement activities.
■ Monitoring and evaluating the sub-capability to ensure that any changes relating to it are effective, address relevant risks, and meet organizational needs and requirements.
■ Appointing suitable contacts/delegates to help meet the above responsibilities.
■ Handing over the sub-capability owner's role to the person who occupies their position, during leave or other extended periods of absence.

Policy Owner

Policy Owners are department or divisional heads responsible for undertaking or coordinating day-to-day business relating to their allocated policy subjects. This includes:

■ Providing input into policy advice on the subject, including legislative change or any other changes required for policies mapped to any business capability changes.
■ Initiating reviews on policy issues relating to their subject, in consultation with Strategy and Policy. Reviews may be in response to general monitoring of the subject, risk assessments, internal or external reviews, or continuous improvement activities.
■ In collaboration with Strategy and Policy, assess policy proposals initiated by other employees or work units.
■ In collaboration with Strategy and Policy, prepare policy development plans for the conduct of policy reviews, whether initiated by themselves, other organizational units, or directed by the Accountable Officer.
■ Oversee the conduct of policy reviews and providing advice/direction on the recommendations of reviews.

- Ensure policy change is properly implemented, including identifying implementation requirements, associated costs and coordinating delivery.
- Monitoring and/or evaluating the subject to make sure that any policies relating to it are effective, address relevant risks, and meet organizational needs and requirements.
- Appointing suitable policy contacts/delegates to help them meet the above responsibilities.
- Handing over the Policy Owner's role to the person who occupies their position during leave or other extended periods of absence.

Business Owner

The business role accountable for managing the business process and its objectives implemented by the application, and ensuring it is fit for the purpose according to agreed and documented standards, and that it meets the objective of the process definition.

Information Owner

An Information Owner is responsible for the management of specific information assets on behalf of the organization. The context of the information determines information ownership. Information owners are responsible for:

- Identifying impacts of legislative or organizational changes on the information requirements of the business.
- Ensuring that appropriate security and processes, consistent with the organizational policy, are implemented for information assets.
- Determining appropriate security classification or sensitivities of information assets and the associated access restrictions.
- Reporting and assisting in investigation of security breaches or issues.

The information owner is also the work unit manager for information or records not stored in a corporate application, such as hardcopy documents or images, digital documents, or audio/visual material whether stored on removable devices/media, personal drives, or network drives.

When information or records are stored in a corporate application all information, or significant subsets of the information, has a nominated information owner who is responsible for managing that information on behalf of the organization. The information owner's approval is sought whenever there is a request to access, modify or enhance information held in an application. To fulfill this obligation, application information owners are an appropriate appointment for that level of responsibility and in a position of sufficient authority to make decisions on behalf of the organization.

System Owner

A system owner for corporate applications and/or IT infrastructure is ultimately responsible for the secure management and support of critical information on behalf of the organization. To fulfill this obligation, system owners of applications or IT infrastructure have an appropriate appointment for that level of responsibility and in a position of sufficient authority to make decisions on behalf of the organization.

System Manager

The system manager is responsible for the management of all resources required to maintain the application and to perform other duties as delegated by the System Owner.

Application Owner

The application owner is responsible for controlling the development, testing, maintenance, use, and record keeping of an application.

Each application owner has ultimate responsibility and accountability for all components of planning and management relating to the:

- operating environment
- system availability
- enhancement and development
- change implementation
- use of the application and associated resources
- compliance with legislation and applicable standards
- strategy and corporate alignment

These responsibilities and accountabilities are multifaceted, and include:

- Detailed application requirements (including user, technical, architectural, functional, security, and public records) are identified and documented.
- Appropriate risk-based business decisions are made to ensure that technological "solutions" fully meet business requirements and are properly developed and implemented.
- Governance activities necessary for the effective, ongoing, and secure management of the application and creation of public records are implemented and maintained.
- Application-specific policies and procedures for efficient, secure application management, and use are documented, and that training in their use is provided to all relevant personnel.

Infrastructure Owner

The infrastructure owner ensures design and management requirements are adequately identified, documented, and addressed during the design, enhancement, development, and implementation of any infrastructure or component thereof. The owner holds the ultimate responsibility and accountability for all elements of planning and managing of infrastructure including:

- security
- operating environment
- availability and disaster recovery planning
- change control
- capacity management and planning
- use of infrastructure components and associated resources
- compliance with applicable legislation and/or standards
- overall administration of the system including agreed service level agreements with service providers

Business Capability Assessment

Developing business capabilities is an iterative and incremental process. It starts with the business capability assessment, which determines the current and required state of the capabilities based on predefined criteria for the assessment. The business criteria for capability assessment are defined before embarking on this activity. The purpose of the capability assessment is to collect sufficient information for prioritizing capabilities and assessing initiatives across the organization to align with business capability building. The objective of the assessment is to develop a program of works to address capability gaps.

A number of methods such as surveys, interviews, or a hybrid of the two is used to assess capability gaps. The method selected provides realistic assessments of the capabilities. The capability assessment provides ground for small and large investments by the organization in achieving strategic goals. Collecting and evaluating this information defines the following:

- Articulate and gain consensus on business capability requirements for each business unit
- Ensure that the enterprise is prepared for growth and profitability
- Ensure that investments of time, resources, and money support the business strategy
- Maximizing transformational opportunities
- Discover harmonization opportunities that cross business units and functional areas to drive efficiency and reduced costs
- Understand the implications of cost optimization efforts on current and future business capabilities
- Provide a reference point for governance

Initiation Phase

The capability assessment is a program of work comprising projects. The initiation phase defines the scope of the project. This has a finite timeline to assess capabilities and is managed as a proper project using the skills of project management, so it does not run in perpetuity. The capability assessment is part of the enterprise project management office or similar unit within the organization. For example, based on a context such as introducing a new product or assessing business capabilities of an acquired or planned acquisition, the scope of the project is defined as identifying the advantage capabilities of the product or organization. The scope of the project is based on the expected business outcomes. The scope defines the level of assessment as well as the business capabilities. Table 4.2 describes the activities required during the initiation phase with the expected outcomes.

Planning Phase

The project planning phase defines the process for assessment. The stakeholders are selected for the roles described in the previous sections, such as capability owners or application owners. For example, a quick assessment of the business capabilities is done to shortlist capabilities for a detailed analysis in one or more dimensions. The quick assessment may highlight gaps in the IT or process dimensions for the prioritized capabilities and the follow-up project scope is defined based on the current project outcomes. Table 4.3 describes the activities required during planning phase with the expected outcomes.

Table 4.2 Business Capability-Building Planning Phase

Activities	Outcomes
Analyze stakeholder list	Organizational changes are common, and the assessment is based on roles and responsibilities. In some cases, a small pool of people with knowledge of operational effectiveness and deficiencies are included in the assessment list.
Plan stakeholder engagement	Key stakeholder engagement is scheduled to get maximum input for the assessment. In most cases, one approach does not fit all. Key stakeholder engagement is defined with multiple approaches to get the right candidates for the capabilities assessment.
Define taxonomy	Capability assessment is driven from a standard taxonomy that is agreed upon with the stakeholders.
Plan sequence for the data gathering (based on location/priority)	Previous data is validated without compromising data collection from interviews or other current collection techniques.
Socialize data gathering schedule	The schedule is published, so the participants are aware of the information collection. In some cases, this assessment provides an avenue for the participants to give feedback to senior management.
Create data collection templates	Data collection templates provide confidence to the participant the information provided is secure and not used against the participant. The truthfulness of information is imperative in the capability assessment.
Create assessment criteria	The assessment criteria is set up and approved by the senior leadership team in advance. This reduces the time and effort in getting the results of the assessment accepted after the evaluation exercise is finished. In some cases, the capability assessment leads to the ground realities that senior management is not aware of or may be ignoring. The attempt to not agree with the data is mitigated by pre-approval of assessment criteria by senior management and executive leadership teams.
Create straw man process and application maps	In some cases, the process of capability assessment approves application development projects. It is recommended to map the processes, sub-capabilities, and applications supporting these capabilities.

Execution Phase

The project execution phase requires senior executive sponsorship to collect data from the key stakeholders. The activity needs feedback sessions with the senior executive team, and they are actively engaged through a project steering committee framework or a defined engagement method agreed upon with the team. The capability assessment requires time commitments from the executives and senior managers. The senior executive sponsorship to this initiative makes sure the data is collected in a timely method. For example, the business capability assessment

Table 4.3 Business Capability Building Delivery Phase

Activities	Outcomes
Gather information from key stakeholders to understand: Business pain points Key drivers for growth Business priorities	Information gathering depends on the stakeholder engagement plan but the information gathered from each source depends on the key drivers, and is published. The information gathering session is focused to avoid becoming an avenue for unproductive venting. The information is gathered within the scope and time defined. These projects are time bound, and data gathering of data is planned with enough margin to revalidate data and work with the participants' work schedules.
	The information gathered provides an outcome of capability, is defined and understood. A heat map approach is used to visualize the information.
	The objective of capability assessment is to create and initiative and roadmap to achieve the desired capability maturity level. The outcome of the assessment is creating projects to develop desired capabilities. This is important to keep employees' trust in organizational acceptance of their recommendations. The information gathered provides an outcome of well-defined and well-understood business capability assessment/description. The findings are documented and published (within context and security of the information) without compromising the organizational competitive edge and sustainability.
	The information shared is designed to provide the stakeholders with adequate information and what is shared depends on the organizational culture. The information is masked before disclosing to the competitors.
Create to-be state	The outcome of the assessment and initiatives to achieve the desired capability maturity level is published in the form of actions taken by organization.
Create migration roadmaps	The business capability 'to-be state,' when compared with the current state, highlights gaps. The migration plan from 'current state' to the 'to-be state' identifies initiatives and projects which are prioritized and subsidized.
Create list of projects	The list of initiatives or projects is created and agreed on with the executive team.
Document findings	A report with the outcome of assessment and next steps.
Socialize findings	Communication to the stakeholders and list of next steps.

executions phase could include the method of the data collection, such as interviews or surveys, and also the assessment criteria. The success of this phase depends upon the strength of the sponsorship by senior executives. In many cases, the surveys and interviews may not be taken seriously by the respondents if senior executives have not indicated the compulsion of responses.

Table 4.4 describes the activities required during execution phase with the expected outcomes.

Table 4.4 Business Capability Building Deliverables

Artifact	Description of Artifacts
Project scoping document	Defines the outcomes expected from the project and scope of assessment.
Resource plan	A clear resource plan.
Stakeholder engagement plan	List of the stakeholders' along with roles and responsibilities, communication methods, and results of stakeholder engagement.
Current/future business capabilities assessment templates	A number of templates are reused for detailed assessment and any future assessments. The effectiveness of assessment is measured if the assessment criterion is maintained and is the same for multiple assessments.
Data gathering schedule	The information gathering schedule provides adequate time to engage with the key stakeholders and to work with their schedules. The engagement and information gathering plans are socialized with the key stakeholders.
Current assessment of business capabilities	A detailed assessment of the business capabilities and recommendations.

Business Capability Building: Deliverables

Business Capability building, including assessment, at the initiation phase identifies and delivers a number of artifacts. Table 4.4 identifies some of these artifacts.

Prioritization

Capabilities are categorized in a high to low priority order. They are listed in alphabetical order within each business category based on the business capability framework in use. For example, if APQC framework is used then the business capabilities are listed based on the category number such as "1.0 Vision and Strategy."

The business capability prioritization is critical for business outcomes. The business capability prioritization is treated as a project. The project is managed with the Board of Management's approval. A number of methods for prioritization can be used. One option is to conduct surveys and individually interview all division executives and their direct reports. The survey is initiated by the board of management as an organizational-wide initiative. This ensures the participation by key stakeholders. The survey is based on organizational strategic requirements and divisional strategy. The business capability assessment survey results are reviewed by survey area where the capability gap is >2 and risks or challenges are identified.

The results of the survey are assessed for alignment with other divisions. Each division's harmonization workshops are conducted and the divisional top-five capabilities gaps are prioritized for short- and long-term plans. Divisional reports are documented and distributed to each division's participants for approval and accuracy of the results. For each priority area, the report includes recommendations on how to address closure of the capability gaps. Based on the divisional priorities, a consolidated enterprise view of organization priorities is developed and presented to the BOM. The business capabilities prioritization is endorsed by the board of management.

Issues

Issues surrounding the successful delivery of each capability is identified and summarized by reviewing known IT risks (infrastructure, application, information, and security), and organizational risks relating to that capability. The assessment is a multistage process. The corresponding supporting Information and Communication technology capabilities (ICT capabilities) are defined. ICT capabilities are a combination of systems, communication networks, IT infrastructure, and other components required for the capability. For example, to provide ICT capability of billing, a number of application systems, interfaces, infrastructure, and communication network is defined as ICT billing capability. The business capabilities are mapped to ICT capabilities. For example, business capability of "Managing Billing" is mapped to ICT Capabilities "Manage Billing," "Send communication," "Process payments." In some cases, all the ICT capabilities are using a single set of ICT assets such as an ERP system. The issues or risks of each of the ICT capabilities are individually assessed using a standard organizational risk management framework. The mapping of the business capability with the ICT capabilities provides visibility to understanding key risks and issues organizations face in the ICT capabilities dimension. This approach is also applicable in other dimensions such as skills management and financial resources allocation.

Policy Mapping

The business capability-based approach may be a new approach for many established organizations. In most organizations, policies and ownerships are prevalent. A policies framework is recommended to suit needs, fits the purpose, and aligns with the business capabilities. The organization's policy framework and, if relevant, the existing policy owners defined in the organization is used as a starting point to align business capabilities and assist in developing stakeholder and target owners for capabilities.

Application Mapping

In most cases, the reason to create a capability framework is to manage IT projects, portfolios, and investment. In many organizations, function and activity model mapping of organization's applications to predefined functions are existing. These activities are designed to provide a pictorial view with high-level descriptions for the various functions and associated activities that are managed by the organization. These documents are intended to help the organization understand the range of functions managed by the organization and are used as a reference point in support of any project or initiative. These documents assist in aligning areas of responsibility and information systems to support those functions.

Example of Priority Calculation

This section details the calculations used to determine the priority rating for the intelligence capability. Table 4.5 shows a sample capability assessment report. This methodology is used consistently throughout the capability maturity assessment (Based on APQC capability framework, 7.4

Table 4.5 Sample Assessment of Manage Enterprise Information Capability

7.4 Manage Enterprise Information	
Description	• Develop information and content management strategies • Define the enterprise information architecture • Manage information resources • Perform enterprise data and content management
Issues	• IT solutions in place to support the KPIs are not adequately orchestrated to deliver to organization's pace requirements • IM maturity is low • Information Systems landscape is complicated as we are part way through ERP Transformation • Too many tools required to extract the information required
Impact	• The organization is constrained in their ability to make decision in an appropriate timeframe • The immaturity of this capability has a significant impact on the '8.0 Mange Financial Resources' capability set
Recommendation	• Enterprise focus on developing IM capability required • Assess ways to accelerate development of BI and data warehouse(DW) capability to close this key capability gap ASAP • Continue to focus on Information Governance and Master data management (MDM) implementation

shows the capability level as per APQC PCF framework). Table 4.5 shows the assessment report for "7.4 Manage Enterprise Information." The assessment heat map is shown as color dots. The traffic lights are used as capability assessment representation: red means need immediate attention, yellow means the capability is partially aligned with the business outcomes, and green means the business capability is fully aligned with the business outcomes. The report as shown in Table 4.5 provides an overview of the business capabilities in the description row. The description is aligned with the capability framework and capability descriptions. The report describes the assessed issues and risks with the assessed business capabilities to meet the business outcomes. Table 4.5 describes a number of IT issues required to be addressed for achieving desired business outcomes. For example, the issue of "IT solutions in place to support the KPIs are not adequately orchestrated to deliver to organization's pace requirements" needs to redefine the key performance indicator (KPI) as per the organizational pace requirements. For example, a required business outcome is better customer interaction with a KPI of length of time a service agent spends with the customer. This KPI could cause the service agent to try and complete the call without resolving the problem. The assessment report should describe the impact of the issues and risks with the capabilities in achieving the business outcomes and the next steps recommendations as described in Table 4.5.

Risk Mapping

Each capability is linked to any risks that limit effective delivery. These risks are mapped in many to many combinations. Each capability has multiple risks and each risk has multiple capabilities. The same method of calculation is applied consistently to all sub-capabilities and capabilities within the assessment.

IT Risk

Incorporating four categories, the IT risk assessment of each capability includes registered risks (including architectural debt) related to—application, infrastructure, information, and security. Risks are assessed according to the architectural patterns, standards, and information policies within the organization.

Application Risk

These are risks associated with an existing application, including risks relating to:

- Business requirements
- Application design
- Application code
- Application testing
- Application maintenance

Application risks relate to integration, quality, performance, usability, ease of patching, and maintenance. There are direct risks such as code that allows undesirable behavior and obscure risks such as the end of support for a library or component used to develop the application.

Applications are mapped to risks based on the existing business sensitivity, data classification, intended use, and exposure potential. The assessment is based on internal standards, architecture experience, and established design patterns (both internal and industry best practice).

Information Risk

These are risks associated with IM, including risks related to the IM life cycle:

- Information Acquisition
- Information Processing and Flow
- Information Retention
- Information Disposal
- Information Security

Information risks relate to the flow of information, its use and availability throughout the information life cycle. Information risks consider loss or exposure of information and unavailability of information when required for a particular business need.

Infrastructure Risk

These are risks associated with the physical environment that hosts or directly supports an application and includes:

- Network
- Servers and back-end systems
- Back-up and Restore environment
- Associated environmental components such as High Availability (HA) and Failover
- Supporting back-end equipment such as Enterprise Service Bus (ESB)

Infrastructure relates to the components and systems that form the underlying services and applications, such as disk storage and networks. Many of these underpinnings are shared across different business applications. For example, more than one application server can call the same database, and different servers can share a disk. For this reason, infrastructure risks are distinct from the other categories of risks in that they relate more to service level, capacity, and performance implications—and less to business application delivery.

Security Risk

These are risks associated with security architecture, including cyber security those within IT systems:

- Business data acquisition
- Business data processing and flow
- Business data retention
- Business data disposal
- Data security and controls

Security is traditionally defined as confidentiality, integrity, and availability (CIA). Security risks are widely defined and are exposures related to design, configuration, and implementation of systems and infrastructure. The risk process seeks a balance between achieving controls to address CIA and the cost of implementing those controls.

Discussion Points

1. Explain the relationship between business capabilities and alignment. What are some key ways that ODBA supports the alignment process?
2. Describe the three dimensions of business capabilities. Why are the components weighted differently?
3. How are resources classified? How does each form a competitive advantage?
4. Why do people skills need to be adjusted with ODBA?
5. Explain the relationship between IT and business capabilities, including positive and negative impacts. How is IT currently perceived in organizations and what needs to change to make it part of a capability dimension?
6. What is the importance of business strategies and capabilities to the organization? What are some of the principles that make up this strategy?
7. What are some of the key results of a business strategy implementation?
8. What is the difference between business strategy components and the implementation plan?
9. What is the role of the capability owner? Why is it such an important role in building and implementing capabilities?
10. What are some of the components of the assessment? What are some potential challenges of the assessment and how could these be overcome?
11. What are the different types of risks and the impact of each on ODBA?
12. What is the importance of aligning Business Architecture with Business strategies? And what are the issues and risks in undertaking this alignment?

13. What are the three classifications of resources and capabilities and how does each form a competitive advantage?
14. What are best principles to optimize the business strategy? Which ones are most relevant?
15. Discuss the tasks, roles, and deliverables in developing business capabilities.
16. How does a technology roadmap differ from and support a business capability framework?
17. What are the different types of application risks? How do they differ from Information risks?

Reference

1. Unhelkar, B. and Tiwary, A. (2010). Collaborative intelligence, in *Cutter IT Journal*, Vol. 23 page 13–21 No. 6, June 2010.

Chapter 5

Implementing Business Capabilities—II

KEY POINTS

- Implementing Business Capabilities and Organizational Strategy Roadmaps
- Revisiting Stakeholder Influence on Implementation Initiatives and funding for business capability-based business architecture (BA)
- Planning Stakeholder engagement and their role in business capability implementation
- Conducting Data collection, Surveys, Interviews with Stakeholders to assess business capabilities
- Creating and validating business capability assessment criteria
- Creating a straw man process and applications mapping for the business capabilities
- Following the three horizons roadmap for business capability implementation
- Building Reactive and proactive business capabilities
- Introducing business capability-based Governance-Risk-Compliance (GRC)

The business capabilities implementations in an organization require a process in itself. This chapter presents the process to develop a business architecture framework incorporating business capabilities. The architecture roadmap discussed in this chapter is most helpful in implementing the business capabilities. The implementation of business capabilities discussed here are in the context of outcome-driven business architecture (ODBA). Stakeholders form an important part of successful development and implementation of business capabilities—hence, they are also discussed here. Additional relevant topics such as capability assessment criteria and funding are introduced.

Roadmaps for Capability Building

This chapter discusses defining, developing, and refining a roadmap to successfully implement business capabilities. By using a "current state–future state" perspective and incorporating tools such as Enterprise Architecture (EA), Program Strategy, and Industry Trends, among others, an organization clearly identifies the current capabilities and the gaps between them and the desired future state. The roadmap helps identify capabilities that need to be enhanced, added, or removed in order to enable the organization to reach the future state. As the organization transitions to the future state, activities, tasks, and projects are undertaken iteratively and incrementally. Such an iterative approach helps in the continuous prioritization of capabilities that are fluid during the early part of their implementation. The roadmap helps in handling this fluidity to ensure capabilities still align with desired outcomes.

The roadmap is a step-by-step process to assess and implement capabilities while continuously aligning capabilities to desired outcomes. Stakeholders from varied areas of an organization play an important role in guiding implementation of the roadmap. A roadmap such as Three Horizons allows organizations to manage short-term efforts and initiate business capabilities. This provides the foundation to move into longer-term planning through governance and risk management and ending at the anticipated outcomes. The roadmap is cyclical in nature where continuous alignment and realignment is needed in order to adjust to changes in the business-operating environment.

Capability implementation has several important components that include assessment, definition, and documentation. In addition, it is important to develop a program that has strong projects, activities, and tasks that align with the capabilities. This, in turn, supports successful outcomes for an organization.

Regardless of the point in the process, it is important to work iteratively to allow for assessment, measurement, and evaluation of each step.

Capabilities are the foundation of an organization to achieve business goals. A roadmap for capability building essentially comprises:

- A step-by-step pathway to assess, refine, and implement business outcome-based capabilities.
- Enables continuous alignment of outcomes and business capabilities to ensure that only the relevant capabilities to the outcomes are developed.
- Enables a multidimensional view of capability development and strategy implementation.
- Comprises business capabilities as a means to achieve business outcomes.
- Details of the stakeholders from business and technology disciplines. A roadmap enables stakeholders from cross-functional disciplines to understand, direct, and implement.

Organizational roadmaps are based on the goals and outcomes established as part of strategy formulation. These strategies are iteratively refined through the Outcome-Driven Business Architecture (ODBA). During the process of building business capabilities, they change—as also the outcomes which are revised and changed. It is worth noting the following in terms of capabilities:

- An important part of implementing capabilities is documenting them. The capability assessment is based on the strategic outcomes required and changes when these outcomes change. The changing nature of strategic intent requires the capability assessment be time-bound and "just enough" so that the documentation is easily updated as the capabilities change.
- Business capabilities can comprise sub-capabilities. For example, the capability in finance to perform "revenue accounting" comprises smaller capabilities such as "processing accounts" and "managing collections." There are some capabilities that are active and others that are dormant. Not all capabilities are included in the roadmap. Only those capabilities that help achieve the organizational outcomes are initially assessed.

- Another important part of implementing business capabilities is to assess and define the current state of all capabilities. The future-required capabilities are defined keeping the strategic goals and outcomes of the organization in mind. The roadmap defines the steps that are required to achieve the outcomes. The capabilities are continuously improved to help achieve the outcome. Figure 5.1 depicts a structure and consistent approach required for the development of the organizational roadmaps used in implementing business capabilities.
- As the organization moves forward with its strategy implementation there is a reshuffling of capabilities. In time, it discovers it needs new capabilities to achieve its outcomes. This discovery results when some parts of the strategy are implemented and, in the process, some missing capabilities are discovered. New capabilities are created to achieve the business outcomes and can refine the strategic goals setup at the time of the strategy formation. A roadmap thus also helps in the continuous alignment of outcomes with capabilities. A roadmap illustrates how to apply the required investments for building new business capabilities. Investment and resources are allocated diligently in the roadmap. This is to ensure agility and flexibility of the organization to adapt to quickly changing external environments.

Developing Roadmaps for Implementation

Figure 5.1 suggests following components of a roadmap for capability implementation within ODBA:

1. The "current-state" assessment starts with collecting data, assessment criteria, and information assessment using templates. These templates are business-focused and understood by the operational team members. Following an agile framework development process (iterative process where the next iteration is refined based on current process outcomes), a template is drawn first and then refined as needed.

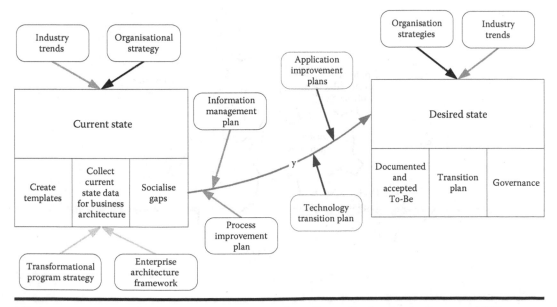

Figure 5.1   Process of developing organizational roadmaps for implementing capabilities.

2. The assessment of the capabilities—Current and desired state is done with a framework (suggested in Chapter 4). The framework is agile to accommodate new capabilities and adopted across the organization.
3. Organizational acceptance of the capabilities gaps is necessary to develop an enterprise-wide approach for capability development. It is important to develop a standard framework that can be repeated, because as external conditions change, the alignment needs another assessment.
4. The future state articulates and documents the capabilities required to meet the business outcomes. The activities required to deliver these capabilities are thus governed by the outcomes desired.
5. A transition plan from current capabilities to desired capabilities streamlines the activities and produces enterprise-wide benefits.

Life Cycle of Building Outcome-Driven Initiatives

Strategies are dynamic because of changing business environments. Every change in strategy requires a change in capabilities. Business capability building is discussed in Chapter 3. Figure 5.2 shows the life cycle of building capabilities based on outcomes. The core stages of the business capabilities building are to understand the current state of the business initiatives. As shown in Figure 5.2, business capabilities and business strategies are evolving and feeding in refinement of IT strategies. The business outcomes expected defines the future state. The current state assesses how the initiatives are progressing and relationship to the business outcomes. The gap between current state and future state as shown in Figure 5.2 determines the program design and also "what next." Once the next phase is designed and implemented, changes in future state or business outcomes are assessed and the cycle starts again. Outcome-driven

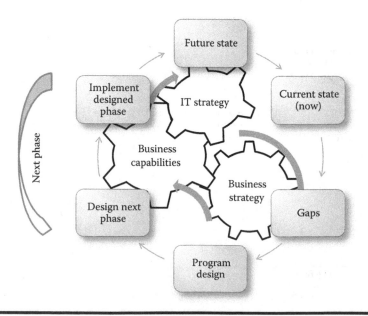

Figure 5.2 The life cycle of building outcome-driven initiatives.

approach does "just enough" with the capabilities. The assessment identifies gaps that prevent the organization from achieving strategic goals. Business strategy, business capabilities, and IT strategies are synchronized to achieve outcomes. The outcomes driving this capability building need to be spelled out. This also assists in measuring the success of program as governance and control is managed easily (Chapter 7).

ODBA, together with the capabilities being built, needs to evolve to handle the following outcomes of the ODBA initiatives:

■ Create a common language and taxonomy of architectures and solutions with the organization
■ Create an Enterprise information management framework
■ Ongoing alignment of data to needs of the business
■ Separation of data categories (structured and unstructured; transactional and analytical)
■ Well-organized and well-documented processes for enhancement of data quality
■ Improved integration between systems
■ Tightened security and privacy of data in hybrid data environment
■ Quality and timeliness of information
■ Understand the cost-benefits of data storage and usage
■ Break down data siloes and bringing them together dynamically to satisfy analytical requirements
■ Establish good Governance, Risks, and Control (GRC)

Planning the Capability Portfolio: Three Horizons Roadmap

In practice, the plans to implement capabilities are based on a 10-year rolling outlook, incorporating three time horizons.[*] This three-horizon approach is based on the premise that planning itself needs to be Agile and is not set in concrete. Planning gives appropriate consideration to current imperatives, likely medium-term scenarios and longer-term emerging trends. In addition to focusing on near-term initiatives and benefits, the three-horizon roadmap contextualizes the importance of investing in foundational capabilities for the future.

The three-horizon approach supports repeatable and logical prioritization and sequencing of capabilities. These decisions are based on identifying the scenarios most likely to occur, and those that have the greatest impact on the current situation. The ultimate goal of the three-horizon planning approach is to support the organization in establishing an ongoing state of readiness.

Figure 5.3 shows this roadmap covering 0–24 months, 24–60 months, and >60 months. Such a roadmap provides the following advantages to the organization:

■ Support the organization in establishing structured and repeatable changes to its plans
■ Support organization in establishing an ongoing state of readiness for managed, planned, anticipated, and reactive change
■ Achieve optimal and sustainable information and technology practices supported by informed decision-making
■ Address pressing requirements from organizations, employees, and partner agencies
■ Respond with Agility to changing business environment

---

[*] http://www.mckinsey.com/business-functions/strategy-and-corporate-finance/our-insights/enduring-ideas-the-three-horizons-of-growth.

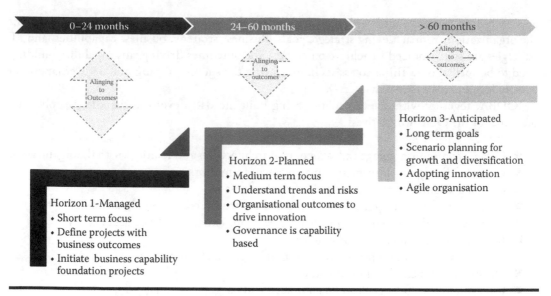

Figure 5.3   Three horizon roadmap for planning.

Horizon 1: Managed

Horizon 1 has a zero to 2-year field of focus. It deals with the delivery and operational transition of project outputs, and management and reporting of tangible business benefits in line with the strategic objectives. In this, concepts possibly identified in Horizons 2 or 3 (in a previous iteration) can progress to projects. Quick-win opportunities are capitalized on and tactical responses to unforeseen events undertaken. Both quick win opportunities and tactical responses are incorporated into the portfolio plan after impact assessments. Conducting tightly controlled trials of the business capabilities enhancement prior to large-scale deployments mitigates deployment risk in this horizon. For example, launching a major product normally goes through a controlled product trials with a selected group of users before general release.

Horizon 2: Planned Building Medium-Term Roadmaps

Horizon 2 has a 2- to 5-year field of focus. It deals with advanced trends that have a reasonable likelihood of a significant impact on the organization. Opportunities and risks associated with these trends are now translated into hypotheses that drive innovation and shape validation activities of the new concepts. The validated outputs forecast changes in capability and capacity requirements. Conducting well-defined "live" pilots in this horizon minimize design risk.

Horizon 3: Anticipated Building Long-Term Roadmaps

In Horizon 3, long-term trends are identified and assessed. This assessment is conducted relative to the perceived likelihood and consequence of risk (positive and negative). Those capabilities that have a probability of a major impact on policy are progressed into scenario plans and later into proof of concept testing. Proof of concept testing explores new capabilities and those developed in Horizon 2.

The three horizons planning is not a linear task. The suggested timelines are guidelines. The competitive market determines planning and changes to it. The three horizons develop initiatives that help bridge gaps in the organization capabilities.

Addressing Business Gaps

Figure 5.4 depicts a combination of the gaps that are addressed in successful implementation of a business strategy. A number of gaps can affect the organization at a given time. The roadmap identifies and prioritizes capabilities that are used to bridge the gaps.

Initiate prioritization based on the impact of any of the following gaps on the business outcomes:

- Business system gaps: Business capabilities that are better in other organizations such as branding or market, product development cycle, or utilization of resources.
- Positional gaps: Business capabilities previously developed by other organizations or strategic investments in products or positioning of the products such as location, resources allocation; or early entry into market advantages such as proprietary product features.
- Regulatory/legal gaps: Governmental restrictions on competitor actions, such as in airline industry allocation of routes allowing only a certain number of participants. The utility industry such as telecommunication, airlines, electricity, and gas sector is heavily regulated in many countries.
- Organizational/managerial gaps: Due to organizational constraints in the current resources it is hard to readjust quickly to the changing external conditions.

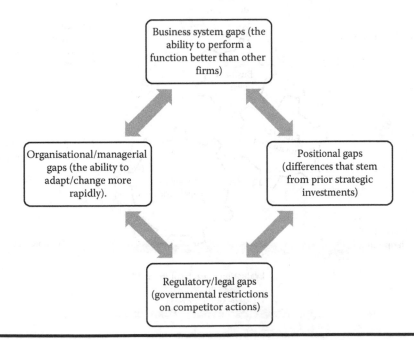

Figure 5.4   Business gaps need to be addressed to ensure roadmap success.

Building Roadmaps

The building of business capability roadmap for Horizon 1 is initiated after the business capability framework is implemented, as discussed in Chapter 4. The building roadmap requires a business capability definition and alignment with nominated dimensions such as people, process, and technology.

Rational Decision-Making

The roles and responsibilities for the business capabilities, policies, and application and information management area are allocated to organizational positions. The implementation plan has a defined framework for rational decision-making in the organization as described in Figure 5.5. This framework is important to undertake agile decision-making develops capabilities. The processes, policies, and templates of the business capabilities development are defined for initiatives and their measurement.

The rational decision-making framework defined in Figure 5.5 is iterative process of an organizational vision and strategy based on business prioritization and business capabilities. The organizational framework and tools supporting it initiate a rational decision-making process as and when any changes are detected in organizational vision, business prioritization, or capabilities and initiate activities to realign roadmaps. For example, when a business decides to launch a new product, business capabilities assessment provides any gaps or change in prioritization.

The roadmap defines the assessment measurement criteria for the new or updated business capabilities and also any change in business prioritization. The assessment of the business

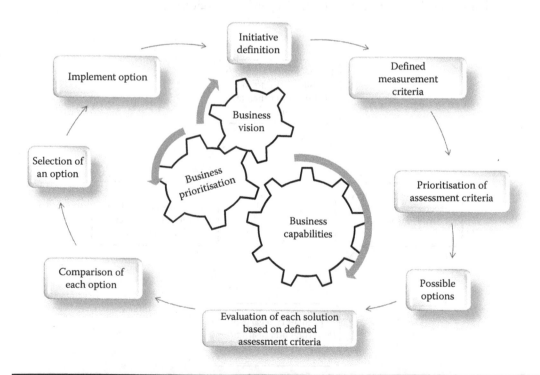

Figure 5.5   Stages of rational decision-making using business capabilities.

capabilities provides a number of options to implement change in strategy or vision. The roadmap evaluates each of these options and selects an option aligning the business visions with the activities. The implementation of the selected option updates the business capabilities assessment.

For example, if the organization has a change in strategy to attract new markets. The assessment criteria as shown in Figure 5.5 are updated with the new capabilities or expected capabilities requiring upgrades. The capability upgrades could be introducing new customer interaction channels or improving Demand Management" capabilities. The prioritization of the upgrade or changes required in the capabilities provides the input for the solution options. The decision-making process depicted in Figure 5.5 implements selected option and capabilities are reassessed and updated.

Stages of Rational Decision-Making Using Business Capabilities

Initiate definition occurs through formal templates with assessment and prerequisites to consider the initiatives. In many organizations, the innovation or ideation process encourages every employee to create an idea. This process generates a large number of ideas and it is time consuming to assess and implement all of them. It may create an environment where the demand for assessment of these initiatives takes most of the resources and actual implementation suffers. On the other hand, a restrictive organizational process can restrict ideas if there are too many assessment steps.

■ The organization defines a process to encourage responsible idea generation and assessment process. This idea-generation process, if governed properly, creates an encouraging atmosphere for employees to thrive.
■ A well-defined measurement criterion is required for assessing an idea and benefits the whole organization. This process of measurement is not used to camouflage delayed tasks if demand processing is hampering the implementation.
■ The prioritization criteria is socialized within the organization for the idea creators. The criteria changes based on organizational vision, business prioritization, and business capabilities required to achieve the vision.
■ The roadmap has multiple components and includes building foundation capabilities and initiatives to achieve business outcomes. The roadmap for each Horizon has a different level of detail and confidence to achieve the desired goals

The implementation investment roadmap is based on expected business outcomes. The scope of the initiative dictates the reasons for the investment. The business capabilities assessment goals understand areas of concern and proactively invest in mitigating organizational and operational risks. These risks reduce organizational preparedness for the new challenges. Market dynamics change and there are new entrants in the profitable market space. The organization creates a program of work to handle development of capabilities and allocating investments.

Developing a Vision

Organizational growth depends on business system gaps, regulatory legal gaps, positional gaps, and gaps in its business capabilities. The vision defines the achievable business outcomes. Figure 5.6 shares development of such a vision. The organization is pushed to achieve better

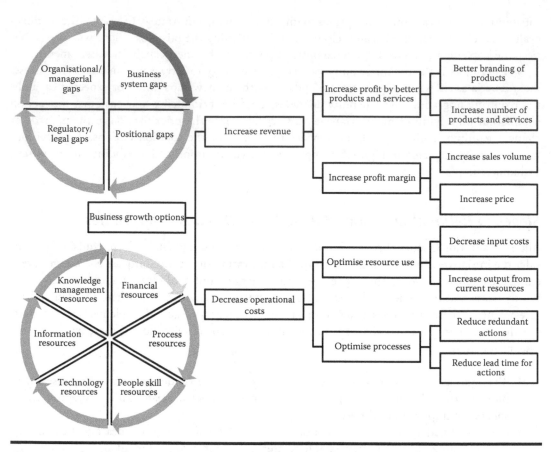

Figure 5.6 Developing a vision for rational decision-making or rational decision-making.

outcomes with the available resources. The organizational vision and strategy are also business capabilities of the organization. Maturity of these capabilities contributes to organizational success. The business capability assessment can highlight gap dimensions shown in Figure 5.6. The understanding of capability gap dimension such as process, people skills, and technology determine the investment focus. As shown in Figure 5.6, if the gap dimension is people skills then the business capabilities of hiring right skills and developing right skills must be the focus of the capability-building initiatives. The organizational profit outcomes can be increased either by increasing the revenue or decreasing the operational costs. In many cases, the business capabilities-based assessment assists in the direction to select right capabilities to invest in. When the business capability gap dimension is because of low maturity of the processes or people skills, it is important to select the decreased operational cost path by optimizing the resources and processes. The organizational revenue increases due to reduced input costs and better productivity because of the optimized processes and better people skills. Business outcomes can be achieved by understanding the area to invest to achieve desired business capability maturity. In many cases, the organizations that take the path of investing more in technology without optimizing processes and developing people skills are unable to realize business goals and desired business capability maturity.

Measuring the Capabilities Implementation

Challenges in Measuring Capabilities

The key challenges in the measurement of the business capability are:

- quantifying intangible benefits
- isolating and accruing the benefits attributable to IT investments
- establishing a baseline for value measurement
- estimating value generated from investments in foundational capabilities many of which support the entire enterprise and not specific business outcomes/initiatives

There are also challenges in communicating this value in business terms and finding appropriate forums to discuss capability framework-driven value with the right stakeholders.

The metrics used are decreased costs, increased productivity, increased revenue, return on investment, IT operation returns, foundational investment, portfolio prioritization, and business value creation. In addition to the IT value, it is also important for business capabilities to enable the organizational sustainability in competitive market by collaborating with other organizations. Measuring value of these capabilities improves the business perception and enables principled investment decisions that drive and track improvement efforts.

There are different types of measurement methodologies for each measurement challenge. Models to measure value to organizations include tools such as "Balanced score card" [1] or implied value of reuse of components developed using various frameworks. Metrics need to undertake ongoing assessment and not at the end of implementation.

The value of business capability-based approach is measured based on resultant business value (cost reduction and increased benefits). The aforementioned tools like the balanced scorecard are unable to successfully measure business value in these terms. This is because these measures mainly relate to projects delivering the expected outputs rather than the value-based outcomes. The value of the re-usable components developed in previous projects also provides an indication of cost-saving. Therefore, measurement tools are required to accumulate the values over time and over multiple initiatives. There is a need to develop a set of quantitative variables that are measured in practice.

Total Capability Index

"Total Capability Index (TCI™)" [2] is a metric designed to measure the total impact of the capabilities of an overall organizational ecosystem. TCI is derived from mathematical models and game theory. TCI provides dynamic assessment of roadmap initiatives and their contributions. TCI also helps organizations assess their cumulative capability contributions. The use of TCI as an organizational measurement framework provides a holistic approach in measuring the success of business capabilities building.

For example, the marketing department is planning to introduce another channel (self-service) that reduces the paper-based marketing currently being pursued. By introducing this channel, the marketing department saves around the same amount of paper and the sustainability index is ×1. The introduction of the web channel now demands the ICT systems to be available 24 × 7 where as previously they were only available 8 am–7 pm on weekdays. The new channel increases the ICT electricity usage and also requires extra infrastructure such as high speed disks and DR systems to cater for high availability. This changes the capability Index of Information and Communication Technology (ICT) to ×2. The tendency is to use the option that provides a better capability index. Hence, continue with current channel if ×1 > ×2 and proceed otherwise. The decision to develop capabilities using capability Index method provides organizations a framework in prioritizing the right investment.

The business capabilities framework success is measured based on holistic gains instead of optimizing the local gains based on capability index. Whereas if the index is calculated over a sequence of future states with global consideration, this leads to a different answer than the simple calculation above. It is necessary to look at this situation as two different alternative choices available at that particular moment. Using an appropriate tool with a combination of game theory and utility theory provides the more sustainable option in the long term. The TCI is also useful to achieve strategic outcomes by balancing the resource allocation in developing dimensions of the capabilities. For example, if people skills are good or capability index is high this could compensate for the other areas such as processes or knowledge management dimensions.

In another example, an ICT department is optimizing ICT infrastructure and consolidating centers, where previously the ICT infrastructure was distributed and based on user system requirements. By consolidation, ICT achieves reduction in power, but increases the response time for various users. Here again, there are two alternative game play choices. The first choice is to proceed with consolidation and the second choice is to proceed with distributed infrastructure. By analyzing the future states with multiple variables, the game theory and utility theory indicate whether to consolidate or not, but also at what point to optimally consolidate in terms of sustainability index and other variables.

Program Structure for Projects That Help Build Business Capabilities

The program of work follows a structure shown in Figure 5.7. The overall building and maintaining of business capabilities is a program of work. Building of business capabilities is treated as a project with defined tasks, a schedule and is part of a new project with associated overheads. The three phases of the program (discover, program planning, and design delivery) identify the gaps and define the business outcomes. Senior executives sponsor business capability owners and handle the building of business capabilities.

Any business capability-building program of work requires multiple phases. Each phase of the program defines the vision and business outcomes required. This refines the phase of organizational structure, the future state and prioritization. The discovery phase provides the input for the program planning. The design and deliver phase focuses on delivering the required business outcomes. The implementation of a phase is an input to the next planning phase. The steering committee and program director roles are defined and assigned to senior executives where the critical activity is organizational acceptance of the program of work. The senior executives sponsor the program of work and business capability owners facilitate the building and ongoing management of business capabilities. The program of work is supported by resources required to manage and govern appropriately.

Chapter 7 defines the enterprise governance and Chapter 8 defines establishing and managing the practice. Business is changing while the business capability initiatives are implemented. Therefore, it is important for the organization to undertake portfolio analysis. Depending on the cost and benefits of each portfolio, systems and applications are linked into different initiatives as per capabilities building or upgrades. For example, the projects that are required to enhance

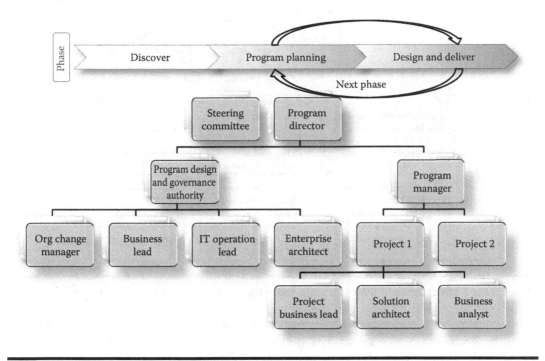

Figure 5.7 Developing a program structure for projects that help build business capabilities.

or build capabilities to maintain status quo or just normal growth are considered in "lights on" portfolio, initiatives whereas projects developing differentiating or next frontier capabilities are categorized as "strategic" initiatives.

Chapter 8 discusses in detail how to establish this practice within the organizational structure. The key stakeholder roles, responsibilities, and scope of program are clearly defined, where senior executives are responsible for business outcomes. This provides stability, credibility, and traction to the program. The organization creates standard templates that are re-usable and acceptable across the organization for collecting data. These templates also define the re-usable criteria for initiating business capability-building activities, investment options, and expected key outcomes (Figure 5.8).

Business Capabilities Based Organizational Analysis

The business capability assessment needs to be in phases. The first pass of assessment must prioritize the capabilities required for further assessment. The capability dimension to analyze depends on the framework and alignment achieved so far within the organization. The analysis phase is pragmatic and time bound to avoid "analysis paralysis." The focus on the various dimensions selected for building the organization depend on the outcome required. The assessment for the various dimensions is as follows:

Resources—Identify which valuable and rare resources/capabilities of the company deliver superior financial performance and decide on each capability's key performance indexes. The key capability resource gaps are identified. The assessment must identify the roadmap and resources required to improve this capability

Culture—Culture of the organization is analyzed and understood to develop the assessment framework. Culture is an important dimension of business capabilities and hardest to change. The

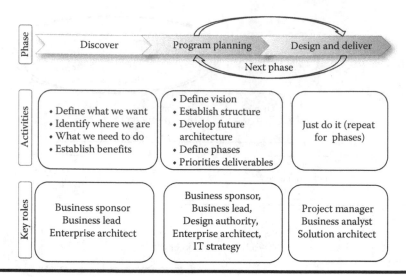

Figure 5.8 Business capability as a continuous improvement program of work.

culture dimension provides the organizational effort that is required in developing roadmap to uplift the capabilities. Most organizations' culture can be divided into two categories: Mechanistic and Organic. These category views are understood as follows:

- In a mechanistic structure, the effort of the organization is focused only on internal systems and processes. This type of culture incurs heavy administrative overhead and internal procedures consume more resources than external customer-focused operations. The mechanistic culture is slow in responding to external change and may lose touch with customers and external stakeholders. In this culture, a narrow outlook occurs within divisions and also between roles and responsibilities. Employees develop unhelpful and closed mind-sets. Job and departments have boundaries and processes are unnecessarily lengthy and red tape prevails.
- The organic structure is suitable for unstable, turbulent, and changing conditions. The organic firm tries to re-shape itself to address new problems and tackle unforeseen contingencies. Instead of a rigid, highly specialized structure, organic firms have a fluid organizational design that facilitates flexibility, adaptation, and job redefinition. In organic structures, departments and divisions are formed as needed and communication is both horizontal and vertical—with importance given to networking rather than a hierarchy. Organizational members are personally and actively committed beyond what is operationally or functionally necessary.

The assessment of the culture is a factor in roadmap implementation. The organizations with mechanistic culture require a well-planned roadmap and a sequential life cycle. For the organic culture organizations, agile and small-step roadmap is more suitable.

Skills—Skill maintenance and the recruitment process of an organization are traditional in methods of employing and coaching employees. This needs to be realigned to adjust to new industry demands of selective hiring, extensive training, and reduced status/wage distinctions (Pfeffer [3]). There is a strong need to change current structure to a structure that nurtures innovations. A high percentage of teams need to have an environment of collaboration and innovation (Burns & Stalker [4]) where team members are empowered to take quick and innovative decisions and provide high-quality services.

In some cases, the organization cannot compete in a dynamic market with their current skill set. The evaluation of the skill level is documented and defines any need to restructure in style, structure, culture, skills, or staff to build an ambidextrous organization (Bandura [5]) in order to achieve the targeted goals. It may need to clearly move away from the current position to be a prospector for change by extensively changing current **skills mix, structure, style,** and **shared values (culture).**

This alteration from the traditional to a transformed view is required where the structure is unable to adapt to the changing external environment. Leadership provides an environment of innovation and empowerment; and skills require a workable mix of technology and functional consultants.

Knowledge—Knowledge management and its availability to the wider set of employees is becoming imperative for success in the new digital world. Though there are various technology-based knowledge-sharing initiatives, they, alone, cannot create a culture of collaboration and creativity. Knowledge contribution is often dominated by a few employees, thus making any knowledge-sharing initiative based on such platforms ineffective. Employees are often reluctant to share their knowledge. Employees often consider their personal knowledge as their key competitive asset and sharing means losing their competitive edge. Instead, deliberate and planned initiatives are required to change employees' behavior and promote knowledge sharing.

Technology selection is an important decision point in developing business capabilities. IT enables a culture of sharing knowledge. There are different technologies on the market that can help organizations build a knowledge repository, but they are expensive, and their focus is on creating a repository rather than promoting interaction. Employees working in these processes not only gain strong domain knowledge but also develop heuristics to reduce turnaround time and improve productivity. These heuristics reside in the minds of employees, and when they move to new roles, their knowledge might be lost.

Risks in Implementing Business Capability and Mitigation

The roadmap to building business capabilities moves an organization from a risk-adverse to a risk-taking culture. The change in culture occurs with the business capabilities improving in the areas of project and program management and also making right investment decisions. Table 5.1 defines sample risks. The organizational risks are assessed based on enterprise risk assessment framework. In the absence of an enterprise risk assessment framework, a tactical framework is used. The implementation plan includes establishing "enterprise risk assessment framework" as an initiative. Table 5.1 defines the changes of category and the risks it creates. The organizational capabilities required during the disruptive changes are listed using the organizational analysis of the current culture, style, and strategy of organizations and the risks anticipated during the disruptive changes.

The organizations assess any gaps between the positioning strategies and execution strategies, including skills, style, structure, and culture conflicting with goals and missions. The main areas of concern in competitive advantages for increase in market share, economy of scale, and new product introduction are:

■ Unable to compete for major engagements based on cost price with other companies due to current structure and overheads. The reasons could be gaps in key capabilities that are categorized as advantage capabilities.

Table 5.1 Sample Risks, Obstacles, and Mitigation Strategies

Category	Risk	Symptoms	Mitigation Strategy
Culture and style	Losing key people due to changed culture and miscommunication.	High attrition rate compared to previous years.	Identify key resources Effective communication plan Have a one-on-one sessions with these key resources to reassure them.
Culture and skills	Reduced innovation due to lack of capabilities.	Low morale of the staff due to communication gaps. Cynicism on new initiative.	Communicate revised business strategy and ensure an effective rewards structure is in place.
Structure	Size and scope of transition of the structure.	Failure in transition.	Transition in small chunks with efficient change management strategies.
Style	Existing talent leaving organization due change in environment.	Staff leaving due to change in culture.	Communicate revised business strategy Ensure that new career contracts are specific and understood by all employees. Matching rewards with responsibilities.
Culture and strategy	Taking the eyes off the crystal ball during the transitioning.	Disruption and doubt by current staff, business as usual activities.	Allocating required resources to business as usual activities. Key resources have a transition plan for their positions.

- The current organizational structure of the company may be highly fragmented along product lines and needs to realign with the positioning strategies.
- Current resources are mostly focused on one area of expertise and need business-oriented personnel or a blend of business and people-oriented skill-set (soft skills). The skill maintenance and recruitment process is based on traditional recruitment views; this needs to be realigned with the new industry demands of business.
- In case of multinational projects are operated in a known environment with only a limited number of staff exposed to the varying cultural demands of the customers. This is refined to include multi-cultural teams from across the globe working together. To succeed in the new global world, it is crucial that employees understand the behavioral differences between various parts of the world. If the company can understand these differences and cater to them, it can fast forward its journey toward its coveted goals—especially in the area of servicing its customers.
- A number of projects are developing similar capabilities in detached groups of the company. These take up valuable resources of time, money, and people. The projects are prioritized for a planned period of time to better utilize the assets in a focused manner.

Analysis of the Current State

The roadmap building identifies an organization's current state of business capabilities maturity. Organizations can start with the desired goal in mind and then do a current state; or start with current state and define the pragmatic "to-be" state. The decision is based on business outcomes. If assessment and building capabilities are based on being competitive then it is better to start with the current state as a starting point. This way, based on the resources available, the organization can decide the expected "to-be" state. This could be called as "pro-active capability building" initiative.

Reactive Capability Building

Business goals and desired outcomes can be a result of changes imposed on the business. As a result, the goals and outcomes are a result of external environment and competitor actions. In such situations, the capability building starts with the end state in mind. These capability-building initiatives are called "reactive capability building." The underlying reason for building capability determines the amount of resources required. For example, with reactive capability building, if the survival of the organization is at stake, all resources are put there to build the missing capabilities. In many cases, reactivity capability building becomes tactical and not strategic.

When using "reactive capabilities building" as shown in Table 5.2, the organizational current state initiative has quick analysis to define the approach of building roadmap initiatives. The analysis focus is on capabilities assessment against a desired business outcome; for example, cost. Cost of the product needs to be reduced in order to be competitive. As shown in Table 5.2, this exercise identifies capabilities that need more resources, for example, "Create and manage organizational performance strategy," "Benchmark performance," and "Manage change." Projects and actions are taken to bring these capabilities to the level required, depending on the importance to the organization.

Proactive Capability Building

When the business outcome expected is to introduce a new or upgraded product and services lines, the assessment of current state focuses on this result. In this case, two levels of current state analysis may be required. The first level of analysis identifies the capabilities that need attention. Table 5.3 depicts the first level of capability the current state identifies: "Define and manage channel strategy," "Define the business concept and long-term vision," and "Develop and manage human resources (HR) planning, policies, and strategies" are the key capabilities that needs attention. The current state for the lower level capabilities is required to define what the organization should do to realize that business vision.

Irrespective of "proactive" or "reactive" current state assessment, shelf-ware documentation (i.e., documenting every current process) is avoided. The assessment team takes a quick inventory of assets such as technology in use, people, skills, and the mapping with the business capabilities. The Business Capability Framework (Chapter 4) directs and identifies appropriate tools (frameworks, system analysis tools, etc.) for the analysis to move to the desired state. The organization defines the approach as part of the assessment initiation.

The stakeholder's assessment picks the right roles and tools for the assessment. Depending on availability of tools and the right roles that can assess the dimension, options such as a survey or a desktop assessment are considered. The organization culture is understood by the team (internal or external consultants) to gather the right data from the stakeholders. It is understood that questions are answered honestly only if the employees believe that the information is confidential.

Table 5.2   Business Capability Analysis for Reactive Capability-Building Initiatives

Business Vision	Business Outcomes Expected	Business Capabilities	Business Capability Current State	Business Capability to-be State	Gaps
Value chain management Through reducing waste and creating processes to achieve value and reliable service at the minimum possible cost	Step change in waste elimination across all functions (process, people, activities)	Create and manage organizational performance strategy	2.92	4.56	**1.64**
Eliminate all waste throughout the value chain from; R&D, production, sales and marketing and distribution.		Benchmark performance	2.97	4.56	**1.59**
		Manage change	2.86	4.44	**1.58**
	Focus on product portfolio's Return on Investment component in support of the overall company	Develop business strategy	3.04	4.09	1.05
	End-to-end value chain mapping	Design products and services	3.45	4.54	1.09
	Ensure products and services are not over engineered beyond customer requirements and what they are willing to pay for	Design products and services	3.45	4.54	1.13
		Develop and manage marketing plans	3.32	4.45	1.13
	Ensure optimal supply sourcing to enable us to compete domestically on globally sourcing competitors— Aggressively pursue lowest cost of goods	Procure materials and services	3.59	4.62	1.03
	Remove complexity in what we do	Create and manage organizational performance strategy	2.92	4.56	1.64
		Manage change	2.86	4.44	1.58
	Benchmark and challenge our practices	Benchmark performance	2.97	4.56	1.59

Table 5.3   Business Capability Analysis for Profitable Future Growth Platforms

Business Vision	Outcome Required	Business Capabilities	Current State	REQUIRED STATE	Gaps
Profitable future growth platforms Identify and invest in cost-effective and sustainable new growth platforms aligned to the vision. Seek new business opportunities to reach the stated goals of higher ROIC revenue.	A concerted effort toward establishing an alternative distribution modes	Define and manage channel strategy	2.83	4.35	**1.53**
	Invest in new product trends	Develop business strategy	3.04	4.09	1.05
		Design products and services	3.45	4.54	1.10
	Align resources to evaluate commercial viability of new technologies	Define the business concept and long-term vision	2.15	4.57	**2.42**
		Develop, maintain and manage HR policies, its strategies and planning planning	2.79	4.02	**1.23**
	Trade-off our infrastructure and strategic alliances	Develop business strategy	3.04	4.09	1.05
		Define the business concept and long-term vision	2.15	4.57	**2.42**

Managing Stakeholders Engagement

The assessment requires managing a large amount of stakeholder input. This includes the key business outcomes and the operational level input from the staff. The level of input required from these stakeholders depends on the scope and number of capability levels being appraised. A standard template is defined for data gathering, analysis, and dynamic roadmaps. The organization develops a stakeholder engagement plan from the data gathering to socializing the results.

The collection, assessment, and measurement criteria of business capabilities are clearly defined and transparent. The capability assessment method requires the information collection to be accurate, realistic, and authentic (i.e., senior executive preferences). This creates trust with future capabilities assessments and ensures investment in right capabilities to achieve the business outcomes.

Table 5.4 defines the plan for the stakeholder management. The business capability assessment data identifies capability gaps to achieve the strategic goals. The outcome-driven approach provides the lists of the capabilities that need to be uplifted. The key stakeholders are the cumulative list of each business capability stakeholders. The list includes internal stakeholder such as business owners of business capabilities and users, and also all the external stakeholders.

The Scope of Transformation

The transformation scope depends on the business outcomes. The organization determines the affordability of the program by assessing an overall organizational budget (now and for the next few years). The organization assesses the difference between operational activity (business as usual) and strategic projects. The resources required to develop the roadmap and those needed for operations to run smoothly are assessed and allocated appropriately.

Table 5.4 Business Capability Analysis for Winning Culture

Business Vision	Outcome Required	Business Capabilities	Current State	Required State	Gaps
Winning culture Actively develop employees, their knowledge, and skill set so that the performance of the team can be lifted up. Environment driven by innovation and a passionate can have attitude. Actively developing employees and building a culture of high performing teams.	Emphasis on high performing teams	Develop and counsel employees	3.35	4.31	0.96
		Create and manage organizational performance strategy	2.92	4.56	1.64
		Develop HR planning, and strategies so that it uplifts the organization	2.79	4.02	1.23
	Recognize team effort and celebrate success	Reward and retain employees	3.14	4.22	1.08
	Creative an agile innovation process	Create and manage organizational performance strategy	2.92	4.56	1.64
		Benchmark performance	2.97	4.56	1.59
		Manage change	2.86	4.44	1.58

The transformation plan of business capability uses the financial and structural metrics for the organization. The scope of organizational transformation combines the following:

■ **Business focus:** The products and services align with the customer's expectations, and where possible, internal production systems are aligned with the customer products and services forecasts. The production systems are capable and agile to allow for changes in the design. The scope of transformation requires better information management and knowledge management capabilities.

■ **Organizational structure:** Operational staff participate and provide input at the design phase to optimize the production time and total cost of solutions.

■ **Business metrics** are used to change from current product-based metrics to the total capability building-based metrics. The performance management system is realigned with business metrics.

■ **Marketing focus:** The marketing and sales focus are total product or service solutions. The marketing strategies are realigned with the new positioning of the products and services.

■ **Technology focus:** Innovations in technology are adopted to provide solutions to customer's requirements and/or reducing cost of ownership.

■ **Alignment of internal and customer-centric processes:** A customer-centric approach requires the business processes and system to work in sync with each other.

GOVERNANCE—RISK—COMPLIANCE

(Discussed in detail in Chapter 7)

Enterprise-wide GRC have effective and efficient control over the business capabilities.

Governance is the overall management approach and controls to direct the organization.

Risk Management supports governance through which management identifies, analyses, and, where necessary, responds appropriately to risks.

Compliance means conforming to stated Requirements, Standards, and Regulations.

A good governance model understands and manages risks. Governance provides control and risk management. Eventually, this is helpful in maintaining compliance with both external and internal legal, audit and accounting requirements. Governance-Risk-Compliance (GRC) is an activity that brings together corporate governance, controls, and reporting and enterprise risk management (ERM) in order to ensure compliance with rules and regulations.

ODBA, in turn, eliminates redundancies and duplications in the activities of governance and risk management. BA is about efficiency and effectiveness that reduces operational costs, project costs, and risks. BA facilitates integration. Governance and risk management are activities that benefit by such integration. The business capability-based governance is discussed in detail in Chapter 7.

Key Considerations for the Roadmap

The business transformation is a program of work with built-in phases. The scope of each phase is based on achievable business outcomes within the organizational assessment performed during current state analysis, and understanding the stakeholder's key priorities. The roadmap defines key success factors for each phase and project, and the cumulative effect on overall business outcomes. The project manager's key success factors include the overall business success as a key criterion to avoid a focused approach of just achieving the project goals.

Clear direction: Translate business strategies into outcomes that provide clear direction on the organization's intentions. The primary task is to bring about change by clearly articulating the business outcomes desired. The investment in IT and its enablement of the business strategies is not always visible. It is important to set a clear direction and business outcome so the organization's investment can be measured against the outcomes. Since strategic intents change while IT projects progress they nullify the benefits that were articulated in the business cases at the start of the IT project.

Allow ample time for evaluation and planning: The capability-building program requires analysis of current business process, cultures, and IT systems topology. Time is allocated to build a robust roadmap. The recommended projects based on the roadmap require a vision for 3–5 years and are included in the program of work over multiple years. This requires a change in process from annual to a program of work for the next 2–3 years for foundation projects.

Have a big vision, but take small steps: Capability-building program defines the vision and components or "big picture" before starting any technology projects. The "big picture" includes the required changes to processes, organization, and cultural refinement. It is hard to achieve this goal in one go and a well-planned phased approach is required to optimize the benefits of enhancement in technology, iterative refinement of processes, and organizational structure [2].

Consider performance [6]**:** The information distribution and complexity of each system due to organic growth usually requires multiple transformations and extractions of data. This may create a performance problem in accessing the data (transactional versus analytical data). The roadmap considers potential performance problems and design systems and processes to address the problems.

Prioritizing requests: Assess the business/IT impact of proposed initiatives to define the business outcomes expected. As described in Figure 5.7, organizations are swamped with new ideas. Without the anchor of business capabilities it is hard to prioritize these initiatives. This kind of assessment results in building the capabilities that are not required for the business outcomes.

Building a program plan: Once a road map is laid out, a 12-month plan of projects is built to deliver the capabilities. The plan uses the classic program management disciplines and include setting objectives, adopting plan/do/review approach, Responsibilities can be categorized in Responsible, Accountable Consulted and Informed(RACI) planning to assign accountabilities. It is critical that the process and people elements are considered along with data and technology.

Continuous improvement [2]**:** The most compelling reason to implement a capability-building program is the strategic imperative for more revenue, improved profit, and demonstrable compliance. Once an initial project in developing business capabilities is completed there are limitless opportunities to improve update processes and add more information to the standard customer record.

Enabling Organization Changes

The data organization change is necessitated due to the information flow when including Big Data in the organizational decision-making and operations. An organization using social media data to decide on product design requires the information flow to be seamless across the organization. This uses following key foundations (if not already existing in the organization):

■ Create a common information collection mechanism where information is entered once in the system and is distributed across other systems, giving access to information required for the job at hand.

- A basic reporting and analytics system to provide immediate needs of the front office.
- Minimum changes to existing systems.
- Skills required for the strategy: Current recruitment policy is changed to a proactive HR policy of identifying resources required over the next number of years and a plan set to develop these resources. Additional streams and new skill sets required are identified. A planned approach to acquire these resources (building in house or targeted outsourcing) is defined.
- Structure change plans: The section heads support the recommended structure in recruiting additional members. These members include career managers, HR managers, and resource managers. These additional members identify the current and future skills required and proactively manage recruitment as well as development of these skills. These managers also channelize resources toward relationship-building trust, motivating, and supporting people necessary for managing continuous change.

Standardizing Reporting

Each division and application may have developed their standalone infrastructure, format and systems for the division and corporate level reporting, resulting in multiple formats and duplication of efforts. A substantial percentage of time is spent in collecting and formatting the reports. In addition to divisional or departmental effort, corporate sections have to employ additional resources to align these reports with the corporate format. This necessitates the need of standardized reporting across organization. To achieve the required standardization, it is important to consolidate currently disjointed systems and solutions.

Iterative Data Transformation to Knowledge and Intelligence Management: Part of Capability Building

Previously in Chapter 4, Figure 4.1 identified knowledge management as a business strategy and component.

Business intelligence (BI) is understood as the creative use of data and information within the organization in a way that results in new bodies of knowledge that can be applied in practice. Collaborative intelligence (CI) takes BI to the next level, where intelligence is synergized within and across multiple organizations to produce actionable value to the collaborators.

Such use of BI and CI requires a robust underlying architecture. This architecture is not a single entity but a combination of various architectures that typically include business, enterprise, and solutions level architectures. BI is the use of insightful analysis to make decisions that impact business direction. BA is a mechanism to make use of BI and related technologies in a cohesive manner to enable decision-making. Although BI can mean the use of technical and analytical intelligence in decision-making, it can also represent the tools, technologies, and platforms that enable intelligence (Figure 5.9).

The success of CI depends on how organizations cooperate in contributing to and sourcing from the services on the CI platforms (Figure 5.10). The following appear to be major challenges in CI:

- **Trust:** Each agency deposits information based on quality parameters and is trusted by all collaborators. The organization also needs to comply with the withdrawal rules.
- **Timeliness of the information:** Today organizations require information to be available 24/7/365. Therefore, it is necessary for collaborating organizations to deposit information in a timely fashion.

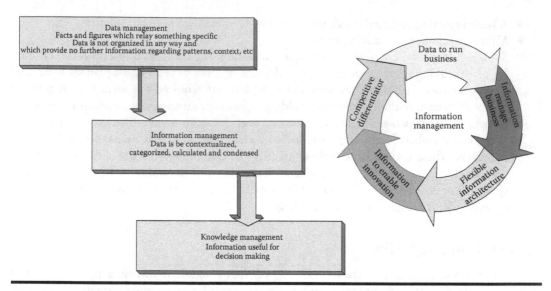

Figure 5.9 Iterations and increments in transforming data from information to knowledge following the roadmap.

- **Delivery of information:** It is also important that information be delivered in a format consumable by the subscribing organizations. If the information requires multiple translations before it can be used, organizations are reluctant to adopt CI.
- **Resources required establishing the CI platforms:** Organizations need to find a cost-effective approach to implementing CI. If the costs of CI are prohibitively expensive, organizations revert to old BI.
- **Legislative and contractual framework:** Collaborating organizations develop a framework to define quickly the contracts required for information sharing.
- **Security:** The safety of the published information is defined collaboratively.
- **Rules for information sharing:** Lack of uniform standards and legislation for sharing personal information impedes creating CI. In different countries, legislation is different for personal information sharing.
- **Discrimination between competitive and collaborative information:** This determination is crucial to the overall CI enterprise, and can change from time to time and place to place.

Discussion Points

1. Discuss the components of a business capabilities implementation roadmap and the importance of each. Give an example of each.
2. What is the importance of each component in the ODBA initiatives?
3. Describe the three Horizon roadmaps and why it is important or valuable to an organization.
4. Why is gap analysis important? Describe different places where gaps can exist.
5. How does the rational decision-making process impact success or failure of ODBA? Provide examples for each state of the rational decision-making process.
6. How does developing a vision move from a macro-view to a micro-view?
7. Describe the components in a business capability program and the importance of each.

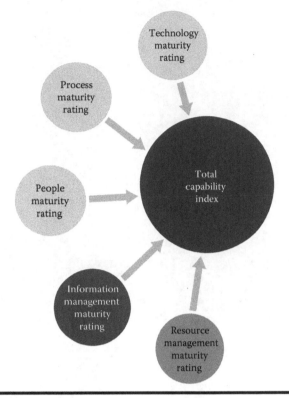

Figure 5.10   Total capability index.

8. Expound on 2–3 key risks in implementing business capability and potential mitigations.
9. Why is it important to analyze the current state? What benefits does the analysis provide?
10. Explain the differences between proactive and reactive capabilities.
11. What elements are included in organizational transformation?
12. Summarize the key considerations for the capability roadmap.

References

1. Kaplin, RS. and Norton, DP. (1992). The Balanced Scorecard—Measures That Drive Performance, *Harvard Business Review*, Feb. 1992.
2. Tiwary, A. and Unhelkar, B. (2011). Extending and Applying Business Intelligence and Customer Strategies for Green ICT, p. 83, B. Unhelkar (ed.), in *Handbook of Research in Green ICT: Technical, Business and Social Perspectives*, IGI Global, Hershey, PA.
3. Pfeffer, J. (1998a). Seven Practices of Successful Organisations, *California Management Review*, 40(2), pp. 96–124.
4. Burns, T. and Stalker, G.M. (1961). *'Mechanistic and Organic Systems of Management'*, The Management of Innovation, Tavistock Publications Ltd., London (revised and reprinted in 1994 by Oxford University Press, Oxford).
5. Bandura, A. (1986). *Social Foundations of Thought and Action*, Prentice Hall, Eaglewood Cliffs, NJ.
6. Unhelkar, B. and Tiwary, A. (2010). Collaborative Intelligence, *Cutter IT Journal*, 23(6) pp. 13–21.

Chapter 6

Metrics and Measurements with Outcome-Driven Business Architecture

KEY POINTS

- Understanding the role of metrics and measurements in Business Architecture (BA)
- Explaining the need for and basis of a maturity model for outcome-driven business architecture (ODBA)
- Developing a five-part maturity model for ODBA
- Assessing an organization's BA against the maturity model
- Progressing the maturity levels of an organization
- Applying ODBA maturity model in Practice

This chapter discusses the metrics and measurements related to implementing Outcome-Driven Business Architecture (ODBA). The five factors—people, process, technology, information management (IM), and knowledge management (KM)—that make up the business capabilities are discussed here in the context of their maturity levels. The business capability maturity frameworks are currently worked by many organizations. Outcome-driven and business capability-based investment frameworks are different from traditional organizational operations frameworks. The authors believe standardized frameworks for measurements are evolving and will have their own maturity cycles. This is because the maturity of ODBA is also the maturity of the capabilities and the way they align with the outcomes. Capability Maturity Model (CMM) is by far the most popular model for measuring maturity. Although CMM primarily deals with process maturity, this chapter builds on the concepts of CMM and applies them to the ODBA capabilities.

Metrics and Measurements in Organizations

The maturity of an organization is reflected in how its projects are estimated, planned, and implemented. The task of estimation involves answering questions, such as *"How long will it take; How much will it cost;* and *How many people are needed?"* with a reasonable amount of confidence. To answer these questions, it is important to know how an organization behaves. Enterprise-wide surveys and historical data on any previous such endeavors, performance of current systems, leadership experience, and the style (or culture) of the organization are all important ingredients in estimating the effort for current initiatives.

Metrics measure specific attributes of a product or process. Metrics also measure organizational key performance indicators (KPIs) or key success indicators (KSIs). Metrics enable an organization to estimate, track progress, determine complexity, identify quality, analyze defects and validate best practices. As a result, metrics contribute to improving processes and, in turn, higher-quality products.

Metrics are, therefore, important in the current discussions on Outcome-Driven Business Architecture (ODBA). Metrics play a creative role in measuring the maturity and success of ODBA. This success is a result of not only excellence in the measurable implementation of ODBA but also increasingly improved estimations for various phases within the implementation effort. Metrics and measurements, however, require time and resources which limit the extent to which metrics and measurements can be applied to ODBA.

Success of a metrics program in organizations heavily depends on collecting useful data that relates to the entity being measured. Lack of useful data and lack of management support can foil a metrics program. Therefore, it is important to commit to a metrics program with management support and over a longer period of time, typically ranging from 3 to 5 years.

Measuring Capabilities and Risks

Measuring business capabilities is an important part of measuring the overall impact of ODBA in an organization. Such measurements are a means to improving and optimizing the value of ODBA. This value is in addition to the value the ODBA provides to the rest of the organization. In many organizations, maturity is based on measurement criteria related to a business category. These category measurements are based on organizational risk or performance-based metrics called KPIs. With ODBA, the application of metrics shifts from the individual category-based measurement to outcome-driven capability-based maturity assessment. This shift requires a number of existing measurement frameworks in the organization to be reassembled to provide a holistic organizational assessment for the capabilities.

In addition to measuring the capabilities, the organization also needs to measure risks and risk levels. The organizational risk metrics are also redefined when ODBA is implemented in the organization

Relating Metrics to ODBA

Metrics and measurements help control and monitor the progress of the ODBA initiative. While metrics help businesses improve estimation and control quality, they are also helpful in understanding how to approach ODBA implementation and measure its success.

There are two parts to the metrics discussion here:

■ The maturity level of the ODBA.
■ The effect of ODBA in improving the organization's processes.

Maturity of ODBA is also a measure of the current state of the organization in terms of how it executes all its projects. In fact, implementing ODBA is also a project. An understanding of the organization's baseline state helps chart a pathway to improve the levels of maturity of the architecture and the processes.

In the context of the ODBA, the relationship of projects to build capabilities and the resultant outcomes becomes important. While metrics are a mechanism to improve the maturity in an organization, those metrics function better with improved maturity.

The organizational business capability maturity is a combination of multiple dimensions such as organizational systems, processes, people skills, financial resource allocation, information, and knowledge management. These capability dimensions are assessed individually using a CMM™. The BA uses these standard assessments to identify each dimension gap.

Factors Influencing Organizational Systems and Product Metrics

Alignment and measurement of capabilities is critical for their sustenance. Identifying what is being measured formalizes an approach to maintain and improve capabilities.

Information technology is a critical business capability to realize the business strategies. However, the pervasive nature of information components in every business capability categories requires organizations to shift from technology and systems to outcome-driven metrics.

The outcome-driven metrics for all the capability dimensions have common factors, where standard assessment frameworks are available, as follows:

- **Quality:** Is a key issue in the capability measurement for maintaining and/or proposing products on the market. The quality of product is important as the cost of rework for the organization is high and negatively affects customer satisfaction. Quality factors include reliability (time to failure), fault density, maintainability (effort required to modify), and the size of these changes, usability, and marketability of the products.
- **Productivity:** Time taken to complete a task as a basis for productivity (size/effort). New development, enhancement, and maintenance have different productivity ranges or averages. Hence, the environmental characteristics are a very important part of the metrics program.
- **Process Improvement:** Process improvement requires established, stable processes for project management, methodologies, work patterns, product design and development, delivery and customer management. Metrics are applied to improve each element. Improvement processes create other sub-processes to direct the efforts toward useful and meaningful tasks which, in turn, reduces defects. It also helps with better utilization of employees and higher team satisfaction.

Metrics programs collect information about quality, productivity, and process improvement. As a result, the overall value proposition of the organization improves. Because ODBA is also aimed at improving the value proposition, this measurement helps in ODBA's total value output. The various metrics used to collect such information are categorized as follows:

- **Corporate-defined** metrics with operational definitions are standardized across the organization. These metrics are collected and stored for organizational activities, and are captured continuously (e.g., financial goals and size). To realize the strategies, the corporate-defined metrics align with the business capabilities being developed. ODBA requires a few prescriptive metrics defined at the corporate level.
- **Organization-defined** metrics are common across a strategic unit or division, such as a telecommunications industry around the globe. They are captured by all teams within the

organization and are designed to give insight into a process that is of critical importance to the organization. Each organization has their own requirements for measurement (e.g., rework required).

■ **Local-defined** metrics are collected to give insight into one process. The operational definitions are common across one project, team, or site. They may be captured continuously or for a specific purpose and discontinued when that purpose is achieved, (e.g., code complexity and the amount/depth of testing done on the project).

Success of each initiative depends on the organizational capabilities in managing and governing these projects. The business capability-based governance (discussed in more detail in Chapter 7), requires the Enterprise Program Management Office (EPMO) to maintain and manage these initiatives.

Business Capability Maturity and Assessment

Often, external management consultancy firms provide assessments of capability maturity and roadmaps. Such external assessments may not always serve the desired purpose of measuring the capabilities within an organization. This is because a business capability embeds itself deeply in the organization and, as a result, it makes sense to define standards for maturity and assessment for continuous improvements within the organization. Metrics developed within the organization—as opposed to an external agency—also enrich the internal knowledge of the participants who are entrusted with the metrics development and usage.

In the meantime, organizations adopting business capabilities are struggling to provide a maturity assessment plan to provide transparency to prioritization of capabilities and investment decisions. The challenges faced in business capability maturity modelling are compounded because each organization chooses their own definition of business capability. The definitions combined with a different set of dimensions such as people, process, technology, information management (IM), or resource allocations makes standardization difficult.

Maturity Assessment in Practice

The "Business Architecture" adoption in any organization is a continuous project and should be dynamic to meet the changing requirements of the business.

The maturity assessment of this project is divided into three distinct phases:

1. Establishing a BA Framework
2. Assessing Business Capabilities to support current strategy
3. Re-assessment of Business Capabilities to support future planned strategies

The first phase, Establishment, creates a re-usable and foundational framework, and the subsequent phases leverage (and iterate upon) this framework. However, the "Business Architecture Framework" use and value extends beyond its initial use.

This stage develops a "Business on a Page" model. This model, as the name suggests, represents the key capabilities of the organization's business on a single page. Thus, a Capability Reference model is created. Usually, most of the effort of this phase goes in setting a common and accepted definition of capabilities across the organization.

There are many ways to establish a framework of capabilities. An existing process framework provides a good starting point as a base. The purists argue that business capabilities are not the same as policies or process. However, in most organizations, one of the dimensions of the business capabilities is processes. The processes are well understood within the organization and in some cases, maturity assessment is already in place. Thus, it becomes easier to utilize the existing standard, where naming of capabilities and processes is similar and already accepted across the organization. This can make adopting change easier.

The other method is to define organizational capabilities without using any previous work. The effort and time required for setting business capabilities in this way requires resources and commitments from senior executive.

The third method is to use an external standard framework. There are many standard frameworks in use. The authors recommend The American Productivity Quality Center (APQC). As discussed in Chapter 2, this Capability Model is used by many organizations for their process frameworks.

Essentially, this framework is the "base map" upon which various layers of information are developed and uncovered during BA capability development and are overlain and presented. The information is presented as Capability Assessment heat map as discussed in Chapter 8.

Once the framework is established, the next phase is to assess the current level of the capabilities. Both current and future phases (2 and 3 as above) are discussed here as the approach of assessment is similar.

Questionnaire and Survey

One of the popular methods of assessment for business capabilities is to develop a questionnaire or survey. The questionnaire requests three pieces of information.

- The current maturity state of a capability (based on a CMM where one represents low maturity and five represents best-in class)
- Where the maturity state of the capability needs to enable the strategy
- The importance of this capability to the business

The questionnaire comprises questions covering all business capability categories. In conjunction with the questionnaire, a follow-up interview with the respondent is recommended to provide detail behind significant gaps of the current and future capability assessment. This information provides supporting content to justify the capability gaps uncovered from the survey. This becomes the diagnostic which reveals strengths and weaknesses of an organization and provides enough detail for action. Eventually this survey becomes the frame of reference for the capabilities over time, is accepted as a standard in the organization, and provides valuable support for the metrics program.

A challenge when implementing metrics is to gain organizational consensus around the priority capabilities for the organization to address. In the absence of this, companies tend to invest in capabilities which management believes important. The process to establish consensus is designed and agreed upon with senior executives during this phase. It is based on facts agreed upon by most in the company. Capabilities most likely to have the biggest impact or provide competitive advantage take priority. Harmonization workshops are recommended to gain a consensus on capabilities that the organization needs to focus on in the immediate and mid-term.

It is also important to focus on only a few capabilities (under five—ideally two to three) at a time. Capability enhancements involve big changes that sweep across a large part of the organization. This takes time and effort and focusing on too many dilutes the effort.

Steps for Assessing Financial Resource Management

To arrive at the assessment values of the capability, an overall assessment formula is used for capabilities like people skills, process, and technology. In the example below, the company is using CMM methodology to assess people skills, processes, and technology, and using Gartner* assessment method for financial resource management:

- **Step 1:** Individual people skills maturity is 3 based on CMM assessment, Process maturity is 2 based on CMM maturity and technology maturity is 2 and so is the financial resource management maturity based on industry standard such as Gartner.
- **Step 2:** Use an organizationally agreed formula to derive the organizational maturity, for example, "30% People + 20% Process + 30% Technology + 20% financial resource management" results in $(0.30 * 3 + 0.2 * 2 + 0.30 * 2 + 0.2 * 2) = 2.31$. This is closer to 2 so overall capability rating can be defined as 2.
- **Step 3:** Using the same techniques, the expected organizational rating for achieving the business strategy outcomes is calculated, resulting in expected business capability rating of 4.
- **Step 4:** Steps 1–3 are repeated for all the business capabilities in the basic framework.
- **Step 5:** Prioritize the business capabilities that need attention.
- **Step 6:** For the prioritized business capabilities, assess each dimension and identify focus areas. For example, if two business capabilities that are prioritized for implementation are "Manage Strategic initiatives" and "Manage enterprise information." The required business capabilities maturity for the two capabilities may need different initiatives. Business capability "Manage Strategic initiative" requires investment in people skills, and enterprise-wide program office and changes in processes. In other case, "Manage enterprise information" requires investment in technology.
- **Step 7:** Based on detailed analysis of the business capabilities, initiatives to improve the business capabilities are managed and outcomes of these initiatives are measured.

Metrics and Estimation Techniques

Measurement gives an empirical value to an event. The empirical value is in accordance with some predefined rules. A system to collect statistics and analyze the results in a timely manner is required to measure capability level. This allows a comparison of the project to improve the capability against a previous level of capability. Bringing the capability to a satisfactory level is defined and operational metrics are identified. The capability enhancement project results from these metrics in an effective way to change its performance.

Risks associated with capabilities and processes are also part of a metrics program (i.e., system to collect, analyze, and provide feedback). A metric tool performs various functions such as recording and maintaining risk analysis processes, storing data, and undertaking analytics to predict conditions that could materialize these risks and steps to minimize the risks. A good metric tool also has templates for the projects of identical nature. These templates ease collection of data, enable comparison, and provide historic information collected and stored from previous projects. The templates also provide an excellent basis for new project estimations.

---

* https://www.gartner.com/technology/home.jsp.

Poor estimations result from a lack of well-defined metrics, relevant data, and estimating expertise. Estimation techniques need quantitative factors to be carefully defined. In particular, the factors driving costs need to be carefully established. Metrics should reflect the range of the deviation between estimates and actuals. Resource metrics determine the deviation of the project estimates to actuals in terms of time, cost, and quality of the final product.

The availability of resources depends on multiple factors that may be outside the control of the project manager. For example, if there are multiple projects starting within the same timeframe requiring similar skills there is a shortage of skills. These skills may have been readily available at the time of estimation. Other factors may differ from estimated to actual, thus producing larger than expected deviations in the actual cost or time required to complete the project. The quality of the output can suffer if the project managers sacrifice quality to save on time and budget.

Cost Estimation Projects

Cost estimations are by far the most important factors influencing a project. Cost estimation methods include *expert judgment,* where a team of experts sit down and consult in various ways to arrive at an approximate cost; *analogy,* where a new project is compared to a similar older project; *Parkinson model*, when the resources available for the project determine the cost for it; *price to win*, where the cost is the price required to win a situation (e.g., the first product of its kind in the market); *bottom-up*, in which individual cost factors are added to give an aggregate figure; and *top-down*, where an overall figure is subdivided into individual cost factors.

These estimating techniques are not perfect. Sound judgment is also required to ascertain which technique or combination of techniques is used to arrive at estimates.

Use of past project historic data needs to be used with extra care. This is because of the need to consider the effect of changes to the environment. Estimates do not always account for the soft issues that impact projects. Estimation is always a combination of data and an educated guess.

Capability metrics are used to measure the key aspects of a capability development process. These metrics make a base level estimate and then periodically check on the progress of the initiative. Capability metrics help compare the complexity of the project to other projects which provide a benchmark for the capability-building metrics. Looking back and analyzing the decisions made during the project enable a more accurate estimation for the capability initiative.

Apart from estimations, a metric tool also helps identify the root cause of the defects. For example, program design, analysis, requirements, construction, and testing tasks are all linked to this tool. Errors occurring in these linked tasks are recorded in the metric tools databases. These errors are recorded in categories such as requirement documentation, construction, or design. Data of resource usage, analysis and report techniques are used for predictions. Analytics on errors result in changes to rectify them in subsequent iterations of the project.

An integrated and practical approach to the ongoing acquisition of project data requires minimal interference with staff resources. Metrics tools address implementation concerns of managers and provide team members with an integrated and secured approach to estimate and manage projects.

Scale for Measurement

The following four types of measurement scales are popular:

Nominal Scale: This scale allocates random numbers to the selected entities. For example, the numbering of entities in a business intelligence report is a nominal scale. This numbering has no order of preference and each has equal importance.

Ordinal Scale: This scale introduces rank, and is derived from ordering relations, less-than and greater-than. For example, cost drivers, such as the size of database, are placed on a scale ranging from very low to extra high. Although it is determined empirically that a low-sized database has less data, it is not possible to ascertain the exact size differences.

Interval Scale: This scale is qualitative and is used within the possibility of comparing measurements intervals empirically. For example, the age range of customers can be under 18, under 30, under 40, and so on.

Ratio Scale: Here the measurement is compared in ratios. Software measurement offers such examples, such as errors to line of code (LOC) ratio.

The type of scale chosen influences meaningful, statistical manipulation, and observation of the data. For example, a common confusion is when a statistical mean is attempted over the ordinal type of data.

CMM levels define an evolutionary path for maturity of processes for an organization. Each maturity level provides a layer in the foundation for continuous process improvement. It comprises a set of process goals that, when satisfied, stabilize an important component of the process. Achieving each level of maturity framework establishes a different component in the process, resulting in an increase in the process capability of the organization. These levels are defined in incrementing models of product quality, risk of doing business with the organization and its stability.

Measuring ODBA Maturity with CMM-I

CMM-I is one of the best-known benchmarks for organizational process maturity. The five levels of CMM-I are popular in driving project initiatives within organizations. CMM has also formed the backdrop of governance within organizations. As the organization moves up the five levels, its control over its predictions, effectiveness and attainability of goals improve. CMM-I is used in this discussion as a basis for measuring the maturity of ODBA as applied in practice. Figure 6.1 shows the five levels of maturity model for ODBA.

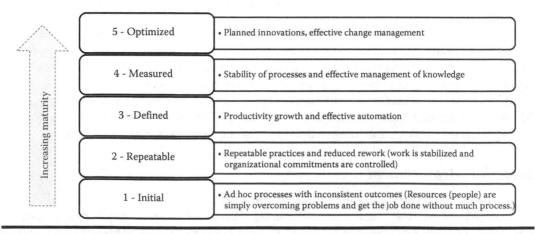

Figure 6.1   Maturity model for ODBA.

The ODBA makes use of the maturity metrics by applying them to the business capabilities. The purpose of the metrics is to define creating or enhancing business capabilities. Measurements are linked to outcomes such as enhanced "marketing capability" or "reduce data security risks."

Following are the factors to consider for ODBA maturity model implementation:

- Define the measures based on the desired outcomes from the capabilities that feed in ODBA.
- Criteria for measurement including what is assessed and why. The criteria for measurement is linked to the business outcomes or strategic actions outcomes.
- The assessment plan is pragmatic and implementable with the right resources and organizational buy in for the capability measurements.
- Flexibility in measurement are specifics for the collection of data and compare with industry-standard benchmark.

    The maturity levels for ODBA are not achieved in quick succession. Practical experience suggests each level might take 6 months to a year to achieve (Table 6.1).

Challenges in Implementing CMM for ODBA

These maturity levels are accompanied by Key Process Areas (KPAs) which characterize that level. Each KPA has five factors: goals, commitment, ability, measurement, and verification. These factors are not necessarily unique to CMM as they represent the stages that organizations go through as they mature. In the context of this discussion, these factors are applied to measure and improve the maturity of ODBA.

The CMM provides a theoretical continuum along which process maturity is developed incrementally from one level to the next. ODBA makes use of these levels to improve its own maturity. Skipping levels is not feasible.

Assessing organizational maturity is vital for an organization's quality improvements. Following are some of the challenges faced by an organization when they apply CMM to ODBA.

- **Lack of a robust model to measure against:** Capability measurement is still being developed by organizations as a formal process and as each organization needs a different set of capabilities. A formal model for ODBA is not available.
- **Lack of time to implement measurement practices:** This is a typical situation with capability development. Consistent improvement of processes and product are the norm. But if projects have unrealistic estimates and the only real requirement seems to be 'meet the schedule,' then this demonstrates a lack of commitment from senior management. In reality, the net result is counterproductive.
- **Lack of useful data collection:** Risk analysis uses mathematical methods to estimate project cost and time. Some of these methods rely on historic information. Recording these incidents or creating metric databases after the project do not provide a complete picture because key people leave the project, or the information stored in individual project files is unavailable for future projects in a meaningful and useful format. For any metrics program to be successful, it is important to establish a program as early as possible in implementing ODBA. This provides definition of measures and the rules to repeat the cycle. This approach requires commitment from top management and developers alike to collect the

Table 6.1 Maturity Model for ODBA

Level	Original CMM Description	ODBA Application of Business Capabilities
Initial (chaotic, ad hoc, individual heroics)	The starting point to use a new or undocumented repeat process.	Resources (people) are simply overcoming problems and get the job done without much process. The business operations succeed only due to motivated and experienced people. This level of capability maturity results in inconsistent outcomes and rework. The movement of key factors such as people or other resources exposes the business to major issues.
Repeatable	Process is documented sufficiently so to enable repeating the same steps.	At this level of business capability maturity, work is stabilized and organizational commitments are controlled. At this maturity level, repeatable practices reduce rework and satisfy internal and external stakeholders.
Defined	Process is defined/confirmed as a standard process; and further decomposed to levels 0, 1 and 2.	The work practices, policies, and training of resources are standardized and IM and knowledge management dimensions of business capabilities enable informed decisions. This capability maturity results in productivity growth, effective automation and better economy of scale for organization.
Managed	Process is quantitatively managed in accordance with agreed-upon metrics.	ODBA is highly beneficial as business outcomes are predictable at this capability maturity level. The organizational processes are stable and reusable across the organization.
Optimized	Deliberate process optimization and improvement is undertaken across the organization.	Level 5 occurs when innovation and continuous proactive improvements to achieve business outcomes are encouraged. The strategic intents are easy to measure and achieve.

data corresponding to the definition of the metrics program. This step is very important at level 1 or 2 of the CMM.

■ **Issue of privacy of data:** Managers and team members are usually reluctant to collect data to measure their performance. This reluctance is possibly based on the fear that the data will be used against them. The project team must be assured that the data will not be used against them. Data should not be available in raw format that identifies people for any analysis. The metrics program ensures the data is not traced back to the individuals. The more assured the teams are about the privacy and use of the data collected, the more accurate will be the available data. Sensitivity of people for measurement should be respected. To measure people instead of processes is a probable cause of failure for metrics implementation. In such cases, even though forcibly implemented, data may not represent the true nature of the measurement.

- **Lack of resources:** Metrics program need resources, such as extra time needed to record metrics, analysis tools, and any automated recording tool need to be budgeted in the indirect costs of the project. Resources are also required to maintain such programs. This is a deterrent to adopting any metrics process, especially if delivery schedules are very tight and budgets are low. Organizations are required to maintain such programs long enough to be effective. This may need dedicated resources to analyze, record, and distribute data. If a few key people are required to work over time because of their skills and involvement in multiple tasks, the organization should consider training more people in similar areas, or hiring more people with similar experience. Training is also required to enforce the metrics program within an organization. Automated tools require training managers, data collectors, and developers.
- **Pressure to report success:** The metrics program requires commitment from top management to enforce realistic and effective measurement. Unfortunately, organization leadership sometimes sets unrealistic goals or expectations which are difficult to meet. Creating a non-threatening environment without the pressure to report the success is a responsibility of leadership.
- **The need for integrated project management tools:** Project management tools are used to monitor the progress of an ongoing project. But once the project is successfully or unsuccessfully completed, it is difficult to create a database of knowledge of key attributes for the success or failure of the project. This collected knowledge is used as a guide for future projects, which may be similar in nature. Integrated PM tools start collecting data while the project is progressing rather than at the end of the project.

Applying Capability Maturity to Architecture

Capability maturity requires growth in multiple dimensions of the organization. This includes processes, resources, technology, IM, and knowledge management. Figure 6.2 shows the maturing of BA of an organization over approximately 5 years. Starting with a typical siloed situation 2 years back, the organization today is applying technology standards and platforms. The reusable and optimized core and processes, modularization of functions and systems, and development of collaborative functions facilitate maturity of the architecture.

OBDA: Maturity

Level 1: Initial

A number of organizational processes are complex and organically grown. These processes are created to either manage risks or resolve issues from expected events. For example, some financial processes are developed to respond to a particular crisis or demand from the regulatory bodies. The process and its impact on overall business capabilities of the organization is not analyzed and the impact on the workforce or resource allocation is chaotic. Processes at this stage are usually

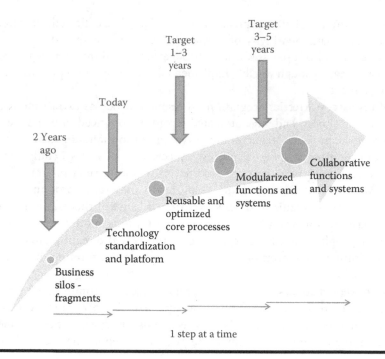

Figure 6.2 Maturing the BA of an organization.

undocumented and in a state of dynamic change, tending to be driven in an *ad hoc*, uncontrolled, and reactive manner by users or events. This provides a chaotic or unstable environment for the processes.

People: People (skills and associated capabilities) are an important measure of the overall organizational capabilities. At this level, the organization has difficulty retaining talented individuals. Managers are poorly equipped to respond to talent. Innovation and creative thinking are not nurtured. People are not trained regularly to keep their skills current. Team work is occasional. Accountability rests with managers. There is inconsistency in performing practices. Employees often run jobs with ritualistic practices. The mindset and behavior of employees is emotionally detached from the workplace.

Process: Processes are the basics of measuring the overall organizational capabilities. At this level, they are (typically) undocumented and in a state of dynamic change, tending to be driven in an ad hoc, uncontrolled and reactive manner by users or events. Groups support different techniques for operations depending on their individual preference. There is no formal coordinating body to manage the processes.

Technology: Technology is the key enabler of the organizational capabilities. Technology at this level has no formal asset management, version control of hardware, software and systems are disparate and many. Not much is done to streamline systems and create a database of what technology is used in which group. Technology is fragmented and legacy systems support the process. There are probably too many different types of software and hardware that are not managed centrally and resources required in the company to maintain and manage these tools are varied. This makes it difficult to cross-skill and senior executives do not have an appreciation of the number of different tools in use.

IM: Information is mainly in the heads of the employees and is not formally documented. The end-to-end process management, where interfaces are understood and links to enterprise-wide system and data architecture is not known.

Knowledge Management (KM): There is no formal process to train inexperienced employees with the knowledge of experienced employees. There is not much awareness of how the work of teams links to customer satisfaction and enterprise performance.

Level 2: Repeatable

At this level, some processes are repeatable, possibly with consistent results. Process discipline is unlikely to be rigorous, but where it exists it may help to ensure existing processes are maintained during times of stress.

People: The workforce practices are implemented at the Managed Level. Focus is on activities at the unit level. There are unclear performance objectives or feedback. Lack of relevant knowledge or skill for the job is present in many units. The communication from senior management is poor and the morale is low.

Process: The process is here for a single unit of work; however, it is not designed from end to end. Legacy designs are used and process improvement is not given much thought. Enterprise-wide business concepts are not widely understood by process designers. However, there are repeatable aspects of some processes and giving business some confidence in their capability of giving information.

Technology: Technology is still not aligned to enterprise goals. There are pockets of programs setup to integrate some processes but they still lack governance and senior executive support.

IM: Information is mainly in the heads of the employees and is not formally documented. The end-to-end process management, where interfaces are understood and links to enterprise-wide system and data architecture is not known.

KM: Knowledge is limited to pockets and the enterprise is still at a risk of losing valuable information if some key employees leave.

Level 3: Defined

Characteristics of processes at this level are sets of defined and documented standard processes and subject to some degree of improvement over time. These standard processes establish consistency of process performance across the organization.

People: They understand their role and cross-training is happening in some areas. Employees take ownership of their own work, but the bigger functional unit picture still resides with managers.

Process: Documentation is functional and identifies interconnections with other processes. Suppliers and customers are identified.

Technology: IT is aligned to business and programs are setup to define processes and integrate them to achieve goals.

IM: Process owners understand the flow of information to and from their process. They understand the responsibility that lies within the process and how their work affects the rest of the function.

KM: Process owners have some ideas on how to redesign their own work, but still need training on how to align it to enterprise goals. End-to-end documentation is available for some processes.

Level 4: Managed

At this level, management identifies ways to adjust and adapt the process to projects without measurable losses of quality or deviations from specifications. Process capability is established from this level.

People: Users can describe and take ownership of their process. They are skilled in problem-solving and process improvement techniques.

Process: Documentation is functional and identifies interconnections with other processes. Suppliers and customers are identified. End-to-end documentation exists. The process owner understands performance goals and a vision of the future. He/she can sponsor the redesign and improvement efforts, plan implementation, and compliance with process design.

Technology: Process owner controls IT and has control over changing the processes to suit the enterprise.

IM: Information is available easily and the architectural and business knowledge is well documented.

KM: Performance goals and standards are widely known and understood. Knowledge is constantly shared between employees, and in the process, the intelligence of the organization is getting richer.

Level 5: Optimizing

Processes at this level focus on continually improving process performance through both incremental and innovative technological changes/improvements.

People: Employees are skilled at change management and change implementation. They can develop a rolling strategic plan for the processes and take redesign initiatives to achieve strategic goals. Reward and recognition reinforce personal growth and learning.

Process: Process is designed to fit with customer and supplier processes to optimize enterprise performance.

Technology: The architecture adheres to industry standards. It is integrated and designed with enterprise-wide goals in mind.

IM: Information is communicated inter- and intra-enterprise level. The metrics are designed with the strategic goals in mind. Managers review progress at regular intervals.

KM: The dashboards regularly state the growth clearly and the lessons are applied back in the system. Managers regularly review the statistics and knowledge gathered, and use them to further enhance the organizations' customer, supplier, and employee relationship.

ODBA Metrics in Practice

To successfully introduce metrics in any organization, the first thing to do is increase the understanding of the metrics within the organization. In addition, an appropriate metrics implementation model and techniques for modifying the process of development and controls are selected. A guided assessment process, maturity and capability determinations, instruments in the form of questionnaires, and guidelines for process improvement (standards for action plan generation), and assessor training programs are established.

Any metrics program depends on the intended use of the data.

Planning, an interactive process which involves characterizing the current project and its environment, setting the quantifiable goals for successful project performance and organizational improvements, choosing the appropriate process model, and supporting methods and tools;

Execution, requires a closed loop cycle of product development using selected processes and collecting information as planned;

Analysis and Packaging, requires constructing reports and postmortems analysis of the gathered data and information.

Table 6.2 lists how to identify capability gaps to metrics in ODBA. Table 6.2 shows the current gap of the organization with its processes and the impact unmanaged processes have on the organization.

Bridging the Gap: Example of an IM Dimension

Bridging the capability gaps brings the organization to a higher level of capability maturity. Information Management System (IMS) is a differentiating and important capability dimension used as an example here to demonstrate how the dimensions are improved. The organization progressively drives IM maturity and capability alignment across organization, enacted and supported by appropriate governance.

The IMS prioritizes four key aspects of the organization IM. These four strategic priorities represent the set of achievable objectives that constitute greatest value, greatest risk treatment, or are important foundations in progressing toward the overarching IM vision. These priorities are consistent with those identified by senior management when establishing the framework.

Organizations have limited capacity which is considered when identifying achievable and sustainable strategies and plans. This strategy outlines a significant change agenda for the organization, which necessitates a clear and endorsed scope (Table 6.3).

- Identifies the starting point for change
- Comprises logical work packages that represent tangible benefit
- Resources with consideration to current and forecast resource constraint
- Realizes and demonstrates tangible value in appropriate timeframes for stakeholders
- Ensures achievements and improvements progressively extend to the whole of the organization.

Prioritization Approach

The prioritization approach focuses on selecting a set of existing functions within the organization that together, represent a set of end-to-end policing services, which;

- represents a high proportion of overall information collected by the organization
- has the potential for tangible efficiency improvements
- has the potential for rapid improvements
- has the potential to provide significant benefit for the whole organization (e.g., data quality improvement)
- enables improvements in end-to-end information security

The IMF is developed and applied to the set of prioritized functions, before being extended to the entire organization. An extended approach is showcased in case studies in Chapters 11 and 12.

Table 6.2 Known Gaps in Capabilities and Their Impact on the Organization

Gap	Definition	Impact
Limited ability to effectively control and manage information.	No defined platform to effectively control and manage information in a repeatable and structured manner. More specific gaps are: Governance, taxonomy of information, including roles and entities, support for operations so they are fit for purpose and have repeatable flows of information enabling key business processes.	Inconsistent governance processes, including decision making and unintended consequences of poor decisions that are costly to fix. This reduces or limits the potential return on investment. There is degradation in the quality and usability of information, and effectiveness of systems. Perpetual evolution and creation of new sets of rules and standards for managing and defining information with each new system or process, making it increasingly more difficult to share and/or integrate information from different holdings.
Limited capabilities in the organization.	Capabilities required for the design, development and implementation of fit for purpose solutions contributing to an improved control and management of the information are not available within the organization.	The current level of IM maturity reflects the existing capability of the organization.
Unmanaged and unrepeatable business processes.	Unable to be supported by managed information flows.	Lack of standardized processes reduces the ability to leverage technology to deliver efficiency.
Fragmented organizational structures.	No current division, that manages information, has either the scope or the capabilities required to manage information consistently throughout the organization.	Overlapping and at times conflicting roles result in a lack of clear leadership to set the direction and vision for IM, define accountability or provide authoritative advice and guidance to the organization.
No appropriate data model is present.	There is no single data model adopted as standard across all functions and business areas to support the management of information in the organization. A number of data models exist; however, they are not aligned and in some cases conflict.	Multiple data bases exist containing the same fundamental information (names, locations, etc.). The data held in different sources cannot be matched as it does not share a unique identifier, the same properties or definitions. Therefore, data cannot be integrated or validated to support a single source of truth, such as a single view of an entity.

Table 6.3   Strategic Priorities and Benefits

Strategic Priorities	*Objectives*	*Enablers*	*Benefits*
Control and manage information	Shape and use information to increase organization performance.	IM framework as a platform for management, IM governance framework and education and training.	Process efficiencies, lower error rates, collaboration, effective work hours.
Information security	Reduce information security breaches and improve safety of employees and community.	IM framework as a platform for security, IM governance framework and body education and training systems.	Controls security breaches, reputation Confidence.
Collection-to-share lifecycle	Make information available and shareable at the collection point.	IM architecture, Managed business processes, Fit for purpose data model.	Higher Information quality, response efficiency and risk management.
Compliance	Information fully compliant with standards and requirement.	IM framework, Education and training, IM governance framework and body.	Increase in reputation, Increase in interoperability and integration.

Governance of ODBA Metrics

To govern progress of capabilities, it is essential to develop a standard of performance, and set of conditions or measurements that make a project successful. These conditions/measurements become the goals for rest of the projects to be successful.

Reporting systems with required data and metrics are established with clear guidelines on how often and where these reports are received. These reports determine how the project is progressing, and highlight any corrective action to be taken.

Goals are adjusted if any re-planning is done because of a deviation that was noticed in the reports. Documentation of controls, measures, and any decision points create the standards to avoid any ambiguity.

Reward and recognition of employees are part of the regular standard program. Leadership sets programs to build enthusiasm in workers and development knowledge. This knowledge is spread and employees are given incentives to share their knowledge.

Discussion Points

1. What is the importance of metrics and measurements to the success of an ODBA program?
2. What are the risks associated in using metrics in measuring ODBA maturity? *(hint: metrics can be misleading; or measuring a part of the organization)*

3. Why are the measures of business capabilities important to ODBA? What will happen to the organization, if the business capabilities are not measured?
4. What are the five elements of business capabilities that are measured? Answer with examples.
5. An organization you know quite well is, in your opinion, at a maturity level 1. This is based on your experience of dealing with that organization as a consultant. However, you are now invited to undertake a formal assessment of their BA and, to your surprise, you find them to be at a maturity level 2. You have a gut feel that this is not right. What do you think are the likely reasons for your gut feeling? Discuss keeping in mind the key elements of that organization's BA that make it at Level 2? And what would be your recommendations (including estimated time) for the organization's BA to move to Level 3?

Chapter 7

Governance, Risk, and Compliance and Quality

KEY POINTS

- Understanding Governance-Risk-Compliance (GRC) and Quality
- Managing GRC and enhancing Quality with outcome-driven business architecture (ODBA)
- Reviewing Governance processes for business investment decisions
- Ameliorating and managing risks in organizations with the help of ODBA
- Ensuring organizational compliance with ODBA
- Discussing the Quality of and with Business Architecture (BA)
- Separating the Quality functions in an organization—Quality environment, Quality Assurance, and Quality compliance
- Applying Quality to data, models, processes, and architectures
- Applying the quality techniques and levels (syntax, semantics, aesthetics) to a BA
- Understanding the quality of operational (non-functional) parameters and BA

ODBA as the basis for investment decision-making requires due consideration to risks. Risks are balanced with the return on investment. Organizational risks include financial, people, technology, and quality risks. Mitigation of these risks is a multidimensional affair that also influences processes, quality, and outcomes. Governance in organizational processes is also a quality issue. Together, governance and quality ensure the organization is legally compliant—both externally and internally. This chapter discusses GRC and quality issues, and how they relate to the ODBA.

Introduction to Governance Risk and Compliance and Quality

Governance, Risk Management, and Compliance (GRC) is a crucial triad of functions that contributes to the success of an organization. GRC enables senior leaders (decision makers) to manage risk and ensure regulatory compliance. Handling complexities of the business needs knowledge about what is going on within the organization (visibility), make appropriate decisions to ameliorate risks, and ensure the organization is compliant with the myriad rules and regulations of the ecosystem in which it operates.

Quality intersects with GRC. This is because quality enables good governance, risk mitigation, and compliance, and, in turn, these factors enhance the quality of products and services of an organization. As a result, the perception of the organization is suitably enhanced.

The business capability framework, discussed in earlier chapters can help improve governance risk management and compliance. Governance is balanced with organizational risks including financial, reputational, and market capabilities that enable an organization to improve its risks by controlling and directing its efforts. Governance also assists in compliance with legislation and business rules. Lack of proper governance exposes the organization to risk of financial losses and non-compliance with rules or regulations.

Under-governance exposes the organization to legal or other punitive damages. Under-governance also impacts quality in a negative way and damages the reputation of the organization in the customer's mind. Over-governance, on the other hand, can throttle creativity within the organization. A relaxed atmosphere is essential for contemporary innovations. Thus, it is important for senior management to pragmatically balance compliance and process implementation in GRC.

More often than not, risks in large organizations tend to get managed in siloes. For example, the financial risk is assigned to the financial compliance professionals, people risk to human resources, reputational risks to corporate communications and Information Technology risks to the corresponding IT department. These siloes in risk management are a result of the organizational structure itself. Silo-based approaches to risks are detrimental to quality.

As discussed in earlier chapters, the outcome-driven business architecture (ODBA) plays a crucial role in enabling a holistic view of the organization. ODBA helps in dismantling the siloes and, as a result, provides a holistic, outcome-driven view of the organization. Such a holistic view is helpful in managing organizational risks in a holistic way. ODBA forms the basis of a holistic, well-aligned approach to organizational functioning.

Risks related to legal compliance are prominent in Internet-based digital business models. The social and mobile media used by the organization exposes it to compliance risks among legislations across the globe. The way the organization approaches its existing and potential customers in the digital space impacts these legislative risks. For example, the perception of the organization plays a role in whether the customer resolves issues amicably or follows the legal route. Interestingly, the quality of products and services of the organization is viewed through perceptions expressed by the customers in an open digital environment.

Reputation of an organization is a complex phenomenon that is made more so in the digital age as organizations cannot directly influence. And yet, it simply can't be ignored. Loss of reputation results in loss of brand equity, low sales, and legal liability. False reputation (e.g., when a criminal creates false information causing it to show up first in search engine results), results in loss of market value. Failure to influence digital compliance results in loss of customers or at least an inability to reach and serve customers.

In addition to the externally facing challenges primarily from customers, there are also internal operational challenges resulting from lack of GRC and quality. For example, failure to control the forecasts in production results in excess inventory costs or lost sales due to the unavailability of inventory or resources. Aging products result in failure to meet changing customer demands which has revenue and competitive implications. Research and Development (R&D) brings an inability to bring new products to market, which reduces market share and revenue.

The following describes Governance, Risk, Compliance and Quality (GRCQ) (based on Figure 7.1) in the context of ODBA:

- Governance is a part of the overall management approach to control and direct the organization. Governance needs a balance between the aspirations and limitations of the organization. ODBA provides a sound basis for governance as it enables an understanding of the structure of systems and projects of an organization in line with its desired outcomes. Alignment of projects with outcomes results in fewer well-directed projects that capitalize on new technologies and processes. For example, with the advent of Big Data, organizations need specific projects that add direct value to decision-making. The multilayered data sources (structured and unstructured) growing rapidly need to be placed under rigorous governance. Appropriate use of governance methods that enable focus on outcomes help control the risks associated with data proliferation.
- Risk Management supports governance by identifying, analyzing, and, where necessary, responding appropriately to risks. ODBA is most helpful here because of the holistic view it provides of the organization. As a result, cross-departmental communications open up and risks are reduced. Furthermore, risks associated with new technologies and analytics (typically Big Data) are extremely dynamic—they change from moment to moment. This implies risk can come at any time and from completely unanticipated directions. Sound ODBA structure helps handle these risks due to the integration and alignment it provides with the organizational outcomes.
- Compliance is organizational conformance to stated Requirements, Standards, and Regulations. ODBA ensures discipline in documenting, reviewing, auditing, and managing the conformance required of an organization. Due to the complexity and exposure of widely varying sources of Big Data, compliance assumes greater importance than before. Compliance trickles down to many layers of businesses which are responsible for the ultimate outcome.
- Quality is complex primarily because of the elements of the subjectivity that influences it. What is considered high quality in one context may not be considered of that high quality in another context. The subjectivity of quality is also based on the perception factor. What is perceived by the users as poor quality becomes that. Since perceptions are built upon opinions of groups (particularly social media groups) as much as an individual's experience, they are not always based on facts, and quality becomes challenging to handle. ODBA aids in

Figure 7.1   Governance, Risk, Compliance, and Quality—integral part of ODBA.

enhancing the quality of an organizations products and services—especially as it optimizes both external and internal processes of the organization. For example, in ODBA implementation, customer's queries can be handled by a single point of contact rather than multiple departments and divisions. This handling of queries starts to change the perception of the organization and the quality of its sources to a positive one.

Governance is usually top down. The priorities of the business, based on its capabilities, are set by the senior-most leaders of the organization. This leadership comprises both business and technical decision makers of the organization who sets and justifies the business priorities. This ODBA-based alignment of priorities is achieved by a synergy of people, processes, and technologies that support the organization's outcomes. The architecture governance framework ensures the architecture principles, standards, and guidelines are expressed along the lines of the desired organizational outcomes and strategies.

Key Characteristics of GRC as a Sub-Framework

GRC is considered a sub-framework within the overall ODBA. Following are the key characteristics of this sub-framework:

- Discipline—GRC presents consistent criteria to assess multiple projects across the organization in terms of how they impact the outcomes. In the absence of an organization-wide discipline, assessment of projects tends to be subjective and influenced by individual decision makers. Rapidly changing technologies (e.g., IoT, Cloud, Machine Learning) are disruptive requiring rigorous discipline in their adoption.
- Transparency and fairness—projects are assessed based on enterprise-wide principles and standards that are part of the ODBA. Disruptive technologies need transparency to ensure all stakeholders in the organization understand the impact of these technologies on the business.
- Independence—Business and Enterprise architects need independence to provide a range of solutions based on organizational demand. This is vital to ensure decisions based on information management are realistic and the organization has the capabilities to incorporate and absorb the new technologies.
- Accountability—architects and project managers are accountable and responsible for documenting any deviations and exceptions from the original decisions and implementation plans. The compliance aspect of GRC ensures accountability.

The above characteristics of GRC are valuable in providing stability to the organization as it embarks on a transformation. Changes to GRC itself are permitted only when there is a change to the overall organization, responsibility reporting model of the business, the makeup of operating facilities, or after a crisis event that results in gaps in the overall Business Capability Modeling (BCM). For the most part, though, it is important that GRC is kept independent of line management. The key characteristic of GRC is to ensure that the accountability of line managers is maintained separately from the responsibilities of GRC and Quality managers.

GRC and ODBA

ODBA is a valid representation of the business. The richness of the business architecture (BA) grows over time as the initial maps that represent the business are supplemented by additional information. GRC ensures effective and efficient compliance of the BA—and, as a result, of the business itself. A good BA model requires understanding and management of risks. GRC brings together corporate governance, compliances and reporting, and enterprise risk management (ERM) in order to ensure compliance with rules and regulations. Thus, ODBA is benefitted by GRC as much as it provides a central coordination place for GRC.

While ODBA drives the change in organization, IT supports the change and is the enabler of change (Tiwary and Unhelkar [1]). Key business outcomes define and impact ODBA. The BA definition requires an understanding of the reason for BA and its tangible benefits to the organization.

ODBA eliminates redundancies and duplications in the activities of governance and risk management. ODBA brings efficiency, effectiveness and reduces operational costs, project costs and risks. ODBA facilitates integration, which benefits governance and risk management. ODBA enhances GRC as follows:

- Enables prioritization based on alignment. As a result of the prioritization, there is direct focus on high business value adding activities and capabilities. Governance is driven by business capability. The governance process spans multiple business areas resulting occasionally in overlapping and conflicting governance bodies. ODBA supports the governance activities by making them holistic.
- Establishes a metrics regime to monitor and improve governance and control by providing the measurement criteria as (discussed in Chapter 6).
- Adopts globally accepted architectural standards and processes. These standards enable a common language of communication and a common understanding of compliance rules and terms within the organization, and with its business partners and stakeholders thereby reducing risk with communication.
- Sources reference models and artifacts from specialist vendors and adopts them in the context of the organizational requirements. These reference models provide the basis for governance and control.
- Provides risk profiles and adoption risks based on organizational business outcomes expected. While legislative risks and compliance are mandatory, other business risks need to be prioritized.
- Ensures the organization for GRC application to disruptive technologies. Ensures that investments of time, resources, and money are made in a way that best supports the organizational strategy and maximizes transformational opportunities.
- Discovers harmonization opportunities across organizational and functional areas to drive efficiency, reduce costs, and understand the implications of cost optimization efforts on current and future business capabilities. This provides the reference point to stop non-essential projects and activities.

In addition to the above characteristics of the governance, risk, and compliance sub-framework, it is also worth noting the advantages of its implementation:

- The Governance sub-framework defines the overall governance structure that is adopted across the organization. This framework is formally adopted and the work force is trained in using the framework. A GRC framework is a vital, strategic function providing internal and external compliance for successful functioning of the organization. GRC in the context of ODBA is understood as an important mechanism to influence the opportunities for strategic investments based on business and technical capabilities.

- Processes to define the steps and checkpoints for the governance. The pre-requisites to initiate the governance and the expected outcomes are defined and approved by senior executives to be adopted in the organization. The governance is clear, concise, and well defined.
- Governance body's membership has the right roles defined for the members as it is relevant to the governance outcomes. In many cases, the membership is not at the right level for effective decision-making. For example, governance cannot be made up of only one discipline—typically IT. Cross-functionality, a well-known concept of Agility in organizations, is also relevant to the governance team of the organization. Without such cross-functional representation, the decisions made by the governance body may not be accepted by the rest of the business. On the other end, a business representative making technical decisions without full understanding of the complexity of the issues can lead to failures.
- Scenarios outlining variations of the governance processes. Governance scenarios highlight the common elements and variation or exceptions. In some cases, the exceptions are handled separately where higher authority or specific expertise is required. Exceptions are presented to specific forums for decision inputs. For example, for organizational reputation risks, corporate communication provides the input. The governance process identifies exceptions to the governance body authority where approval is required by a different set of stakeholders. In this case, the exception stakeholder is not included as part of the governance body.
- Properly defined and formalized terms of reference of a governance body provide authority. The term of reference defines criteria required for the acceptance of submission to governance body. The metrics for measurement of the effectiveness of the processes and decisions are maintained and reviewed regularly to update their term of reference.
- Predefined governance document workflow enables compliance on the governance process itself. The document flow includes all steps of the governance process. Governance processes demand meetings of stakeholders, requiring relevant documents be presented well in advance. The frequency and time of the governance meetings can cause delays due to time constraints and prioritization of agenda items. The ODBA-based business capabilities assist in defining the priorities of the agenda. For example, if a project is developing business capabilities identified as critical then the governance frequency is carried out more often and so also the reporting of the project to the senior executives.

Appropriate levels of governance reflect the needs of the enterprise and a realistic assessment of its capabilities. Organizationally agreed business outcomes and priorities are the anchor of the governance sub-framework. And since ODBA has an overbearing focus on outcomes, it plays an important role in enhancing the governance function of the organization.

Business Risks

Business Risks and Their Impact

Business risks range from those related to inappropriate technologies, lack of skills or motivation in the staff, failed product and failed marketing, missing leadership and security—to name but a few (See Appendix C for a comprehensive list of business risks). Most risks are identified by organizations when risks appear in other organizations within the industry—or their own experiences. There are many more risks, however, that are entirely new and organizations need a strategy to handle the new risks. Having a robust business and enterprise architecture (EA) is one way to plan for this scenario. Architecture provides stability to the organizational systems. Therefore, introduction of a new solution or business process is controlled by the architecture. As a result, risks are better understood and obviated even before they occur. Many non-technical advantages of an architecture (e.g., consistent terminology and enhanced communication) also come into play in reducing risks.

Business Risks and Capabilities

Business capabilities are discussed earlier in Chapters 3 and 4. Business capabilities need governance process by identifying upfront risks and placing effective controls to handle them. Eventually, this is helpful in maintaining compliance with both external and internal legal, audit, and accounting requirements. This is vital to pave the path for sensible technology investments—which assume significant importance and demand high attention from decision makers in the era of Big Data-driven technologies and businesses [2].

Once the risks are visible, effective compliances to mitigate those risks are implemented. For example, disruptive technologies (e.g., Big Data) have significant business impact which need to be identified quickly and handled effectively [3]. The wide gamut of business and technology options in Big Data expose the organization to a suite of uncertainties in terms of business and technology strategies and their execution. Including GRC in strategy planning, helps in identifying risks and protecting systems. Apart from this, GRC has a core task in maintaining compliance with legal, audit, and accounting requirements.

GRC protects business investments. Investments are valued significantly higher when protected by GRC and carefully mapped to business capabilities. This is because apart from ensuring compliance, GRC also ensures value-for-money. Thus, Business Capabilities enhance governance processes which, in turn, help identify risks upfront and position effective plans to ameliorate those risks. GRC based on Business Capabilities helps in technology strategy planning; it also eventually helps in maintaining compliance with legal, audit, and accounting requirements.

Balancing Governance with Risks

Good governance is pragmatic governance. Such governance balances organizational risks with opportunities. Governance and risk mitigation help achieve business objectives without sacrificing quality. The GRC effectiveness and efficiency is enhanced by understanding the business capabilities and limitations. Understanding organization-wide business capabilities, business and technology strategies, and the way in which the organization views opportunities and risks are important in balancing risks. GRC succeeds only when coupled with sound business capabilities—resulting in an effective and enterprise-wide anchor and decision-making tool.

Constraints in Following GRC

Balancing between quality and risks is due to many business constraints. These constraints and their impact on organizations are depicted in Table 7.1:

ODBA's Risk Alignment

Outcome-driven EA defines and positions business outcomes. The GRC sub-framework using ODBA ensures risk-adjusted value. Implementing the GRC framework keeps the organizational

Table 7.1   Business Constraints in Following GRC Sub-Framework

Business Constraint to Use GRC	Impact on Organization	ODBA as a Resolution to Constraints
Demand for resources is higher than the available resources and GRC adds steps in the process workflow to comply with governance.	The pragmatic GRC framework requires identifying and adequately managing the risk profiles. The risk profile is defined with business and legal aspects in mind.	The business outcomes define activities for each unit/division. The unit/division manages demand based on alignment with the strategic actions.
High percentage of resources currently engaged in managing demand and need to comply with the GRC. The GRC framework is managed by the resources having adequate authorities to enforce the GRC requirements on projects.	In some cases, the constraint of delivery time is used to bypass some of the governance processes. This generates a number of gaps in organizational capabilities. The GRC processes are clear and implementable in the organizational context.	The organizational skills, resources, requirements are defined for the prioritized business capabilities. The resources are acquired and managed via enterprise project office for the demand and supply and timelines. The resource both people, assets, and systems are planned and managed based on business capabilities development. The capability assessments after the activities completion must identify the gaps in skills and plan to acquire them.
Projects are assessed on cost and benefits and are not looked at holistically. This creates organizational risks to be addressed later on.	The remediation of these risks is expensive and time consuming. The reports from the GRC are visible to the executives with each business capabilities the risks carried forward. Initiatives are planned to reduce these risks.	Prioritization criteria is defined and socialized within the organization. These criteria are applied for each project assessments. The governance process is managed by senior executives and any exemptions are granted after due dalliance.
Projects are more tactical and may only service one unit or department requirements so may not require to comply with GRC.	The tactical projects have a tendency to become long term and expose the organization to the risks of financial or reputational damages.	The EA roadmap is approved for short term (0-18M) and (18-36M). The implementation plans for the short-term activities must be resourced and required investment is allocated. Each unit/division has understanding of the priority of their idea and initiatives. Focus on modular and enterprise activity.

culture, maturity, and approach in mind. Furthermore, project portfolio management, application portfolio management, and investment decision processes are also kept in mind to maximize business outcomes.

ODBA specifically helps manage risks as follows:

- Supports the otherwise fragmented and overlapping communities of interests within the organization
- Recommends tools and services to provide optimal balance of physical policing and online information and services
- Enables empowerment of decision-making at the customer point of contact by providing contextualized information
- Assists in aggregated information across multiple agencies, jurisdictions, and information as needed
- Assists in Integrated across commands, external jurisdictions, partners, and agencies
- Helps the management and makeup of IT costs and information is one of the largest cost items for IT

Governance and Business Investment

From a business investment decisions viewpoint, GRC is most helpful in facilitating decisions based on the desired outcomes. Factors such as regulatory demands, competition, and technology breakthroughs also dictate investment decisions. Business Intelligence (BI) is brought in, internally, in these decision-making processes (Unhelkar and Tiwary [4]).

Figure 7.2 shows a traditional stage-gate process based on cost and benefit analysis. In this figure, each project is assessed to be based on the project costs and benefit it offers to the organization. This approach examines every idea and initiative independently of each other. This is

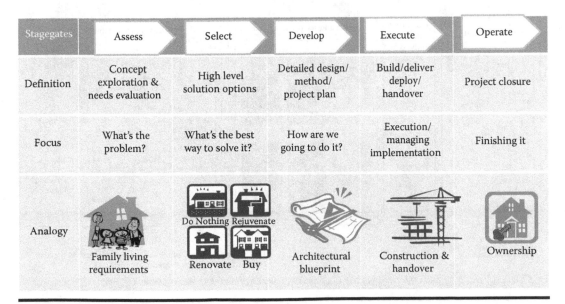

Figure 7.2   Traditional governance model based on cost and benefits.

the traditional and popular approach to investment decisions. This approach, however, lacks the holistic viewpoint of a program of development for the entire organization.

This is particularly true of data-intense applications and solutions (Kleppmann [5]). The linear nature of this process leads to a fragmented governance of the projects. As such, it does not mitigate the risks associated with execution of multiple projects simultaneously. GRC, in such cases, becomes a variation of multi-gating process, where at each gate multiple projects are assessed based on predefined criteria. This approach runs the risks of project sponsors ticking the boxes and getting projects through these loops. Apart from the risks of project conflicts, this approach also results in building duplicate capabilities.

The governance rules being linearly defined do not result in a cohesive whole to provide the strategic direction to the organization.

Correlating Business Capabilities to GRC

Business capabilities describe what the business does, and what it needs to do differently in response to strategic challenges and opportunities [6]. Business capabilities combine technologies and processes to create value. Dynamic business capabilities focus on what needs to be done differently in response to new and strategic challenges (e.g., Big Data). Examples of Big Data-based capabilities include Analytical capabilities (e.g., Predictive, Net Promoter Score—NPS), Unstructured Databases, Networks and Security infrastructures and Business Agility.

A capability gap assessment is portrayed in a heat map as shown in Figure 7.3. Such capability assessment is based on a simple map superimposed with additional layers. The visualized gaps

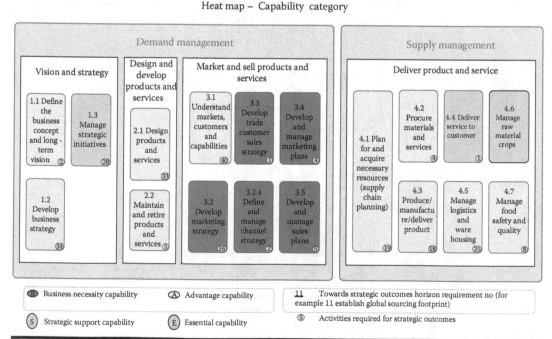

Figure 7.3 Capability assessment.

shown in Figure 7.3 are further enhanced with the help of GRC to identify the organizational risks and prioritize the capabilities. There is an enterprise-wide effort to develop a prioritized list of capabilities and implementation plan. For example, such prioritization considers not only the capabilities needed, but also existing capabilities, maturity levels, and efforts needed for alignment and integration, and ensures uniformity in capability-building activities. This in a way is governance on GRC (based on White et al. [7]).

The Governance Process

Effective governance ensures investments are planned in accordance with the current and future business outcomes. As depicted in Figure 7.4, effective governance is also required across the project management office (PMO) to plan and implement projects holistically (especially IT). The PMO is encouraged to reflect upon multiple projects and ensure avoidance of siloes and duplications.

Capability prioritization is undertaken keeping outcomes in mind. Once projects are prioritized, it is possible to define a corresponding business investment plan. The process for capability prioritization and investment planning is shown in Figure 7.5. There is a need to communicate and gain acceptance across the organization on capability prioritization. This is done at the highest level of management so that it can be acknowledged and included in programs across the organization. Eventually, as shown in Figure 7.6, a process based on business capabilities and GRC is used to undertake investment decisions.

GRC and Investment Decisions

The investment decisions for GRC require the following as pre-requisites:

■ Future state assessment as a continuous process. Each project, at completion, updates the enterprise current state and includes any extra efficiencies required to achieve the final future state. This process is included as part of the project governance and completion process. The architecture team keeps the future and current state up-to-date.

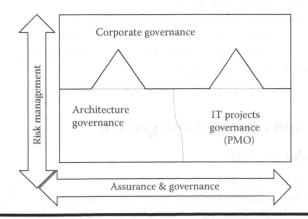

Figure 7.4 Governance structure.

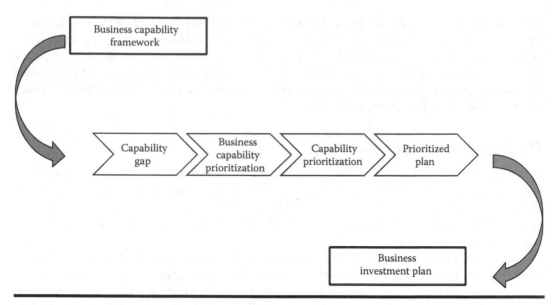

Figure 7.5 Capability prioritization and investment planning.

- The organizational strategic plan includes any investment governance. The required business capabilities to achieve the strategy and their assessment are a pre-requisite in assessing the initiatives. Business capability framework establishes and assesses projects based on assessment methods currently in use by the organization.
- The assessment and prioritization for the initiatives are formalized by the senior executives and the intent to use this list for project prioritization is agreed upon by all departmental heads and project initiative decision makers.

The pre-requisites provide the governance team a list of the business capabilities, future directions and targeted architecture to define the initiatives. In case the departments need to initiate their own projects, departmental decision makers assess these initiatives against the business capability priorities. Exemptions to some initiatives are granted due to legal requirements, business environmental impacts, and similar urgent situations.

Good governance processes also provide an avenue for exemptions. For example, a tactical project to comply with some legislative changes may be approved with some sunset conditions. The enterprise team then re-assesses the tactical solution and defines the project to achieve the targeted stage based on tactical project impact.

Value of GRC and Change Management

The Business Value of GRC

A GRC mapped to business capabilities ensures that investment decisions of time, resources, and money are made in a way that best supports the strategic directions of the business. Specifically, with the advent of Big Data technologies (Buytendijk and Oestreich [8]), the advantages an organization gains in its technology investments are as follows:

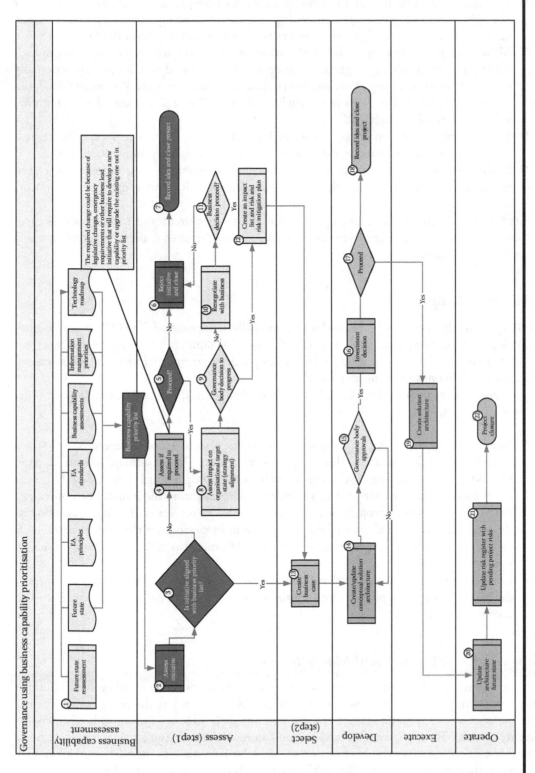

Figure 7.6 The proposed governance process.

- Provides visible evidence of Big Data technologies investment as well as strategies. For example, a technology investment requiring a multi-node Hadoop installation is undertaken based on an understanding of what the business wants to achieve from Big Data.
- Maximizes the transition needs of the business, for example, use of Big Data analytics requires both existing organizational data and the new, dynamic, perhaps externally sourced, unstructured Big Data. The need to transition to a new suite of Data and Analytics is acute and, more often than not, fraught with risks. This risk is reduced and transition value maximized through GRC.
- Discovers harmonization opportunities for Data, Analytics, and the user experience across various functional areas of the organization, resulting in efficiency and reduced costs.
- Provides a sound reference point for investment decision-making—as investments are placed under governance, and returns the risks on investments while remaining legally compliant.

Understand the implications of cost optimization efforts on current and future business capabilities as, very often, initial costs are daunting and result in erroneous decisions on postponing technology investments.

GRC and Change

ODBA governs all activities whether performed internally or outsourced. The ODBA also controls technology, information, solution, and security changes. The same applies to outsourced functions performed on behalf of the company, including design, deployment, maintenance, modification, and repair and decommissioning activities.

The business capability-driven GRC brings about changes in the organization. These changes occur at two levels:

- Level 1 change defines an organizational investment plan based on business capability prioritization and the roadmap. This is a proactive measure. This roadmap, in turn, initiates one or many projects. The GRC monitors each project's progress and uses a method to assess the progress toward the target that is fulfilled by implementing the project. This provides a better measurement of project success. The success of the project is measured based on traditional cost/benefit analysis and also improvement in capabilities that either reduce costs to the organization—enterprise wide or provides additional capability to increase revenue of the organization.
- On level 2, when a project is initiated, it is assessed for the business capability it enhances or develops. In some exceptional cases, legislative or operational demands may supersede this aforementioned demand.

Governance Adoption and Maintenance

GRC adoption is continuously reviewed and revised as the business changes and evolves. The architecture governing the organizations' systems and processes matures as the requirements change. The architecture is as dynamic as the business—both should be able to adjust quickly to the changing environment. The objective of the architecture forums ensures technology investment decisions are made efficiently and on the basis of the best available information, including development of options, in the enterprise context. The GRC framework is thus kept aligned to ODBA.

Quality and ODBA

Quality is of paramount importance in the discussions of ODBA. In addition to the overlap of quality with GRC, it also has an independent role with respect to ODBA.

The effort of quality in the discussions on business architecture has two aspects:

- Quality as a result of architecture in the overall organization; and quality of the architecture itself.
- Quality includes many elements—each contributing to the overall success in decision-making for the business.

For example, quality of data impacts quality of analytics which, in turn, impacts the insights provided by the software solutions. Confidence in the analysis by the decision makers is another essential part of quality. Thus, reliability of the business architecture comes into play—which is vital to build confidence in decisions. Regulatory acts, such as SOX, GLB, Basel II, HIPAA, and HOEPA, necessitate further focus on quality. This is because it is obligatory for the organization to be compliant with these acts—and quality goes a long way to ensure that the organization's data and processes are compliant.

The dynamicity of the business environment indicates a need to understand quality as a rapidly changing concept. The underlying theme in understanding quality is—*it depends.* ODBA accepts the dynamic nature of the business environment and therefore does not proceed with a rigid definition of quality. ODBA continuously focuses on alignment and quality is an important result of such alignment. Quality initiatives in an organization, however, help in enhancing the processes associated with ODBA. The following points are worth considering in terms of ODBA and Quality:

- ODBA provides the necessary context to handle quality issues appropriately.
- Having an ODBA with rich semantic details is a major step in quality.
- Well-defined interfaces for collaborative services define the contracts for exchange of data and information—and ODBA enables rigorous definition of these contracts.
- ODBA provides mechanisms to store, retrieve, and archive the data accurately and securely. These mechanisms can be appropriately handled in terms of the business context with the help of ODBA.
- Quality (like GRC) is benefitted by having a detailed ODBA, good governance, aligned outcomes, astute leadership, and the right tools.
- Weakness in data quality and data integrity puts the business at risk.

Quality Levels and Architecture

Goals, methods, and performance are three major aspects of organizational quality [9]. The key aspects of quality shown in Figure 7.7 expand on Perry's basic definition. Goals lead to outcomes, methods translate to processes and performance is defined by the operational parameter. Thus, ODBA (with its focus on outcomes) remains at the heart of quality enhancement initiatives in an organization.

Understanding quality in the context of ODBA is based on its various levels. For example, goals of data quality ensure filtering and safe storage of data. Information quality focuses on the

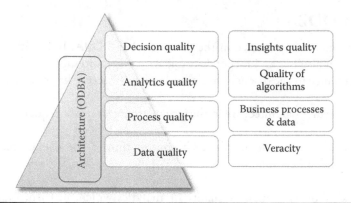

Figure 7.7   Key aspects of quality in Business Architecture.

most efficient ways to decipher meaning from data. ODBA influences four highly interconnected elements of quality (Figure 7.7):

- Data Quality
- Process Quality
- Analytics Quality
- Decision Quality

Data Quality

Data quality at the base of the triangle in Figure 7.7. In the world of Big Data, there is no limit to the volume of data—spanning from terabytes to petabytes, exabytes and more. Ensuring the quality of this data is part of both quality control and quality assurance. Numerous techniques are popular in handling the quality of data. For example, Equivalence partitioning, boundary values, and so on, are used in sampling, checking, and correcting the data. Data, however, are not independent entities. Data across the enterprise have multidimensional relationships. These relationships provide insights for decision-making. The logic of the program, as well as standards, like naming of attributes and operations and layout of code specific to a particular language impacts information quality. Since the code deals with and manipulates the data, the quality of the code influences the quality of the data.

Process Quality

Process quality deals with the functional aspect of a business process. Processes are meant to directly provide value to the user. This user can be external (typically a customer) and also internal (e.g., a staff). Process quality is primarily concerned with semantic issues rather than syntactical issues. Modeling of a process is a discipline in itself which makes use of the BPMN [10] suite of standards. All process modeling starts with the user (Actor) in mind—and the way in which the actor interacts with the user is documented in a Use case. ODBA, with its focus on outcomes, provides value in ensuring process quality. This is mainly because ODBA ensures that the processes are also aligned and optimized for the users (actors).

Analytics Quality

Analytics are highly popular in the Big Data space in particular because they enable businesses to discern patterns and trends within those data. Analytics quality is assured when the problem is modeled in detail and followed by a detailed model of the solution. The problem and solution models are influenced by models of the architecture that stay in the background. The models improve the quality of the solutions. The quality of the models themselves is also important [10]. The models are subjected to the quality assurance. These models play a crucial role in improving the quality—by improving the communication among project team members and among projects.

There are many popular analytics such as descriptive, predictive, and prescriptive analytics. The quality of these analytics is influenced by the quality of the algorithms on which they are modeled.

- Descriptive Analytics—is based on techniques, such as segmentation, classification, clustering, and association. The quality of these analytics dictates the quality of decisions taken by businesses. Businesses are keen to identify the patterns that exist within their data to improve their decision-making capabilities.
- Predictive analytics—as the name suggests, attempts to predict trends based on the data. Empirical methods together with Machine Learning (ML) algorithms are used in predicting trends. These predictions are only as good as the quality of data that is used for analytics.
- Prescriptive analytics goes beyond simply predictions and, instead, also recommends a course of action. Thus, these prescriptive analytics are far more advanced in their analytical capabilities as they make use of optimization and simulation techniques. The prescriptions enable decision makers to make their decisions with minimum tacit input as the analytics offer detailed insights and recommendations on the most optimum decisions.

Decision Quality

Data, processes, and analytics eventually feed into the quality of decisions at all levels within an organization. Decisions relate to BI—which brings together information from many different systems and applications in order to enhance decision-making. ODBA provides for quality in decision-making. For example, it facilitates a common language for communication. ODBA also enables discipline in handling data, modeling processes, and coding the algorithms that produce insights.

ODBA's alignment translates into projects that build capabilities—including capabilities to make better and more effective decisions. Enhancing decision-making is an ongoing process that requires excellence in modeling, design, algorithms, and, above all, data. With the advent of Big Data, the availability of data has exploded and so have the technologies that make use of such data.

Managing the Quality Environment

Figure 7.8 shows the high-level impact of quality on the overall business. This impact is seen in enhanced decision-making and, therefore, better business outcomes. The operational processes of an organization are also optimized and, therefore, perform more efficiently due to the quality of operational parameters. Various types of architectures (within ODBA), projects, and people are impacted by quality as summarized in Figure 7.8.

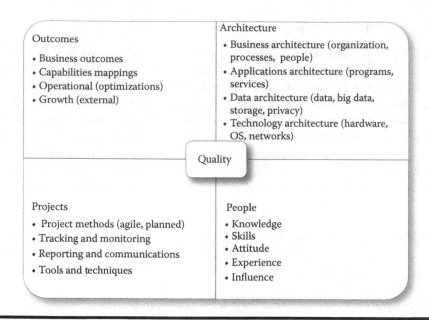

Figure 7.8 High level impacts of quality on business (organization).

Managing this overall quality environment of the organization is "Management Quality." This quality includes organization of resources, forming of teams with appropriate roles, setting objectives for the project and its ensuing priorities, managing risks, and multi-channeled communication. These are standard project management tasks that become important in building business capabilities. Quality has a direct bearing on the success or failure of these tasks and, as a result, on the project.

An improvement in the management quality leads to an overall improvement of the way in which risks are managed, governance is implemented, and compliance is ensured. Furthermore, the objectives for initiative are clearly scoped and people are motivated. There are additional important tasks in managing the quality environment—and that includes managing the quality assurance personnel, organizing the quality meetings, procuring the quality control tools, and managing the risks associated with quality.

The quality environment is responsible for information, analytics, and decision quality. Furthermore, it is also responsible for itself—that is, organizing the quality management functions itself is subject to the quality criteria setup in the quality environment [11].

Specifically, in terms of a process, the quality environment deals with the tools and techniques of the process itself. It deals with process transition issues, training issues, pilot project selection, process deployment with a case tool, and quality control organization.

ODBA and Quality Improvement

Data forms the basis for process, analytics, and decisions in an organization. Therefore, in discussing the quality of organizational decision-making, data deserves a special place. ODBA rests on the quality of data—followed by information, processes, analytics, and eventually decisions. The challenge with quality, as alluded to earlier in this chapter, is it is based on a combination of facts and perceptions. For example, the consistent and concise representation of data elements in a schema is a factual quality dimension, but the reputation and relevancy of data and information changes the context of quality. Similarly, non-functional (also known as operational) parameters of a solution dictate the perception of quality. A slow responding web page (even if factually correct) results in a perception of poor quality from the end user's viewpoint.

Architecture and Quality

An architecture helps reduce risks. A quality environment also helps reduce risks. For example, architecture provides a strong foundation for development and deployment of business processes. Since business processes are the key mechanism for interaction between an end user and the organization, improvement in business processes enhances the perception of quality and reduces risks.

The ODBA is thus a repository for organizational capabilities and their alignment with the outcomes. With such an ODBA, the business processes are optimized—resulting in value to the end users, business process-centered orientation, and lately, into a business capability-centered view, becoming even more resilient to business changes and transformations.

ODBA brings together business processes, business capabilities, and desired outcomes in the most efficient and effective way. These entities within ODBA form multiple layers—typically represented by Unified Modelling Language (UML) standardized notations (e.g., activity diagrams for business process model and class diagram for showing the entities and their relationship) [12].

Quality and Context

ODBA influences quality because it impacts the development of solutions over their entire life cycle. Starting with elicitation of requirements, through to designing, coding, and testing, ODBA influences all stages of solutions development. This influence, of course, starts with specific focus on data quality. With ODBA, the overall quality environment has data as its starting point.

Data quality has been driven by the Pareto Principle [13] which can be understood as "80-20" principle in the sense that 20% of data is used 80% of the time and vice versa. This principle is helpful in establishing the relevance and context of data. Quality of data requires an understanding of the context in which it operates. A set of data items describing a patient can be totally different from each other depending on the context—whether it's the medical data or the billing data. This understanding of data context is the basis for quality of large datasets. A data analyst together with a process modeler can figure out the purpose and flow of a business process that results in an improved understanding of data context.

Furthermore, the way the data elements connect with each other also changes their context. The same 'Name' element for a Patient can be related to her medical history, and that same 'Name' element deals with her billing history. Electronic Medical Record (EMR) initiatives strive to eliminate redundancies between multiple occurrences of the same data element. The challenge with data elements is that many a times the meaning of the data depends on where it is used which is not always an easy task. For example, if a patient process is flagged as "completed" it can mean multiple things—completed from a medical point of view but the bills are yet to be paid.

When a data is annotated with the likely context, that annotation is called metadata—as it describes more things around the data. Thus, a metadata (e.g., a tag or a stereotype) provides contextual information about the data. As a result, it is possible to improve the mechanism to filter data and enhance its quality. The standardization of data also enhances the ability to share the data across multiple systems. This is particularly important when it comes to quality of Big Data—as that is where metadata provides a much better understanding of especially unstructured data (e.g., an audio file or an image) resulting in improved filtering and sharing of data.

Architectural Quality Practices

ODBA provides a set of practices that are applied to data, in particular, to enhance its quality. Following are some of these practices:

- Provides Governance framework around incoming data, its storage, its usage, and its decommissioning.
- Incorporates industry-wide accepted policies and standards and applying them with the use of tools and techniques within the organization to handle data.
- Defines data which is tremendously helpful in describing data in a consistent manner thereby improving communications and sharing.
- Contextualizes data by annotating data with metadata and thereby providing pertinent meaning to that data.
- Provides data standardization and validation techniques to ensure new data is appropriately labeled, tagged, and cleansed before storing.
- Supports metrics and measurements related to quality of data.
- Understands the full data supply chain that ensures the source of data is known—and thereby eliminate anomalies in new data by anticipating areas of error.

Syntax, Semantics, Aesthetics of ODBA Quality

ODBA enhances overall quality environment within the organization. However, ODBA also benefits with quality techniques. "Verification and Validation" describe the way in which the quality of solutions (outputs of project initiatives) is enhanced. Verification and validation are essentially quality techniques preventing as well as detecting errors, inconsistencies, and incompleteness in project outputs (Figure 7.9).

Verification is concerned with the syntactical correctness of a model or architecture whereas validation deals with its meanings and value. Verification focuses on ascertaining the architecture is correct whereas validation ensures it meets the needs of the business. Validation of architecture deals with tracing the solutions to the requirements.

Verifying and validating a solution has three levels of checks: syntax, semantics, and aesthetic checks. Syntactical correctness, semantic meaning, aesthetical beauty, and eventually business value cover the various aspects of quality as data gets analyzed. The words syntax, semantics, and aesthetics reflect the techniques or means of accomplishing the validation and verification of the models. Following is a brief description of the syntax, semantics, and aesthetic checks.

- All quality models should be syntactically correct, thereby adhering to the rules of the modeling constructs they are meant to follow. Numerous programming and modeling tools ensure the quality of syntax. For example, visual tool scans validate the rules of the association relationship between datasets and ensure correct interface formats. Variations to the analytical models and complying with the meta-model become a project-specific part of the

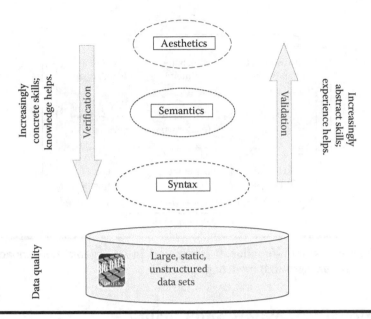

Figure 7.9 The verification and validation of architectural models for their syntax, semantics, and aesthetics quality.

syntax checks. Conforming to syntactical correctness is a great aid enhancing the overall quality of a solution and reducing the pressure on testing.

■ All quality models represent their intended semantic meanings consistently. The semantics aspect of model quality ensures the diagrams produced represent the underlying of the domain. For example, semantic quality ensures that the business objectives as stated by the users are correctly reflected in the process models, business rules, constraints, and pre- and post-conditions documented in the corresponding use case documentation. In this context, the traditional and well-known quality techniques of walkthroughs and inspections (Unhelkar [14]) are highly valuable and are used more frequently and more rigorously than for syntax checking.

■ Quality in architecture and models also needs aesthetics—which exhibit the creativity and long-sightedness of their modelers. This means that models are symmetric, complete, and *pleasing* in what they represent. Very simply, aesthetics imply style. Often, while reading a piece of code, one is able to point out the 'style' or programming and hence trace it to a programmer or a programming team. Although the code (or for that matter any other deliverable) is accurate (syntactically) and meaningful (semantically), difference arises due to their styles. This style of modeling has a bearing on the readability and comprehensibility of the models. Example of a factor that affects styles is that of 'granularity' of designs. In good object-oriented designs, the level of granularity is considered, as it strongly affects understandability. This aesthetic "size consideration" is studied under the granularity of the UML-models [15]. This also requires a good metrics program within an organization that enables improvement of aesthetics of the entire quality environment and the resultant outputs. Aesthetic considerations offer a high level of satisfaction to the organisation that goes beyond the basic needs of the solution.

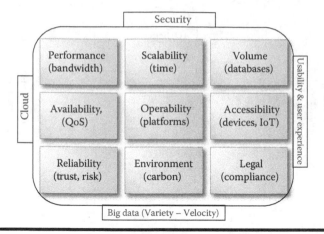

Figure 7.10 Operational (non-functional) parameters in an organization impacting quality—[part of architecture (background) modeling space].

Non-Functional Parameters and Quality

In addition to the functionality and behavior of a suite of solutions used by an organization, there is also a need to consider the non-functional aspect of the solutions. The alignment of solutions to outcomes (as professed by ODBA) is a major step in the direction of handling the operational parameters of a solution. Figure 7.10 depicts these non-functional (operational) parameters of a system (or, a collaborative suite of solutions comprising multiple systems). It is vital for any architectural initiative to keep these parameters in mind right from the beginning of an initiative. For example, performance and security have a major effect on the way an entire organization is perceived by its users. Unhelkar has discussed these parameters in detail as part of Model of Architectural (background) Space (MOAS) [14]. These parameters are discussed in greater detail next:

- Performance (Bandwidth)—is usually specified in terms of the speed of response expected from a system. The performance requirement for an Internet-based deployment depends on the available bandwidth. Factors such as available processing power, amount of data to be processed, etc. also impact performance.
- Scalability (Time)—this is the expected growth and use of the system over time. Scalability includes system parameters, such as data storage and performance related to the system as the number of users grow. Scalability requirements are dependent on the time factor (growth and demand over next day, month, or year).
- Volume (Databases)—this is the size of the database expected when the system is in operation is an example of this requirement. Data space for current usage as well as backup and mirroring of operational databases is part of this requirement.
- Availability (typically known as QoS—Quality of Service)—examples of these requirements include permissible downtime for maintenance, number of times a system is allowed to be offline, and expected quality of service for different types of system failures.
- Operability (Platforms)—almost all systems in operation today require a back-end-operating system and a front-end browser technology. This requirement specifies the type of operating platform and the browsers used for the system. Due to dynamically changing devices

and locations (in the case of mobile interfaces) the specifications of browsers become very important. The entire range of browsers and operating systems and their versions is vital in specifying this Non Functional Requirements (NFR).

- Accessibility (Devices, IoT)—these non-functional requirements deal with the ease of access for user devices. This ease of access needs to consider users that may have special needs (e.g., if users are asked to enter Captcha characters to authenticate they are not robots, then those characters should also be available in an audio format to ensure some users are not disadvantaged). Accessibility is not limited to the needs of the users; it is also a mandated, regulator requirement.

- Reliability (Trust, Risk)—this non-functional requirement is based on the criticality of the system. For example, an aircraft navigation system can have a reliability specification that is closer to Twelve-Sigma (as against Six Sigma)—implying a one in billion, rather than a one in million defect.

- Environment (Carbon)—the increasing importance of environmental consciousness in business implies a requirement to specify its carbon content. While some business systems may not directly contribute to carbon emissions, the effect on the back-end data servers increasingly comes into calculations for overall carbon emissions of the organization [15]. Alternatively, Carbon Emission Management Systems (CEMS) have a more detailed specification for its carbon capacity that is specified as non-functional as well as functional requirements.

- Legal (Compliance)—financial systems invariably have requirements for tracking and auditing. While some of these requirements are functional in nature (e.g., logging the details of the auditor), others that deal with creating an audit trail and backups may not directly be functional. Instead, the legal requirements are specified as non-functional and require careful walkthroughs and inspections for their verification in the system.

Each of the above NFR is impacted by four additional non-functional (operational) factors. These four factors, also shown in Figure 7.10, are as follows:

- Security (Levels)—this requirement varies widely going from a specific function or use case in a system through to the organizational policies in terms of access to its web portals. Examples of security requirements include encryption (e.g., 128 bit), password policies, and browser requirements.

- Usability and User Experience—this requirement applies to all other requirements shown in the center of Figure 7.10. While usability itself deals with the ease of use of a typical user interface of the system, user experience deals with the overall "take away" of the user when interacting with the organization through the system. Thus, all non-functional parameters within the middle of Figure 7.10 influences and are influenced by user experience.

- Big Data (Velocity and Variety)—this is shown as a higher-level requirement in Figure 7.10 that influences and is influenced by all other requirements in the center of that figure. While Big Data-related requirements are newer (as compared with the early procedural and also object-oriented approaches to software engineering), it is important to factor these requirements within the overall NFRs of any new system. This is particularly true with the velocity of data coming into the system—such as when an IoT device (a fitness wrist watch, a blood pressure-monitoring device, or a carbon emission recording device) collects and sends data to the system. Furthermore, Big Data also adds to the challenge of non-functional parameters due to the variety of data—audio, video, and graphics, for example.

- Cloud—Cloud computing has brought a vital parameter in the discussion on non-functional requirements, because most new software systems (including and especially mobile applications) store their data on a Cloud. Even corporate systems which had in-house databases are moving those databases in a private cloud. For example, the capacity, availability, scalability, and reliability parameters are influenced by the Cloud computing architecture. With the back-end data on the Cloud and the processing (analytics) also shifting to the Cloud, the availability of the system and its reliability depends on that of the Cloud—and the intermediate network that carries the connectivity to the Cloud.

Discussion Points

1. What is GRC and why is it necessary in an organization?
2. Why is Quality so closely associated with GRC? Discuss with an example.
3. What is the role of ODBA in enhancing the Quality environment in an organization? How does ODBA relate to GRC?
4. Name five business risks and the potential impact to an organization.
5. What is the importance of GRC in mitigating organizational risks? Also discuss the importance of balance in risks with examples? *(Hint: total risk mitigation or taking no risks is a bad business strategy)*
6. Summarize the advantages and disadvantages of implementing GRC in terms of the quality environment of the organization
7. Why is Quality considered subjective? What are the challenges resulting from this subjective nature of quality?
8. What do you understand by data, process, analytics, and decision quality? How are these qualities related to each other?
9. What is the difference between verification and validation of an artifact?
10. What are the three types of checks that can be applied to any model including ODBA? Why are all three important (as against any one or two of them)? Discuss with examples.
11. List three distinct operational (non-functional) parameters affecting a solution. Provide examples in your answer.
12. What is the importance of security in the age of Cloud and Big Data? Why should one be concerned with security in discussion on ODBA?

References

1. Tiwary, A. and Unhelkar, B. (2011). Extending and Applying Business Intelligence and Customer Strategies for Green ICT, p. 83, B. Unhelkar (ed.), in *Handbook of Research in Green ICT: Technical, Business and Social Perspectives*, IGI Global, Hershey, PA.
2. Tiwary, A. and Unhelkar, B. (2015). Enhancing the Governance, Risks and Control (GRC) Framework with Business Capabilities to Enable Strategic Technology Investments, *SDPSnet Conference* (1–5 Nov, 2015. Dallas, TX). 2015 Society for Design and Process Science (www.sdpsnet.org).
3. Unhelkar, B. (2017). *Big Data Strategies for Agile Business,* CRC Press, Boca Raton, FL.
4. Unhelkar, B. and Tiwary, A. (2010). Collaborative Intelligence, *Cutter IT Journal,* 23(6) pp. 13–21.
5. Kleppmann, M. 2014. *Designing Data-Intensive Applications, Early Release,* O'Reilly, Sebastopol, CA.
6. Balasubramanian, P., Kulatilaka, N., and Storck, J. (1998). *Managing Information Technology Investments Using a Real-Options Approach,* School of Management, Boston University.
7. White, A. and Logan, D. (2015). *Governing the Information Governance,* Gartner Inc. Stamford, CT.

8. Buytendijk, F. and Oestreich, T.W. (2015). *Organizing for Big Data through Process and Governance*, Gartner Publications.

9. Perry W.E. (1991). *Quality Assurance for Information Systems: Methods, Tools and Techniques*, Wiley-QED.

10. Unhelkar, B. (2005). *Verification and Validation for Quality of UML Models*, John Wiley and Sons, (Wiley Interscience).

11. Evans, P. and Wolf, B. (2005). Collaboration Rules, *Harvard Business Review*, July–Aug 2005.

12. Unhelkar, B. (2003). *Process Quality Assurance for UML-Based Projects*, Pearson Education (Addison-Wesley), Boston. ISBN 9 780201-758214.

13. Unhelkar, B. and Henderson-Sellers, B. (1994). ODBMS Considerations in the Granularity of a Reusable OO Design, *Proceedings of TOOLS 15 Technology of Object Oriented Languages and Systems, Fifteenth International Conference*, Christine Mingins and Bertrand Meyer (Eds.), Melbourne, November 1994, Prentice-Hall, pp. 229–234.

14. Unhelkar, B. (2018). *Software Engineering with UML*, CRC Press, Boca Raton, FL.

15. Unhelkar, B. (2011). *Green ICT Strategies & Applications: Using Environmental Intelligence*, CRC Press Boca Raton, FL.

PRACTICE AND TOOLS   B

Chapter 8

Establishing and Managing the Business Architecture Practice

KEY POINTS

- Developing Business Architecture (BA) as a professional practice within the organization
- Creating a Center of Excellence for BA practice within the organization
- Establishing an external BA practice that provides Consulting, Coaching, and Training in the BA space
- Collaborating among various business functions as part of the BA practice
- Identifying and promoting the Returns on Investment (ROI) of a BA practice

This chapter describes establishing and managing Business Architecture (BA) as a professional practice. Such a practice is externally a consulting service or, internally a center of excellence. The purpose of a BA practice is to capture, store, and disseminate knowledge across the organization. The discussions in this chapter are relevant more to organizations that have already initiated outcome-driven business architecture (ODBA).

Sharing Outcome-Driven Business Architecture Knowledge

Outcome-driven business architecture (ODBA) is a long-term activity that is continuously enhanced with time. The resultant knowledge is captured, stored, and made available for subsequent activities in the organization. This is the basic need for creating a practice. An ODBA practice is setup internally (as a Center of Excellence) or externally (as a consulting practice). The sponsorship from senior executives that initiates and enables business architecture (BA) alignment (discussed in Chapters 4 and 5) is also the basis for establishing BA as a discipline.

Once established as a disciplined function, BA is ideally treated as a practice unto itself. Establishing and running the architectural practice includes responsibilities for the ODBA as well as the more technical enterprise architecture (EA). BA is closely associated with EA and both are part of the architectural practice. The architectural practice is made up of various functions and each of these functions has a key responsibility of collecting, storing, and sharing information and knowledge related to architectures within the organization. The functions of an architectural practice are summarized in Table 8.1.

The BA has a strategic, business focus. An architecture supports IT functions and business processes including the corresponding technical or solution levels. As a result, business outcomes are better aligned with business capabilities in a strategic manner.

Table 8.2 further describes the architectural discipline in relation to stakeholder scope and impact on the organization. The scope of the BA practice is understood first as a part of developing

Table 8.1 Functions of the Architecture Practice

Architecture Discipline	Description and Relevance of Architectures to the Organization
EA	Definition of EA strategy and vision. Assessing the enterprise environment. Providing support for enterprise architectural principles and supporting framework. Governance of the EA framework, standards, guidelines, and practices. Supporting metrics and measurements related to EA
Domain Architecture	Responsible for managing knowledge and advice with a specialization, maintains and governs compliance with the EA framework. Assists with analysis of models and using a variety of techniques and tools, contributes to the maintenance of the EA framework.
Business Architecture	Framework to support the functioning of the organization. Focus is on capabilities that are organizational priorities. It is essential to identify areas of improvement or weakness and drive change through capability uplift. Achieved through: process, information, knowledge, and infrastructure management.
Solution Architecture	Deals with the architecture of a specific software solution—ensuring the new solution fits in with the existing systems ecosystem. Solution architecture is the fundamental organization of a system solution. System architecture defines key system elements and their relationships.

Table 8.2 Architecture Disciplines, Stakeholders, and Impact

Discipline	Stakeholder	Scope	Impact
EA	Business decision makers	Collaborative (across businesses)	Strategic
BA	Business decision makers	Across organisation	Strategic
Domain Architecture	Technical—Business decision makers	Across single business	Strategic—Operational
Solution Architecture	Technical decision makers	Limited to the solution	Tactical—Operational

BA practice. The organizational culture defines the key skills such as decision making collaborative approach, strategic thinking, effective stakeholder management, and resilience required for the BA.

BA is treated as a Business Capability Competency that aligns strategies to relevant IT systems, services, and platforms. Therefore, architectural competency centers store, manage, and share principles, patterns, and enterprise level policies and standards. The centers also provide technical input to the Business Capability Competency Groups. Establishing a competency center brings together concerned parties and ensures that business and IT are aligned and working in conjunction to achieve common objectives. The many layers of governance are also reduced as a result of a well-managed competency center.

Figure 8.1 shows how the business and technology capabilities are built and dispersed in an organization through the BA practice. The BA practice is an internal consultancy service. Initially, it is resourced with external consultants, but once the practice is established, the organization trains its own staff for continuing and maintaining the rigor and direction. The BA practice utilizes the ODBA concepts to make the organization more effective. The business architects focus on defining and analyzing business outcomes. The architects then plan the required changes in products and processes. The BA practice recommends and plans roadmaps for improving and implementing an organizational change.

Business architects advise the organization on possible scenarios. It is a strategic role requiring adequate responsibility and authority. The BA practice continuously analyzes products and

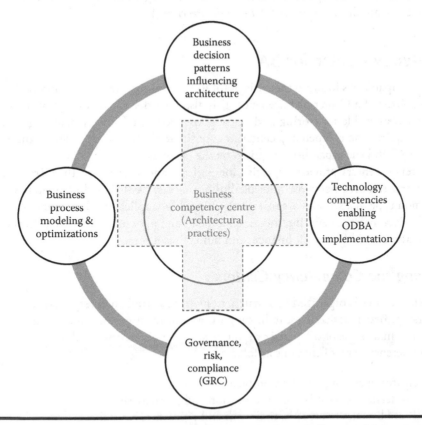

Figure 8.1 Business and technology capabilities are built and dispersed in an organization through the BA practice.

services. It uses framework and tools to provide guidance and roadmaps to align business outcomes with capabilities. The business outcome-based metrics provides measures of success.

Agility as Part of BA Practice

Traditionally, the BA practice followed a linear life cycle. The size and complexity of architecture implies risks. Even a small oversight can result in great losses. Undocumented mistakes or missed deadlines have repercussions beyond a single project. With advancing technology, there is a need to iterate solutions. This iterative and incremental approach to developing and deploying a BA practice is most successful by incorporating the principles and practices of Agile.

Agility is a characteristic that plays an important role not only at a project level but also at organizational level [1]. When it comes to BA practice, Agile is used as an underlying culture in small, goal-oriented collaborative teams. Therefore, the BA practice is not only an advisory and controlling role but also participates in the work. Agile helps the BA practice leaders respond quickly to a changing organizational environment. While there is an understandable need to get enterprise initiatives functioning in an Agile manner, it is equally important for BA practices to incorporate agility within their own activities. A phased and iterative life cycle is the core of Agile. But when agility is applied in practice, the need for a composite approach that combines the agility with necessary planning and formality is imperative. This balanced way of working for the BA practice uses CAMS—Composite Agile Method and Strategy. Further details of how CAMS can help architecture are discussed in *The Art of Agile Practice* [1].

Competency Center for BA

The business capabilities forming the basis of ODBA are served through the internal service. This service is considered a Center of Excellence. It is also considered a competency center within an organization responsible for storing and sharing knowledge, effectively enabling sharing of services. This requires the competency center to coordinate skills at various levels and ensure their availability to fulfill the capabilities required by the business.

Competency centers provide expertise for projects and programs. They are repositories of knowledge and resource pools for multiple business areas. Skills-based competency centers, the most common type in a services organization, are used for application development, software language skills, data management, internet development, and network design. Within the enterprise, services are also shared for travel, finance, and human resources.

Organizing the Competency Centers

A competency center is organized as a matrix to manage shared an enterprise-wide vision to provide leadership, best practices, research, support, and/or training for a focus area. The BA competency center makes use of the matrix to source and provide cross-discipline services and value.

The competency center functions as follows:

- Participates in solving the right problem
- Fully understands the effect of intervention and participation
- Identifies obstacles to organization work and overcomes resistance
- Finds the right support in the organization to mobilize the program
- Develops a long-term relationship with internal resources

Competency centers support projects. Projects, based on a business case are related to outcomes. A project team is a non-permanent structure. Usually, the team is disbanded when the project is handed over to an operations team. Introducing new functionality requires establishing a new project team and executing associated processes.

Project-Based Approach Compared to Competency Center

BA represents a program of work where the business needs, benefit realization, and supporting tools and processes are constantly moving. Figure 8.2 depicts the best-practice approach competency centers use to manage this type of problem. The needs of the organization are quickly met without significant waste searching for expertise, understanding the problem, executing project initiation phases, and ramping up project efforts. Without this approach, benefits from the initial investment in a solution quickly diminish and fragmentation starts to impact the organization's efficiency.

As depicted in Figure 8.3, competency centers increase innovation and improves delivery speed. The organizational structure provides the environment for innovation and future proofing the solutions. The competency centers are resourced with budgets and skills for the enterprise level BA practice. The overall organizational IT investment governance includes roles and responsibilities. This ensures the organizational IT and other investments are aligned with the organizational strategies. The investment management framework includes business capabilities priorities as a major factor in investment decisions.

Competency centers accelerate the use of new technologies and optimize core capabilities with higher efficiency and lower costs. Technical professionals within competency centers embrace non-technical skills and cross-discipline collaboration in addition to core technical expertise to operate at peak efficiency and deliver optimal value to the enterprise. The competency center facilitates the development of enterprise-wide standards and architectural principles across the organization. The enterprise-wide standards provide uniform templates for assessing business cases and ensuring stakeholders are represented in decision-making.

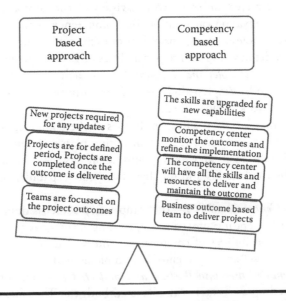

Figure 8.2 Traditional project-based approach compared to BA competency center.

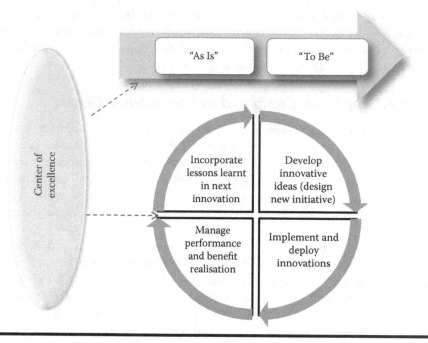

Figure 8.3 Competency center manages projects and innovation as continuous cycle.

The BA competency center assists in rationalizing tool selection across the organization and disseminating knowledge and best practices. The overall governance of the organization investments requires the competency center to identify competing requirements and resolve conflicting conclusions.

The competency center or center for innovation creation needs to be treated as a project in itself. The project outcome is to build business capabilities for innovation.

The competency center creation starts with a vision of the competency center. The vision articulates the required innovation capabilities. The competency center organizational structure defines the team structure, roles and responsibilities of each team member, and its operating processes. Table 8.3 defines the key roles and responsibilities of BA competency center.

Identify Competency Center Roles and Responsibilities—Each competency center has roles and responsibilities that need to be developed. These roles are summarized in Table 8.3. This ensures the skills required for BA work are identified.

Develop Communications Strategy—Responsibilities of the competency center are distributed and duplicated across the organization. A communication plan is developed and executed which identifies the impacted individuals and work groups, identifies the critical success factors for the competency center, sells the benefits and highlights the new capability to the organization and external stakeholders.

Embed Competency Center Capability—The competency center is designed to embed process, work practices, standard operating procedures, operating level agreements, and reporting lines within the roles and responsibilities of competency centers. The standard operating procedures reflecting changes in processes are documented and implemented.

Transition Competency Center into Business as Usual (BAU)—The competency center, once established, is considered a cost center with allocated budgets. The roles and responsibilities of the competency centers are defined and communicated within the organization. The competency

Table 8.3   Competency Center Team Roles and Responsibilities

CC subject matter expert	Business architects, IT architects, and enterprise architects who are business outcome focused, understand business capability and IT and are able to be a bridge between business and IT departments.
Business expert	Knowledge about business and business value. Experts from each business units or major business units for the priorities business capabilities.
Tool expert	Knowledge and skills in using various architectural tools. Develop reports and dashboards for communicating and reporting to executives.
IT expert	Knowledge and skill in current IT environment. Expert in developing tools and frameworks required for BA practice.
Architect	Knowledge of future direction and reference architectures. Solution designers and architects for IT initiatives
Center lead	Knowledge of outcome delivery. Allocate resources, manage stakeholders, measure and report progress.

center is also responsible for the activities that were done within the organization by various units. The competency center is responsible for the development and implementation of a business capability development. The organization is reorganized, and resources such as professionals and budgets are realigned with the competency center's operating resources and budgets.

Metrics and Value in Managing a BA Practice

Figure 8.4 demonstrates the value derived from the center of excellence and provides clear direction to the organization in building the business capabilities. The clear direction and better investment

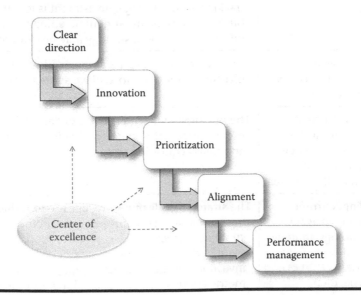

Figure 8.4   The value of clarity derived from the center of excellence for a BA Practice.

plan provides the environment for innovation. The business competency center provides continuous improvement plans and prioritizes the initiatives that are aligned with the business outcomes.

The outcomes expected from the BA practice are defined upfront. The measures of success are clearly articulated. The BA practice is responsible for the executive level reporting. The strategy reports from the BA practice include key metrics shown in Table 8.4.

Strategic Imperative

The competency center provides business capabilities as a service across different divisions and business units. Competency centers also provide input in re-engineering the organization. This re-engineering results in changes to the structure and operations of the organization.

Organizational Structures and BA Practice

The mechanistic–organic typologies of organizational structures are an important consideration in the restructuring of organization. Two contingency theorists, Burns and Stalker [2], proposed these structures which underlie restructuring attempts even now.

Table 8.4 Key Metrics and Value Measurement for BA Practice

Key Metrics	Outcomes Expected
Emerging issues and key events	The enterprise-wide issues and key events are linked to the business capabilities. This assists in prioritization of the initiative as well as refining the business capability priorities.
Current investment priorities	Provides a governance mechanism to invest in areas aligned with the key capabilities. It is expected there is some investment required for the business as usual activities. This metric identifies how investment is tracking. If the strategic investment is less than the business as usual investment (keeping the lights on), a different investment strategy may be required.
Estimated current year investment towards business technology strategy	This assists in refining the strategic directions and investment required to achieve strategic goals.
Initiative progress (current year/entire strategy) against business technology strategy (filter by capability, architectural debt, theme, etc.)	The outcome of this metric tracks demand and supply of the resources. This metric assists in developing resources and skills acquisition strategies
Initiative funding (current year/entire strategy) against business technology strategy (filter by capability, architectural debt, investment type, etc.)	The strategic goals of BA practice are to reduce the investment in tactical projects and increase investment in strategic projects. In case of foundational deficits identified by capabilities assessment, additional investment in some initiatives may be required. This metric assists with fund allocation based on ongoing progress of the initiatives.

Mechanistic

Consider an organization which performs specialized manufacturing tasks, where job design is simplified, and the organization is traditionally authoritarian, has fixed procedures and policies and values, and respects the hierarchy and authority. Such an organization is suited to efficient production in a stable external environment, using relatively unskilled labor.

This organization has systems, an architecture and culture which are consistent with each other and suited to the environment within which the organization operates. This is, in effect, a mechanistic organizational type. For example, electricity utilities traditionally have relatively stable technologies and operated in fairly stable environments. As a manager in these organizations, many management practices are more mechanistic in nature.

In such a mechanistic organization, it may not be realistic to enrich jobs by introducing empowered, creative, self-managed teams at the frontline. Such people management methods would not 'fit' with the existing culture, architecture, environment and systems. Rather, time sheets, performance measurement systems, formal grievance systems, and policies and procedures typify people management in a mechanistic organization. Architecture and systems are very central to organizational performance.

Organic

Conversely, professional organizations such as lawyers' offices, medical teams, and research units are notoriously difficult to control with methods such as rules, hierarchical power, performance reviews, and job design. Rather, they are controlled by such factors as shared professional values, peer review, and strong personal motivation and capabilities. Rigid systems rarely get in the way of interpersonal interaction and processes; rather, they loosely define the boundaries of the group. Culture is central to organizational performance.

Tools for Business Strategies

There are multiple strategic tools and concepts utilized by the business world in assessing and developing strategic intents, vision, and goals. These tool sets offer analysis methods to assess and identify organization focus.

- Porter's 5-Forces analysis [3]
- Industrial segmentation*
- Sustainability analysis
- Resource and capability analysis
- Value chain and relative cost analysis
- Portfolio analysis
- Financial analysis

Each analysis type has its own set of assessment methods, focus, assessment criteria, and expected benefits and advantages for the organizations. However, each also comes with some potential shortcomings.

---

* https://en.wikipedia.org/wiki/Industrial_market_segmentation.

Effective strategy formulation in complex and ever-changing business settings combines the insights inherent in the specific concepts and techniques with the intelligence that comes with human enterprise. In this latter respect, strategy formulation can never be off-the-shelf.

The assessment could follow any of the traditional tools, but if the strategy is anchored with the business capabilities development, it becomes easier to assess and change course of action when the strategy changes. Hamel and Prahalad [4] suggest that enduring success flows to those companies whose senior managers maintain and adhere to a clear and workable strategic intent, all the while allowing the strategic specifics, as well as implementation issues, to be worked out lower down in the organization. The BA provides an anchor to clarify intent and a governance process as discussed in Chapter 7.

BA as a practice helps organizations dynamically manage their strategic intents. BA is incorporated within the organization by utilizing existing frameworks. BA frameworks in an organization support long-term strategies, priorities, and business goals. BA provides relevant standards and operational performance against agreed business capabilities.

The outcome of BA practice is an Architectural Investment Roadmap that addresses the following:

- Ongoing and increasing requirements for security, accessibility, and agility to be embedded in all IT systems enabling the organization to transform and change quickly to meet a more dynamic environment;
- Requirements to make better decisions through the ability to analyze information across all information systems quickly and accurately;
- Ability to securely and quickly access timely, accurate and relevant information in the field;
- Ability to optimize processes that draws on information from a wide range of IT systems.

Organizational Centers for Knowledge Sharing

Structural transformation is needed to integrate the customer into the business value chain. The structure has capabilities of being seamless and transparent in business and domain expertise. The following changes are considered to achieve the expected business outcomes:

- **Creating a Centers of Excellence (COE)**—Using the three horizons theory,* these centers are designed to extend and defend core business (Baghai et al. [5]). This means migrating from siloes of multiple teams providing different package maintenance, interfacing software, and infrastructure services. The COE builds a view of the customers, products, and services offered around the complete solution. Business solution architects, business analysts, domain experts, and structures are aligned to include key skills required to service customers' maintenance effectively.
- **Creating a Centre of Alliances (COA)**—Current structures may not have any identified group with the relationship built within the organization. This center of alliance develops horizon two* capabilities by improving proactive skills in future technologies and improvements in the packages (Baghai et al. [5]).

---

* http://www.mckinsey.com/business-functions/strategy-and-corporate-finance/our-insights/enduring-ideas-the-three-horizons-of-growth.

■ **Centre of Innovations Excellence (CIE)**—In many cases, solutions fall in "building yesterday's system tomorrow" but need to innovate into horizon three* by "building tomorrow systems today." The structure of the organization is more organic and the measurement is based on the total value of innovations. The input to innovation comes from the other parts of the organization such as the CEO (Baghai et al. [5]).

Figure 8.5 lists the key roles required in building a business competency center. The roles defined for the competency center are a mix of the subject matter experts, business architect, tool makers for the BA practice such as maintaining the business architecture frameworks, business competency assessments, and business investment portfolio reporting.

Table 8.5 depicts the organizational risks in developing the competency center and a migration strategy. The development of a competency center addresses the risks of culture and style, skills, organizational structure and strategy.

A mechanistic organization structure is hierarchical and roles and responsibilities are defined based on the position within hierarchy. An Organic structure is flat with the roles and responsibilities based on tasks. The business capabilities and business architecture development are defined based on organizational culture.

Table 8.6 discusses the overall cultural impact in implementing BA as a practice.

The Process to Establish the BA Practice in an Organization

The investment in BA practice requires a planned approach with the outcome-driven approach. Figure 8.6 defines a process in setting up the BA practice.

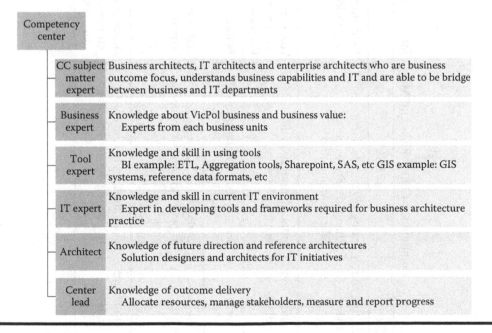

Figure 8.5 Competency center roles.

Table 8.5 Competency-Center Risks and Mitigation Strategies

Category	Risk	Symptoms	Mitigation Strategy
Culture and style	Losing key people due to changed culture and miscommunication	High attrition rate compared to previous years	Identify key resources Effective communication plan Have one-on-one sessions with these key resources to reassure them
Culture and skills	Reduced innovation due to lack of capabilities	Low morale of the staff due to communication gaps. Cynicism on new initiative	Communicate revised business strategy and ensure an effective rewards structure is in place
Structure	Size and scope of transition of the structure	Failure in transition	Transition in small chunks with efficient change management strategies
Style	Existing talent leaving organization due to change in environment	Staff leaving due to change in culture	Communicate revised business strategy Ensure that new career contracts are specific and understood by all employees. Matching rewards with responsibilities
Culture and strategy	Taking the eyes off the crystal ball during the transitioning	Disruption and doubt by current staff, business as usual activities	Allocating required resources to business as usual activities. Key resources have a transition plan for their positions

Table 8.6 Cultural Impact in Implementing BA as a Practice

Practice Dimension	Mechanistic Organization Culture	Organic Organization Culture
Over all culture impact	Creativity and effort focus on internal problems only—systems and procedures Heavy administrative overhead—internal procedures consume more resources than external customer-focused operations Slow in responding to external change—lose touch with customers and external stakeholders Parochialism, defend-my-patch behaviors occur. Organizational members can develop unhelpful, bounded mindsets—perceptions of external and internal Job and departmental boundaries can lead to the rational-legal organization becoming bogged down in a spaghetti of tortuous processes and "need-to-consult" everyone and anyone	Suitable for unstable, turbulent, and changing conditions The organism firm re-shaped itself to address new problems and tackle unforeseen contingencies Rather than a rigid, highly specialized structure—a fluid organizational design which facilitates flexibility, adaptation, job redefinition Departments, sections, and teams are formed and reformed. Communication is lateral as well as vertical—with emphasis on a network rather than a hierarchy Organizational members are personally and actively committed beyond what is basically operationally or functionally necessary
Role definition defines how job descriptions of the enterprise architect are defined	Roles are defined as specialized for roles and responsibilities EA roles are fully defined with responsibilities articulated Requires senior management sponsorship EA group reports in CEO or CIO to be effective in governance	Roles are broad and loosely defined EA roles depend upon the sponsorship It is important to get the right person rather than the right definition of the role
Understanding of task	Only senior management have understanding of organizational vision Job definition and organizational structure is very important in EA program Governance is sponsored by senior management	Lower level employees have an understanding of whole system The governance is communicated to the teams and team members Document management is a must in changing environment

(Continued)

Table 8.6 (*Continued*)   Cultural Impact in Implementing BA as a Practice

Practice Dimension	Mechanistic Organization Culture	Organic Organization Culture
Commitments of the employees to the organization and the roles and responsibilities	Thought of as functionaries and are not asked to be committed beyond an exact performance of their allotted duties EA roles cross organization horizontally, requiring necessary authorities to change the organizational processes	Employees are expected to be committed to the successful completion of the whole task Need to define and agree on the framework to use (change may import different frameworks)
Communication and knowledge and information	Vertical Knowledge and information about the enterprise, its tasks, and the jobs within it are concentrated in the upper levels of hierarchy EA objectives are documented and accessible to all	Horizontal Knowledge and information is distributed around the organizations Communication methods are defined and agreed upon. Regular meetings with stakeholders and participants re-enforce EA objective
Interaction and relationship between teams	Relationship between superordinate and subordinate is one of command and control EA governance is defined EA objectives are communicated to all the teams	More consultative approach Communication and stakeholder awareness is important Regular formal/informal meeting with business and IT stakeholders

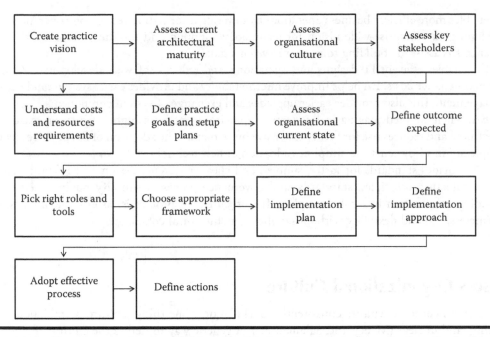

Figure 8.6 The process for establishing the BA Practice in an Organization (including for ODBA).

Create Practice Vision

Organizational strategies enable better use of technology, improved matching of resources to demand, improved capability through workforce reform and enhanced collaboration across partners. This requires user support of the information, better communication and information-sharing across the organization and with partners. The increasing interconnectedness of information internally and with external partners brings many benefits and also creates more vulnerability because of different levels of sensitivity attached to data.

The Enterprise Architecture (EA) strategy sets up a high-level plan including establishing a framework. This framework develops and delivers business-driven initiatives and implements efficient and cost-effective solutions. The EA strategy states principles and actions required to ensure that the organization provides timely and accurate information to the frontline staff. The EA creates a mechanism to incrementally develop solutions that refresh the technology solutions. The recommendations are to adopt "**Business driven, outcome focused.**"

A business-driven, outcome-focused EA has these key attributes:

■ Clearly defined business outcomes and ensures that BA is positioned to achieve those outcomes.
■ Risk-adjusted values are part of the criteria for designing BA governance.
■ Matches EA governance, decision-making and assurance to organizational culture.
■ Integrates EA governance with other processes, such as project portfolio management, application portfolio management, and investment decision processes to maximize business outcomes for the organization.

EA enables more efficient business operations by lowering information technology operation costs, developing an enterprise-wide vision for technology adoption and building adoptable and agile systems. EA assist in "building tomorrow's systems today."

EA enables efficient IT designs and operations, and reduces software development, support, and maintenance costs. EA helps improve interpretability and provides easier systems and network management. This also provides easier upgrades and exchange of system components.

EA, when adopted pragmatically creates an environment for a higher return on existing IT investment and reduces risk for future expensive investments. The adoption of EA practices reduces complexity in IT systems and simplifies adoption of new technology.

EA provides standards for faster, simpler, and cheaper systems design and IT procurement. The architecture principles, standards, and governance processes simplify buying decisions by providing information in a coherent plan. The procurement process is faster—maximizing procurement speed and flexibility without sacrificing architectural coherence.

Assess Organizational Culture

Research on corporate culture consistently concludes only one thing: culture is ambiguous, fluctuating, and unclear (Mabey and Salaman [6]). A generic way to define the culture of any organization is 'the way we do things around here.' A formal definition of culture is the social glue that binds organizational members together, and the one that members share or have consensus about. This includes beliefs, values, routines, behaviors, patterns of meaning, expectations, understanding, and assumptions. These shared beliefs are invented, discovered, or developed through organizational activities and are considered valid because of their ability to frame organizational decisions and maximize organizational performance.

Consider an organization which performs specialized manufacturing tasks, where job design is simplified, and the organization is traditionally authoritarian, has fixed procedures and policies, and values and respects the hierarchy and authority. Such an organization is suited to efficient production in a stable external environment, using relatively unskilled labor.

Such an organization has systems, an architecture, and culture which are all consistent with each other and suited to the environment within which the organization operates. This is, in effect, a mechanistic organizational type. For example, electricity utilities traditionally have relatively stable technologies and operated in fairly stable environments. As a manager in these organizations, many of your management practices would be more mechanistic in their nature.

Cultural Signatures

The visible parts of the cultural signature are:

- **Artifacts** are an important element of culture. These refer to the observable forms and practices within the organization. Rituals, ceremonies, symbols, norms, and language are common examples of cultural artifacts: Rituals are elaborate and planned sets of activities often which are enacted time and time again, usually for the benefit of the audience (Beyer and Trice [7]).

■ **Values** are expressed beliefs about how and why things are done, for example, mission statements or credos. Schein calls these expressed values 'overt espoused values.' The 'value set' of an organization may be recognizable at the top level and/or shared throughout the organization (Armstrong [8]). Examples of areas in which values can be expressed are care for customers, productivity, teamwork, and excellence and performance orientation.

■ **Basic assumptions**, according to Schein, are the essence of culture. These are the taken-for-granted interpretations of reality or unquestioned basis on which people act. They are highly resistant to change and are often not able to be readily identified, particularly by members of a culture. The have generally become so taken for granted that one finds little variation within a cultural unit. Basic assumptions relate to matters such as the appropriate degree of hierarchy, how to compete in the market (the relationship to one's environment), and how conflict is treated.

Organization culture contributes to the success or failure of strategy. The business capabilities framework includes culture as an attribute of the business capabilities. This assists in dealing with the culture in a planned and holistic approach. Culture is very important and hardest to change within an organization. Culture of an organization contains the following:

■ A shared set of values and beliefs fulfills a number of important functions in organizations.
■ Creates a sense of identity and belonging among an organization's members.
■ Feelings of identification and belonging encourage commitment to the organization.
■ Shared values and beliefs enhance social system stability by avoiding potentially disruptive conflicts of interest
■ Culture directs and shapes behavior. It is a form of behavioral control.

Management culture defines the organizational structure. Challenges such as globalization, deregulation, and technological developments are constantly changing the nature of work and need constant monitoring of the organizational capabilities to deal with these challenges. Flexibility in management is necessary to absorb the economic shocks that occur as the business environment changes, and to adjust employment levels accordingly.

The employee's perspective of looking at the problem is influenced by his/her professional training and also the cultural background. The management culture is different in different areas of the organization. For example, in accounting the culture is defined as managing at a micro-level with the accuracy of the information being paramount. The marketing department culture is defined at a macro-level and the delivery of message (branding) is more important. This, when mixed with the cultural background, impacts the delivery of the strategic outcomes.

Table 8.7 discusses the impact of the diversity groups on organizational capability of implementing BA as a successful practice.

Key Performance Indicators

Establishing the business architecture practice is combined with an EA practice, if it does not already exist in the organization. The organizational structure in the format of the center of excellence or a department within the organization needs sponsorship from top executives. The practice establishment requires commitments for the number of resources for a defined time in mind. The outcome expected is defined in advance along with the measurement criteria for success. The following items are analyzed and planned:

Table 8.7 Impact of the Diversity Groups on Organizational Capability

Group Type	Diversity Type	Positive Outcomes	Negative Outcomes
General organizational	Gender, race, education	Variety of ideas, shared experience, not re-inventing the wheel	Absenteeism, Psychological commitments, social relationships, and communications
Top management team	Age, functional background, company tenure, education, education background	Growth, shareholders value increases, innovation and changes	Overall performance, strategic planning
Operating workgroup	Gender, race, job level, functional	Performance, communication	Turnover, group process
Project team	Age, company tenure, team tenure	Outside team performance, Communication, task processes	Inside team communication may impact the performance and successful project implementation

- Key Performance Indicators (KPI) of the program to measure value expected from this investment is defined and resourced. The ODBA practices what it expects from the organization. The business capabilities required for the practice are defined and assessed. The resources regardless of type (e.g., financial, skills) are defined to achieve the outcomes. The purpose of business architecture practice maintains the business capabilities dynamically to assist in realizing strategic goals.
- Program initiation is defined and communicated to the organization. The program has resources to bring in expert skills on demand during the strategic goals realization. In many cases, only a few resources are permanent with the option of additional resources on and as needed basis. This keeps the current skills within the practice and provides technical and business guidance.
- Program governance is defined for capabilities building, prioritization of capabilities and managing organizational investments based on organizational-wide capability-based investment plans. The governance discussed in Chapter 7 is pragmatically adopted and socialized within the organization.
- Identify stakeholders of the program and socialize the program objectives, governance, and roles and responsibilities for each. The program structure, governance, and investment plans are included in the organizational-wide induction programs for new employees.
- Analysis of the organization current state identifies gaps and prioritization of these gaps. Business capabilities prioritization changes with the change in strategy, requiring a measured approach to the task. Quick analysis is important to define the approach to manage capability assessment. Avoid shelf-ware documentation (documenting every current process). It is recommended to take a quick inventory of current assets without extensive documentation.

- Identify appropriate tools (frameworks, system, analysis tools) for the practice. Avoid expensive and extensive tool sets as the skills if these tool sets require investment of resources and time.
- Gap analysis (current state versus to-be state), is based on the strategic outcomes required, defines the approach for the assessment and roadmap planning (incremental versus big bang) and in roadmaps, identifies if new technology is useful (e.g., Service Oriented Architecture (SOA) or not?)
- Picking the right roles and tools, and understanding the culture of organization is very important; this includes the hierarchy of the organization chart. The new team, EA teams or employees are independent from business and IT and bring an internal consultant culture.

The Vision

The EA strategy assists in developing information architecture framework to enable informaton flow access across multiple agencies or jurisdictions. Information is available as needed and an environment established to design and implement services that enable integrated and standardized services across commands, external jurisdictions, partners, and agencies. The vision of EA and BA practices are aligned. Alignment includes establishing architectural processes and artifacts to support and guide IT, and business decision-making, ensuring optimal alignment of IT investment with the organization's business strategy. The adoption of this EA strategy activates the EA Framework. This is achieved by architecture defined in following three phases.

Phase 1—Defining Enterprise-Wide Components

Architecture scope or **phase 1** defines enterprise-wide components that are required to develop BA framework, processes, and governance. Phase 1 is the foundation of the business and EA practice and includes:

1. Define architecture principles agreed upon by key stakeholders. The architecture governance follows these foundation principles.
2. Develop architecture guidelines and standards for the "Application Architecture," "Information Architecture," and "Technology Architecture" to guide the business through the framework.
3. Build a governance structure and process to optimize the value of each investment.
4. Develop a business capability model and business priorities for short term (0–18 months) and medium term (18–36 months). The business capability-building priority list drives investment decisions.
5. Develop architecture processes for architecture governance and assurance of right solutions.
6. Develop architecture risk register to manage the risks not mitigated during project life.
7. Commence the master data management approach.

Phase 2—Planning Activities

Phase 2, based on the business capability framework, is planning activities to create the information lead architecture in support of the strategic implementation plans:

1. Develop projects to provide a consolidated single information source.
2. Optimize the cost of the information collection and exchange; develop strategies for the optimized and robust infrastructure including cloud adoptions where possible.
3. Develop solutions to manage the digital assets.
4. Develop required reporting for operational and strategic goals.

Phase 3—Extend to Include Intelligence

Phase 3 extends the platform to include the intelligence lead strategic implementation. In this phase the following detailed strategies are developed:

1. Master data management (MDM) implementation strategy.
2. Contextual view capability strategy.
3. Cloud adoption strategy.
4. Enterprise Resource Planning (ERP) adoption strategy.
5. Define EA to deliver targeted business outcomes.
6. Create enterprise-wide view to support the communities of interests.
7. Provide tools and services to enable optimal balance of operational and online information and services.
8. Contextualized information to enable empowerment an active community by providing:
   - Aggregated information to assist in seamless access across multiple agencies, jurisdictions
   - Provide access to information where it is needed
   - Design and implement integrated services across departments, partners, and government agencies.

Establish the BA Practice

The objectives of BA adoptions are to create an enterprise-wide framework to assess projects. It is recommended that key business processes and capabilities are reliably documented and supported by the relevant information flows. The future state requires the organizational capabilities and business functions are defined and visible. In a large number of organizations, operational and analytical information availability is siloed, requiring effort to collect and manipulate information from the various sources.

In changing circumstances of real-time information analytics, systems colloborate internally and with external partner systems to automatically collect and analyse information. Future information needs require scalability and performance more than current systems. Systems need to be secure and sustainable. Systems store and report on structured (data tables), semi-structured (Reports, documents), and unstructured (images, video) with quick accessibility. Information is stored based on a corporate data model.

The following outcomes are desired:

- Fully implemented SOA with updated Enterprise Service Bus as the only means to interface between systems.
- Systems are scalable and adoptable with the increase in data demands and number of users.
- Standard packages are used with minimal customization and enable cost-effective future upgrades.

- Increase in the number of systems/services delivered via cross-agency collaboration.
- Percent delivery of systems/services identified in service delivery plans and the realization of defined business benefits.

Establish the Supporting Architecture Governance

Architecture governance is the practice and orientation by which architectures and other architectures are managed and controlled at an enterprise-wide level. The current architecture governance process is focused on solution design and therefore more targeted toward project solutions and options. This sometimes results in projects not delivered as designed. The architectural risks created during projects are not managed post-project closure.

The new EA governance process has the following key characteristics:

- **Discipline**—all projects are assessed for architectural impact.
- **Transparency**—projects are assessed based on enterprise-wide architectural principles and standards.
- **Independence**—architects have independence to provide solution options based on organizational demand.
- **Accountability**—architects and project managers are accountable and responsible for documenting any deviations and exceptions from the architectural principles.

The following focus areas for EA governance are implemented as part of the EA strategy:

- Articulate the value of BA in a way that is relevant and applicable to individual operational areas. This embeds the function rapidly and steers the levels of IT investment toward long-term competitive outcomes.
- Establish consistent BA across the organization, including common principles, processes, and capabilities.
- Work with various divisions to ensure that IT investments are made in the correct EA context.
- Establish a transparent and effective means of assessing local versus enterprise optimization trade-off decisions to assist in managing IT at an enterprise level.
- Enhance business agility with the goal to make IT an enabler of business change.
- Percent of existing/new systems which have availability and business continuity requirements assessed, implemented, and maintained.
- Percent of systems/services with Service Level Agreements.
- Percent of projects compliant with EA strategy, governance.

Strategies for Future Technologies

The nature of information management is changing. The organizational goals are to be more efficient and provide better service to stakeholders. Technological architecture is developed once business priorities are known.

Technology is an enabler in most of the organizations but current systems may have aged. This restricts adopting new capabilities from current applications suites and other systems in the market. There is focus to upgrade the technology platforms and application but architecturally it is important the new systems are implemented timely and enterprise wide. The deployment of technology continues to raise questions of balancing effectiveness with efficiency of current and future technologies.

The key objectives of the new technology introduction are:

■ Percent delivery of systems/services identified in service delivery plans and the realization of defined business benefits.
■ Improvements in efficiency/performance related to the introduction of new technologies/systems/services.

BA Practice Implementation Style

The architecture community works together with IT delivery and business stakeholders to achieve desired maturity levels across all architectural dimensions. The following guidelines are followed to implement pragmatic and workable models:

■ Communicate and champion enterprise IT and architecture value.
■ Establish a connected, diverse, and collaborative architecture community.
■ Actively manage development and progression of architecture maturity.
■ Implement a diversified and scalable architecture model.
■ Execute a balanced top-down and bottom-up architecture agenda.
■ Architecture cycle to maintain currency of content and build longevity of practice.

The implementation of architecture practice requires a number of established project management practices. Table 8.8 defines the leadership styles of various practice leaders and desired outcomes. Table 8.8 discusses the reasons to adopt these styles, what to do and what not to do. The BA practice leaders adopt leadership styles based on organizational culture and the scope of the architecture practice.

People Management

The architecture practice is resourced with diverse skills and resources. The team is constituted from highly technical to business subject matter experts. Table 8.9 defines the interaction style of the leaders with the team members.

The diversity of the tasks within the BA practice requires a defined task management approach. The tasks vary from defining the business strategy to advising the technical aspects of the projects. This requires diverse task management styles. Table 8.10 defines task management styles.

The BA practice tasks leadership requires different way to manage the stakeholders. Table 8.11 defines the task management styles and recommendations when these styles are adopted based on the desired outcomes.

The BA practices success within the organization is based on the performance and outcomes. The performance goals of the practice are a combination of the evaluative tasks performance and also building business capabilities. Table 8.12 defines the key performance measurement for evaluative and development tasks. The business practices select a number of evaluative and development KPI and manage and report the performance of the practice based on selected KPIs.

Table 8.8 Leadership Styles of Various Practice Leaders and Desired Outcomes

Leadership Practice	*Desired Outcome*	*What Does This Mean?*	*Why Do It?*	*What Can Individuals Do?*	*What Is Too Much?*
Leading by example	Staff follows behavior exhibited by leaders	Overcoming "do as I say, not as I do" hypocrisy	Provides a clear picture, increases trust	Modify own behavior, communicate desired state, reward, be visible	Example without instructions. Being far removed from normal self
Networking	Provides support for plans	Make an effort to network before problems occur	Organizations are made of people not machines	Work out who is in one's network. What actions to take to improve it?	Overreliance on network for 'favors' to do regular work
Pride and enthusiasm	Staff enjoy their work	Everybody feels like a valued part of the team	People follow if they believe the leader has their interests at heart	Notice achievements and provide recognition	Too much can seem insincere
Communication	Staff trusts leader	Primarily downward	Avoids poor decisions based on invalid assumptions	Create the opportunity. Be relevant to the audience	Cc: without thought to the relevance
'People' values	enthusiastic cooperation	Personal ('the right way') or organizational (consideration, commitment, recognition and rewards)	People respond to respect for who they are, not just what they do	Find out what people value. Share one's own values	Fundamentalism

Table 8.9 Interaction Style of Leaders

Leadership Practice	Desired Outcome	What Do We Mean?	Why Do It?	What Could You Do?	What Is Too Much?
Interest and concern	Staff work at optimum level of stress	"Connecting," noticing, responding	Best way to achieve optimum stress level (*Yerkes-Dodson law*)	Show an interest. Ask how people are going	Being a nosy parker
Teamwork	Resolve harmful conflict and achieve synergy	Ranges from 'Nominal', 'Interdependent' (*see negotiation*), 'Committee' to 'Working group' (best)	Synergy -> efficiency	Be aware, hold team meetings, accept *some* conflict	Duplication, cloning, too much or too little conflict
Delegation and trust	Maximize leverage from staff ability	Delegation, Involvement, Development	"Pygmalion effect": create high expectation	Check attitude; Group problem-solving	Confusing delegation with abdication. Management by consensus
Listening and learning	Higher-quality decisions, staff feel valued and work harder	Acceptable to have disagreements. Giving undivided attention.	Staff know more than you, what is going on!	Decide to listen more. Eliminate bad listening habits	Losing balance with own time management
Recognition and reward	Satisfaction and motivation -> high effort	Positive feedback. Encouragement	Motivates	Notice achievements. Must be *Appropriate, Precise, Timely (APT)*	Praising everything, even if not exceptional

Table 8.10 Task Management Styles

Leadership Practice	Desired Outcome	What Does This Mean?	Why Do It?	What Could You Do?	What Is Too Much?
Performance improvement	Improved performance	Search for *continuous improvement*	Staff need to know when to improve. Gives message that manager is interested	***Appropriate***—detail ***Precise***—avoid "good… but" ***Timely***—just before staff perform	When not balanced with positive feedback
Resources and infrastructure	Decrease wasted time and energy	Environment, equipment, supplies, processes, decisions	Creates environment for people to achieve	Get the facts. Deal with problems. Plan, organize, control.	Mindlessly following the plan. "Plans are for aborting" (Beer)
Quality and productivity	Increased performance, effectiveness, and safety	Maximize Value of output/Value of Input	No need to ask!	Identify resources and outputs, measure and compare over time	Cost of systems outweigh productivity gains
Rationality	Help achievement of organizational or unit objectives	Making most appropriate decision *in the circumstances*, given available information	Using good information and good reasoning gives better answers	Check that you have sufficient information. Stick to the facts. Focus on desired outcomes	Not making decisions. Seeking perfection or certainty. "paralysis by analysis"
Roles and objectives	Focusing effort and skill	Aligning staff by setting goals, minimum and maximum levels of achievement	Without goals, efforts are dissipated	Be clear on your own role and objectives	Not allowing enough freedom, too much freedom

Table 8.11 Task Management Styles

Leadership Practice	Desired Outcome	What Do We Mean?	Why Do It?	What Could You Do?	What Is Too Much?
Decisive action	Removal of uncertainty, faster achievement of objectives	Making decisions under pressure, taking control in crises, risk-taking, initiative, sense of urgency	Staff want bosses to be decisive	Force yourself to make decisions, behave with urgency	Appearing arrogant, ignoring evidence, insensitivity
Dealing with blockages	Unimpeded progress and minimum waste of time and energy	Assertively challenging or getting around intractable problems, procedures, or people blocking progress	Solving problems rather than escalation welcomed by business	Get the facts, devise options, deciding what to do, learning to be more assertive, building support, triggering change	Trampling better informed people
Outward looking	Activities and achievements that contribute or respond to, and benefit from external world	Organizations are really open not closed systems	Understand opportunities and threats	Read more papers, magazines, etc. Join associations, conferences. Create and use informal opportunities	Not leave enough time to focus on your own patch
Innovation	Fundamental breakthroughs	Think of, find, or promote new ideas	Solving problems	Trust staff to overcome their own problems. Respond to their ideas, not just yours	Not allowing good ideas to bed in
Future orientation	Better responses to predictable events and clear picture of end goal	Contingency planning. Identify trends	Works for sports people	Write mission statement	Being unrealistic

Table 8.12 Key Performance Measurement for Evaluative and Development Tasks

Evaluative	*Developmental*
• Documenting good versus poor performance • Identifying specific deficiencies • Deciding whether to extend or renew a contract • Pay, promotion, demotion, and dismissal decisions • Dealing with grievances • Deciding who needs training • Collect data for external review	• Foster open communication, understanding, and respect • Clarify expectations, roles, responsibilities, and resources available to achieve goals • Building motivation by expressing recognition and thanking • Fostering outcome-focused culture • Timely feedback regarding strengths and opportunities for improvement • Establishing agreed SMART goals and performance improvement, linked to corporate strategy

Table 8.13 Performance Management Tasks and Leadership Skills

Performance Management Tasks	*Component Skills*
Setting goals	Strategically aligned, consistent, SMART, both qualitative and quantitative, challenging but achievable, criteria and standard based, consider individual and cultural differences, learning goals, individual or group, build goal acceptance, and commitment
Empowering	Understand, delegate, provide resources, give encouragement, know when to do it, appreciate blocks
Providing feedback	Descriptive, specific, tentative, positive, timely, validating, confidential, owned
Evaluating	Comprehensive information, prepare, avoid biases, appraisal meeting, acceptable feedback, deal with poor performance, plan performance
Rewarding	Consider diversity of preferences, ability to influence, respond to changing preferences and constraints, be consistent with org. strategize, align with team and individual goals

The success of the BA practices within the organization is based on the performance and outcomes. Table 8.13 defines the performance management tasks and the leadership skills required.

Discussion Points

1. What are the differentiating characteristics among architecture functions?
2. How does BA disperse business and technology capabilities throughout the organization?
3. How does CAMS fit into the BA picture?
4. Why is it important to define competency center roles and responsibilities? What is the impact if these are not defined?

5. Describe the differences between mechanistic and organic organizations. Provide examples of when each provides value.
6. How does culture impact BA implementation? Why is it important to consider culture when implementing BA?
7. EA strategy has three phases—How does each build on the previous phase and why is it important to include all three phases?
8. Explain the key differences between managing stakeholders and managing tasks.

References

1. Unhelkar, B. (2013), *The Art of Agile Practice: A Composite Approach for Projects and Organizations*, CRC Press, Boca Raton, FL.
2. Burns and Stalker. (1961). *The Management of Innovation*. Cambridge University Press, Cambridge, UK.
3. Porter, M.E. (1979). How competitive forces shape strategy, *Harvard Business Review*, 59(2), pp. 137–145.
4. Hamel, G. and Prahalad, C.K. (1989). Strategic intent, *Harvard Business Review*, 67(3), pp. 63–76.
5. Baghai, M., Coley, S., and White, D. (1999). *The Alchemy of Growth: Practical Insights for Building the Enduring Enterprise*. Orion Publishing Group, London.
6. Mabey, C. and Salaman, G. (1995). *Strategic Human Resource Management*, Blackwell, Oxford.
7. Beyer, J. and Trice, H. (1988). *The Communication of Power Relations in Organisation through Cultural Rites*, Sage, Newbury Park, CA.
8. Armstrong, M. (1995). *A Handbook of Personnel Management Practice*, Kogan Page, London.

Chapter 9

ODBA, Big Data, and a Functioning Agile Organization

KEY POINTS

- Understanding a Functioning Agile Business and the role of Big Data and outcome-driven business architecture (ODBA) within
- Envisioning an Agile Organization with Rapid Response Capabilities to Internal and External Stimuli
- Balancing Planning with Agility—a Composite Agile Method and Strategy (CAMS)
- Enhancing decision-making in Agile Organizations with Collaborative Business Intelligence
- Achieving Collaborative Holistic 360° view of an entity from both a customer and organization perspective

The discussions until now focused on Outcome-Driven Business Architecture (ODBA). 'Agile Business' is the goal of all initiatives in an organization and ODBA is no exception. Therefore, this chapter focuses on Agile business. The value proposition of ODBA is based on alignment of organizational initiatives with desired outcomes. The end result of such an alignment is the ability of the organization to take rapid and more accurate decisions. This enhancement of decision-making is described as Agility. Composite Agile Method and Strategy (CAMS) has been discussed in the past, and a corresponding Big Data Framework for Agile Business (BDFAB) is also developed. This last content chapter (as the ensuing three are case studies) focuses on Big Data technology adoption as a means to enhance Agility in the organization—including its operation and growth. This chapter further outlines the ongoing agility and knowledge synchronization between users and systems is outlined.

Envisioning an Agile Organization

Agile as a Business Value from Big Data Adoption

Agile means different things to different people—and sometimes, depending on the context, the meaning changes even for the same person. For a developer, Agile is a method to produce a solution. Scrum and XP are examples of such Agile methods. For an architect, the entire effort with outcome-driven business outcome (ODBA) is to provide the necessary opportunities for business value through people, processes, and technologies. For a product manager, Agile is a mechanism to develop products and services that enable growth in market share. For a regulator, agility can be used in real-time transaction reporting for compliance. For business leaders, however, Agile holds the promise of a faster and more accurate response to a changing business situation.

Figure 9.1 depicts this business agility. The change shown in Figure 9.1 can arise from either a problem, a new business initiative, or an unimagined risky situation. The transactional gap is the distance between the change and the organization coming to know about it. The business reaction or response depends on how well the organization has prepared for the event. The time gap between the change and the organization's response can be considered as the 'sensitivity' of the organization. The shorter the time gap to respond, the higher the organization's sensitivity. Reducing the transactional gap and increasing the sensitivity is the purpose of any initiative in an organization. Thus, the discussions on ODBA—with specific focus on alignment of initiatives with outcomes—also has the eventual goal of enhancing the Agility of the organization.

Agile is thus the eventual business value and Big Data adoption as a means to achieving that value. Agile is also a method to produce Big Data solutions and is described as a culture and a mindset [1,2]. Thus, the keyword Agile has a lot to offer to this discussion on ODBA and vice versa. For example, ODBA brings together the business outcomes and solutions development viewpoint—both of which are essential in deployment of new technologies and solutions (in particular, Big Data-driven solutions).

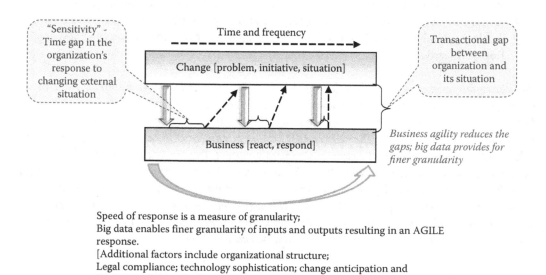

Figure 9.1   Big Data facilitates organizational Agility by ensuring a very small gap between the organization and the situation impacting it to enable faster and more accurate decision making.

A Big Data Framework for Agile Business (BDFAB) is described in detail by Unhelkar [3]. The starting point for BDFAB is an Agile mindset. This mindset deals with the psyche of the decision makers. For example, a decentralized, fine granular decision-making process dilutes the power of hierarchical decision-making. This can be unsettling for some users. Similarly, the collaborative and cross-functional nature of Agile teams can also come as a surprise to some business stakeholders.

Discussions on ODBA in the previous chapters have highlighted the need for a holistic view. Such a holistic view is possible with a team that is Agile because one characteristic of such an Agile team is cross-functionality. With such cross-functional teams, business stakeholders suddenly realize they are expected to actively participate in the upkeep of ODBA and the development of new solutions. These business stakeholders discover they are 'too busy' running the business to participate on a daily basis in the prioritization and decision making process. Yet, when quizzed they say they are totally "committed" to Agile. These contradictions are anticipated in Big Data adoption using Agile principles and skilled adoption champions have to deal with these challenges.

Business agility can be understood as a time measure of changes to the operating environment of the business and the time it takes for an organization to respond to that change. An agile organization is able to quickly respond to a change in the environment; however, as the rate of change of stimuli increases there is corresponding challenge to business agility. An interesting aspect of enterprise agility is the correlation it has with a lean organization [4]. Being lean is a precursor to becoming agile—in fact, leanness and agility are intricately tied together. Changes to the business requirements are considered inevitable and, therefore, welcomed in an agile organization. Agile principles and methods enable the solution providers to cope with the changing business requirements.

Agile is a holistic and comprehensive enterprise-wide approach that brings together the tools/methods/processes/standards/frameworks/costs across multiple tiers of an organization, resulting in what is called a Composite Approach. Such an approach focuses not only on the practices of Agile, that are commonly understood as daily standups and user stories, but also the best practices, phases, and deliverables from the planned family of methods. Business agility stands to benefit by understanding how to apply an Agile culture value system across all organizational functions.

Thus, despite the popularity of Agile in the software development arena, enough care needs to be exercised when agility is applied across an enterprise. Consideration needs to be given to the role of agility in the following examples:

- Production Systems—Mission critical production systems need to be supported and kept operational. Ongoing iterative releases of a solution can be potentially risky to the operation. Therefore, a balance between the continuity of existing services and introduction of new services needs to be managed.
- Supported Users—Software releases impact users. Any changes impacts one or more users and these need to be supported. For example, if a business process used by a million customers and thousands of branches in a bank has to change to incorporate analytics, then the users of that process need to be trained to successfully implement the change. This support function can take time and effort and it needs to be planned from the outset.
- Regulatory—Within complex regulatory environments, such as health, aviation, and financial services, regulatory approvals are a key compliance requirement. Obtaining these approvals can take time to implement and adopt. Therefore, iterative solutions

releases may have to be grouped together in a major release that is compliant with the regulatory needs.

- Customer Understanding—Customers often seek stability so they can learn to use the service. Multiple release cycles of vendors are often resisted. Release cycles need to be planned, keeping the customer confidence high.
- Migration—Big Data adoption requires data and process migrations. For example, the use of NoSQL databases in the background require movement and/or integration of the unstructured data with the existing enterprise systems. This migration also requires use of Application Program Interfaces (APIs) provided by tool and database vendors.
- Legal—Change often means revisions or new contracts and agreements. From additional vendor services through to customer onboarding, agility is required but is tempered against the necessary legal obligations.
- Risk Management—Agility is the counterpart of risk. Every change has an associated risk. The more changes made, the greater the risks and the greater the risk of realization. Conversely, not changing has its own risks. It is the balance of risk management against agility that is important.
- Freeze Periods—Whether it is compliance, such as SOX or audit or investigations, systems and business operations are subject to freeze-periods where changes cannot be made. These periods are part of the business environment and need to be accommodated within agile businesses.
- Cost—Ongoing iterative software development has costs associated with it. These costs include those of Release cycles, integration with existing data, regulatory and data migration. These costs need to be considered within agile.

Advantages of Agility and Big Data

Enterprise-wide Agility implies small, cross-functional teams involving customers, users, and producers (developers) of solutions working in short, sharp iterations producing visible results. Once the overall deliverables are achieved by the team, it is dismantled and the members revert back to a common pool of resources. A composite approach to Agile makes use of a community of practices and knowledge sharing within the organization. Therefore, while self-organizing small, Agile teams implement features in a solution, the larger pool of talent in the organization gets nurtured and developed. This occurs through upskilling and also socializing team members and is vital for development of Big Data skillset within an organization.

Agile is thus a socio-cultural phenomenon across an organization that includes agile methods, agile style of working, and applying agility across the organizational space. The advantage of using agility is creating business value rather than creating software solutions and packages.

Envisioning an Agile Organization

What makes an organization Agile? And what does an Agile organization look like? First and foremost, an Agile Business has an agile vision that aligns with strategy but evolves in response to changes in the business environment. Within Agility, fluidity in the vision of an Agile organization is essential. This means that while the vision and mission of an organization is meant to provide direction and guidance for its growth, it is not unchangeable. Figure 9.2 envisions such an Agile organization.

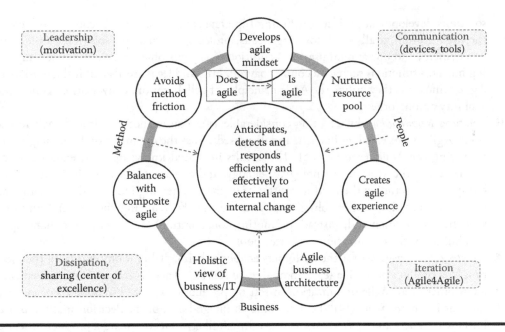

Figure 9.2   Envisioning an Agile organization.

At its very core, an Agile organization anticipates, detects, and responds efficiently and effectively to change, both external and internal. This is a collaborative, highly interconnected, and communicative organization that is in sync with the ecosystem in which it exists (comprising industry, government, and society). Providing Agile business value implies moving the organization from where it is right now (presumably slow-moving, inefficient, rigid, hierarchical, and disconnected with the environment in which it exists) to an organization that is well aligned and well connected with its customers and partners. Big Data used in a strategic manner offers significant opportunities to achieve this transformation and eventual business agility. This is because Big Data analytics highly enhance an organization's ability to detect and respond to external and internal stimuli.

Precisely measuring the level of Agility of an organization, however, is not easy. An Agile organization is much more than the sum total of the individuals who make up the organization and the sum total of their Agile practices. While "Doing" Agile is easier to measure and justify, "Being" Agile is 'fuzzy' and not easily measurable. But it is "Being" Agile that provides maximum value to all the stakeholders. BDFAB works to create a synergy between technology, method, people, and business in order for an organization to 'Be' Agile.

Figure 9.2 summarizes some of the key ongoing characteristics of an Agile organization that are embedded in the psycho-sociology of its people, methods of work, and business decision-making. These are the characteristics that facilitate easier and smoother adoption of Big Data and, at the same time are provided added impetus with Big Data. These Agile organizational characteristics are as follows. An agile organization:

■ *Develops Agile Mindset* by welcoming change across all functions of the organization. This is the starting point for the business transformation process. The Agile mindset is one that is used to spot a problem to solve or an opportunity to grasp. Analyzing the problem (or opportunity) results in understanding business needs, proposing initiatives, and undertaking solutions development projects (including Big Data solutions). Agile becomes a mindset of the organization at all levels covering needs, projects, alternatives, solutions, validations, deployment, and operational usage. In addition to key customer-centric processes, supporting business functions such as accounts, payroll, HR, and legal are also all influenced by the Agile mindset as they utilize the Agile principles of collaboration, conversation, collocation, visibility among others.

- *Nurtures Resource Pool* by devoting considerable attention to individuals and their interactions. Agile is preserved, enhanced, and dispersed across the organization by managing and nurturing the Agile resource pool. This results in shared knowledge and experiences categorized into the areas of psychology, sociology, and culture. Cohesion within and among groups, understanding the natural resistance to change, helping individuals overcome their biases and phobias, and enabling trust and sharing (by reducing the internal and often wasteful competition and, instead, promoting collaboration)—all results in enhancing the capabilities of the organization's resource pool.

- *Creates Agile Experience* for the customers enabling their collaboration right from the inception of a product or service (e.g., an analytical service). There is maximum involvement of a customer of an Agile organization in setting product or service directions. For example, the Net Promoter Score (NPS) can become an integral part of the decision-making process for new products and services. If customers are unlikely to recommend a product or service, then a major debriefing needs to be carried out to ascertain the root cause for potential rejection. Agile is not just confined to the boardroom; is implemented and visible across all levels of decision-making. When the customer-driven experience results in satisfied and supportive customers, it in turn, also leads to the service staff of the organization feeling satisfied with what they served to the customer.

- *Implements an Agile BA* that enables and supports internal structural changes to facilitate business response to internal and external pressures. ODBA, encompassing technical (Enterprise) architecture can sometimes be stuck in time. This may happen with the good intention of providing stability to the organization. More often than not, this technologically slow-moving entity and corresponding organizational structures reduce organizational agility. Agile extricates an organization from the dungeons of rigid hierarchy and endless planning and into the real world where change is the impetus for every decision [2].

- *Maintains a Holistic View* of Business rather than a 'siloed,' function-driven view of business. This is important for ODBA. Agility as a culture results in a collaborative and communicative problem-solving approach within the projects of the organization. Due to its holistic nature, Agility also helps an organization deal with maintenance, operations, and infrastructure processes in line with the desired business outcomes. These non-project activities provide as much contribution in providing a holistic customer view as the project activities dealing with a solution [4].

- *Balance with Composite Agile* by ensuring proper utilization of the existing assets of the organization. In non-agile organizations, planning has been the key to reducing the risks associated with any change and its impact on the business. A risk adverse organization was once considered a stable organization. This stability was viewed as indicative of the ability of the organization to handle the impact of change. However, flexibility rather than rigid stability is the key to absorbing change [5]. For example, a flexible, flat, and cross-functional internal organizational structure can withstand the impact of government policy changes that result in the opening of a region to global markets, while a hierarchical and rigidly stable organization struggles to adapt. Changes to labor laws leading to changes in relationships with trade unions, is another example where the flexibility of an organizational structure can provide positive value in successively adapting to change. Needless to say, *balance* plays a crucial role in bringing together planned and pure Agile aspects of activities within an organization—as espoused by CAMS.

■ *Avoids Method Friction* by giving due attention to the many friction points within the organization. These friction points arise on the project level due to multiple projects, multiple methods within those projects (e.g., project management, IT governance, software development methods, and quality assurance) with each stakeholder focusing on their own roles and goals. The fundamental and philosophical differences between Agile and planned approaches add to these friction points. On the organizational level, there are numerous Business As Usual (BAU) activities that follow their own processes and standards. For example, the architecture, infrastructure, operations, and maintenance disciplines have their standards that are potentially in conflict with the project standards—mainly because the latter focuses on delivery of solutions as against maintaining stability and optimized operations. This aspect of Agile that helps avoid method friction has been discussed under the CAMS umbrella [6].

In addition to the characteristics of Agile organizations, Figure 9.2 shows four defining activities of such organizations:

■ *Leadership* plays a crucial role in motivating and sustaining change toward agile. Agile business value is considered strategic and leadership helps maintain focus on that value. Big Data is considered an enabler rather than an end goal in itself, and leadership continues to direct the effort of the organization keeping the role of Big Data as an enabler in mind.

■ *Communication* in its many different forms, channels, and frequencies is yet another cornerstone of an Agile organization. Big Data adoption needs continuous communication—almost becoming a routine part of every meeting, briefing, and organization-wide updates.

■ *Mindset* of such an organization is *iterative* and incremental and therefore it uses Agile even in Agile adoption. While the strategy of an organization is clearly set, the way the strategy is implemented changes with the business environment. This alignment to strategy while adopting the implementation is the mindset of an agile organization.

■ *Sharing* and diffusion of knowledge and experiences, typically through a Center of Excellence. Just as organizations have mentoring schemes and specialization support for project managers, so it is with Agile and Big Data within the context of the respective business areas.

It's worth noting that the above characteristics of an Agile organization are fluid. Hard metrics seldom provide correct measures of the business outcomes. These characteristics of Agile discussed above can vary depending on the type of business, size of the organization, and industry to which an organization belongs. For example, in banking, which is in the service sector, a holistic view of the business is based around business processes and their agility. In a product-based organization, such as an auto manufacturer, a holistic view of the organization focuses on the inventory and supply chain processes. The level of Agility desired by the business can also dictate the level of granularity in its analytics. For example, a government organization, which is bureaucratic by nature, may not aim for the fine granularity, like that of a commercial bank. Bureaucratic organizations, however, need to place special emphasis on avoiding method friction, whereas a Big Data-based technology organization (e.g., a vendor) focusing on providing Analytics-as-a-Service (AaaS) will have to ensure an agile enterprise architecture to facilitate changes to its business policies resulting from analytics.

Functioning Agile Business with Embedded Big Data Analytics

Holistic, Fine Granular, and Sensitive Business

Business agility is less of an activity or a method and more of a value system. This is also an indicator of holistic, fine granular and sensitive business that capitalizes on the technical and analytical capabilities of Big Data. Composite Agile Method and Strategy (CAMS)—mentioned in earlier chapters—plays an important role in balancing such business agility. CAMS supports formal methods and frameworks (e.g., business methods, governance frameworks, and project management approaches) needed within the organization but also facilitates application of pure agile principles and practices in developing solutions.

Understanding the Agile touch-points within these methods helps the organization reduce "methods friction." Incremental changes are made to the practice of these methods to ensure a balance between the formality of control and the flexibility of Agility. For example, a formal contract (deliverable) mandated by a governance framework is produced through negotiations—but the Agile value of customer collaboration and face-to-face communication is also carried out. Similarly, other elements of a method or framework, such as its roles, tasks, techniques, and practices are examined and adjusted to overcome the method friction points.

People issues are considered paramount in producing agile business value. Not only are individual workers affected when an organization shifts to overall agility but so also are the senior managers and decision makers whose style of working is affected by the changes to the business methods and processes. Thus, the rate of transition of a business to agility is continuously adjusted to ensure high comfort level for people. Dynamicity in terms of skills, attitude, and knowledge of individuals is factored in as the organization adopts a composite Agile approach. Formal policies and Key Performance Indicators (KPIs) need to be tied in with risks and leadership to achieve a balanced business agility.

Figure 9.3 summarizes the internal and external (dependent) areas of consideration for a functioning Agile business that capitalizes on Big Data business strategies. These considerations are grouped into two parts. Those factors that are directly under the control of the organization are shown inside the organizational boundary. The relatively bigger circles are dependent on external collaborations as well and are shown traversing the organizational boundaries. Big Data and Agile together bring about fundamental changes to the business. The internal changes to an organization are as follows:

- Business Policies—this is forming new business actions and updating existing ones to incorporate agile values. These business policies elevate the focus of agility from project-based to organizational, strategic agile. Business policies play an important role in enabling collaboration between partnering organizations. Such collaboration is important for the Big Data analytics based on wide-ranging data sources.
- Business Ecosystem—considers the change brought about not only in the business shift to agility but also to the many partnering organizations and their relationships. Techniques, such as SWOT and PESTLE analysis, are very helpful in ascertaining the impact of collaborations and agility on the business ecosystem and vice versa. These techniques are also a part of BDFAB* as a business decides on adopting Big Data.

---

* Big Data strategies.

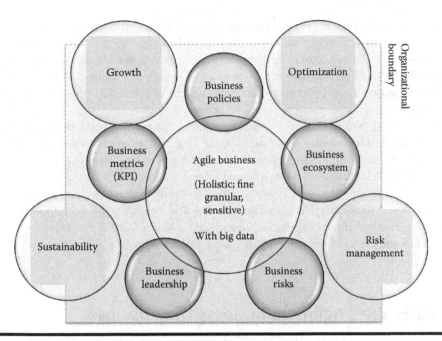

Figure 9.3 A functioning Agile business (Holistic) capitalizing on Big Data strategies: Internal and external impacts.

■ Business Risks—associated with changes in internal management structure as agility is embraced; as also the changes to external relationships. These risks start emerging as soon as an organization makes attempts to inculcate Agile values and behaviors in its interactions— as compared with the original contract-based interactions and relationships.

■ Business Leadership—is affected and, in turn, affects the agile changes. Visionary agile leadership changes the way in which an organization is structured, its culture, and the way in which it operates. Agile as a value system relies more on leadership and less on management. This, in turn, requires changes to the way in which management functions in an organization. Relinquishing control, facilitating sharing of tasks and accepting informality in reporting are important changes brought about by leadership rather than management. These same leadership qualities are required as Big Data is adopted by the organization—as the value derived from Big Data is achieving business agility.

■ Business Metrics—comprise the measures and indicators in terms of what constitutes success in terms of an agile business. The Key Performance Indicators (KPIs) change their focus—as a business transforms to agile—from being purely objective measures to include a certain amount of subjectivity in them. For example, an agile business will not index employee reward structures to merely an objective measure of customer satisfaction; instead, the business metrics for customer satisfaction includes subjective discussions and insights gained from interacting directly with the customer.

The factors that are not directly under the control of the organization but are dependent on other external factors and which impact the business agility of an organization are also summarized in Figure 9.3.

■ Growth opportunities for the business based on improving customer satisfaction/experience, development of innovative products and services, establishment of collaborations with vendors and business partners, and ensuring value in mergers and acquisitions.

■ Optimization of business operations based on innovative problem-solving, use of external tools and technologies, process modeling, re-engineering, and optimization and establishing decentralizing decision-making through big data analytics.

■ Risk associated with the business including security and privacy, compliance and documentation, audits, and traceability of transactions. Big Data technologies and analytics help ascertain these risks (which are both external and internal). However, Big Data adoption has its own risks that need to be handled—by using a formal framework like BDFAB in undertaking adoption.

■ Sustainability that intends to reduce a carbon footprint, enhances carbon metrics and measurement through analytics, and used training and coaching for developing positive user attitude. Successfully incorporating sustainable, environmental considerations within an agile, holistic business requires collaboration and participation with internal and external entities [7,8].

Big Data Enables Agility in Business Dimensions

While a business aspires for 'Agility,' a number of its business functions and its organizational aspects undergo change. These business functions are also affected by external and internal factors. Figure 9.4 shows the external factors that affect business agility (shown on the outside of the box)

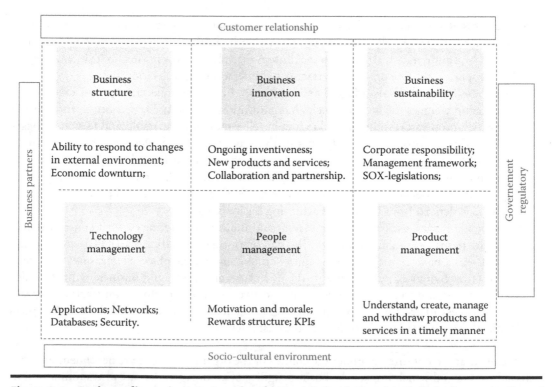

Figure 9.4   Business dimensions (external and internal) that becoming Agile by incorporation of in Big Data-driven business strategies.

and the way in which the business responds to these factors internally (shown on the inside of the box). These external and internal factors affecting agile business transformation are discussed in greater detail next:

External Influencing Factors

The external influencing factors in an agile business transformation include Markets, Customer Relationship, Business Partners, Government and Regulatory requirements and the Socio-Cultural environment in which the business exists. Many of these manifest through the costs of a business. These factors are discussed next.

Customer Relationship

Agile business transformation impacts the customer relationships of the organization. Through agility, the organization becomes more flexible in its offerings (customer centric). This, in turn, enables the customers to configure their own requirements from the organization. With agility, customers can also be invited to participate in business decision-making in terms of product design and service expectation. The transforming organization needs to ensure it aligns its agile changes with its customers. For example, if an organization changes the way in which it offers a product (e.g., making it self-serve), the customers need to be made aware of those changes. In an agile bank, the customer is offered the ability to put together accounts in different formats for her individual needs. This requires bank staff educate and align the customer to the offering. The demographics of the customer also need to be considered in adopting agility. For example, an elderly demographic of customers who are dealing with their superannuation accounts may not be able to utilize the Self-serve analytics (SSA) features and flexibility that a bank is offering. These customers need to be treated differently than the ones who are comfortable in exclusively dealing online with the organization.

Business Partners

Collaboration, Agility, and Big Data are closely related. Adopting Agile, especially in its composite format across the organization, implies a definite impact on the business partners of the organization. For example, the relationship of the organization and its business partners expands based on agile values of trust and honesty. This has relevance to the way in which an organization communicates physically and technically. For example, a business process analyzing production schedules of an organization are exposed to a supplier electronically to reduce inventory. An agile organization thus has many processes that cannot be executed in isolation. Business partners are affected by the transformation and, therefore, they need to be involved in the very early stages of agile transformation.

Internet-based communications are the backbone of business processes which also means businesses are invariably dependent and sensitive to changes in the applications and behavior of their business partners. This is because any change in any business process of an organization has immediate ramifications for the processes of the business partners. Starting right from the ubiquitous spreadsheet used by a small business through to the comprehensive Enterprise Resource Planning solutions used by large corporations and multinationals, sharing information with business partners through Information and Communication technology (ICT) plays a core role in business decision-making. Partners influence every aspect of an organization's marketing, management, growth, and expansion. These business partners demand services, implementing new technologies, and upgrading their own business processes as a result of agile adoption by a business. Sharing information with these partners not only avoids issues relating to process mismatches with them, but the partners can themselves also provide assistance in enabling a comprehensive agile transformation (especially if they have adopted the agile values themselves).

Government Regulatory Factors and Sustainability

Adopting agility at an organizational level requires careful consideration of the legal and regulatory requirements that are usually external to the organization. While agility promotes collaboration and open communication, there is still a need to document the interactions from a legal viewpoint. Understanding the regulatory requirements, ongoing changes to legislations across multiple, collaborative partners and their regions, and the impact of these legal requirements on the organization are crucial factors in organizational adoption of agility. Interactions of the organization (especially large and global organizations) with its governmental structures may have to be documented in detail—facilitating traceability and audit. Irrespective of the desire of the organization to be agile, some of these government-business interactions cannot be agile in the pure sense. A combination of agile values and corresponding formal documentation is required in dealing with this factor during transformation.

Socio-Cultural Environment

The socio-cultural environment in which the organization exists and operates is immediately affected when Agility is adopted by the organization. Similar to the consideration of customer demographics, the social environment of an organization requires due consideration in terms of its acceptance of agility. For example, a business dealing with selling goods online to a teenage audience will find it relevant to investigate the social media frequented by these potential customers. Agility at the business level changes the way in which goods are sold online. Collaborative-agile, in particular, expands the reach of the organization to beyond its geographical boundaries. In such cases, proper study of the socio-cultural environment and the way it is affected by agility is required as a part of agile business transformation.

Internal Factors and Responses

Business Structure

Structural flexibility of the business is its ability to change internally so as to respond to external pressures. The structural model of the business needs to be flexible enough to allow it to respond to external demands. The global economic downturn came upon businesses without much warning. A flexible business model and associated agile corporate culture can become capable of handling such sudden external changes. Accompanying the need for structural flexibility of business is the need for the underpinning systems (e.g. human resources (HR), customer relationship management (CRM)) to facilitate such nimbleness. Communications technologies remove duplicate activities, eliminate redundant activities, merging manual processes with electronic and mobile processes, and improve the overall process flow within and across the organization [9–11]. BDFAB (fifth module in particular) aims to integrate these technologies and tools with processes and people, thus paving the path for flexible business structure.

Business Innovation

Business innovation is the ability of the business to creatively generate new products and services, come up with innovative ways of handling the competition, and prioritize its risks [5]. An agile business creates many opportunities within itself to be creative and innovative. Enabling an innovative approach to business often calls for changes in business practices, business operations, and business culture. These changes are facilitated by keeping agility in mind during Big Data adoption. Agility understands the type of business, the domain in which it exists, its available resources, and its strengths and weaknesses, as well as a supportive culture. Conversely, the need to foster innovative culture is also high in agile business transformation that enables people to experiment with processes and technologies to improve and optimize them.

Business Compliance

Business compliance is the need for the business to develop capabilities to meet regulatory compliances. The external demands for government and regulatory requirements alluded to earlier need to be satisfied by businesses by internally reorganizing itself. An agile internal business structure is able to respond easily to ever-changing legislations. Consider, for example, SOX legislation. This legislation provides protection from fraudulent practices to shareholders and the general public and at the same time, also pins the responsibility for internal controls and financial reporting on the CEO and the CFO of the company.

Agile transformation enables the business to carry out this accountability and responsibility through changes in the internal processes, updating of ICT-based systems to enable accurate collection and timely reporting of business data, and changes in the attitude and practices of senior management. Another example of the need for the business to comply is the rapid implementation of regulations related to carbon emissions. This legislation requires businesses to update and implement their carbon collection procedures, analysis, control, audit, and internal and external reporting.

Technology Management

Technology management in agile adoption involves handling the changes to underlying technologies that support the business and its processes. Challenges in managing technologies include changes to the wired and wireless networks, service-oriented applications, distributed data warehouses, and complexities of security as the organization transforms to an agile one. Businesses rightfully aim to capitalize on the connectivity accorded by the ubiquitous Internet [12]. This ICT-based communication results in an enhanced customer experience and improved internal business efficiency.

For example, an agile organization wants to provide services to a customer at the location of the customer. This change requires the organization to be flexible in its customer service processes and be able to move those processes around by utilizing its mobile networks. Corresponding data relating to the customer also has to change to accommodate the context and the changing mobile contents.

People Management

Adopting agility impacts the people within an organization. Managing the employees and other contract staff within an organization, keeping motivation high and keeping abreast of changes is a crucial ingredient of successful agile adoption. In adopting agile across the organization, careful attention needs to be given to the career aspirations of individuals, their personal job satisfaction criteria, and their attitude toward agility. Large, global organizations employ people in numerous ways including permanent employment, contract labor, and consulting/advisory roles. The approach to each of these engagements differs when agile is adopted as an organizational culture. For example, a permanent employee is interested in finding out what happens to his next promotion if the tasks to be performed are 'shared.' The contract employee may be happy to share tasks but would like to index his contract rates to quality and time. The human resources (HR) systems and processes supporting these engagements need to be flexible and capable of handling these differences and the changing scenarios. Agile business transformation investigates, updates, and ensures a flexible approach to resourcing people, managing them, motivating them, and enabling them to provide their best to the organization and its customers.

Product Management

Product management refers to the need to produce new products and services and to continue to produce existing products with improved parameters (such as time and cost). Agility changes the way the organization captures data related to products analyzes it, and incorporates the output into product development and deployment. For example, an agile organization eschews long-winded analysis of product feedback, but, instead directly collaborates with the customer to derive instantaneous updates on product feedback. This information is immediately made available to the decision makers through Internet-enabled collaborative systems. With the adoption of agility, the processes for product development change and also the corresponding supporting ICT systems. While the organization develops consistency across its various product lines and its development and deployment activities, collaborative agility also offers opportunities for 'mass customization' (i.e., the ability to produce customized products for each customer, but on a mass, production scale). This occurs in an agile organization due to reduced touch-points during a production process. Disposal of used products and withdrawal of a product line in a timely and coordinated manner are also a part of product management. The new agile organization has a lean inventory, reduced paperwork, and continuous change incorporated in its product life cycle management (PLM).

CAMS: Balancing Agility with Formality in Big Data Adoption

CAMS facilitates the application of methods at various levels of an organization depending on their relevance, principles, and practices. In bringing together planned and agile behaviors, and business, technology and operational views of an organization need to come together based on 'balance.'

Leadership from all collaborating organizations should focus attention on competencies and frameworks that go beyond the commonly known software development life cycles. Thus, the use of psychology and sociology knowledge and bringing in innovative techniques to overcome the cultural differences becomes an important function in such outsourced projects.

For example, with the overwhelming focus of Agile on face-to-face communications, the outsourcing parties are naturally inclined toward holding physical meetings at least before the initiative—even if it is not possible to do so on a daily basis as specified in Agile methods. Effective global outsourced contracts base themselves on a balance between electronic and physical communications—the latter going a long way in overcoming the socio-cultural differences and developing much better working relationships.

AGILE PRINCIPLES IN PRACTICE

Big Data solutions development includes database design, modeling of algorithms and applications, and eventually their coding and testing. Many of these solution level activities can occur in an outsourced environment. Agile principles (discussed in Ref. [1]) at solutions development level can be kept in mind for their uniqueness in an outsourced environment. Following are the four groups or types of Agile principles:

Customer-Centric. These principles focus on the external aspect of a project and encourage provisioning of value to the end user. In outsourced contracts, the client side can find these principles valuable and apply them to their own customers in their markets. The customers of the client can be invited to be a part of the outsourcing initiatives to make it easier for the vendor to understand their core needs. These principles apply particularly well where the solution is indeed a customer-facing solution. For outsourced infrastructure and maintenance activities, the role of these customer-centric Agile principles is limited to gathering the requirements for enhancements and the fixing of errors.

Developer-Centric. These principles are focused internally on a project and enable team members to function effectively and efficiently. These are the principles that have immense opportunity to be applied by the vendor of an outsourcing arrangement in arriving at the solution. These Agile principles, however, are more tactical than strategic in nature, more suitable for product development, and are derived from pure Agile methods.

Architecture-Centric. These principles provide the basis for work that offers stability and ongoing improvement in the product as well as the working style of the team. These Agile principles revolving around technical excellence and design are applicable more on the vendor side of an outsourcing arrangement but with substantial inputs from the client side. These principles express a strategic, long-term view of the environment in which a solution operates.

Management-Centric. These principles enable the team to focus on organizing itself to reduce administrative overheads of time and effort, and at the same time, enhance its working style. These Agile principles, including acceptance of changes and self-organization of teams, play a crucial role in BPO and knowledge process outsourcing work.

Collaborations and Intelligence as Functioning Agile

In order to understand the evolving complexities of processes, they are categorized as individual (carried out by a user), organizational (carried out by multiple users), and collaborative (occurring across organization). Technically, they can also be categorized as physical (occurring through face-to-face and paper-based interactions), electronic (occurring through the Internet-based communication medium), and mobile (occurring independent of location).

This categorization of processes is based on original work on processes by Unhelkar [13] and later by Unhelkar and Murugesan [14], wherein a finer categorization is attempted. Figure 9.5 shows the evolving complexity of Agile organizations from a business as well as technical viewpoint. The increasing levels of complexities from business process viewpoints (starting with Broadcast processes and going up to full Collaborative processes) are shown on the left. The right side of Figure 9.5 shows the evolving complexities of information technologies (starting with

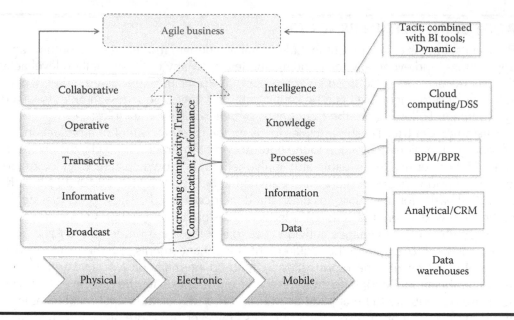

Figure 9.5   Agile businesses make substantial use of business intelligence at all levels.

data and going up to Intelligence). The types of collaborations and the evolving complexities of a collaborative–agile business are discussed in greater detail next.

Types of Collaboration

Physical Collaboration

This is the traditional way in which businesses relate to each other. This is the people-to-people, face-to-face, manual process of collaborating with each other. Physical collaboration is understood as working together. Legalities of such collaborations can be long-drawn and bureaucratic, limiting opportunities for collaborations and agility.

In physical collaborations there is a need to establish partnering organizations, and then setting up an alliance which encompasses both formal and informal agreements, followed by legal contracts and eventually execution of the collaboration. This physical collaboration can be slow and time consuming, leading to a lost market opportunity. Whenever physical collaborations are formed, it is imperative that stakeholders and players in these partnering organizations quickly understand and establish working relationships. The socio-cultural issues in physical collaborations are most crucial. Agility in such physical collaborations is limited as each organization is required to maintain full, and independent operability. Yet, understanding the structure and dynamics of physical organizations provides the basis for their collaborations through electronic and mobile communications technologies.

Electronic Collaboration

An electronic collaboration uses Internet-based technologies to enable automated and continuous exchange of information between suppliers, customers, and intermediaries. This electronic collaboration is supported by tools that facilitate communication and information sharing needs of collaborators either as individuals or in groups. Electronic collaborations, although tool based, still face the challenges of mapping the trust between collaborating organizations during the collaborative work establishment and life cycle. Web service-based solution architectures provide opportunities for organizations to collaborate through their portals. The enhanced ability of information systems to connect and communicate with each other leads to a collaborative opportunity for Agile enterprises. Electronic collaborations open up agile opportunities as they also enable organizations to re-use their IT infrastructure and databases.

Mobile Collaboration

This is an extension of the electronic collaboration with the additional characteristic of being independent of location and time. This is based on the features of mobility that enable multiple parties to connect and collaborate with each other using mobile/wireless devices and networks. Mobility leads to dynamicity in collaborations, enabling real-time sharing of information and knowledge between the different parties that take part in the collaborative work. This results in flexibility and support, and ad hoc relationships between multiple parties, coming together to work together for short-term customer-focused goals. Agility in mobile collaborations is most enhanced as the infrastructure associated with physical and electronic organization is further reduced due to both location and time independence.

Reaching Collaborative Intelligence in Agile Business

Collaborative Intelligence (CI) was discussed by Unhelkar and Tiwary [15] where CI was shown to facilitate the sharing of intelligence across a group of collaborative organizations. CI is achieved through an incremental rise in technologies and complexities starting with data, then information, process, knowledge, and intelligence. The self-serve analytics (SSA) on the Cloud enables collaboration at all levels within and across the organization (see Sidebar).

COLLABORATIONS AND SSA

The type of service offered impacts upon the support and costs. The type of service may vary over time and a mixed approach may be required. The two main types of services:

Self-service—This is mainly where the data products are provided as a service. Others undertake use these products to undertake analysis and value-adding processing. Self-service is often easier to establish, maintain, and cheaper to run. Self-service is often popular with more technologically experienced and those who consume the service as a major part of their job.

Managed Service—This is where the service undertakes much of the analysis and value-added processing on behalf of others. Managed Services often require more effort to establish, maintain, and may incur higher costs. Managed Service is often popular with those who just want a valued-added product for decision-making and do not have the time for Self-service.

Self-service versus Managed Service is often a key in the implementation of Big Data services within an organization as well as being a pathway to adoption. When establishing a Big Data service within a Government transport management agency, concerns around jobs was a prominent theme. To implement the service, the agency started with a selected product offering (an extension of familiar report rendered in real time with selected enhancements) to key stakeholders. As the service becomes valued, funding was secured, and a range of effective easy-to-use products were offered. As the comfort level with the products increased and demand for services increased, more advanced analytics services were supplied.

Self-service was found to be popular with more technically aware people at a desk in back-office roles whose job it was to utilize data. A greater range of products were provided with a Self-service tool but some level of support was still provided. Those with a greater awareness of technology and in back-office roles were more accepting of minimal viable products and more frequent upgrades and iterations.

In contrast, frontline staff or those traveling around more preferred a Managed Service where by highly refined products were provided and the processing was completed for them. Frontline staff also preferred consistency and uniformity of products and showed greater frustration with more agile product releases.

As Big Data grows in maturity and the data analytics capacities and capabilities increase, more of the value-added analysis will be automated. This is especially the case where data are automatically analyzed as part of artificial intelligence, that is, many Big Data services provided will be used by computers rather than people directly.

Collaborative Data and Agility

Collaboration in the electronic form starts by sharing of data with well-connected, reliable, and trustworthy partners. The data sharing allows greater opportunities to re-use data and provide solutions that are based on a variety of data sources. For example, demographic data of a customer, such as her name and address, usually stored by another organization (e.g., a telephone company) need not be stored by the bank. Instead, the data source for this data is made available through a collaboration with a telephony company under "contracts." Such basic collaboration reduces the data storage overheads and contributes toward Agility.

CI and Agility

This is the next level of sharing, that of information, in a generic way so that the customer behavior is also personalized. For example, the bank now provides information on the demographic behavior patterns such as spending styles, income groups, and geographical nuances (e.g., beach or hills or next to a large sporting arena) to the telephone company—once again, under contracts. Sharing of information creates opportunities for timely services and new products—thereby enhancing the agility of the organization.

Collaborative Process and Agility

Collaborative approaches aim to model and share business processes across multiple organization. This collaboration of processes among businesses is the evolving step after the sharing of data and information. For example, there are opportunities to share the process of opening an account in a bank through a commonly created process model by a third party. Alternatively, the process of account opening from a bank can collaborate with the process of verifying the details of a person or, re-use the basic 'name, address, phone number' data and related information from yet another service provider. While the variation in each of these processes is accepted, many of the fundamental processes in modern businesses are streamlined. There is limited value in businesses trying to re-invent the processes that are now routinely known in respective sectors, such as banking, airline, and hospital.

The collaborative advantage comes from re-using and sharing the processes across multiple organizations. Collaborative business processes are built on electronic and mobile communications and, as such, enable businesses to put together new customer-centric processes that they would not be able to do on their own creating process-models for commonly known processes and making those processes available across organizations provide many advantages to those collaborating organization—the most important one being their enhanced ability to respond to changes or, in other words, business agility.

Collaborative Knowledge and Agility

This level shares knowledge about an individual or a group of customers/users across multiple organizations. For example, location, information about a mobile customer (person) is correlated with other bits of information about that customer, such as their buying history, to produce knowledge about that customer and, additionally, about that customer group. This knowledge is invaluable in designing new products and services dynamically—rather than going through a full iteration of market research, prototyping, and customer feedback.

CI and Agility

This is a fully mature implementation of collaboration by a group of organizations within and across multiple industrial sectors with a common goal of enhancing customer experiences. Conversely, a group of organizations at this level could also be the customers themselves, acting in a collaborative manner to achieve higher value. What is most important in a CI environment is that not only are the aforementioned data, information, process, and knowledge being shared, but it is also made available at the right time and place for the participating organizations. Right from data hubs and warehouses through to operational processes and new product development, CI is a positive influence on business agility. The real advantage of CI comes from having a strategy for multiple organizations to share these elements in a timely and succinct fashion.

Reaching Collaborative Business Process

Collaborative business processes were discussed earlier as a part of evolving complexities of collaborative agile business processes. The entire process discussion itself is made up of five increasing levels of complexities—as shown in Figure 9.5, on the left. These are the broadcasting, information, transactive, operative, and collaborative processes that are employed by an agile business. It should be noted that these business processes may themselves not be exclusive to each other, but may coexist within a business as it strives for agility through collaboration. However, understanding each of these types of businesses can also help understand the approach to collaborative business.

Broadcasting Business Processes

This is the unidirectional aspect of the business that provides large-scale broadcasts of its products and services. Physical broadcasting is through print media—including newspapers and brochures. Electronic broadcast includes advertisements and related marketing material on professional and social website. At a very basic level, it is scanning of the company's product brochures and putting them up on the Internet, resulting in what has been known as the brochureware. Mobile broadcasts are the messages appearing on individual user's handsets. Mobile broadcasts are the most convenient way to reach globally dispersed customers that may be on the move. The increasing importance of social media also has to be factored.

Informative Business Processes

This informative aspect of the Internet (e-Information) encompasses provision of information to known or registered parties. Alternatively, information can be put up in the public domain for users/customers to pull that information as required (as against the aforementioned broadcast which is 'pushed'). For example, this aspect of business includes providing basic company contact details like phone, fax, and physical address. As a result, informative aspect of business has minimal maintenance and security requirements.

Transactive Business Processes

The transactive business is what is commonly referred to as e-Commerce or transactionware. This is the beginning of collaboration. The earlier EDI (Electronic Data Interchange) has now evolved into Internet-based financial transactions involving multiple parties. Transactive business on the web involves ability to send and receive messages and thereby conduct business transactions, by communicating with multiple businesses behind the web interface. Examples of these transactions include bookings and reservations, posting feedbacks, buying goods, and seeking services (the last two being paid for using another collaborative party—such as a credit card provider).

Operative Business Processes

This is the shifting of the operational aspect of the business on the Internet. Physically, this used to involve detailed administration of the operations of the business. Electronically, this is the shifting of HR, timesheets, payroll, and personnel systems on the web. Furthermore, internal production and inventory processes are also moved on the Web. Operative business results in close alignment of the business to its customers, suppliers, and internally to its employees. As a result, there is a large component of business to business (B2B) transactions in operative businesses.

Collaborative Business Processes

Collaborative business encompasses the previous four levels of business but further expands it for multiple organizations. Electronic communications facilitate data, information, process, knowledge, and intelligence to be shared across many organizations—as and when required. This sharing can result in broadcasting of marketing material, provision of information, ability to conduct multi-party financial transactions and also share the operational aspects of each other's business. This is a truly collaborative business scenario—with the customer being the eventual beneficiary.

Ongoing Knowledge Synchronization in a Learning Agile Organization

Holistic Customer—The Ultimate Goal of Business Agility

A holistic, single, 360° view of a customer can only be supported by a highly synchronized, unified, and minimal-friction organization. While Big Data is an enabler, its ultimate value is in business agility. This agility, however, has to result in a holistic, 360° view of (and for) a customer. Figure 9.6 shows this holistic, single customer view [16]. The view itself is holistic but the various business functions and systems enabling this view are themselves continuously changing. For example, the underlying Master Data Management (MDM) [17] initiative of an organization needs to continuously update itself based on data sourced from the customer.

An Agile organization is not a static organization but, instead, its continuously changing, evolving, and learning. Such a learning organization is augmenting its capabilities with Big Data technologies and analytics. Figure 9.6 shows the need for continuous updates to customer profiles, billing information, products and services, and monitoring the usage of the solutions by the customer—to result in a unified view. These aforementioned activities are further supported by Customer Relationship Management (CRM) systems, market analysis, billing systems, usage statistics, and financial management systems. The parties involved in this holistic exercise are the individual and the organization—whose capabilities are enhanced with Big data analytics and technologies. An important part of this capability enhancement is the knowledge synchronization and usage resulting from Big Data. The users and the organization have to continuously share and enhance their knowledge.

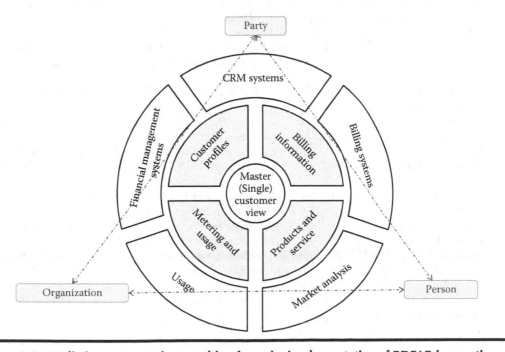

Figure 9.6 Holistic customer view resulting from the implementation of BDFAB in practice.

Discussion Questions

1. Why is it important to discuss Agility in the discussions on ODBA?
2. Describe the practical way in which leadership, communications, iteration, and dissipation plays a role in enabling an Agile organization? Why are each of these important for Big Data? *(hint—because Big Data is a enabler of Agile business)*
3. How would you envision an Agile organization? Discuss how each factor influencing business agility can benefit and utilize Big Data?
4. How does data become intelligence? Discuss the transformational process based on Agile and Big Data utilization.
5. Why is CAMS as a balancing act more appropriate than a pure Agile method in developing Big data solutions? And why is such a balancing act needing good leadership *(hint—because it is dynamic)*
6. What is meant by a Collaborative holistic 360° view from both customer and internal staff? Describe with examples?

References

1. Unhelkar, B. (2013). *The Art of Agile Practice: A Composite Approach for Projects and Organizations*, CRC Press, Boca Raton, FL.
2. Unhelkar, B. (2010). Agile in Practice: A Composite Approach, Cutter Executive Report, Jan 2010, Vol. 11, No 1, Agile Product and Project Management Practice, Boston, MA.
3. Unhelkar, B. (2017). *Big Data Strategies for Agile Business*, CRC Press, Boca Raton, FL.
4. Unhelkar, B. (2014). Lean-Agile Tautology. Cutter Executive Update, 3 of 5, Vol. 15, No 5, Agile Product & Project Management Practice, Boston, MA.
5. Murugesan, S. and Unhelkar. B. (2004). A roadmap for successful ICT innovation: Turning great ideas into successful implementations, *Cutter IT Journal*, 17(11).
6. Unhelkar, B. (2012). Avoiding Method Friction: A CAMS-Based Perspective—Cutter Executive Report, 20 Aug 2012, Vol. 13, No 6, Agile Product and Project Management Practice, Boston, MA.
7. Unhelkar, B. (2011). *Green ICT Strategies & Applications: Using Environmental Intelligence*, CRC Press, Boca Raton, FL.
8. Unhelkar, B. (2010). *Handbook of Green ICT: Technical, Methodological and Social Perspectives*, IGI Global, Hershey, PA.
9. Unhelkar, B., Ghanbary, A., and Younessi, H. (2009). *Collaborative Business Process Engineering and Global Organizations: Frameworks for Service Integration*. Business Science Reference.
10. Ghanbary, A. and Unhelkar, B. (2007). Collaborative Business Process Engineering (CBPE) across Multiple Organisations in a Cluster. *Proceedings of IRMA Conference*. IRMA 2007. Vancouver, Canada. 19–23 May.
11. Unhelkar, B. (2003). Understanding Collaborations and Clusters in the e-Business World. *We-B Conference*, (www.we-bcentre.com; with Edith Cowan University), Perth, 24–25 Nov, 2003.
12. Arunatileka, S. and Ginige, A. (2003). The Seven E's in eTransformation: A Strategic eTransformation Model. Presented at *IADIS International Conference XXTEMPIECTAEXXe-Society* 2003, Lisbon, Portugal; Ginige, A. A New Paradigm for Developing Evolutionary Software to Support E-Business, In *Handbook of Software Engineering and Knowledge Engineering*, Vol. 2. Edited by S. K. Chang. World Scientific, 2002, pp. 711–725.
13. Unhelkar, B. (2003). *Process Quality Assurance for UML-Based Projects*, Pearson Education (Addison-Wesley), Boston, MA.

14. Unhelkar, B. and Murugesan, S. (2010). *The Enterprise Mobile Applications Development Framework*, Computer.org/ITpro, IEEE Computer Society Publication, USA, pp. 33–39.
15. Unhelkar, B. and Tiwary, A. (2010). Business Intelligence 2010: Delivering the Goods or Standing Us Up? *Collaborative Intelligence, Cutter IT Journal*, 23(6), 13–21.
16. Tiwary, A., and Unhelkar, B.
17. David, L. (2009). *Master Data Management*, Elsevier Butterworth-Heinemann Press, Oxford.

CASE STUDIES

C

This section contains three case studies based on organizations that have embarked on the Outcome-Driven Business Architecture (ODBA) journey.

The current state of maturity of the organizations in terms of their business capabilities (based on their existing Enterprise Architecture (EA)—and Business Architecture (BA), if available) are thoroughly examined in these case studies. This is followed by an in-depth exercise in terms of their desired future states. A commonly understood and accepted ODBA within the organization is established in the context of American Productivity Quality Center (APQC). A measure of all capability gaps across the business is established using a variety of techniques including surveys, interviews, and workshops. These assessments also gain consensus on which capability gaps to address most urgently—at both a divisional and an enterprise level. A series of recommendations are developed to close these gaps; the recommendations are then incorporated into strategy execution initiatives.

Case Study Methodology

The case studies included in this book use APQC Process Classification Framework (PCF) to define the business capabilities. The reason to use APQC as a Capability Model is based on wide-ranging use of APQC–PCF for processes definition by many organizations. The assumption is if a process model is well defined, it could be extended for the business capability definitions. The APQC PCF hierarchical model is an internationally recognized model that is tailored to different industry's needs. The APQC model is therefore adopted as the Business Capability reference model for the case studies.

The process for assessing the Business Capabilities is defined in each case study. This process involves determining which capabilities are required to deliver the Strategy. Those capabilities are identified by mapping the strategic initiatives of the Corporate Strategy to APQC capabilities at 'Level 2' of the capability map as discussed in Chapter 5. Each case study has adopted a different method of assessing the business capabilities.

The assessment information is used in developing the "Business on a Page" model, which as the name suggests, represents the key capabilities of each case on a single page. Essentially, this is the "base map" upon which contains various different layers of information to present the information developed and uncovered during the BA. The "Business on a Page" model represents the Business capabilities at the level they were assessed and it is upon this that the Capability Assessment heat map (depicted throughout this document) is layered.

The heat map graphically depicts the status of a capability gap. The assessment criteria are defined by organizations at the time of ODBA framework definition. The assessment layout is depicted in Table 10.1.

Table 10.2 depicts a Sample of the business capability assessment used across all the case studies.

1B Business capability assessment (based on Traffic lights) *Business capability Name (using APQC format should show NN.MM Name. For example, 1.2 Develop business strategy depicts APQC category 1 and process 2*	
Description	Business capability Name (using APQC format should show NN.MM.XX "Name." For example, "1.2.1 Develop overall mission statement" depicts APQC category 1 and process 2 and activity 1.
Issues	• Current gaps in this capability
Impact	• Impact on the strategic outcomes
Recommendation	• Recommendations to fill in this Gap

1.2 Develop business strategy	
Description	1.2.1 Develop overall mission statement 1.2.2 Evaluate strategic options to achieve the objectives 1.2.3 Select long-term business strategy 1.2.4 Coordinate and align functional and process strategies 1.2.5 Create organizational design (structure, governance, reporting, etc.)
Issues	• Need better insight management • No strategy for "Big data" • Not focused on the future; we need to aggressively look at the future; we don't have a group focusing on "Beyond Tomorrow" type of activities • Insufficient focus on innovation
Impact	• Missed opportunities as first mover (opportunity of being the first with an idea/product in the market) advantages in growth categories • We still have silo activities in various categories and brands
Recommendation	• Align with the enterprise approach to strategy development • Corporate strategy needs to embrace a broader perspective at a certain stage • Refreshing strategy needs to be more frequent

Chapter 10

Business Architecture and Capability Case Study 1— Manufacturing Industry

Introduction to the Case Study

Business Context

This business case study is of *GreenFood* Private Limited, a mid-sized fast consumer goods manufacturing company. *GreenFood* is currently producing many ready and pre-cooked meals. The organization has acquired established brands (e.g., a meat business) over several years. The current customers are food and supermarket retail chains. The Board of Management (BOM) of *GreenFood* is putting the final changes on a new strategy to address the next five years growth and goals of the company. This new plan is deemed necessary by a quickly changing market environment *GreenFood* operates in. The indications are showing that most of this change is here to stay and is a permanent structural change rather than cyclical movement.

After many years of making record profits, *GreenFood* finds the profits are decreasing and have halved in the last two years. These profit results are significantly below the target return for the business and for some departments, it is below cost of capital. The BOM finds the current trends in *GreenFood* manufacturing business are not sustainable and change to the way *GreenFood* conducts its business is inevitable. All the divisions that make up *GreenFood* are challenged with the task of seeking out initiatives that improve profitability.

The BOM strategy has three major directions for *GreenFood*, each one with its own action plans and time schedule, and each one very important to the future success of *GreenFood*. The three strategic directions are:

- Secure profitability
- Change from a product focus to a product and services focus
- Invest and grow in new markets

GreenFood's operational and utility costs are increasing enormously. Various taxes, insurance, compliance costs, factory wages, and general overheads are on the rise as well. At the same time, the market is not allowing recovery of these costs, margins are being squeezed and profits reduced. *GreenFood* is maintaining a strong market share in the retail market but this is coming at a high operational cost. Simultaneously, *GreenFood* is feeling a lot of price pressure in the category market from imports flooding in from lower cost countries.

The Supply Chain Division is embarking on a comprehensive cost-saving program using a combination of capital expenditure and a review of processes, both aimed at productivity and efficiency improvements. Making products more price competitive is a must, otherwise volumes start to fall and *GreenFood* loses economies of scale.

The reduction in profits and increase in the operational costs of *GreenFood* necessitate the market assessment of current products and opportunity to introduce new products and services not part of the current offering. It needs a comprehensive review including market forces, competitors, manufacturing, and sourcing. *GreenFood* is going through the difficult task of aligning with the same speed and agility as the market environment. This project's objective is to establish *GreenFood's* Business Architecture. This comprises a representation of the functional capabilities of the business as depicted in Figure 10.1. An enterprise-wide assessment of the current state of maturity of organization's business capabilities as well as a desired future state of these capabilities is conducted to enable the organization to achieve its strategy.

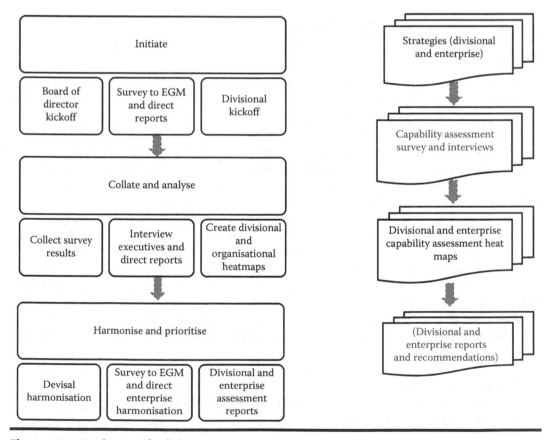

Figure 10.1 Project methodology.

This case study provides *GreenFood's* journey of developing a business architecture framework, capability assessment, and achieving the following objectives:

- Articulate and gain consensus on business capability requirements for each business unit to achieve strategic intents of *GreenFood*;
- Ensure that *GreenFood* is prepared for growth and profitability;
- Ensure investments of time, resources, and money are made in a way that best support the business strategy;
- Maximize transformational opportunities presented to *GreenFood*;
- Discover harmonization opportunities that cross business units and functional areas to drive efficiency and reduced costs;
- Understand the implications of cost optimization efforts on current and future business capabilities;
- Provide a reference point for governance of current and future investments, projects, and actions.

The "Business Architecture" project must adapt to meet the changing requirements of the business. The current strategy is still in vogue and guiding the organization and hence, forms the basis of assessment of business capabilities. The project involves the senior executives of the business and their direct reports in surveys, one-on-one meetings, and workshops right from the beginning so as to gain their support and consensus for such a large sweeping change. The ODBA project as depicted in Figure 10.2 is divided into three distinct phases:

1. Establish Business Architecture Framework to setup the business capabilities framework within the *GreenFood* (as discussed in Chapters 5 and 8).
2. Assess Business Capabilities to support the current strategy based on Business architecture framework as discussed in Chapter 6.
3. Assess Business Capabilities to support new strategy as discussed in Chapters 7 and 8.

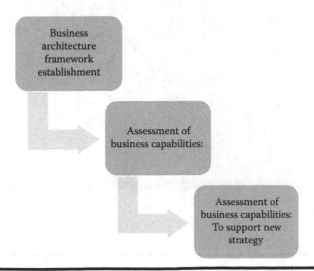

Figure 10.2   Adopting change in strategy.

The Intellectual Proprietary (IP) and capability that is established in the first phase of 'Establishment' is leveraged way beyond (and iterated upon) its initial use, and is re-used and developed further in Phases II and III (discussed in Chapter 4) of the project. This section describes the methodology approach and deliverables of each of these three stages in detail.

Business Architecture Framework Establishment

The current information technology (IT) investment demand and supply is mapped as depicted in Figure 10.3. The initial assessment of *GreenFood* issues established that, due to high demand for IT projects, most of the IT management staff were only servicing the demand requirements. The *GreenFood* employee personal performance assessment required senior managers and executives to generate new ideas and were rewarded on the number of ideas that were generated. The idea creation was recorded in a 'new idea and suggestion' system. The management had to provide details of the idea and how it is beneficial to *GreenFood*. The delivery of most ideas required upgrades or acquisition of new IT. This was working favorably for idea creators as they could tick the box for the innovation part of performance reviews, passing on the responsibility of delivery of the idea to the IT department [1]. The resources of the IT department were stretched in assessing the idea validity, feasibility, and implementation impact as depicted in Figure 10.3, leaving little time and resources for actual implementation.

The information department devised a development life cycle as depicted in Figure 10.4. This life cycle adoption was difficult because the amount of resources required to plan the projects was very high. This was especially busy during the annual employee performance assessment period

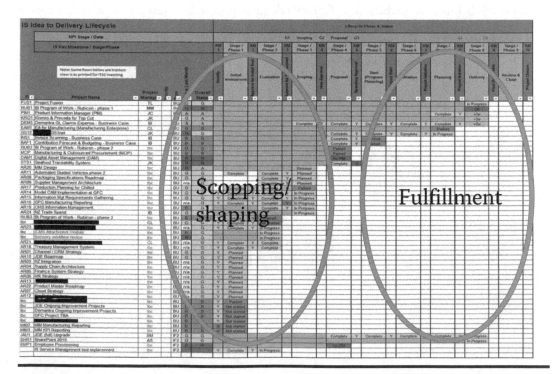

Figure 10.3 Sample of typical IT organization with most of the resources allocated to manage demand.

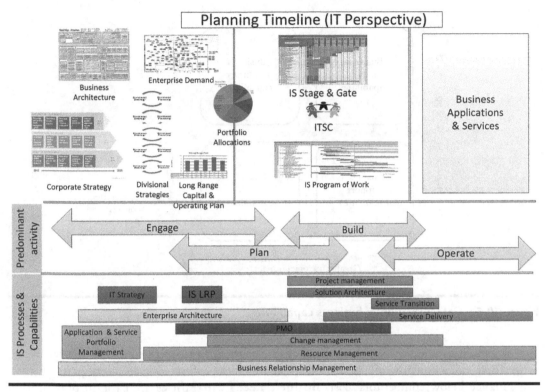

Figure 10.4 Allocating resources to fulfill demand is difficult without knowing where to focus.

as the number of new ideas increased exponentially at that time. In absence of any prioritization by the senior executives, the loudest voice was heard, and projects proposed by these loud voices were implemented. The IT resources were blamed for not being efficient and unable to implement even simple ideas. This perception of "inefficient and ineffective IT systems" was demoralizing to the IT staff and the turnover was higher than industry average. The IT budgets were exhausted in assessments of ideas, scoping, and planning, leaving little resources for delivery.

Initially this phase involved establishing a Capability Reference model that represented the organization's business. The American Productivity Quality Center (APQC) Capability Model was already in use by the Enterprise Architecture (EA) team. Because this hierarchical model is an internationally recognized model that is tailored to manufacturing-type organizations, it was adopted as the Business Capability reference model as shown in Figure 10.5.

The business capabilities assessment results in the following categories:

- **Core capabilities** like Business Advantage, business **essential** capabilities, for example, Business Basic or supporting capabilities, for example, Business **support** or needs.
- **Business Advantage capabilities** directly contribute to the customer value proposition and have a high impact on *GreenFood* financials. These capabilities should be among the best in performance among organization's peers and they should come at an acceptable cost. **Business support capabilities** have a high contribution in direct support of advantage capabilities. These capabilities should be at least at the industry level of performance at a competitive cost. **Business basic capabilities** may not be visible to the customer but contribute to company's business focus and have a big impact on the bottom line. These

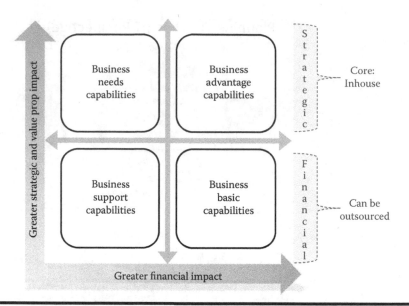

Figure 10.5   Categorization of business capabilities.

capabilities should focus on efficiency improvement; especially in high-volume work. Their value contribution is assured when they are performed at industry parity performance below competitors' cost. **Business needs capabilities** are basic to organization processing. These should run at industry level performance below competitors' cost. They can be candidates for alternate sourcing. Figure 10.6 depicts a sample of the capability assessment of the supply and demand management domains of the business capabilities. The business capability assessment includes mapping business capabilities with the current project initiatives as shown in Figure 10.2. The mapping of business capabilities and projects/actions highlighted some areas have several actions planned but no resources were allocated to these actions. The gaps in *GreenFood*'s capacity to achieve its strategic intents are assessed based on the resources allocated, skills of the resources, information management, and knowledge management dimension of the business capabilities. The initial setup of the BA framework was challenging. In this case, it is appropriate to adopt a pragmatic BA framework. *GreenFood* is facing market-driven challenges and internal resource constraints in delivering new initiatives of speeding up the growth and investing in new markets. This requires organization resources to be allocated to core business activities and reduce the resource allocation from other activities which are not required to achieve strategic outcomes.

The process to assess the business capabilities is also developed during this stage of the project. This process determines the capabilities required to deliver the strategy. Those capabilities are identified by mapping the strategic initiatives of the corporate strategy to APQC capabilities at 'Level 2' of the capability map. A questionnaire is developed that evaluates only those capabilities. The questionnaire requests three pieces of information.

- The current maturity state of a capability (based on a Capability Maturity Model (CMM) where 1 represented low maturity and 5 represented best-in class)

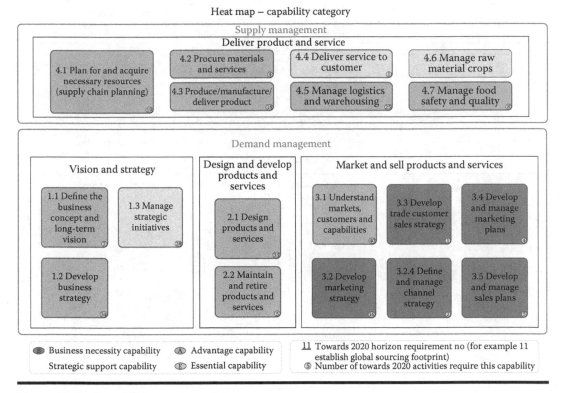

Figure 10.6   Capability assessment.

■ The maturity state that the capability should be at, to enable the strategy
■ The importance to the business of this capability

The questionnaire is comprised of 50 questions covering all 12 APQC categories at 'Level 2' business capabilities. In conjunction with the questionnaire, a follow-up interview with the respondent to the questionnaire is carried out to delve into significant gaps between the current and future capability assessment. This information provides the supporting content to justify the capability gaps uncovered from the survey. Figure 10.7 depicts developing the key capabilities of *GreenFood* Business on a single page. This "Business on a Page" model becomes the "base map" upon which various layers of information that are developed/uncovered are overlain. The model represents the Business capabilities at the assessed level and it is upon this that the Capability Assessment heat map (discussed above) is layered. The heat map graphically depicts the status of a capability gap where the gaps of "High" indicates gap >1.45, "Medium" between 0.6 and 1.45, and "Low" <0.6.

The business divisions of *GreenFood* are quite diverse and it was determined to have a divisional perspective and enterprise assessment of Business capabilities as depicted in Figure 10.8. To provide the means to analyze the data it was proposed to survey and interview 60+ people. A database to house the information was established.

A challenge of the project is to try and gain organizational consensus to address the priority capabilities for the organization. The project set out to achieve a "Bottom Up" assessment of the Business capabilities to support the strategy. In addition to this assessment, harmonization workshops were designed to gain a consensus on immediate and near future priority capabilities for the organization to focus on.

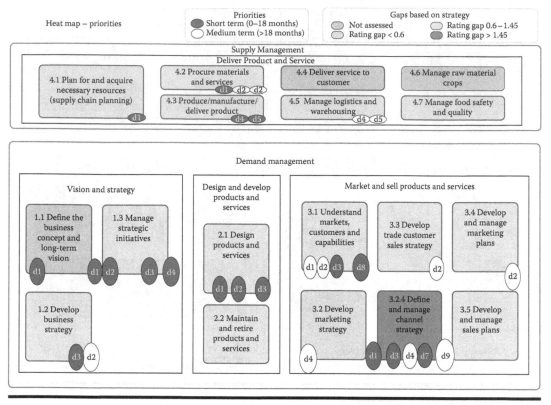

Figure 10.7 Overall capability assessment.

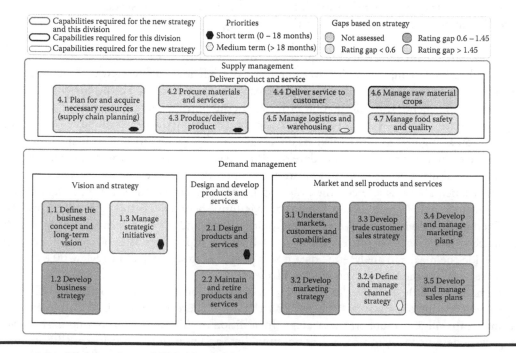

Figure 10.8 Divisional capabilities heat map.

Current Business Capability Assessment

The project was kicked off with the BOM's approval to conduct the surveys and individual interviews of the all divisional Executive General Managers (EGMs) and their direct reports. The selected participants from each division including divisional EGMs are individually interviewed (total of 60 interviews) to understand, among other things:

- Details of their divisional strategy
- Review survey areas where capability gap is >2
- Identify risks and challenges
- Alignment with other divisions

Each division's harmonization workshops were conducted and the EGMs nominated their focus priorities (five short terms-0–18 months and five medium term-18–36 months) capabilities gaps. Divisional reports were documented and distributed to each division's participants. For each priority area the report included recommendations on how to address the closure of capability gaps. Based on the divisional priorities a consolidated enterprise view of *GreenFood*'s priorities was developed and presented to the BOM. The strategic outcome and actions are mapped with the business capabilities and assessment as depicted in Figure 10.9.

Alignment with New Strategy

As the project developed, the organization's senior management independently embarked on a comprehensive re-development of *GreenFood*'s strategy to account for the rapidly changing

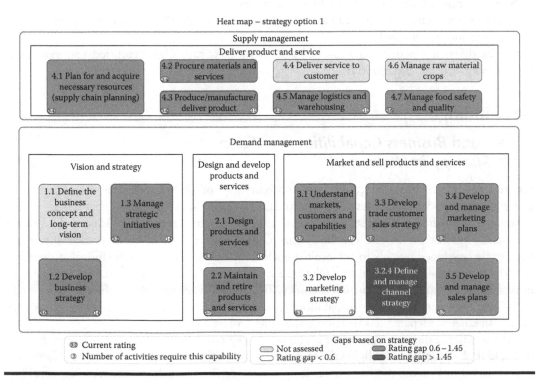

Figure 10.9   Heat map for strategy option 1.

business conditions. While this does not invalidate the work being done in the Business architecture project, it does require some of that work is extended to incorporate the new strategy. The changes in the strategy 'Vision New' were adopted as shown in Figure 10.2. It is at this stage that the BOM requested a third horizon of the BA project to align with the new strategy, which was nearing completion as shown in Figure 10.10. The focus of this phase is to establish BOM consensus on priority business capability gaps to achieve the new strategy. The new strategy outlines three strategic directions as stated before

- Secure profitability
- Change from being a product company to product and service
- Invest to grow in new markets

To expedite this phase, the project assumed that the assessment of capabilities for the current strategy is still be largely valid when it came to the first two strategic horizons. The third horizon is for the long-term future, and was deemed to require a comprehensive evaluation of the capabilities required to achieve that strategy. Coupled with the timing of the third horizon, "invest to grow in new markets" was discounted from consideration in this phase.

The capabilities required for the first two strategic directions (Secure profitability and Change from being Product Company to product and service) are determined by looking at the detailed actions already identified in the project work. This identified additional capabilities that are not required for the current strategy.

A revised Divisional Heat map is drawn up which highlighted:

- all the capabilities required to achieve the strategy,
- the current state of a capability and the gap to desired capability maturity (for current) if it is previously evaluated,
- The divisional priorities are assessed against the new capabilities required new vision and strategies of the organization.

Key Findings

GreenFood *Business Capabilities for 'Vision New' Strategy in Horizon III*

Figure 10.11 depicts the radar graph of the capability gaps of *GreenFood* strategy. The appendices contain further radar graphs detailing each pillar of the *GreenFood* and divisional strategies. The major gaps identified are in systems, processes, and people management. "Vision new" strategy as assessed against the current capability gap highlights a number of business capabilities that need to be developed quickly to achieve the goals setup for "secure our profitability." The project assessed the capabilities required for each of the strategies as shown in Figure 10.1 against the business capabilities required and current maturity. The summarized strategies as shown in Table 10.1 shows the alignment of business capabilities required to achieve strategic outcomes and provides insight in current preparedness to achieve strategies and business goals.

The business capability assessment is mapped to key *GreenFood* planned activities as depicted in Table 10.2. Table 10.2 highlights the capability gaps in achieving strategic outcomes. Table 10.2 is also useful in briefing the focus areas for planned activities to achieve the required capability rating for strategic directions.

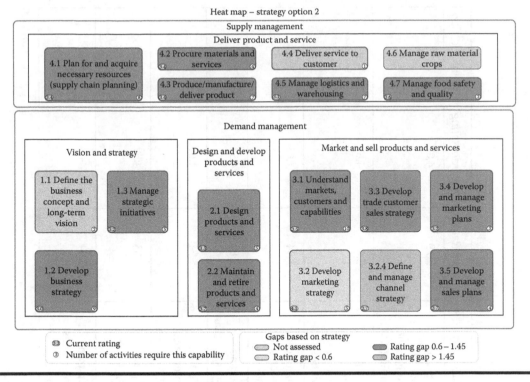

Figure 10.10   Heat map for strategy option 2.

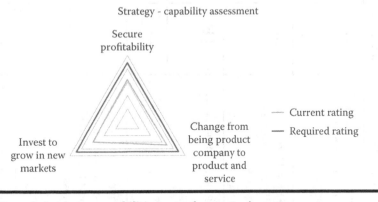

Figure 10.11   Sample business capabilities gaps for strategic outcomes.

Table 10.1   Assessment of the Overall *GreenFood* Capability

Key Strategy	Current Rating	Required Rating	Gap
Secure profitability	3.20	4.46	1.26
Change from being product company to products and services	3.43	4.44	1.01
Invest to grow in new markets	2.97	4.46	1.49

Table 10.2   Assessment Data of the Overall *GreenFood* Capability

Key Strategy Activities	Requirement	APQC_ID	Capability	Current Rating	Required Rating	GreenFood Gap
Supplier of choice • Deliver meaningful solutions through category leadership and strong interdependent relationships. • Customers recognize our expertise and turn to *GreenFood* first to solve their evolving requirements. • Customers trust us and we deliver.	Dedicated teams aligned to our customers and markets.	6.1	Develop and manage HR planning, policies, and strategies.	2.79	4.02	1.23
	Good breadth of intelligence across all categories.	3.1	Understand markets, customers, and capabilities.	3.61	4.62	1.01
	Strong negotiation skills.	3.3	Develop trade customer sales strategy.	3.94	4.63	0.69
		3.5	Develop and manage sales plans.	3.83	4.52	0.69
	Leverage relationships within channels to support the broader business.	3.3	Develop trade customer sales strategy.	3.94	4.63	0.69
		3.5	Develop and manage sales plans.	3.83	4.52	0.69
	Build longer term strategic relationships with key customers.	3.3	Develop trade customer sales strategy.	3.94	4.63	0.69

(Continued)

Table 10.2 (Continued) Assessment Data of the Overall *GreenFood* Capability

Key Strategy Activities	Requirement	APQC_ID	Capability	Current Rating	Required Rating	GreenFood Gap
Consumer loyalty • Develop our insights capability thus providing a superior product offering and building consumers trust in our brands. • Invest in understanding consumers to ensure a leadership position.	Ongoing consumer research.	3.1	Understand markets, customers, and capabilities.	3.61	4.62	1.01
	Agile and innovative leader (fast adoption of trends)	2.1	Design products and services.	3.45	4.54	1.10
	Utilize global networks and alliances to obtain information.	3.1	Understand markets, customers, and capabilities.	3.61	4.62	1.01
	Leverage and invest in our brands and products to drive growth.	3.2	Develop marketing strategy.	4.27	4.61	0.34
	Knowledge of chef and user needs.	3.1	Understand markets, customers, and capabilities.	3.61	4.62	1.01
	Communicate trends such a new food habits, current food hypes.	3.1	Understand markets, customers, and capabilities.	3.61	4.62	1.01
	Become technically savvy and reach consumers in new ways.	3.2.4	Define and manage channel strategy.	2.83	4.35	1.53

(Continued)

Table 10.2 (Continued)   Assessment Data of the Overall *GreenFood* Capability

Key Strategy Activities	Requirement	APQC_ID	Capability	Current Rating	Required Rating	GreenFood Gap
Optimise portfolio value • Use portfolio management to align resources to deliver category goals. • Balance and invest company resources aligned to our desired product portfolio positioning.	Check and measure where our resources are being allocated.	2.1	Design products and services.	3.45	4.54	1.10
		8.8	Manage internal controls.	3.15	4.32	1.17
		8.1	Perform planning and management accounting.	3.01	4.25	1.24
	Specific product and product group targets and investment levels for; invest to grow, reinforce, and expand, maximize profit, hold/analyze, divest, or exit.	1.2	Develop business strategy.	3.04	4.09	1.05
		2.1	Design products and services.	3.45	4.54	1.10
	Consistent message and understanding in relation to what categories received what investment.	1.2	Develop business strategy.	3.04	4.09	1.05
		2.1	Design products and services.	3.45	4.54	1.10
	Fast track growth of highly profitable categories.	2.1	Design products and services.	3.45	4.54	1.10
	Optimize resource allocations.	2.1	Design products and services.	3.45	4.54	1.10
	An optimized portfolio that exploits our strengths and best market opportunities.	1.2	Develop business strategy.	3.04	4.09	1.05
		2.1	Design products and services.	3.45	4.54	1.10

(Continued)

Table 10.2 (*Continued*)   Assessment Data of the Overall *GreenFood* Capability

Key Strategy Activities	Requirement	APQC_ID	Capability	Current Rating	Required Rating	GreenFood Gap
Profitable future growth platforms • Identify and invest in profitable and sustainable new growth platforms aligned to the vision • Seek new business opportunities to reach the stated goals of 14% ROIC and $2.5 billion	A concerted effort toward establishing an alternative distribution mode (Go direct, own shop, on-line).	3.2.4	Define and manage channel strategy.	2.83	4.35	1.53
	Invest in new product trends.	1.2	Develop business strategy.	3.04	4.09	1.05
		2.1	Design products and services.	3.45	4.54	1.10
	Align resources to evaluate commercial viability of new technologies.	1.1	Define the business concept and long-term vision.	–	–	–
		6.1	Develop and manage HR planning, policies, and strategies.	2.79	4.02	1.23
	Trade off our infrastructure and strategic alliances.	1.2	Develop business strategy.	3.04	4.09	1.05
		1.1	Define the business concept and long-term vision.	–	–	–
	Proactively seek merger and acquisitions.	1.1	Define the business concept and long-term vision.	–	–	–

Table 10.3 describes the key findings of the business capabilities assessment. A sample assessment is depicted in Figure 10.11. The heat map depicted in Figures 10.9 and 10.10 is used to determine divisional priorities for the new strategy, and adjustments are made to the previous list of priorities to reflect the new strategies. The consolidated list of divisional priorities then provides the enterprise priorities that are presented and confirmed with the BOM. The combined results are plotted against the activities planned and gaps are identified as shown in Figure 10.11.

Secure Our Profitability

The reasons for the decline in *GreenFood* profitability are attributed to an increase in manufacturing costs combined with retailers exerting their buying power to reduce *GreenFood's* profit margins. At the time of the project the Australian dollar was strong and imported goods were competing on price and quality with locally manufactured goods. Table 10.4 depicts survey data. The current gaps in business capabilities are shown in Figure 10.12 **Secure our profitability** radar graphs. It highlights key areas to improve.

The key findings are that globalization[*] is exacting more demands on manufacturers' abilities to achieve growth and profitability, and meet performance objectives. Pressure is being placed on process and plans to develop real agility to adapt rapidly to volatile business conditions, and simultaneously meet customer demand for products and services with right-first-time production. Right-first-time production means there is minimal scrap, rework, or urgent manufacturing process re-engineering when production begins on a new product. It enables *GreenFood* to reach the market with new products faster, increasing their window of opportunity while reducing costs, defects, and risks. Establishing the right priorities, strategies, and discipline becomes of paramount importance. Equally important is the prioritization of technology investments that enable and support. The organization requires a streamlined product supply—that is, design through production and service processes over the full life cycle. *GreenFood* brings together capabilities from different technology areas such as Supply Chain Analytics and Visibility, Supply Chain Planning (SCP), Supply Chain Execution, Enterprise Resource Planning, Business Intelligence (BI), Sales and operations planning and customer relationship management. Table 10.5 lists the business capabilities required to achieve the goals setup for "**Secure profitability**." Table 10.5 utilizes the APQC notation to define the business capabilities required to meet strategic outcomes. The pre-requisites define the activities to perform to meet the strategic goal, for example, "secure Profitability" requires *GreenFood* to define the business strategy to achieve this outcome, sent to all levels and agreed upon at the departments and division level as to the expected business outcome. The business capabilities required to achieve this outcome are defined in APQC[†] format (12.6.1 means the APQC category, process, and activity).

GreenFood **organizational structure.** The new strategy implementation requires a change in current *GreenFood* Structure and resourcing (6.1). The new structure needs to align with the new vision and skills required. The new vision requires a different skill set in customer management. The customer base and definition are changing due to a change in the vision servicing end customers who are purchasing from retailers. The customer base is also increasing from a handful customers to a larger country population. *GreenFood* needs clear accountabilities

---

[*] This is a summarized extract from the Hype Cycle for Manufacturing Product Life Cycle and Operations Management, 2011 by Simon F Jacobson, Marc Halpern, Leif Eriksen Gartner Publication Date 27 July 2011/ ID Number G00214960.

[†] https//www.apqc.org/pcf.

Table 10.3 Key Findings Summary

Area	*Finding*

Over all observations	• Many activities are planned without due consideration for the skills and resources required. The assumption of *GreenFood's* capacity to take additional tasks and activities is not supported by the assessment of business capabilities and has following issues:
	  – Too many activities in the short term
	  – Multiple stream of activities defined with same EGM owners
	  – Short-term load on capabilities that may need more than 24 months to build

GreenFood structure	• *GreenFood* structure needs to realign from current "Doer" to "Thinker and Doer" skillset. So far, divisions have been autonomous in planning the projects and program; in the new strategy, many of the projects and plans need to be managed as a portfolio to gain maximum value for the investments and realigns the current *GreenFood* structure. • Collaboration within *GreenFood* teams to reduce over-engineering of products and bringing estimated costs closer to actual production costs.
IT	• IT should be used to enable business and requires investment in new technology in the area of consumer contacts. Investigation of the collaboration of Information management and operational technology to optimize operation costs • Acquire resources with specialties of insights, culinary, consumer services, direct to end user and digital skills.
Business strategy	• Limited activity to close Capability Gaps (for advantage capability or strategic support capability). The capabilities required for "Invest to grow new markets" are not defined until the approach to grow in new market is finalized and the operational model is defined ("go to market" strategy).
Program management	• Silo approach for many actions. A silo approach may result in same capabilities being developed differently by different divisions. This may require restructuring some of the program office structures. Implement project management discipline across the teams.
Initiative management	• Multiple customer and consumer service strategies are in place. No holistic approach to tailor customer contacts based on the consumer/customer segments. • Training of staff in LEAN methodology is required. • Evolve manufacturing into a focused center-of-excellence model.
HR and payroll management	• The new strategy initiates a change not seen in *GreenFood* for a long time. This requires change management to be defined and planned with the new direction in mind.

Table 10.4 Secure Our Profitability Assessment Data

Requirement	Current Rating	Required Rating	Gaps
Achieve greater alignment across units	3.27	4.46	1.19
Drive out cost, improve productivity	2.92	4.44	1.52
Fix underperforming *GreenFood* categories, grow others	3.02	4.46	1.44
Optimize supply chains	2.93	4.45	1.51
Retune recent acquisitions	2.89	4.43	1.55

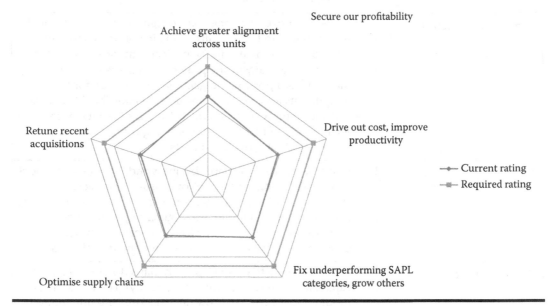

Figure 10.12 Strategy radar graph—Secure our profitability.

and communication of critical priorities to *GreenFood* staff. The gaps highlight overlaps where resources are split across each of the divisions; the new structure minimizes this overlap by realigning resources and acquiring resources with specialties of insights, culinary, consumer services, direct to end user, and digital.

Investment Planning

The current investment plan needs a new framework for the investment. As discussed in Chapter 7, the business capability response is mapped to the agreed IT outcomes of business cost, revenue-based allocation, business satisfaction, and the capability to align with the strategic outcomes. Figure 10.13 provides a sample mapping of the survey information against the business outcomes. The business capability assessment data is mapped to the IT gaps in governance, quality of information, information availability for decision-making, skills of resources managing the life cycle of the information from collection, to analysis. These mappings are then used to define the business outcomes.

Table 10.5 Business Capabilities Required to Achieve "Secure Profitability" Strategic Goals

Pre-requisites	Business Capability Required	Related Capabilities
Business strategy is defined for enterprise and divisions. Divisional strategies defined and aligned with the enterprise strategy.	• 12.6.1 Create and manage organizational performance strategy (11071) • 12.6.2 Benchmark performance (11072) • 7.4 Manage enterprise information (10565) • 12.4 Manage change (11074) • 3.1 Understand markets, customers, and capabilities (10101) • 1.2 Develop business strategy (10015) • 4.1 Plan for and acquire necessary resources (supply chain planning) (10215) • 4.3 Produce/Manufacture/Deliver product (10217) • 4.5 Manage logistics and warehousing (10219)	• 6.1 Develop and manage HR planning, policies, and strategies (10409) • 1.3 Manage strategic initiatives (10016) • 2.1 Design products and services (11681) • 3.2 Develop marketing strategy (10102) • 8.3 Perform general accounting and reporting (10730) • 6.1 Develop and manage HR planning, policies, and strategies (10409)

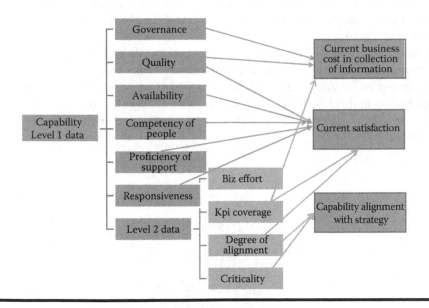

Figure 10.13 Survey response mapping to lenses.

The recommended approach for the investment is discussed with the BOM members. The options for the IT investment plans are:

Allocation of investment budgets based on the average business costs. Figure 10.14 provides a sample allocation of the IT investment budget based on the business cost of individual departments. Figure 10.14 depicts an allocation where major departments are allocated the IT budget leaving

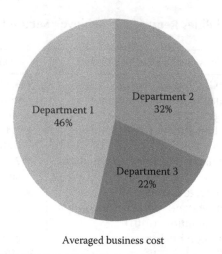

Averaged business cost

Figure 10.14 Options to allocate the resources based on average business cost.

no or little allocation to remaining departments. This model has an advantage of attending to areas where business costs are high and, by automating with an IT investment reducing or optimizing costs. This allocation provides an optimized investment plan. This is then compared to the prioritized capabilities and highlights the investment gaps of those capabilities. In some cases, this isolated investment allocation plan reduces the business cost in one area but multiplies in other areas. In Chapter 6, the "Total Capability Index" was discussed to provide a holistic investment plan.

The option of allocating IT budgets based on business satisfaction (as depicted in Figure 10.15) results in major allocation to the customer facing departments and other support departments receive minimum or no allocation of IT budgets. This IT investment happening outside the centralized budget and is known as "Shadow IT," where individual departments are allocating some of departmental budgets for IT initiatives. In many cases, these initiatives create localized tactical solutions.

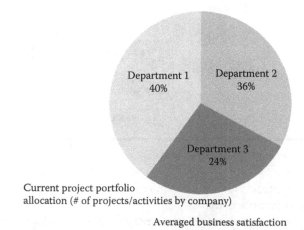

Current project portfolio
allocation (# of projects/activities by company)

Averaged business satisfaction

Figure 10.15 Options to allocate the resources based on business satisfaction.

The option of allocating resources and investment funding based on business satisfaction has similar issues as resources based on the business costs. Figures 10.16 and 10.17 assess the other *options to allocate investment budgets based on the current revenue contribution by individual departments or projects ideas generated by the departments.* Figure 10.16 highlights gaps in allocating funds to the departments not directly generating any revenue but acting as the supporting structure for others.

The option of allocating funding based on new ideas generated as depicted in Figure 10.17 provides a similar picture. The ideation and investment process allocation of past years has discouraged many departments of *GreenFood* to actively participate. The current demand of the projects is also high leaving little or no resources for the implementation of the projects.

Governance

Governance (as discussed in Chapter 7) and quality of investment decisions is difficult as the projects implementing solutions are measured based on the cost and benefits of the individual project and activities. In many cases, the projects complete successfully on cost and benefit criteria but develop business capabilities that are not required because of change in the strategic directions. The duration of the projects also overlaps with the changes in the strategic direction and without an anchoring business capability of managing strategic initiatives, these orphan initiatives (no link to the strategic outcomes) results in critical resources engaging in implementation on the cost of other initiatives.

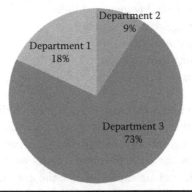

Figure 10.16   Options to allocate the resources based on each departmental contribution to revenue.

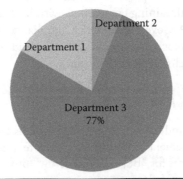

Figure 10.17   Options to allocate the resources based on project ideas from each department.

Governance of the project as 'Bottom Up' results in more projects not aligning with the priority capabilities of the business. Decision makers are the project sponsors, and in many cases, are personally involved and benefit, but *GreenFood* as a company, does not gain any advantage from these projects. For example, a project to provide "Better Health and Safety" systems was seen as an important initiative but only used by a handful of the highly trained engineers and made little impact on the success of the OHS rating. Effective Governance was lacking based on a body that should comprise both business and technical decision makers of *GreenFood*.

Key Recommendations

GreenFood requires considerable planning for a future program of work to manage the challenges faced in people, process, and technology areas. The following are some key recommendations:

- Approve development of a business case for Enterprise Project Management Office (EPMO). At that time, each department provided business project managers and resources required for operational activities.
- Approve development of enterprise information management requirements
- Assign a sponsor for EPMO business case
- Divisional strategy definition and capability prioritization
- Develop strategy to build the following capabilities
  - 3.2.4 Define and manage channel strategy
  - 2.1 Design product and services
  - 3.1 Understand markets, customers, and capabilities
  - 6.1 Develop and manage human resources (HR) planning, policies, and strategies

A new Business Capability Competency Group that aligns to the strategy focus is established. Responsibilities of the group include creating synergy in operational, strategy, and IT professionals and ensuring relevant IT systems, services, and platforms support the organization's outcomes. Assisting these competencies is the EA governance framework that ensures the architecture principles, standards, and guidelines are expressed like the organizational goals and strategies.

GRC returns significant value when it is carefully mapped to business capabilities. Apart from ensuring compliance, GRC is also geared to ensure the organization gets what it has paid for. Business Capabilities benefit organizations provided they are controlled through governance processes, risks are identified upfront and there are effective controls to handle the risks. Eventually, this is helpful in maintaining compliance with both external and internal legal, audit and accounting requirements. A Governance-Risk-Compliance (GRC) body is recommended to pave the path for sensible technology investments. These would become of significant importance in the era of Big Data-driven technologies and businesses.

Design Product and Services

- Refine and localize new product initiation (NPI) process for current products and services
- Implement project management discipline across the teams
- Allocate dedicated resources for "Beyond Tomorrow" products and services
- Collaborate within teams to reduce over-engineering of products and costing estimates differing from actual production costs

- Investigate the collaboration of Information management and operational technology to optimize operation costs
- Develop enterprise-wide strategic management group to manage business initiatives

GreenFood *Organization Structure*

- The new strategy implementation required change in the current *GreenFood* structure and resourcing (6.1). Recommendations for the new structure are:
  - Aligned with the vision, and with clear accountabilities
  - Communicate critical priorities
  - Minimize overlaps where there are split resources across each of the divisions
  - Realign and acquire resources with required specialties
- Evolve manufacturing into a focused center-of-excellence model
  - Achieve economies of scale through specialization, and seek the right balance of "flexibility" per site
  - Drive LEAN culture through whole value chain, eliminate, or redefine ineffective process steps
  - Key performance indicators (KPIs) needs to be aligned and accountabilities clear

Table 10.6 lists the business capabilities required to achieve the goals setup for the **"Secure *GreenFood* Profitability solution."**

Business use of social technologies is expanding beyond the early adoption of business functions of marketing and recruiting into a broad range of industries. Digital marketing and social media for business-to-consumer continues to rise in prominence and opportunity, and there are early signs of a growing interest in using social capabilities to drive workforce effectiveness and to engage with partners and customers in B2B environments.

Table 10.6 Business Capabilities Building Recommended for Secure *GreenFood* Profitability

Pre-requisites	Business Capability Required	Related Capabilities
A business model is worked out to reach our customers. Necessary infrastructure is available. The required analytics capabilities/services are available. A targeted customer segmentation is identified.	• 3.1 Understand markets, customers, and capabilities (10101) • 3.2 Develop marketing strategy (10102) • 5.1 Develop consumer care/service strategy (11592) • 5.4 Develop customer care/customer service strategy (10378) • 11.5 Manage public relations program (11014) • 7.3 Manage business resiliency and risk (11216) • 5.3 Measure and evaluate consumer satisfaction (11609) • 7.6 Deploy IT solutions (10567)	• 1.3 Manage strategic initiatives (10016) • 12.6.1 Create and manage organizational performance strategy (11071) • 7.4 Manage enterprise information (10565) • 12.4 Manage change (11074) • 6.1 Develop and manage HR planning, policies, and strategies (10409) • 5.3 Measure and evaluate consumer satisfaction (11609) • 6.2 Recruit, source, and select employees (10410)

Forward looking IT leaders are now beginning to recognize the possibilities of applying social solutions to IT, as seen in the advance of social IT management and social network analysis for Business Process Management (BPM), and in the introduction of social media strategic impact on EA. Thus, more recommendations are suggested.

- Develop a business strategy for consumer contacts
  - Staff are ambassadors of *GreenFood* brands and products and food services
  - Have list of customers that supply products, for example, Best Meats, Seafood trading
  - *GreenFood* should have functions at venues that they supply to or want to supply
  - Using dinners at *GreenFood*'s key customer restaurants as rewards
  - All staff goes into the field to learn; induction should include education on product range
  - Understand your own palate via sensory testing, for example, display of food
  - Reward and recognition should be food orientated (e.g., not movie passes)
  - Educate food culture and improve food expertise in business.
  - Does a foodie culture apply to all *GreenFood* offers?

Manage Strategic Initiatives (1.3)

GreenFood develops the strategy every 2 years in the enterprise and then individual divisions expend this strategy. The strategic implementation is managed at a division level and no formal team or role is assigned to manage strategic initiatives enterprise wide. The change in strategy as described in "*GreenFood* New vision" requires a high level of activities planned to achieve the "New" goal; this business capability is depicted in Figure 10.18 and required to manage strategic initiative holistically. Figure 10.18 lists the business capability activities and tasks.

Table 10.7 provides the list of the requirements in each direction for enterprise-wide strategic implementation. The gaps highlighted are that strategy to execution is not holistically managed and there is a lack of governance around the stated benefits versus the actual benefits delivered.

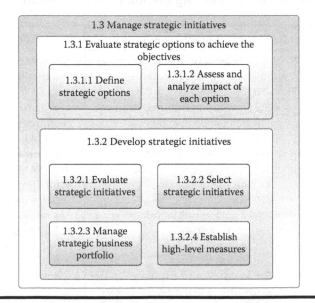

Figure 10.18   Levels 3 and 4 business capability-managed initiatives.

The lack of clarity and consensus around business priorities and missing risk management capabilities has an impact on the deadline of strategic objectives of *GreenFood* not being met and risks not actively managed.

Table 10.8 describes many options for building business capabilities.

Table 10.7 Strategic Alignment with Business Capabilities

Pre-requisites	Co-related Capabilities	New Requirements
• Business strategy is defined for enterprise and divisions • Divisional strategies defined and aligned with the enterprise strategy	• 1.1 Define business concepts and long-term vision • 1.2 Develop business strategy • 10.1 Manage enterprise risk • 12.2 Manage portfolio, program, and project	• Secure our profitability • Drive out cost, improve productivity • Achieve greater alignment across units • Adopt a leading-edge digital platform • Own retail consumer meal solutions • Develop direct to end user models • Establish global sourcing footprint • Devise a business plan for new market • Accelerate brand in new market • Expand presence, skills, and capability in new market

Table 10.8 Option Analysis of Business Capability Building

Option	Description	Advantages	Disadvantages
Develop process and adopt individually in each division	• The process is created for *GreenFood* • Same process is adopted by all the divisions for the definition of initiatives, governance • The responsibility of managing the initiatives remain within the divisions	• Can utilize existing resources supported by few external resources to define the process • The initiatives leverage the departmental expertise and knowledge in managing initiatives (no learning curves or misunderstanding of the imitative directions) • No additional cost in setting up the team to manage strategic initiatives	• Cross-division initiative may not get the same attention as the divisional one • Business capability silos remain as now • Training requirement be high (as may leaders from each division need to be trained in the processes, governance, etc.) • The required rigor may not be applied to the initiatives (based on personal relationships, etc.)

(Continued)

Table 10.8 (*Continued*) Option Analysis of Business Capability Building

Option	Description	Advantages	Disadvantages
Develop process and create a matrix team for implementation across *GreenFood*	• The process is created for *GreenFood* • Same process is adopted by all the divisions for the definition of initiatives, governance • Matrix team is formed to manage the initiatives	• Leverage the skills from cross-division • No additional cost in setting up the team to manage strategic initiatives • Cross-divisional initiatives get attention	• Lead time for the projects may increase • May turn into bureaucratic process
Create a separate group to manage the strategic initiatives	• A separate group is formed with the overall responsibility of managing all strategic initiatives. • The *GreenFood* structure (which group/division this reports to) should be important. • The team may require independence and also authority to govern projects across the *GreenFood*.	• The process is applied holistically to all projects • Enterprise prioritization drives the projects. • No additional cost in training each divisional team.	• Additional cost of the separate team • The lead time for the projects may increase due to limited resources, managing the demands for large number of the project initiatives.

Manage Enterprise Information (7.4)

GreenFood manages IT needs in-house using a mix of permanent and contracted staff. The Information System department has developed systems to allow *GreenFood* to have an interface with external stakeholders. The new strategy has expedited the need for information availability and analytics capabilities in sales, marketing, and customer and consumer analytics for the product portfolios. The current setup of IT has challenges such as current IT solutions to support the KPIs are not adequately orchestrated to deliver to *GreenFood* pace requirements. The current BI capability is not adequate and only provides reactive reporting. There is a lot of manual effort required to extract the information and there are inconsistent tools. Master data is not managed well across the *GreenFood* (e.g., data associated to product deletion is not retired). The impact is *GreenFood* is constrained in their ability to make decisions in an appropriate timeframe. The other impact is information is only available on a weekly or monthly basis; this results in reactive rather than proactive decision-making.

Figure 10.19 using APQC Process Control Framework defines in detailed activity and tasks layers for the "Manage Enterprise Information" capability. Table 10.9 provides the list of the

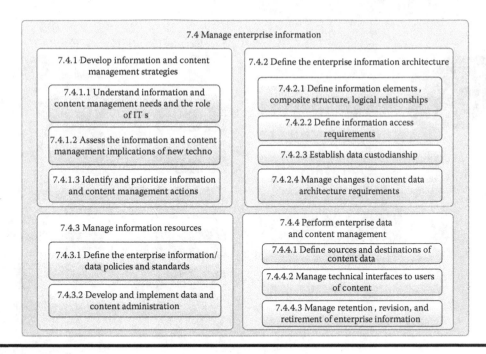

Figure 10.19   Business capability—Manage enterprise information.

Table 10.9   Business Capabilities Required for Improving Information Management Capability

Pre-requisites	Co-related Capabilities	GreenFood *New Requirements*
• Measure and benchmark • Manage the business of Information management • Define and manage channel strategy	• 7.1 Manage the business of IT • 7.1.2 Define the EA • 7.1.3 Manage the IT portfolio • 7.1.4 Perform IT research and innovation • 7.1.8 Manage IT suppliers and contracts • 7.2 Develop and manage IT customer relationships • 7.3 Manage business resiliency and risk • 7.5 Develop and maintain IT solutions • 7.6 Deploy IT solutions • 7.7 Deliver and support IT services • 12.1 Manage business process • 12.2 Manage business portfolio, program, and project.	**Secure our profitability** • Fix underperforming *GreenFood* categories, grow others new categories. • Optimize supply chains • Drive out cost, improve productivity • Retune recent acquisitions • Achieve greater alignment across units • Embrace a passion for food • Adopt a leading-edge digital platform • Own retail consumer meal solutions.

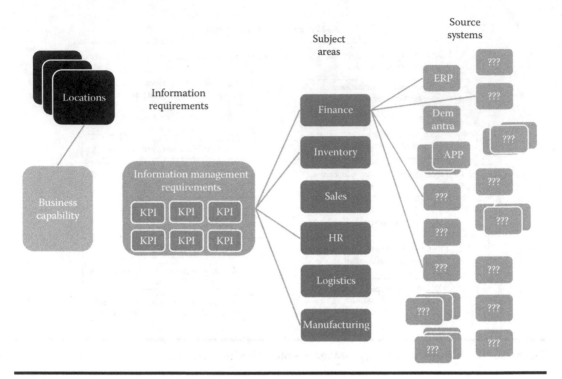

Figure 10.20   Relating the IT environment to metrics.

requirements in each horizon for enterprise-wide strategic implementation and the upliftment required in the co-related capabilities.

It is recommended to allocate resources to develop information management capabilities and accelerate development of BI capability. Figure 10.20 recommends mapping the KPIs with the core business capabilities. This assists in refining the KPIs and measuring against strategic outcomes.

This is the path that *GreenFood* used to align itself to its new strategy. The process of alignment is successful and as the capabilities are empowering the strategy, the growth and the confidence of the market in *GreenFood* has the confidence to grow further. The capability growth is a virtuous cycle and the culture of *GreenFood* is becoming more positive.

Reference

1. Oncken, W. and Wass, D. Jr. (1999). Management Time: Who's Got the Monkey?, *Harvard Business Review*. https://hbr.org/1999/11/management-time-whos-got-the-monkey.

Chapter 11

ODBA and Capability-Building Case Study 2—Energy Market

Introducing the Case Study (Energy Market)

Business Context

This business case study is of *EnTility* Private limited, a large energy retailer that generates and distributes energy. The energy industry is continuously growing and, in the context of environmental consciousness, gaining attention from customers, regulators, and media. Inefficiencies in energy generation and distribution are regularly reported in media due to climate concerns as well as a rise in prices. Governmental policies focus on strategies to develop efficient and renewal energies. The entire strategic approach to energy generation and distribution requires significant collaboration among various parties. These parties include the generators, distributors, retailers, governance agencies, product providers, and consumers. Outcome-Driven Business Architecture (ODBA)-based development of capabilities in *EnTility* promises to offer a much more efficient organization that can handle the generation and distribution cycle in the energy market.

Business capabilities in *EnTility* enable collective sharing of consumers' energy requirements, an efficient approach to energy generation, optimized current generation capacities, and a highly efficient distribution and retail market. This information is generally available and is used in part, but a holistic capability management provides each of the participants with information and intelligence to improve products and services.

The introduction of smart metering capabilities provides the opportunity for energy generators, distributors, and retailers to plan distribution according to customer energy use, whereas product manufacturers could use this information to create new energy-efficient product designs. Governing agencies could participate to better monitor and refine the governing rules.

The Board of Management of the *EnTility* are bidding for acquisition of a major electricity generation, distribution, and retail company. This new plan is deemed necessary by the very fast changing market environment. *EnTility* realizes that this is a permanent future change and needs a deeper look into the workings of the acquired company for its long-term profitability and sustainability. The acquisition of a new organization is an excellent opportunity for *EnTility* to expand its customer base and grow its suite of offerings.

After a number of years in which *EnTility* profits improved strongly within a reasonable distance of forecasted return, its profits have been reduced by half. The energy customers are regularly changing their energy suppliers in the open market. The government has passed a number of legislations that require openness of contracts and reporting back to customers and governing bodies. All of the divisions that make up the *EnTility* are challenged with the task of seeking out initiatives to improve profitability, reporting and managing the cost of doing business.

The plan has three horizons, each one with its own action plans and time schedule, and each one very important to the future success of *EnTility*. The three strategic directions are:

- Secure profitability by retaining existing customers through better products and services
- Increase the customer base by acquisition
- Invest and Grow in new markets such as renewal energy, solar, and wind farms

Business Drivers

Effective and efficient information flow is becoming a necessity to achieve *EnTility*'s corporate goals of "future proofed *EnTility*," market leading performance, delivering value to customers, and becoming a rewarding work place. The business outcome-driven capability framework is required as an enabler (i.e., value is derived from efficient and effective use of capabilities). For example, to increase cross-selling, *EnTility* requires not just a single view of the customer, but skilled sales people with a thorough knowledge of available solutions and an understanding of product gaps. The customer view must capture who a customer is and what he has done, and help employees decide what to do next. The key business drivers are:

- Customer-focused growth—increased customer understanding can position *EnTility* for higher growth and profitability in the future; driving growth and profitability by adopting a 'Value' view of customers—generate actionable customer insights that uncover customer acquisition, retention, and growth opportunities.
- Drive new revenue streams through customer-focused business transformation and strategic differentiation.
- Integrate customer insights into *EnTility* customer management processes to deliver the right treatment to the right customer at the right time—leading to improved customer service, customer satisfaction, and customer loyalty.
- React more quickly to changing market dynamics and competitive threats.
- Achieve real-time access to information to support decision-making.
- Improve communications with partners, leading to additional strategic opportunities such as joint selling through a partner ecosystem, customized offers, and "package deals" involving products from multiple vendors, special discounts that apply to preferred partner products, and so on.
- Improve regulatory compliance and privacy management.

Current Challenges

EnTility has organically grown and currently customer-related information is distributed in multiple systems in different formats and may apply different business rules for validation. For example, a Customer Service Officer (CSO) interacting with the customer for a specific billing inquiry is required to interact with a number of systems to collect the relevant information and customer profile. Different systems, for example, customer relationship management (CRM) system, Customer preference (CRM systems), Billing history (could be multiple Billing systems, depending on products purchased), Payment History (Billing systems and financial systems), Pending service orders (Billing, CRM, and other systems), and major activities in the premise area are all disjointed. The current topology of information technology (IT) systems and processes increase the 'cost to serve' and 'cost to sell.' Following are the key challenges currently faced by the *EnTility*:

Missed Opportunities for Cross-Selling and Up-Selling

If *EnTility* does not have current or complete information about what customers have bought before, the company cannot make informed predictions about what the customers will buy in the future. Sales and Marketing cannot target their advertising and direct-mail campaigns with precision; they can waste money on offers or advertising that are not appealing to their recipients; they cannot cross-sell and up-sell to maximize the total value of each customer to the business. This results in reduced customer satisfaction and brand loyalty. Targeting customers with one-to-one marketing campaigns based on their unique spending activities is a holy grail for all retailers.

Less Effective Customer Service

Higher management cannot focus on improving services without a consolidated view of *EnTility* business capabilities and capability gaps. If the gaps are in un-integrated processes or people skills are limited, customer service agents are not able to improve the services to customers effectively— whether it is providing billing support, offering promotional prices and discounts to preferred customers or other customer-facing activities. With limited integration of processes, customer interaction requires multiple hand-overs between CSOs frustrating customers and service agents.

Poor Employee Productivity

Currently, the CSOs access multiple systems to consolidate customer information. This increases the average per call interaction time and also frustrates the customer and agents while waiting for the information.

Cost to Serve and Sell Is Higher than Market Average for Utility Industry

The engaged external management consultancy reports a high level of exceptions, poor data quality, and complex IT systems with multiple interfaces, increasing the cost to serve and cost to sell. Most of the utilities companies offer similar products with very few distinguishing features. *EnTility* needs to ensure they make a good impression. The impact of customer messages and call durations are central to the feeling a prospect or customer has about that business.

The back-end process then comes into play. Last impressions are equally key to a good customer experience. *EnTility* must ensure they answer customer queries across all channels, maintaining a customer-focused approach not only when sending information to customers, but also in the way in which this is done. This is where many disconnects can occur, with information provided by the customer at one stage of the process not being transferred or applied at a later stage. Nothing leads to dissatisfaction more rapidly than the sense that the business wasn't listening properly.

EnTility's customer information is currently distributed across billing, CRM systems and usage systems and is not easily shareable. *EnTility* users need to log on to multiple systems to collate customer information in their day-to-day activities. *EnTility* IT systems have organically grown and are categorized as highly distributed systems with complex IT systems and equally complex integration. The current systems require a lot of work-around that creates a high number of exceptions as noted below:

- As per reports the "cost to serve" a customer is around 60% of new customer's yearly profit and *EnTility* customer churn rate is high.
- Currently, implemented CRM system's full scope is to reduce "cost to serve," but it could be enhanced with additional planning and providing context-sensitive information to *EnTility* users. The current planned change only impacts data quality of the CRM.

No Single Customer View (SCV)

There is no availability of relevant "context sensitive customer information" to each of the user's touch-points (at the time of sale, campaign, problem resolution, etc.). For example, a contact center user has customer information about current products, history of customers (various locations), and any pending service requests. *EnTility* needs to provide context-sensitive information to its users from a single access point for each of the touch-points. The introduction of new CRM system addresses some of the business concerns. The single customer view requires a well-planned roadmap to build on the current CRM platform to achieve higher efficiencies and reduce both "costs to serve" and "cost to sell" along with other business benefits.

EnTility's operational costs are rising. Various taxes, insurances, compliance costs, factory wages, and general overheads are increasing. At the same time, the market does not allow recovery of these costs, margins are being squeezed and profits are reduced. *EnTility* is maintaining strong market shares in the retail market but at a high operational cost, with reduced profit margins. Simultaneously, *EnTility* is feeling a lot of price pressure in the category market from imports flooding in from lower cost countries.

- **Customer Information is duplicated in multiple systems:** Currently, customer information including customer personal details, contacts, and addresses is duplicated in CRM and billing systems; asset information such as meter information is duplicated in billing systems and usage.
- **Low trust on the information quality:** Currently, customer information is federated between CRM and billing systems. The information is also stored in different formats and business rules are applied inconsistently. Key entities are stored and updated in different systems using inconsistent business rules.
- **Access to most of the customer information is via reports or extraction of data and updates:** Currently, customer and billing information is shared using batch processes. These batch processes extract information from various source systems and apply to the data warehouse systems. On a regular basis the information from the data warehouse systems is extracted and applied to other systems. The end-to-end process of exchanging data between CRM and billing systems could take up to 2 weeks.

- **Lack of "uniform business rules" engine:** Each system currently applies business rules as defined at the time of that system development. This has created disjoint business rule application between various systems. It necessitates multiple formatting and translation of information for the consumptions of each system users. It makes it difficult to consolidate information about customer's profiles.
- **Multiple systems can create and update customer master data:** Post-Customer relationship system implementation, most of the customer, address and contact information is managed by CRM systems. The exception is "New connections" where customers are initially created in the billing system to follow existing complex process of "New connections." Once the address is occupied by a customer, it is created in the CRM system.
- **Process owners and process standardization:** The current business processes and owners are distributed along the organizational boundaries. End-to-end optimized processes and identified single owners are recommended.

Meeting Challenges Using ODBA

Business Capabilities of EnTility

The reduction in profits and increase in the operational cost of *EnTility* necessitate a market assessment of current products and opportunities to introduce new products and services. The acquisition plans for a major energy company requires a comprehensive review including market forces, competitors, manufacturing, and sourcing. *EnTility* is going through the difficult task of aligning itself with the speed and agility of the market environment.

This case study objective is to describe establishing *EnTility*'s ODBA to meet the challenges as described earlier. In this case study, *EnTility* is well aware of the challenges and reasons for the capability gaps. This case study is more focused on managing the IT domain of business capabilities to achieve the desired business outcomes.

The business capability development team conducted an enterprise-wide assessment of the current state of maturity of the organization's business capabilities as well as their desired future state for enablement of their strategy as depicted in Figure 11.1. For the planned acquisition, an organizational business capability assessment is conducted to identify differentiating capabilities of each of the two organizations, and reduce the duplication as depicted in Figure 11.2. The business capability base assessment is used to establish an ODBA in order to get a holistic view of the current processes, people skills, information and knowledge management functions, and operations of the company.

Business capability-based assessment helps management understand the holistic capabilities required across the organization and, in case of mergers and acquisitions, any duplications or redundancies. Understanding business capabilities and a detailed understanding of the priority capability dimension gaps such as people skills, IT or processes, provides a perspective to the extent of solutions required to implement any change. Organizations usually lead changes through projects with limited time, budget, and resources, and in many cases the scope of the projects focus on one of the few dimensions of the business capabilities. For example, a project's scope may be to upgrade technology or processes and successfully implement as per the scope. But what if the scope was not right or implementation of the project widens the gaps in other capability dimensions such as people skills or the resources required? For a successful project, there needs to be clarity on the extent of the change, which business unit needs to be involved, what skills are required for the change, and comprehensive testing scenarios to ensure the change is smoothly integrated into the present structure and processes.

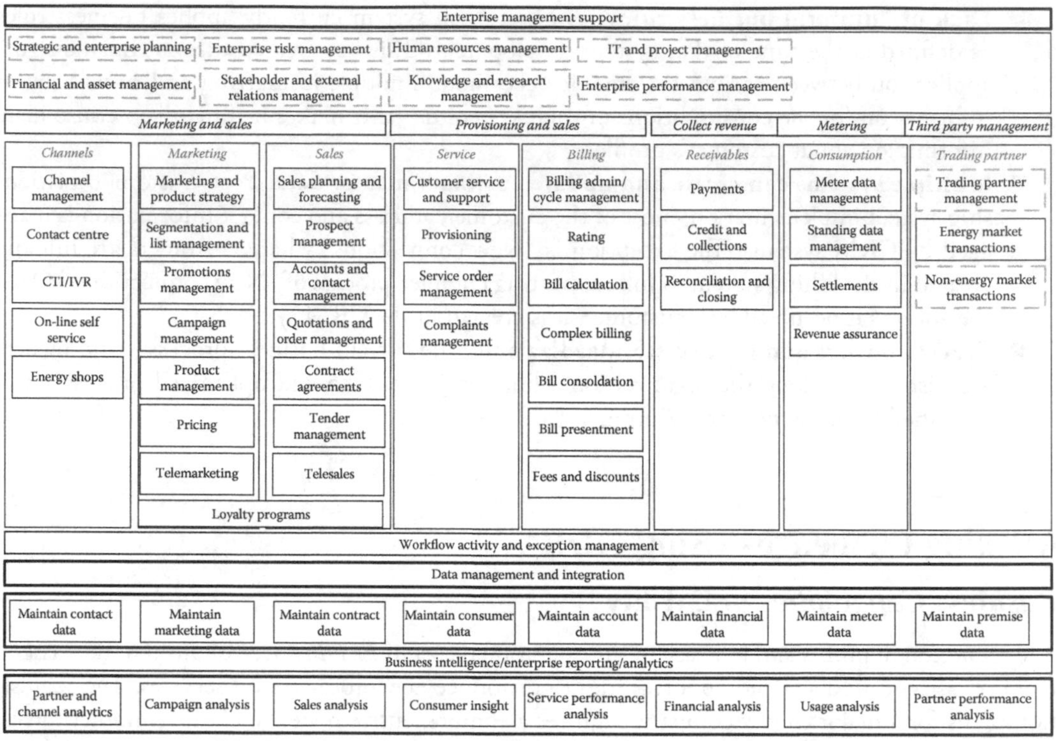

Enterprise management support

Strategic and enterprise planning	Enterprise risk management	Human resources management	IT and project management
Financial and asset management	Stakeholder and external relations management	Knowledge and research management	Enterprise performance management

Marketing and sales			*Provisioning and sales*		*Collect revenue*	*Metering*	*Third party management*
Channels	*Marketing*	*Sales*	*Service*	*Billing*	*Receivables*	*Consumption*	*Trading partner*
Channel management	Marketing and product strategy	Sales planning and forecasting	Customer service and support	Billing admin/cycle management	Payments	Meter data management	Trading partner management
Contact centre	Segmentation and list management	Prospect management	Provisioning	Rating	Credit and collections	Standing data management	Energy market transactions
CTI/IVR	Promotions management	Accounts and contact management	Service order management	Bill calculation	Reconciliation and closing	Settlements	Non-energy market transactions
On-line self service	Campaign management	Quotations and order management	Complaints management	Complex billing		Revenue assurance	
Energy shops	Product management	Contract agreements		Bill consolidation			
	Pricing	Tender management		Bill presentment			
	Telemarketing	Telesales		Fees and discounts			
	Loyalty programs						

Workflow activity and exception management

Data management and integration

Maintain contact data	Maintain marketing data	Maintain contract data	Maintain consumer data	Maintain account data	Maintain financial data	Maintain meter data	Maintain premise data

Business intelligence/enterprise reporting/analytics

Partner and channel analytics	Campaign analysis	Sales analysis	Consumer insight	Service performance analysis	Financial analysis	Usage analysis	Partner performance analysis

Figure 11.1 *EnTility* business capability model.

The ODBA establishment, as discussed in Chapter 8, provides *EnTility* a short- and a long-term roadmap for the business capabilities to be developed. The focus of these projects is on IT and knowledge management dimensions of the capabilities. People skills and resources (financial commitments) are identified and allocated by the *EnTility*. The required capabilities are mapped against current capabilities and gaps are identified as depicted in Table 11.1. These gaps are utilized to define the projects and actions. In this case, the highest gap of 'retention of the customers' (**2.09**) is identified.

The business capability assessment is mapped to key *EnTility* planned activities as depicted in Table 11.2. Table 11.2 highlights the capability gaps to achieve strategic outcomes. It is also useful in identifying the planned activities to focus on within projects to achieve the required capability rating. Table 11.2 utilizes the American Productivity Quality Center (APQC) notation to define the business capabilities required to meet strategic outcomes. The pre-requisites define the activities to meet the strategic goal, for example, "secure Profitability" requires a defined business strategy to achieve this outcome, is communicated to all levels and departments/divisions agree on the business outcome expected. The business capabilities required to achieve this outcome is defined in APQC* format (12.6.1 means the APQC category, process, and activity).

Table 11.3 describes the key findings of the business capability assessment. A sample assessment is depicted in Figure 11.3. The assessment of the customer services capabilities as shown in Figure 11.3.

---

* https://www.apqc.org/pcf.

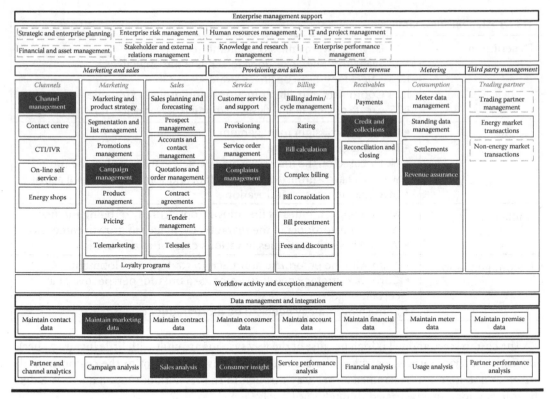

Figure 11.2   Merger and acquisition—other company capability assessment.

Table 11.1   Assessment of the Overall EnTility Capability

Key Strategy	Current Rating	Required Rating	Gaps
Secure profitability by retention of existing customers by offering better product and services-based *EnTility*	2.16	4.25	**2.09**
Increase the customer base by acquisition	2.85	4.5	1.65
Invest and grow in new markets such as renewal energy, solar and wind forms	1.90	3.85	1.95

Developing Effective Customer Service Capabilities

Table 11.4 defines actions required for the strategy of developing effective customer services.

Table 11.5 maps the actions required for the strategy with the business capabilities to develop a lean and efficient organizational structure. The current gap for this capability as in Table 11.5 is 0.76.

1.2 Develop business strategy	
Description	1.2.1 Develop overall mission statement 1.2.2 Evaluate strategic options to achieve the objectives 1.2.3 Select long-term business strategy 1.2.4 Coordinate and align functional and process Strategies 1.2.5 Create organizational design (structure, governance, reporting, etc.)
Issues	• Need better insight management • No strategy for "Big data" • Not focused on the future; we need to aggressively look at the future; we don't have a group focusing on "Beyond Tomorrow" type of activities • Insufficient focus on innovation
Impact	• Missed opportunities as first mover (opportunity of being the first with an idea/product in the market) advantages in growth categories • We still have silo activities in various categories and brands
Recommendation	• Align with the enterprise approach to strategy development • Corporate strategy needs to embrace a broader perspective at a certain stage • Refreshing strategy needs to be more frequent

The cost to serve and sell is high because of the way systems are built with little integrity checks and widely varying processing rules. The back-end processes matter a lot to the customer as the customer queries must be handled all the way through to the resolution. Once a query is lodged the information must be passed through until resolved.

EnTility customer information is distributed among many systems and is in different formats and not easily shareable. *EnTility* users need to collate information from multiple systems which delays their other activities. *EnTility* IT systems have grown slowly over the years with each system defining its own business rules. The resulting IT systems and integration are thus very complex and highly manual. This creates many exceptions which increases processing time and frustrates CSOs and customers.

12.2 Manage portfolio, program, and project	
Description	12.2.1 Manage portfolio 12.2.2 Manage programs
Issues	• Reliability of jobs to support reporting • COGNOS still not supporting sales • Incentives are too egalitarian • Retailers do not see us as agile • Recent focus on cost should have been part of our core values, instead of a reaction to the recent financial results
Impact	• Lack of core values limits the progression of the company through organic growth • Lack of necessary capability development • Individuals lose morale from a lack of individual incentive • Inefficient use of resources regarding COGNOS (two systems working for one process)

(Continued)

Recommendation	• Re-establish confidence in COGNOS • Increase individual incentives • Re-establish core values
12.6 Measure and benchmark	
Description	12.6.1 Create and manage organizational performance strategy 12.6.2 Benchmark performance
Issues	• Business intelligence (BI) strategy requirements are disconnected from where we are now • Reporting capabilities are not effective • COGNOS not effective yet
Impact	• Inefficient use of COGNOS • Reports take too long
Recommendation	• Invest in better reporting capabilities • Re-evaluate COGNOS • Re-establish current position with BI strategy requirements

Table 11.2   Assessment *Data* of the *Overall* EnTility Capability

Requirement	APQC_ ID	Capability	Current Rating	Required Rating	EnTility Gap
Leverage and invest in our brands and products to drive growth.	3.2	Develop marketing strategy.	4.27	4.61	0.34
Knowledge of customer service agents and user needs to communicate trends	3.1	Understand markets, customers, and capabilities.	3.61	4.62	1.01
Become technically savvy and reach consumers in new ways. Check and measure where our resources are being allocated.	3.1	Understand markets, customers, and capabilities.	3.61	4.62	1.01
	3.2.4	Define and manage channel strategy.	2.83	4.35	1.53
	8.8	Manage internal controls.	3.15	4.32	1.17
Develop enterprise project management office	8.1	Perform planning and management accounting.	3.01	4.25	1.24
Align resources to evaluate commercial viability of new technologies.	6.1	Develop and manage human resources (HR) planning, policies, and strategies.	2.79	4.02	1.23

(Continued)

Table 11.2 (*Continued*)   Assessment *Data* of the *Overall* EnTility Capability

Trade-off our infrastructure and strategic alliances.	1.2	Develop business strategy.	3.04	4.09	1.05
Optimize resource allocations.	1.1	Define the business concept and long-term vision.	2.0	4.05	2.05
Proactively seek merger and acquisitions.	1.1	Define the business concept and long-term vision.	3.1	4.47	1.37

Table 11.3   Key Findings Summary

Area	Finding
EnTility structure	• *EnTility* structure needs to realign from current "Doer" to "Thinker and Doer" skillset. So far, divisions have been autonomous in planning the projects and program; in the new strategy, many of the projects and plans need to be managed as a portfolio to gain maximum value for the investments and this should realign the current *EnTility* structure. • Collaboration within *EnTility* teams to reduce over-engineering of products or estimated costing being different to actual production costs.
Information technology	• IT should be used to enable business and requires investment in new technology in the area of consumer contacts. Investigate the collaboration of Information management and operational technology to optimize operation costs. • Acquire resources with specialties of insights, consumer services, and digital.
Business strategy	• Limited activity to close capability gaps (for advantage capability or strategic support capability). The capabilities required for "Invest to grow new market" are not defined until the approach to grow in new market is finalized and the operational model is defined ("go to market" strategy).
Program management	• Silo approach may result in the same capabilities being developed differently by different divisions: this may require restructuring some of the program office structures. Implement Project management discipline across the teams.
Initiative management	• Multiple customer and consumer service strategies are in place. The holistic approach should tailor customer contacts based on the consumer/customer segments. • Training of staff in LEAN methodology is required. • Evolve retail services centers into a focused center-of-excellence model.
HR and payroll management	• The new strategy initiates a change not seen in *EnTility* for a long time. This requires change management to be defined and planned with the new direction in mind.

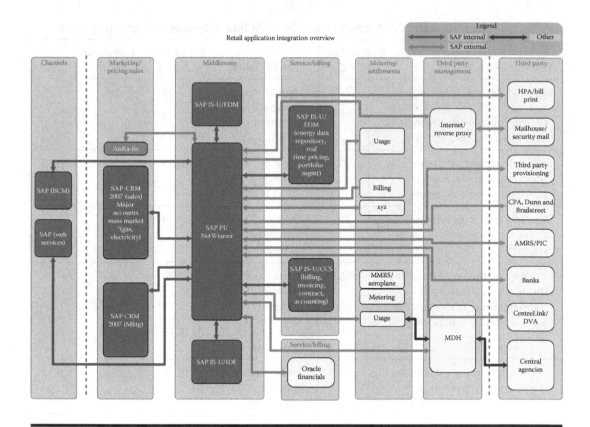

Figure 11.3 Develop effective customer service capability gap.

Table 11.4 Develop Effective Customer Service—Action Gaps

Action—Capabilities	Current	Required	Gap
Drive a lean and efficient structure with a commitment to continuous improvement at every level of the business	2.87	4.49	1.62
Implement best practice procurement models for services as well as inputs	3.11	4.47	1.37
Develop and improve processes to increase the efficiency of 'spend'	3.21	4.33	1.11
Develop a culture of relentless focus on cost down	2.84	4.40	1.55
Eliminate automate or outsource administrative functions	1.92	2.78	0.87
Identify capability gaps and improvement priorities	3.01	4.45	1.43
Ensure full and effective use of IT infrastructure by focused investment in system development, support, training, and education	2.73	4.16	1.43

Table 11.5 Develop Effective Customer Service—Action Mapping to Capability Gaps

Requirement	APQC ID	Capability	Current Rating	Required Rating	Gap
Drive a lean and efficient structure with a commitment to continuous improvement at every level of the business	3.1	Understand markets, customers, and capabilities	3.90	4.67	0.76
Implement best practice procurement models for services as well as inputs	1.2	Develop business strategy	3.65	4.54	0.88
Develop and improve processes to increase the efficiency of spend	3.2	Develop marketing strategy	4.29	4.71	0.43
Develop a culture of relentless focus on cost down Eliminate automate or outsource administrative functions	12.2	Manage portfolio, program, and project	1.90	4.67	2.76
	12.6	Measure and benchmark	2.16	4.71	2.55
Identify capability gaps and improvement priorities	3.4	Develop and manage marketing plans	4.29	4.71	0.43
	7.4	Manage enterprise information	2.67	4.48	<u>1.81</u>

Introducing a new product at *EnTility* engages many business lines of the company. The product successful launch is assessed for business capabilities in areas of Research and Development, marketing, sales, IT, data flows, regulatory, delivery, and accounting departments among other capabilities. Understanding how the current capabilities, processes, and information network of the company are utilized to incorporate a new product is fundamental to the successful launch of a new line of business. The present architectural plan of the company makes it easy to understand what departments is impacted and who should be involved in making the change. This project is driven by the extent of change found from the architectural plan. The mapping of business capabilities to applications, data structures, and IT processes makes it simpler to see the level of change required in the company. The Process dimension needs changes and optimization of the inter-departmental processes that are required to support new product and proactive analytics.

EnTility manages the IT in-house. Systems are for the internal need of the *EnTility* interfacing with few external stakeholders. The new strategy has expedited the need for information availability at a faster pace, with the analytics capabilities in the area of sales, marketing, investment versus value and customer and consumer analytics for the product portfolios. The current setup of IT has challenges. IT solutions in place to support the key performance indicators (KPIs) are not adequately orchestrated to deliver to *EnTility* requirements. The current BI capability is not adequate and provides only reactive reporting. The reason is a lot of manual effort required to extract the information required and

3.1 Understanding Markets, customers, and capabilities	
Description	3.1.1 Perform customer and market intelligence analysis 3.1.2 Evaluate and prioritize market opportunities
Issues	• *EnTility* don't have any a group focusing on "Beyond Tomorrow" type of activities to forecast the market beyond 3 years • Category management required rather than product • People skills are required for understanding the change in consumer dynamics and also find out more alternate solutions • *EnTility* is not considering holistic cost of products • Insufficient focus on innovation
Impact	• Entity is new products are variation of existing products and mostly cannibalize the existing product markets
Recommendation	• Capability is needed in area of people behavior analysis • Develop analytics capabilities around consumer insights, Shopper data, Loyalty Data • Adopt a category Focus approach
3.2.4 Define and manage channel strategy	
Description	3.2.4.1 Evaluate channel attributes and partners 3.2.4.2 Determine channel fit with target segments 3.2.4.3 Select channels for target segments 3.2.4.4 Define and manage channel/store format strategy
Issues	• Retailers controlling range, packaging • *EnTility* don't has adequate channels from retail perspective
Impact	• Current retail channels are shrinking
Recommendation	• Utilize insight management • Invest in CRM for consumer channels
3.4 Develop and manage marketing plans	
Description	3.4.1 Establish goals, objectives, and metrics for products by channels/segments 3.4.2 Establish marketing budgets 3.4.3 Design and execute brand and product marketing programs 3.4.4 Develop and manage pricing 3.4.5 Design and execute consumer promotions 3.4.6 Manage trade pricing, promotions, and allowances 3.4.7 Track customer management measures 3.4.8 Develop and manage packaging strategy
Issues	• *EnTility* is at the highest price whereas customers are seeking lowest costs and our competitors are exploiting this • *EnTility* is not necessarily gaining any quantifiable benefit for green energy products • *EnTility* brands are not strong enough to demand the price we want • Unable to get any price increase from our governing energy pricing bodies

(Continued)

Impact	• Increased cost of generation is reducing our margins • Starting to loose volume of sale • Weather changes are erratic and planned generation and distribution is unable to meet consumer energy
Recommendation	• Develop a pricing architecture and pricing strategy • Review our trade spend strategy

has inconsistent tools. Master data is not managed well across *EnTility* (e.g., data associated to product deletion is not retired). The impact is that *EnTility* is constrained in their ability to make decisions in an appropriate timeframe. The other impact is the availability of information. Because it is on a weekly or monthly basis; this results in reactive rather than proactive decision-making.

7.4 Manage Enterprise Information	
Description	7.4.1 Develop information and content management strategies 7.4.2 Define the enterprise information architecture 7.4.3 Manage information resources 7.4.4 Perform enterprise data and content management
Issues	• Current reports takes a long time to run • Unable to get adequate prioritization for retail reports • *EnTility* do not have a formal roadmap for development of reports • Too much manual effort required to extract the information required • Inconsistent tools • Spend visibility in procurement is very poor • Consumer analytics capabilities are basic and making best use of the information available • Major disconnect between BI strategy requirements and where we are now • Lack of Trust in COGNOS
Impact	• Lack of timely sales information • Information Management Capability not geared up to meet the business current requirements let alone future (Big Data) • Retailers do not see us as agile
Recommendation	• Need to simplify the data collection, adopt more of a high level view • Start with a scorecard and work down to drive out information management requirements • Need to spend some time prioritizing information needs to ensure that highest priority needs are addressed first
12.1 Create and manage organizational performance	
Description	12.1.1 Create organization design 12.1.2 Develop supporting organizational processes 12.1.3 Create enterprise measurement systems model 12.1.4 Measure process productivity 12.1.5 Measure cost-effectiveness 12.1.6 Measure staff efficiency 12.1.7 Measure cycle time

(Continued)

Issues	• No clear linkage between KPI at different level of organization. • Unbalanced KPI set—financially focused • Continuous monitoring of KPI set and their relevance required • Not enough focus on supply of energy side of KPI
Impact	• Not making the best use of resources. When new systems are implemented the opportunity is not taken to improve the way things are done—things stay the same as they were before. • Cannot benchmark ourselves (across a whole range of activities) against competitor's or industry best practice

Recommendation	• Align with the enterprise-wide Performance management strategy
	  – Review of Balanced scorecard
	  – Review Standard Operating Processes

1.3 Manage strategic initiative

Description	1.3.1 Develop strategic initiatives 1.3.2 Evaluate strategic initiatives 1.3.3 Select strategic initiatives 1.3.4 Establish high-level measures
Issues	• Lack of governance around the stated benefits versus the actual benefits delivered • Lack of clarity and consensus around business priorities • Execution of Strategy requires agility, however, complexity is constraining our business "go to customer" situation
Impact	• *EnTility* "go to market" time is high, and is slow to act • Disconnect between some projects versus the strategy • Silo projects with limited governance and accountability • Under communication of initiatives and projects • May not direct or adequately resource project with opportunities to add high value
Recommendation	• Focus on 3 core initiatives prioritized by the board • Align the enterprise approach to strategy management

3.2.4 Manage Channel Strategy

Description	3.2.4.1 Evaluate channel attributes and partners 3.2.4.2 Determine channel fit with target segments 3.2.4.3 Select channels for target segments 3.2.4.4 Define and manage channel/store format strategy
Issues	• Silo approach to channel across the organization • No common definition across the organization for channel • *EnTility* needs to build brand awareness for our products using social media • People skills are required for understanding the change in consumer dynamics and also find out more alternate solutions • Market dynamics demands us to look at multiple channels to reach our end consumers • Currently uses old fashioned techniques to reach customers • *EnTility* need to develop direct selling capabilities • Exploratory stage, need to qualify opportunities

(Continued)

Impact	• Without a strategy we are not in a position to quickly exploit new opportunities across existing or new channels • Communication across the organization is hindered by a lack of clear definition around what existing and prospective channels for communication are • Lost opportunities for synergies across the organization • Missing market opportunities because of limited channels
Recommendation	• Align with enterprise effort to define "Channel Strategy" • Understand Opportunities and profit measures per channel
1.2 Develop business strategy	
Description	1.2.1 Develop overall mission statement 1.2.2 Select long-term business strategy 1.2.3 Coordinate and align functional and process strategies 1.2.4 Create organizational design 1.2.5 Develop and set organizational goals 1.2.6 Formulate business unit strategies 1.2.7 Develop financial strategies 1.2.8 Analyze portfolio positioning
Issues	• Some products are not sustainable
Impact	• Product line is restricted
Recommendation	• Invest in sustainability • Invest in innovation or other sustainable energy products

Key Recommendations

Get Business Involved, or in Charge

Single customer view (SCV) indicates the business value and what strategic or tactical business benefits the organization is planning to achieve. The simple matter is that the SCV plan needs to have the "business metric" not an IT metric of delivery of application. This requires business to define the key benefits that are expected from the SCV. The three key areas of improvements are

- Key Customer Information Management (CIM) processes
- Technology supporting them
- Culture of the organizations

The business needs to evaluate and optimize the key CIM processes before initiating any IT projects. The existing culture within various departments must be analyzed and factored in the roadmap.

Allow Ample Time for Evaluation and Planning

The single customer view requires analysis of current business process, cultures, and IT systems topology. This needs ample time allocation to build a robust roadmap. The project/s that is recommended based on the roadmap requires a vision for 3–5 years and must be included in the program of work for multiple years.

Have a Big Vision, but Take Small Steps

A single customer view requires defining the vision and components or "big picture" before starting any technology projects. The "big picture" includes the "to-be" processes, organization, and cultural refinements required. Once the big picture is defined, it is hard to achieve the lot in a "big bang" approach and a well-planned phased approach is required to optimize the benefits of "enhancement in technology," iterative refinement of processes and organizational structure.

Consider Potential Performance Problems

The information distribution and complexity of each system due to organic growth requires multiple transformation and extraction of information. This may create performance problem in accessing the data (transactional versus analytical data). The roadmap considers potential performance problems and should design systems and processes to address them.

Institute Data Governance Policies and Processes

Data security, including permission, security, and access control in *EnTility* data and systems standardization effort is required to establish organization-wide security policies (*who can access what data and how*). This should begin with an audit of customer permissions, system security, and business rules for accessing customer data.

Developing a complete, correct, and consistent standard for all customer records should be a top priority. This requires standardization of the business rules and data formats across the systems. Current data quality improvement undertaken by CRM project must be included as "business as usual" tasks to maintain achieved cleansing of data and maintain ongoing quality. This requires end-to-end data quality process definition and implementation should be an integral part of the single customer view strategy.

Prioritizing Requests

The context-sensitive information is clearly defined. This assists in developing entities required for SCV. The entities are defined as **mandatory** data elements that must be available (name, address, telephone, etc.), **required** are others that may be necessary (email address, credit worthiness, contract status), and **optional** that are useful (last contact date, customer score, preferences).

Developing a Road Map

Once these priorities are in place, the next step is to layout the overall roadmap. Because of the rate of technological change and the increasing importance of standardized data, it is almost inevitable that the company ends up with several current initiatives that involve customer information. This is both an opportunity and a risk. Part of the benefits case involves aligning and enabling other initiatives. Requested capabilities are delivered simply by coordinating the customer data streams in existing projects. If interdependencies are not given due consideration early in the project, any new single view initiative becomes another standalone project. As such, it is a struggle to gain traction with the topic of data and an opportunity to harmonize existing initiatives is missed.

Building a Program Plan

Once a road map is laid out, a program plan of projects is built for capabilities to be delivered in the next 12 months. All the classic program management disciplines apply here—setting objectives before defining activities, adopting measure/trial/measure, and plan/do/review approaches using Responsible, Accountable, Consulted and Informed (RACI) planning to assign accountabilities, and so forth. It is critical that the process and people elements are considered along with data and technology. To understand the root causes of why a single customer view isn't visible today, each step is examined from a people, process, data, and technology perspective.

Continuous Improvement

The most compelling reason to implement a single customer view is the strategic imperative for more revenue, improved profit, and demonstrable compliance. Once an initial project is completed there are limitless opportunities to improve update processes and add more information to the standard customer record.

Single customer view is the enabler of better customer services and benefits business with lower "cost to sell" and "cost to service." This requires a well-planned roadmap and should only be undertaken after following tasks are completed:

Data Cleansing Process

CRM project has developed data cleansing modules for most of the billing systems. These modules should be extended to CRM systems as well. The success of the single customer view is determined by the data quality and user's trust on the presented data. The recommendations are to use a federated data source and consolidate information using Master data management and "on demand services." Data cleansing processes are defined and data cleansed on a regular basis using scheduled processes. The scheduling takes into consideration any performance issues.

Business Analytics Strategies

This is essential in generating various profiles on a regular basis that assists in realizing SCV.

Foundation Projects as Part Program of Work

This is essential in identifying the customer information necessary to realize business outcomes. The next few years program of work includes a project for "lights on" category (those projects that are necessary to keep basic processes running for the organization's everyday business) and foundation projects to realize the next five years' strategic road maps.

Such recommended directions have led *EnTility* to define a clear path for its future direction and growth, and a successful and effective merger of an acquired utility organization.

Chapter 12

Business Architecture and Capability Case Study 3—Government Services

Introduction to the Case Study

Business Context

Gov4You is a federal government agency responsible for managing and sharing citizen information for large groups of the population. The *Gov4You* department was created almost 15 years ago to meet the election promise of providing better information services to the citizens. The department was setup to provide complete digital services for citizens. The digital citizen services must cater to the large demographic differences, and for those that are digitally savvy as well as those without any access to the Internet. These services are currently provided by several different departments that sometimes require physical visits by the citizens to the departments with a lot of paper work for identification and service request forms. However, citizens demand better services that use digital platforms in 24 × 7 formats. This concept of providing service using a digital transformation is referred to as 'Smart Government' and provides intelligent services to citizens by taking advantage of technological advances. It needs to incorporate new technology such as Cloud storage and Big Data analytics.

The expectation of Smart Government poses a difficult problem for *Gov4You*. The *Gov4You* needs a radical overhaul and redesign of its services to incorporate new technology and provide real-time, efficient services to its citizens. It has current constraints of budget, existing structure of processes, people and tools, an architecture that needs a complete redesign, and is a challenging task.

Citizens expect the same service from government they are getting from social media and other web applications. They want to have access to their personal information and details of activities available online. *Gov4You* must manage the demand for "open data," where information is available to all, without any restriction of copyrights, and "My Data," where individual citizen information is available as requested, based on the context of the inquiry. Such changes in services also allow for local and global data, requiring processing, classifying, and making a significant amount of the data available to other government and non-government agencies.

However, *Gov4You* has a few major challenges in achieving this goal.

Processes

Departments have not streamlined and re-evaluated their processes for many years. Some of the processes have unnecessary steps and require many authorizations and approvals along the way. The relevancy of those steps is no longer valid. *Gov4You* must look at its processes with a fresh perspective, and make them simpler and more streamlined. With online digital services for citizens, some of the activities like physical sign offs, might become redundant. The new system should make self-service easy and fast. This means that the *Gov4You* should redefine structures, roles, and its operating model. Due to jurisdiction changes and regulatory laws, there is duplication of work between departments. Same personal data is processed similarly, but has to be kept private and separate. These processes need to change so only contextual information is sent digitally between the departments and duplication does not exist.

Information Management

Gov4You currently has a limited information management structure available. Knowledge of what the business uses, how and when the knowledge is transformed, and where is it kept is known only to some groups. The security classification and access control is not clearly known. A high level of security is required to safeguard the information from any malicious use and is required for data transfer to other departments. Digitization requires data from several departments, and security and privacy is a high priority. Processes to ensure tight security and privacy of data cannot be defined if rules are not clearly known. Security of data and information is of further importance in Big Data because of the need and opportunities to share data and analytics. Data is not adequately aligned to the needs of the business to provide timely, contextual information if information is not complete. All disparate information from various systems of the agencies becomes difficult to integrate. Not knowing where to fetch the information required makes the cost of retrieving information prohibitive.

The culture of sharing information must be promoted within government agencies and ensures information is current, relevant, and well managed. Structured and unstructured information must be available in the context of knowledge and information requirements of different groups. Information should be synthesized easily as a process to gather knowledge. *Gov4You* must also have the right analytics on top of the Information Management to learn from its successes and failures to develop better services for the citizens.

Gov4You is required to be transparent and accountable for all its decisions, but the lack of an enterprise information management framework means that transparent processes cannot be defined to improve the quality of data and integrate it with systems. There is no single and complete data model within the organization. There are multiple instances of the same customer across three or four different databases. Multiple databases containing the same basic information (e.g., address, birthdate, email) create a nightmare for maintenance, as well as operational use. For digitization, the name and addresses received from external organization have to be matched with *Gov4You* data. As the data is not standard and in multiple places, integration becomes very difficult. Data entry also does not have enough controls, making it an error-prone process.

To get this project of digitization up to speed, online networks, collaboration tools, and the right infrastructure are required to support network and capacity issues. Infrastructure solutions require a careful strategic approach to take advantage of cloud-based storage and analytical opportunities. Understanding data risks and the impact of change across the data architecture involves complex and lengthy analysis. All this sharing of information within and externally requires a robust, well-thoughtout architecture.

Knowledge Management

Knowledge is not readily available because it is in the heads of the employees and mostly undocumented. This needs to be centralized to create a common understanding across diverse locations, and to bring about a feeling of connection with employees that might belong to various divisions. IT can enable this change and create a process to create, organize, and retrieve information via a knowledge repository. This can also make the organization aware of its above average capabilities and areas of expertise. However, employees should be rewarded and encouraged to use the system, so it is useful. Employees should have easy and quick access to knowledge that can help them resolve their issues so better customer service can be given. This Knowledge Management (KM) system should be available across jurisdictions and keep field forces connected.

Correct and timely information and data are essential to get to the next step in any online process, especially when taking real-time decisions and next best actions. Departments are creating their own reports and defining the data structures with different definitions. Hence, the reports cannot be compared to each other and do not provide a view of the bigger picture. As real-time services are expected, business intelligence needs to be dynamic as well to provide up-to-date information to *Gov4You* service agents and executives. The Key Performance Indicators (KPIs) for different departments are often in conflict, leading to data reports unusable by other departments.

Some of the information is on old devices and must be kept for up to 99 years. Transformation of this information on newer and faster devices is also a time-consuming and challenging task.

Knowledge is about not only the file locations or the process used, but also the experience gathered after having worked on a process for some time—for example, knowledge of a geographical location and its intricacies that can help in building and designing roads and highways must be available to *Gov4You*. This experience takes time to build, and is the key factor in a competitive advantage. Technology limitations are prominent in *Gov4You* due to lack of investment. The new disruptive technologies demand organization to adapt to digital business, but the organizational capability to utilize these advancements may be restricted by current technological solutions. The use of agile development methods may assist in achieving the goals of tactical solutions with a strategic mindset, but planning is important in adopting this approach.

Outdated Technology

Gov4You has not invested in information technology due to resource constraints. This lack of investment in technology has created a technology debt. Architectural debt can delay the government's transition from current services to "Smart Government" services. Data structures do not allow the information to flow freely and quickly. Data needs to be transformed and re-calculated at stages, often manually, before it goes to the other departments.

The digital age requires new data structures and the ability to make real-time decisions. This needs information to flow quickly, securely between and within departments and analyzed in real time. *Gov4You* does not have the technology or the skills to get this done.

Any new technology implementation in *Gov4You* goes through legislative checks, risk assessments, and any other compliance rules. This usually takes a long time and employees are discouraged by this red tape so avoid new implementation if they can.

Employees

Gov4You has several employees that have been working there for more than 10 years. Due to inefficiencies described above, their morale, enthusiasm, and hunger for learning new technology needs a boost. Government jobs are secure and HR policies do not provide a challenging atmosphere for employees to learn, grow, and share information.

Employing technically savvy, innovative personnel that comes with fresh ideas would be a great addition to *Gov4You*. This mix of skills and capabilities is quite essential for the step up required for *Gov4You*. However, the remuneration and award policies of HR are not as attractive as in private companies, which makes it harder to retain the young and inquisitive.

Funding Issues

Funding is usually allocated to a department on an annual basis, according to its plans and goals. A digital project of this size has not been able to gather momentum so far. It requires vast resources and needs different agencies to work together and form a common platform for the user. The rules and regulations of each department are different and the data being pooled together needs security, process change, information and knowledge management, and governance at the very least. The sheer magnitude of such a large project needs a good business case and details of implementation such that it would be accepted for funds.

As this project is large and it may take more than one funding cycle (1 year) to finish, chances are high that top management loses direction or government policies shift. Furthermore, as the project initially comprises a number of foundational pieces, any funding delay may impact other projects until the next cycle. There is also a doubt that if the completion of the project is delayed the solutions implemented might not be current with the latest technologically and service offerings that comes with it.

Government funding is generally allocated to a project giving benefits against a certain cost and its maintenance. Funding may not include amounts for improvements or adoption of new technologies. Hence, a foundational project establishes the technologies and architecture as an underpinning structure might not get the funding it deserves.

Currently, each department is approaching digital transformation within its own budget, constraining options.

Organizational Structure Challenges

The different departments of government, including *Gov4You*, have been working in siloes, impeding any digital revolution.

Departments operate relatively independently with their own spending limits and policies as agreed upon by the center. Thus, each agency could have a differing priority or an inconsistent business process. For this project to commence, it is important to reduce redundancies with minimum disruption to existing processes.

Delivering a change at this level, especially where the jurisdiction covers millions of people, is understandably massive and involves many layers and departments. Handoffs between departments can become time-consuming and expensive, as can duplication of data, reports, resources, and processes. Each department might have a different procurement policy.

In the current *Gov4You* organizational structure, roles are distributed across departments, responsibilities are not always clear, and there are no distinct handover points in processes for sharing information and outcomes.

Governance

Governance is the overall management approach that monitors and controls projects in organizations, to deliver value and not lose sight of the big picture. *Gov4You* should ensure this large project is appropriately governed from the start to ensure short- and long-term objectives are met. The strategic alignment of the project with each participating department is essential for the success of such a project. This complexity requires constant monitoring, so that the project achieves critical success factors from each division at each milestone.

Senior management must understand the result of the designed strategy and the capabilities needed to achieve the goal. It should also be clear on its current state of capabilities and the gap between the current and the desired states.

As there is no enterprise view of information, communication within *Gov4You* and other collaborating departments must be clear. Governance must understand both the strategy and the limitations of the organization, to make sensible, cost-effective, and appropriate decisions.

The scope of the project and conflicts of stakeholders must be contained so that joint agreement is reached.

With so many changes and challenges, the senior management has to be practical and proceed in a manner to adopt progressive steps and start the change the organization needs.

Following high-profile criticism in the press and with various citizen forums of a fragmented approach to strategic planning, including a failure to set objectives for the short, medium, and long term, a new strategy for *Gov4You* was developed to set the basis for the development of a new, long-term strategic plan. The vision sets out the organizational transformation needed to maximize effectiveness of *Gov4You* and details how the organization should respond to these challenges in the future. Figure 12.1 defines the project methodology used in this case study for the creation and use of business capability-based framework to provide directions for the investment decisions.

The history of *Gov4You* shows the danger of being swept along by waves of social and technological change and responding only under external pressure. Instead, *Gov4You* should shape its own development through engagement with the citizen community about the strategic choices it must make—including setting priorities. With a high number of disparate systems currently operating across various government agencies, information is commonly duplicated, inaccessible by citizens using online services, stored in siloes, not standardized, and not able to provide the full capability that *Gov4You* requires to perform their functions. As a result, there are multiple cumbersome and ineffective processes for capturing information, which divert *Gov4You* from providing the core digital services.

In line with the agreed Enterprise Architecture Framework, any Information and Communication Technology (ICT) initiatives are established to seek maximum benefit to *Gov4You* by adopting the best value approach to adopting solutions (re-use before buy, buy before build). The strategic framework is designed enable guidance, consultation, and an approval framework for investments in people, process, and technology; ensuring alignment to and support of the defined strategy and vision of *Gov4You*. The *Gov4You* adopted "Think BIG but start small" principle and defined following guidelines for the business capability definition projects:

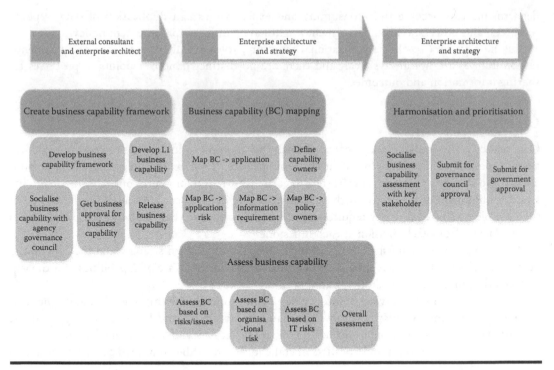

Figure 12.1 Project methodology.

■ Target projects to build necessary capabilities
■ Projects are to either enhance a business capability or develop new required business capabilities
■ Enterprise-wide prioritization is required
■ The mindset needs to change from technical solutions to business outcome-driven solutions
■ Solutions must be pragmatic and timely
■ Value for Money and Return on Investment

Business Technology Roadmap

The Business Technology Roadmap (BTR) was developed in collaboration with external consultancy agency, and provides a business technology reference framework that supports the long-term strategies, priorities, and business goals of *Gov4You*, while supporting the relevant standards and operational performance against agreed business capabilities. The BTR is developed as business capability-based investment governance and roadmaps. The business capability is based on in-house development and supplemented with American Productivity Quality Center (APQC) Process Control Framework (PCF) for government industrial vertical. The following principles are used to guide the development and refinement of a fit-for-purpose, practical, and achievable BTR (Figure 12.2).

To maintain BTR relevancy as an accurate 5-year rolling view of strategic information and systems, it was recommended that the Chief Information Officer accepts Roadmap ownership, and that the Information Management Committee formally sign-off the roadmap on an annual basis (Figure 12.3).

Principle	Description
Effective	Improve the accessibility, timeliness, agility, and effectiveness of information and services.
Efficient	Shape functions, solutions, and priorities to maximize value for money.
Relevant	The needs of *Gov4You*, the community and our partners drive the development of fit-for-purpose solutions.
Business driven	The enterprise wide needs, solutions and priorities are identified and driven by the business, with clear ownership of capabilities and solutions, and an enterprise wide commitment to priorities.
Interoperable	Continually improve information flows and exchanges with all stakeholders.
Secure	Solutions are shaped by security needs and enable security requirements to be met.
Sustainable	Adopt strategies, plans, and practices that meet the needs of the present while providing a platform for the future.
Flexible and adaptive	Based on evidence, we develop and deploy capabilities that enable *Gov4You* to respond to the evolving needs of community and partners in a timely manner. Systems are sufficiently flexible to enable such changes.
Deliverable	Solutions are realistic and achievable, and delivered in a way that enables stakeholder confidence in *Gov4You* systems and information.

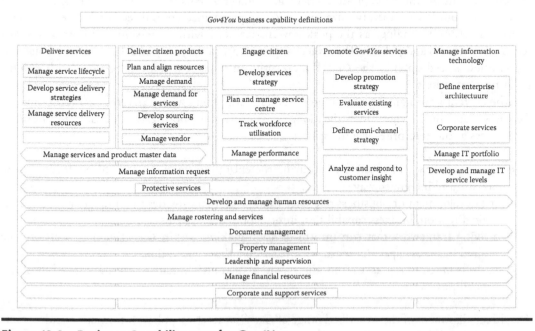

Figure 12.2   Business Capability map for *Gov4You*.

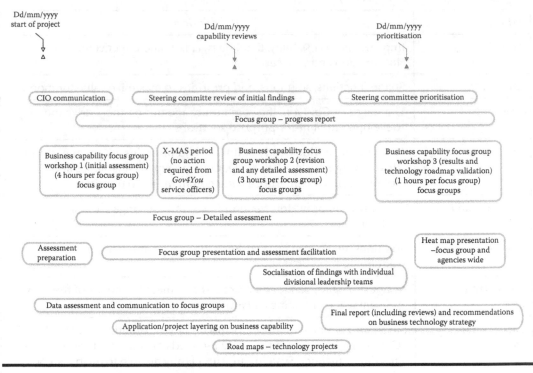

Figure 12.3 Business Capability assessment plan.

Governance Structure

In order to ensure the appropriate level of governance is enabled without creating additional bureaucratic burden on the organization, existing governance committee for Project Approval Committee (PAC) remained as the peak governance body with ownership and oversight across required standards and policies. The project approvals are given yearly and, on prioritized business capabilities, agreed upon by the *Gov4You* executive management committee along with government representations.

The current governance structure provides standards along with providing technical input to Business Capability owners. Identification, assessment, and prioritization of *Gov4You* business capabilities at the enterprise level to assist:

■ the organization in effectively capturing the entire information needs of the business in a holistic and integrated way
■ the development of a business reference framework that provides the linkages between strategic direction, business capabilities, information, and systems
■ a living framework that can inform decision-making within *Gov4You* that relates to the desired business capability maturity levels across the organization
■ to inform *Gov4You* as to the alignment of planned initiatives to the agreed business capabilities

The direct alignment of the prescribed range of *Gov4You* services, policy, information and systems to business capabilities and sub-capabilities incorporating:

- Identifying target business capability owners (agency CEO or directors)
- Identifying target sub-capability owners (Director level)
- Identifying relevant stakeholders
- Mapping organization policies, process, information, applications, systems, and finance
- Mapping organizational, business and IT (infrastructure, information, application, and security) risks
- Assessing the risks and opportunities affecting each business capability
- Identifying highest priority capabilities

Moving Forward with *Gov4You*

Key Tasks and Artifacts Produced

The following key tasks have been completed as part of the development, mapping, assessment, and prioritization process.

Create Business Capability Framework	*BTR*
Business Capability Mapping	Target Capability Owner Target Information Owner Target Application Owner Application > Capability Map Risks > Capability Map Organization Risk > Capability Map IT Risk > Capability Map
Assess Business Capability	*Business Capability Assessment*
Harmonize and Prioritization	Draft Communications package for target owners Draft roles and responsibilities for capability and sub-capability owners

Methodology and Artifacts

The following materials have been utilized:

- People—*Gov4You* Organizational Chart
- Policy—*Gov4You* Policy Framework
- Process—*Gov4You* Manual Policy and Guidelines
- Information and Application
- *Gov4You* Function Framework
- ICT Procurement information
- Finance (incomplete mapping)
- Contract and Procurement reports
- Financial Delegation reports
- Risk
- Business risks

- *Gov4You* Organizational Risks
- Enterprise Architecture Risks:
- Infrastructure
- Information
- Application
- Security

Policy Mapping

The *Gov4You* Policy Owner Framework is used as a base to align business capabilities and existing policy owners where possible to assist in the development of stakeholders and target owners for capabilities.

Application Mapping

The *Gov4You* Function and Activity Model mapped all *Gov4You* applications to predefined functions. The predefined functions are designed to provide a pictorial view, with high-level descriptions, for the various functions and associated activities managed by *Gov4You*. This assessment is intended to help the organization understand the range of functions managed by itself and is used as a reference point in support of any project or initiative. This document can also assist in aligning areas of responsibility and information systems to support those functions. The work undertaken by that project has been validated in workshops with agency participants as part of this process and has been used as the basis for mapping business capabilities to applications.

Risk Mapping

Each capability has been linked to risks that limit effective delivery. Risks affecting the effective delivery of business capabilities have been mapped in a many to many combination. Each capability may have multiple risks. Each risk may have multiple capabilities.

The same method of calculation has been applied consistently to all sub-capabilities and capabilities within the assessment.

Assumptions

The weight of each risk within an area has been considered as equal business risks.

Calculations

The weighting of combined risk has been weighted as follows:
- 40%—Organizational Risk
- 30%—Business Risks
- 30%—IT/Architecture Debt

Risk Threshold

No identified risk: 0
   Low: 1%–16%

Medium: 17%–30%
High: +31%

Example of Priority Calculation

This section details the calculations used to determine the priority rating for the Intelligence capability. This methodology was used consistently throughout the capability maturity assessment.

Business Capability: **Understand constituent needs and align to *Gov4You* capabilities**
Organizational Risks—3 (21%) Medium

Following organizational risks assessed as linked to the **"Understand constituent needs and align to *Gov4You* capabilities"** capability:

Information management and security	The risk of an unauthorized release of sensitive information caused by non-compliance with *Gov4You* security policy resulting in a compromise citizen security.
Cyber threats	Risk of cyber infiltration to *Gov4You* systems by organized crime groups, caused by a lack of appropriate technology and personal capability and capacity to monitor and investigate threats, resulting in compromised *Gov4You* data and an inability to deliver *Gov4You* services.
Physical security of *Gov4You* premises and property	The risk of breaches to the physical security of *Gov4You* premises and property caused by deliberate criminal acts resulting in physical harm to *Gov4You* members, loss or damage to property, and/or a loss of investigation integrity.

Business Risks—37 (26%) **Medium**

Due to the volume of Business Risks (37) linked to the **"Understand constituent needs and align to *Gov4You* capabilities"** capability, the following three have been used as a sample extract:

- Failure of Applications to meet business needs, for example, Freedom of Information Manager.
- The risk of failing to adequately capture evidence and provide support caused by insufficient telecommunications infrastructure and equipment resulting in reduced capacity to service technical investigations.
- Failing to identify information about behavioral patterns and trends caused by inadequate processes and systems to support capture of information resulting in an increase in poor ethical behavior and diminished public confidence in *Gov4You*.

IT Risks—20 (63%) **High**

The following IT Risks were linked to the **"Understand constituent needs and align to *Gov4You* capabilities"** capability.

Risk	Infrastructure	Information	Application	Security
Decentralized information inhibiting organizational view		X	X	
Multiple copies of data resulting in the use of incorrect information.		X	X	
Data leakage or misuse due to inconsistent Classification.		X		X
Data is stored Inappropriate applications/systems	X	X	X	X
Availability exposures due to lack of mature BCP and DR processes		X	X	

Infrastructure—2 (6%) **Low**	Information—7 (22%) **Medium**
Application—7 (22%) **Medium**	Security—4 (13%) **Low**

Weighted Risk Combined

Organizational Risk at 40% + Business Risk at 30% + IT Risk at 40%

$$(0.4 \times 21\%) + (0.3 \times 26\%) + (0.3 \times 63\%) = 34.5\% \text{ High}$$

Risk Categories

Capabilities are colored using traffic light colors of green, red, and amber depending on the number of risks mapped to each business capability.

Organizational Risk

The *Gov4You* Organizational Risks are managed at the strategic level and include risks assessed as those of the highest priority, scrutiny (public and media), cost, and risk to the organization.

These risks have been determined by *Gov4You* executive team as the most significant risks and issues affecting *Gov4You* and as such have been weighted at 50% when calculating overall risk to business capabilities.

The highest priority capabilities in this category were:

■ Understand constituent needs and align to *Gov4You* capabilities
■ Leadership and Supervision

Business Risks

Figure 12.4 depicts the business risks of the capabilities. The model aims to put an end to standalone processes and different timelines for strategic assessment, business planning, and risk management regimes. The model brings together intelligence, business planning, service delivery, and performance management across the organization.

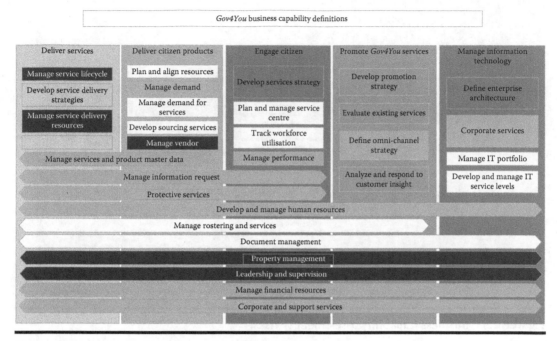

Figure 12.4   Business Capability assessment of business risks.

The highest priority capabilities in this category were:

■ Understand constituent needs and align to *Gov4You* capabilities
■ Leadership and Supervision

IT Risk

Figure 12.5 depicts the IT risks incorporating four categories: the IT risk assessment of each capability includes registered risks (including architectural debt) related to application, infrastructure, information, and security. Risks are assessed according to the architectural patterns, standards, and information policies within *Gov4You*.

Application Risk

These are risks associated with an existing application, including risks relating to:

■ Business requirements
■ Application design
■ Application Code
■ Application testing
■ Application Maintenance

Application risks relate to the integration, quality, performance, usability and ease of patching, and maintenance. They range from direct risks such as code that allows undesirable behavior, to oblique risks such as the end of support for a library or component used to develop the application.

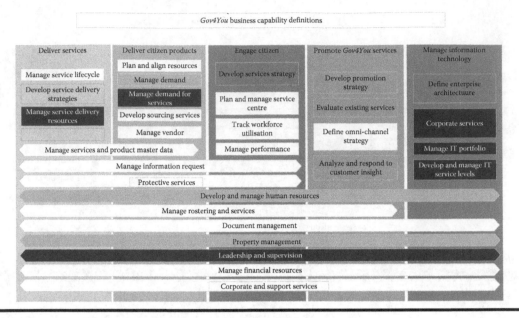

Figure 12.5   Business Capability assessment IT risks.

Applications were mapped to risks based on the existing business sensitivity, data classification and the intended use of the application, and the potential for exposure. The assessment is based on internal standards, architecture experience, and established design patterns (both internal and industry best practice).

Information Risk

These are risks associated with information management, including risks relating to the Information Management life cycle:

- Information Acquisition
- Information Processing and Flow
- Information Retention
- Information Disposal
- Information Security

Information risks relate to the flow of information, and its use and availability throughout the information life cycle. Information risks do not just consider loss of or exposure of information—but also information not being available when required for a specific business need.

Information risks are mapped in consultation with responsible stakeholders and based on assessment of controls, data classification, and business usage requirements, in accordance with the data governance standards.

Infrastructure Risk

These are risks associated with the physical environment that hosts or directly supports an application. This includes:

- Network
- Servers and back-end systems
- Back-up and Restore environment
- Associated environmental components such as High Availability (HA) and failover
- Supporting back-end equipment such as Enterprise Service Bus (ESB)

Infrastructure relates to the components and systems that form the underpinning for services and applications that run on top of them, such as disk storage, networks, and so forth. Many of these services are shared across different business applications—more than one application server can call the same database, for instance, and different servers can share disk space. For this reason, Infrastructure risks are different from the other categories of risk in that they relate more to service level, capacity, and performance implications—and less to business application delivery.

These risks have been assessed based on technical assessment of the underlying components being capable to meet the specified service levels agreed with the business, both at a point in time, and throughout the life of the solution.

Security Risk

These are risks associated with security architecture, including those within IT systems:

- Business Data Acquisition
- Business Data Processing and Flow
- Business Data Retention
- Business Data Disposal
- Data Security and controls

Security is traditionally defined as Confidentiality, Integrity, and Availability (CIA). Security risks are largely defined in the reference documents and are related to exposures related to design, configuration, and implementation of systems and infrastructure. The risk process seeks the balance between achieving controls to address CIA and the cost of implementing those controls. Business stakeholders were engaged to identify security risks that are related to gaps in controls or perceived exposure of the organization to loss, theft, damage, data leakage, compliance, etc. that exceed our regulatory framework. The highest priority capabilities in these categories were:

- Understand constituent needs and align to *Gov4You* capabilities
- Leadership and Supervision
- Corporate Services sub-capabilities:
  - Information Technology
  - Strategy, Planning, and Policy
  - Change/Project
  - Quality and Compliance
  - Internal Audit

Priority Capabilities

Figure 12.6 depicts the capabilities which have been calculated as the highest priority for the organization are those with significant and consistent barriers to the relevant and timely access and

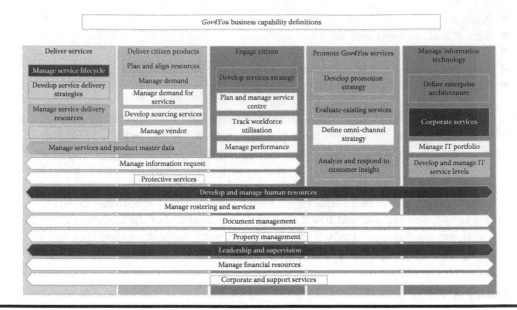

Figure 12.6 Business Capability assessment overall risks.

exchange to the information needed, impeding organizational ability to respond to requests for service both externally and internally within *Gov4You*. These limitations include:

- Lack of system integration
- Insufficient data storage
- Significant manual processing (including data duplication)
- Functional and non-functional obstacles to individual staff access
- Inability to respond quickly to new technology requirements (cyber-crime, social media)

The capabilities with the least functional maturity and the greatest challenges and risks have been designated as the overall highest priority:

- Understand constituent needs and align to *Gov4You* capabilities
- Leadership and Supervision
- Corporate Services sub-capabilities:
- Information Technology
- Quality and Compliance
- Strategy, Planning, and Policy

Business Capability Assessment

The "inadequate investment in technology" over a sustained period has resulted in a wide array of inefficient, ineffective, and in some cases unsustainable IT systems. *Gov4You* requires the investment of resources toward its IT systems to become a truly modern, agile, and well-equipped organization. To achieve this objective, the investments are guided by the following principles where information must be:

- Provided from a single source of truth;
- Accurate and up-to-date;
- Available instantly regardless of location;
- Presented within the context of the specific scenario experienced by the user;
- Drawn from multiple systems in a coherent manner to allow the best-informed decision-making;
- Able to be shared securely, quickly, and seamlessly with other personnel in the field, and
- Services delivered in a secure and trusting manner that allows digital services to the citizens

Gov4You does not and is unlikely to have unlimited access to the financial resources to address the substantial legacy resulting from the previous under-investment. As a result, analysis was performed to assess the maturity and risk level of each *Gov4You* Business Capability, informing the future ICT direction for *Gov4You* through:

- An enterprise-level view of the key challenges and risks affecting *Gov4You* 's business capabilities;
- An overview of the business problems from an operational perspective and potential opportunities to leverage information in a more effective manner; and the
- Summary identification of the highest priority business technology capabilities within the organization.

To understand the maturity required by the organization to deliver the capabilities, each capability was evaluated within a context of the information and functionality needed for optimum performance and assessed against the applications and technology used; policy and governance in place and known risks, business problems, and information gaps that hinder effective service delivery.

With a focus on ICT functionality, risks, and business problems surrounding non-ICT capabilities (e.g., training, education, and supervision of staff) were excluded from the assessment.

The capabilities that have been calculated as the highest priority for the organization are those with significant and consistent barriers to the relevant and timely access and exchange of information. A combination of enterprise technology gaps (lack of integration planning and capability, insufficient storage, disparate and siloed systems) and obstacles to individual access for staff has been assessed as the greatest impediment to effective service delivery. The identification of the highest priority capabilities can be used by the organization to inform enterprise level investment analysis and ensure that system initiatives and resultant program of work are aligned and prioritized to these areas with the greatest need.

1.3 Manage Service Delivery Resources	
Description	1.3.1 Evaluate strategic options to achieve the objectives 1.3.2 Develop strategic initiatives
Issues	• Strategy to execution is not holistically managed • Lack of governance around the stated benefits versus the actual benefits delivered • Lack of clarity and consensus around business priorities • Missing risk management capabilities • Benefits identified in strategy are not being delivered

(Continued)

Impact	• The strategic objectives of the organization are not being met • Risks are not actively managed • IS does not execute on strategy and will constrain business
Recommendation	• Develop an enterprise approach to strategy implementation • An enterprise-wide prioritization is required for resource allocation • Implement a risk management methodology.

7.4 Corporate Services	
Description	7.4.1 Develop information and content management strategies 7.4.2 Define the enterprise information architecture 7.4.3 Manage information resources 7.4.4 Perform enterprise data and content management
Issues	• IT solutions in place to support the KPIs are not adequately orchestrated to deliver to organizations pace requirements • Information management maturity is low • Too much manual effort required to extract the information required • Information Systems landscape is complicated • Too many tools required to extract the information required • Master data is not managed well across the organization
Impact	• The organization is constrained in their ability to make decision in an appropriate timeframe • Availability of information is on weekly or monthly basis; results in reactive rather than proactive decision-making
Recommendation	• Enterprise focus on developing information management capability required • Assess ways to Accelerate development of BI and DW capability to close this key capability gap asap • Continue to Focus on Information Governance and MDM implementation

7.1 Manage the Business of Information Technology	
Description	7.1.1 Develop the enterprise IT strategy 7.1.2 Define the enterprise architecture 7.1.3 Manage the IT portfolio 7.1.4 Perform IT research and innovation 7.1.5 Perform IT financial management 7.1.6 Evaluate and communicate IT business value and Performance
Issues	• IT is lately recognized as strategic enabler of the business and needs to transform itself and uplift its capabilities to manage this change in expectation • Current demand spike and lot of latent demand, processes for managing demand are not effective • Business is actively looking for alternate providers due to responsiveness • Current Project methodology is too heavy weight and needs to be streamlined • Legacy of poor governance and systems documentation needs to be addressed

(Continued)

Impact	• Business which is increasingly reliant on IT misses out on new opportunities and cannot fully leverage IT solutions to deliver efficiencies. • Complexity of the systems landscape will increase if business bypasses Information Services and seeks alternate solution providers. • Information collection is slow and manually collected in many cases using paper-based, excel and access database. • The IT investment is not optimized
Recommendation	• Develop comprehensive Demand Management process • Transition to a service-based organization where costs of service are fully understood • Establish a culture of measurement within IT • Revise Project Methodology to ensure the overheads introduced are truly adding value

7.2 Develop and Manage IT Customer Relationships	
Description	7.2.1 Develop IT services and Solution strategy 7.2.2 Develop and Manage IT service Levels 7.2.3 Perform Demand Side Management for IT services 7.2.4 Manage IT Customer Satisfaction 7.2.5 Market IT Services and Solutions
Issues	• IS's customers does not feel that IS understands their particular issues and is responding to them appropriately • Business requirements are being fed to IS in an unqualified state and IS spends a large amount of resource qualifying these requirements and turning them into projects. • The Business is seeking alternate providers for IT services
Impact	• Project timelines are stretched as much of the project is spent clarifying requirements • Irrespective of how much IS delivers it will fail to meet business expectations on service delivery
Recommendation	• Grow the Business Relationship Management (BRM) capability and dedicate resources to hot spots • Establish the e-business manager role with a mandate to have much greater customer intimacy • Further establish the Enterprise Architecture disciplines and framework to underpin the Business engagement, requires clarification and fulfillment capabilities of IS

Prioritization

Capabilities have been categorized in high–low priority and listed in alphabetical order within each category.

Target Owner

A target owner has been identified for each capability by linking the policy, application, financial delegate, and process owners to each capability. As a rule, the target owner of each capability is the major or majority policy owner within a subject. The Responsibility section of this document contains detailed description of roles and responsibilities.

Descriptors

The description of each capability or sub-capability is taken from the 'Business Technology Roadmap' that was confirmed with senior representatives from across *Gov4You*. The capabilities were based on a business capability reference model that has been defined using internal definition and utilizing standards definitions such as APQC PCF for *Gov4You*.

Issues

Issues surrounding the successful delivery of each capability are identified through reviewing known IT risks (infrastructure, application, information, and security), business risks, and organizational risks relating to that capability and summarized.

Key Recommendations

This case study assessment provides recommendations about which foundation activities are best aligned to reducing the risks and challenges surrounding each business capability. Each capability and sub-capability assessment includes brief examples of current issues and potential future experiences should the recommended position papers be endorsed and those solutions implemented.

Allow Ample Time for Evaluation and Planning

The citizen services definition **requires** analysis of current business process, cultures, and IT systems topology. This needs ample time allocation to build a robust roadmap. The project/s that is recommended must be based on the roadmap requiring a vision for 3–5 years and must be included in the program of work of multiple years. This requires change in process from current yearly program of work to program of work for 2–3 years for the foundation projects.

Consider Potential Performance Problems

The information distribution and complexity of each system due to organic growth require multiple transformation and extraction of information. This may create performance problem in accessing the data (transactional versus analytical data). The roadmap should consider potential performance problems and should design systems and processes to address them.

Institute Data Governance Policies and Processes

Data security, including permission, security, and access control in *Gov4You* data and systems standardization effort is required to establish organization-wide security policies (*who can access what data and how*). This begins with an audit of customer permissions, system security, and business rules for accessing customer data.

Developing a complete, correct, and consistent standard for all customer records should be a top priority. This requires standardization of the business rules and data formats across the systems.

Developing a Road Map

Once these priorities are in place, the next step is to layout the overall roadmap. Because of the rate of technological change and the increasing importance of standardized data, it is almost inevitable that *Gov4you* ends up with several current initiatives that involve customer information. This is both an opportunity and a risk. Part of the benefits case involves aligning and enabling other initiatives. Requested capabilities may be delivered simply by coordinating the citizen services data streams in existing projects. If interdependencies are not given due consideration early in the project, any new single view initiative is become another standalone project. As such, it is a struggle to gain traction with the topic of data and an opportunity to harmonize existing initiatives are missed.

Building a Program Plan

Once a road map is laid out, a program plan of projects is built for capabilities to be delivered in the next 12 months. All the classic program management disciplines apply here—setting objectives before defining activities, adopting measure/trial/measure, and plan/do/review approaches using RACI planning to assign accountabilities, and so forth. It is critical that the process and people elements are considered along with data and technology. To understand the root causes of why a single customer view isn't visible today, we need to work through each of the steps from a people, process, data, and technology perspective.

Data Cleansing Process

Customer Relationship Management (CRM) project has developed data cleansing modules for most of the billing systems. These modules should be extended to CRM systems as well. The success of the citizen services is determined by the data quality and user's trust on the presented data. The recommendations are to use a federated data source and consolidate information using Master data management and "on demand services." Data cleansing processes must be defined and data cleansed on a regular basis using scheduled processes. The scheduling must take in consideration of any performance issue.

Business Analytics Strategies

Develop the citizen services performance management systems using the business analytics strategies. This assists *Gov4you* in developing citizen-centric services.

Foundation Projects as Part Program of Work

This is essential in identifying the customer information that is necessary to realize business outcomes. The next few years' program of work should include project for "lights on" category (those projects that are necessary to keep basic processes running for the organization's everyday business) and foundation projects to realize the next 5 years' strategic road maps.

Such recommended directions have led *Gov4You* to define a clear path for its future direction and growth, and successful and effective management of citizen services. *Gov4You* prioritized its projects and activities and reduced the list of planned projects. The reduction in managing project or initiative demand provides resources available to plan the implementation of the strategic activities. This assisted in enhancing the digital services framework for optimized services to the citizens.

Bibliography

This book is result of number of years of establishing business capability-based business architecture practices across private and public organizations. The business capabilities definitions have been in the domain of management consultancy organizations for a number of decades and have a number of frameworks that are proprietary to them. This book is bringing business capabilities based-business and enterprise architecture adoptable across all cross-section of organizations irrespective of size (small, medium, or large corporations) or industry base. This requires amalgamating business management principles, frameworks, and tool sets with the information technology disciplines. This bibliography lists a number of books from the management and technology domains to enhance the understanding of the concepts defined in this book. The book list is arranged in the order of the concepts introduced in the chapter numbers but is applicable to a number of other chapters where the concepts are discussed in details or referred.

Chapter 1

General Management

Alex Berson, Larry Dubov (2007), *Master Data Management and Customer Data Integration for a Global Enterprise*, McGraw-Hill, New York.

AnHai Doan, Alon Halevy (2012), *Principles of Data Integration*, Morgan Kaufmann, Waltham, MA.

Bonnie Biafore (2011), *Successful Project Management: Applying Best Practices and Real-World Techniques with Microsoft Project*, Microsoft Press (O'Reilly), Sebastopol, CA.

David C. Hay (2002), *Requirements Analysis: From Business Views to Architecture*, Prentice Hall, Upper Saddle River, NJ.

Eric Verzuh (2013), *The Portable MBA in Project Management*, John Wiley & Sons, Hoboken, NJ.

Hans J. Thamhain (2014), *Managing Technology-Based Projects: Tools, Techniques, People and Business Processes*, John Wiley & Sons, Hoboken, NJ.

Jack J. Phillips, Lynn Schmidt (2011), *The Leadership Scorecard* (Improving Human Performance Series), Routledge, New York.

James A. George, James A. Rodger (2010), *Smart Data: Enterprise Performance Optimization Strategy*, John Wiley & Sons, Hoboken, NJ.

Joel L. Naroff, Ron Scherer (2014), *Big Picture Economics: How to Navigate the New Global Economy*, John Wiley & Sons, Hoboken, NJ.

Keesook J. Han, Baek-Young Choi (2013), *High Performance Cloud Auditing and Applications*, Springer-Verlag, Berlin, Heidelberg.

Linda M. Orr, Dave J. Orr (2014), *Eliminating Waste in Business: Run Lean, Boost Profitability*, Apress, New York.

Olivier Blanchard (2011), *Social Media ROI: Managing and Measuring Social Media Efforts in Your Organization*, Que, Indianapolis, IN.

Paul Smith (2012), *Lead with a Story: A Guide to Crafting Business Narratives That Captivate, Convince, and Inspire*, Amacom, Nashville, TN.

Rini Van Solingen, Egon Berghout (1999), *Goal/Question/Metric Method*, McGraw-Hill, New York.

Rod Stephens (2015), *Beginning Software Engineering*, John Wiley & Sons, Hoboken, NJ.

William McKnight (2013), *Information Management: Strategies for Gaining a Competitive Advantage with Data*, Morgan Kaufmann, Waltham, MA.

Reading on ROI

Alain Verbeke (2009), *International Business Strategy: Rethinking the Foundations of Global Corporate Success*, Cambridge University Press, Cambridge.

Allan Afuah (2009), *Strategic Innovation: New Game Strategies for Competitive Advantage*, Routledge, New York.

Bernd H. Schmitt (2007), *Big Think Strategy: How to Leverage Bold Ideas and Leave Small Thinking Behind*, Harvard Business School Press, Boston, MA.

Charles C. Poirier, Lynette Ferrara, Francis Hayden, Douglas Neal (2003), *The Networked Supply Chain: Applying Breakthrough BPM Technology to Meet Relentless Customer Demands*, J. Ross Publishing, Boca Raton, FL.

Clifford M. Gross (2013), *Too Good To Fail: Creating Marketplace Value from the World's Brightest Minds, Management for Professionals*, Springer-Verlag, Berlin, Heidelberg.

Damon Golsorkhi, Linda Rouleau (2010), *Cambridge Handbook of Strategy as Practice*, Cambridge University Press, Cambridge.

David Archer, Alex Cameron (2009), *Collaborative Leadership: How to Succeed in an Interconnected World*, Routledge, New York.

Deepa Prahalad, Ravi Sawhney (2010), *Predictable Magic: Unleash the Power of Design Strategy to Transform Your Business*, Prentice Hall, Upper Saddle River, NJ.

Don Debelak (2009), *Perfect Phrases for Presenting Business Strategies (Perfect Phrases Series)*, McGraw-Hill, New York.

Fons Trompenaars, Maarten Nijhoff Asser (2010), *The Global M&A Tango: How to Reconcile Cultural Differences in Mergers, Acquisitions, and Strategic Partnerships*, McGraw-Hill, New York.

Gary Cokins (2009), *Performance Management: Integrating Strategy Execution, Methodologies, Risk, and Analytics*, John Wiley & Sons, Hoboken, NJ.

Graham Hooley, John Saunders, Nigel F. Piercy, Brigitte Nicoulaud (2008), *Marketing Strategy and Competitive Positioning* (4th Edition), Prentice Hall, Upper Saddle River, NJ.

Ian Wilson (2003), *The Subtle Art of Strategy: Organizational Planning in Uncertain Times*, Praeger Publishers, Westport, CT.

Jason Wingard (2015), *Learning to Succeed: Rethinking Corporate Education in a World of Unrelenting Change*, Amacom, Nashville, TN.

Joe Calloway, Chuck Feltz, Kris Young (2010), *Never by Chance: Aligning People and Strategy through Intentional Leadership*, John Wiley & Sons, Hoboken, NJ.

John E. Silvia (2001), *Dynamic Economic Decision Making: Strategies for Financial Risk, Capital Markets, and Monetary Policy*, John Wiley & Sons, Hoboken, NJ.

Laura Stack (2014), *Execution IS the Strategy: How Leaders Achieve Maximum Results in Minimum Time*, Berrett-Koehler Publishers, San Francisco, CA.

Lynda Applegate, Robert Austin, Deborah Soule (2009), *Corporate Information Strategy and Management*, McGraw-Hill, New York.

Lyndsay Wise (2012), *Using Open Source Platforms for Business Intelligence: Avoid Pitfalls and Maximize ROI*, Morgan Kaufmann, Waltham, MA.

Marty Poniatowski (2009), *Foundations of Green IT: Consolidation, Virtualization, Efficiency, and ROI in the Data Center*, Prentice Hall, Upper Saddle River, NJ.

Michael Armstrong (2006), *A Handbook of Management Techniques: A Comprehensive Guide to Achieving Managerial Excellence and Improved Decision Making*, Kogan Page, London.

Nilofer Merchant (2014), *The New How: Creating Business Solutions through Collaborative Strategy*, O'Reilly, Sebastopol, CA.

Orville C. Ferrell, Michael D. Hartline (2010), *Marketing Strategy*, South-Western College, Chula Vista, CA.

Rich Horwath (2014), *Elevate: The Three Disciplines of Advanced Strategic Thinking*, John Wiley & Sons, Hoboken, NJ.

Sergiu Hart, Andreu Mas-Colell (2013), *Simple Adaptive Strategies: From Regret-Matching to Uncoupled Dynamics* (World Scientific Series in Economic Theory), World Scientific Publishing, Singapore.

Shiv Mathur, Alfred Kenyon (2001), *Creating Value, Second Edition: Successful Business Strategies*, Butterworth-Heinemann, Oxford.

Terry Schmidt (2009), *Strategic Project Management Made Simple: Practical Tools for Leaders and Teams*, John Wiley & Sons, Hoboken, NJ.

William Weir (2001), *50 Battles That Changed the World*, Career Press. Franklin Lake, NJ.

Chapter 2

Information Technology strategies

Balasubramanian, P., Kulatilaka, N. and Storck J. (1998), *Managing Information Technology Investments Using a Real-Options Approach*, School of Management, Boston University, Boston, MA.

Buytendijk, F. and Oestreich, T.W. (2015), *Organizing for Big Data through Process and Governance*, Gartner Inc., Stamford, CT.

Carlopio, J. (1998), *Implementation: Making Workplace Innovation and Technical Change Happen*, McGraw-Hill, Sydney, pp. 1–10.

Cruz-Cunha, M.M. (2010), Social, managerial, and organizational dimensions of Enterprise Information Systems, business science reference.

Davenport, T.H., De Long, D.W. and Beers, M.C. (1998), Successful knowledge management projects, *Sloan Management Review*, 39(2), pp. 43–57.

Goel, A., Tiwary, A. and Schmidt, H. (2010). Approaches and initiatives to green IT strategy in business. In: B. Unhelkar (Ed.), *Handbook of Research on Green ICT: Technical, Methodological and Social Perspectives*, IGI Global, Hershey, PA.

Goel, A., Tiwary, A. and Schmidt, H. (2010). Green ICT and architectural frameworks. In: B. Unhelkar (Ed.), *Handbook of Research on Green ICT: Technical, Methodological and Social Perspectives*, IGI Global, Hershey, PA.

Harryson, S. (2000), *Managing Know-Who Based Companies: A Multinetwroked Approach to Knowledge and Innovation Management*, Edward Elgar, Northampton, MA.

Hosbond, J.H. (2004), *Automating Knowledge Creation: A Critical View*, Aalborg University, Aalborg.

Johnson, L. and Furlong, G.P. (2001), *Knowledge Management and the Competitive Edge*, Faculty of Business, University of Greenwich, London.

Kleppmann M. (2014), *Designing Data-Intensive Applications, Early Release*, O'Reilly, Sebastopol, CA.

Kotter, J.P. (1995), Leading change: why transformation efforts fail, *Harvard Business Review*, 73(2), pp. 59–68.

Manyika, J., Chui, M., Brown, B., Bughin, J., Dobbs, R., Roxburgh, C. and Byers, A.H., (2011), Big data—The next frontier for innovation, competition and productivity, *McKinsey Report*, June 2011, Retrieved August, 2015.

Metrics collection and implementation: An integrated and extensible approach in *World Multiconference on Systemics, Cybernetics and Informatics (SCI 97)* at Caracas, Venezuela in July 1997.

Miles, R.E. and Snow, C.C. (1978), *Organisational Strategy, Structure and Processes*, McGraw-Hill, New York.

Miles, R.E. and Snow, C.C. (1984), Fit failure and the hall of fame, *California Management Review*, 26(3), pp. 10–28.

Nonaka, I. (1994), A dynamic theory of organisational knowledge creation, *Organisational Science*, 5(1), pp. 14–37.

Scott Morton, M. (1991) (Ed.), *The Corporation of the 1990s: Information Technology and Organisational Transformation*, Oxford University Press, New York.

Stace, D. and Dunphy, D. (1994), Translating business strategy into action: transitions, transformations and turnarounds. In: *Beyond the Boundaries*, McGraw-Hill, Sydney, pp. 99–122.

Tiwary, A. and Unhelkar, B. (2011), Extending and applying business intelligence and customer strategies for green ICT, pp. 83. Chapter 6 in B. Unhelkar (Ed.), *Handbook of Research in Green ICT: Technical, Business and Social Perspectives*, IGI Global, Hershey, PA.

Tiwary, A. Collaborative Intelligence. Alinement Network, 10 May 2010 http://alinement.net/component/content/article/50?Itemid=34.

Unhelkar, B. and Tiwary, A. (2010). Business intelligence 2010: Delivering the goods or standing us up?, *Collaborative Intelligence, Cutter IT Journal Page 13–21*, 23(6).

Unhelkar, B., Tiwary, A. and Ghanbary, A. (2009), Transitioning business processes to a collaborative business environment with mobility: An action research based on a service organization. Chapter 7 in B. Unhelkar (Ed.), *Handbook of Research in Mobile Business: Technical, Methodological, and Social Perspectives*, 2nd Edition. IGI Global, Hershey & New York.

Usability of metrics collection system on November 97 at Australian Software Metrics Association's, "Better Business Through Metrics" Conference in Canberra.

White, A. and Logan, D. (2015), *Governing the Information Governance*, Gartner Inc., Stamford, CT.

Chapter 3

Enterprise Architecture

David Wood, (2010), *Linking Enterprise Data*, Springer-Verlag, Berlin, Heidelberg.

Dominic Duggan, (2012), *Enterprise Software Architecture and Design: Entities, Services, and Resources (Quantitative Software Engineering Series)*, John Wiley & Sons, Hoboken, NJ.

Jaap Schekkerman, (2013), *How to Survive in the Jungle of Enterprise Architecture Frameworks: Creating or Choosing an Enterprise Architecture Framework*, Trafford Publishing, Bloomington, IN.

James Luisi, (2014), *Pragmatic Enterprise Architecture: Strategies to Transform Information Systems in the Era of Big Data*, Morgan Kaufmann, Waltham, MA.

Jason Bloomberg, (2013), *The Agile Architecture Revolution: How Cloud Computing, REST-Based SOA, and Mobile Computing Are Changing Enterprise IT*, John Wiley & Sons, Hoboken, NJ.

Stefan Bente, Uwe Bombosch, (2012), *Collaborative Enterprise Architecture: Enriching EA with Lean, Agile, and Enterprise 2.0 Practices*, Morgan Kaufmann, Waltham, MA.

Knowledge management

Alan Eardley, Lorna Uden, (2010), *Innovative Knowledge Management: Concepts for Organizational Creativity and Collaborative Design (Premier Reference Source)*, IGI Global.

David E. McNabb, (2006), *Knowledge Management in the Public Sector: A Blueprint for Innovation in Government*, M.E. Sharpe, Armonk, NY.

Murray Jennex, (2005), *Case Studies in Knowledge Management*, Idea Group Publishing.

Pak Yoong, (2009), *Leadership in the Digital Enterprise: Issues and Challenges*, Business Science.

Tuba Kocaturk, Benachir Medjdoub, (2011), *Distributed Intelligence in Design*, John Wiley & Sons, Hoboken, NJ.

Chapter 4

Balasubramanian, P., Kulatilaka, N. and Storck, J. (1998), *Managing Information Technology Investments Using a Real-Options Approach*, School of Management, Boston University, Boston, MA.

Berson, A. and, Dubov, L. (2007), *Master Data Management and Customer Data Integration for a Global Enterprise*, McGraw-Hill, New York.

Biafore, B. (2011), *Successful Project Management: Applying Best Practices and Real-World Techniques with Microsoft Project*, Microsoft Press. Redmond, WA.

Blanchard, O. (2011), *Social Media ROI: Managing and Measuring Social Media Efforts in Your Organization*, Que, Indianapolis, IN.

Brandenburger, A. and Nalebuff, B. (1995), The right game: Use game theory to shape strategy, *Harvard Business Review*, 76(7), pp. 57–71.

Buytendijk, F. and Oestreich, T.W. (2015), *Organizing for Big Data through Process and Governance*, Gartner Inc., Stamford, CT.

Camerer, C. (1991), Does strategy research need game theory? *Strategic Management Journal*, 12, pp. 137–52.

Cruz-Cunha, M.M. (2010), Social, managerial, and organizational dimensions of Enterprise Information Systems, IGI Global.

Dixit, A. and Nalebuff, B. (1991), Ten tales of strategy. In: Dixit, A. and Nalebuff, B (Eds.), *Thinking Strategically: The Competitive Edge in Business, Politics and Everyday Life*, W. W. Norton & Co., New York, pp. 7–30.

Eisenhardt, K. (1990), Speed and strategic choice: how managers accelerate decision making, *California Management Review*, 32(3), pp. 39–54.

George, J.A. and Rodger, J.A. (2010), *Smart Data: Enterprise Performance Optimization Strategy*, John Wiley & Sons, Hoboken, NJ.

Goel, A., Tiwary, A. and Schmidt, H. (2010). Approaches and initiatives to green IT strategy in business. In: B. Unhelkar (Ed.), *Handbook of Research on Green ICT: Technical, Methodological and Social Perspectives*, IGI Global, Hershey, PA.

Goel, A., Tiwary, A. and Schmidt, H. (2010). Green ICT and architectural frameworks. In: B. Unhelkar (Ed.), *Handbook of Research on Green ICT: Technical, Methodological and Social Perspectives*, IGI Global, Hershey, PA.

Han, K.J. and Choi, B-Y. (2013), *High Performance Cloud Auditing and Applications*, Springer, New York

Hay, D.C. (2002), *Requirements Analysis: From Business Views to Architecture*, Prentice Hall, Upper Saddle River, NJ.

Hogarth, R. (1987), *Judgement and Choice*, Wiley, Chichester.

Kleppmann M. (2014), *Designing Data-Intensive Applications, Early Release*, O'Reilly, Sebastopol, CA.

Manyika, J., Chui, M., Brown, B., Bughin, J., Dobbs, R., Roxburgh, C. and Byers, A.H., (2011), Big data—The next frontier for innovation, competition and productivity, *McKinsey Report*, June 2011, Retrieved August, 2015.

McKnight, W. (2013), *Information Management: Strategies for Gaining a Competitive Advantage with Data*, Morgan Kaufmann, Waltham, MA.

Metrics collection and implementation: An integrated and extensible approach in *World Multi-conference on Systemics, Cybernetics and Informatics (SCI 97)* at Caracas, Venezuela in July 1997.

Naroff, J.L. and Scherer, R. (2014) *Big Picture Economics: How to Navigate the New Global Economy*, John Wiley & Sons, Hoboken, NJ.

Orr, L.M. and Orr, D.J. (2014), *Eliminating Waste in Business: Run Lean, Boost Profitability*, Apress, New York.

Oster, S. (1994), *Understanding Rivalry: Game Theory, Modern Competitive Analysis*, 2nd edition, Oxford University Press, New York, pp. 237–51.

Phillips, J.J. and Schmidt, L. (2011), *The Leadership Scorecard* (Improving Human Performance Series), Routledge, New York.

Russo, J. and Schoemaker, P. (1989), *Decision Traps: The Ten Barriers to Brilliant Decision-Making and How to Overcome Them*, Simon Schuster, New York.

Schwenk, C. 1985, Management illusions and biases: their impact on strategic decisions, *Long Range Planning*, 18, pp. 74–80.

Simon, H.A. (1987), Making management decisions: the role of intuition and emotion, *The Academy of Management Executive*, 1(1), pp. 57–63.

Smith, P. (2012), *Lead with a Story: A Guide to Crafting Business Narratives That Captivate, Convince, and Inspire*, Amacom, Nashville, TN.

Spender, J.C. (1989), *Industry Recipes: The Nature and Sources of Managerial Judgment*, Basil Blackwell, Oxford.

Stephens, R. (2015), *Beginning Software Engineering*, John Wiley &Sons Inc, Indanapolis, IN.

Thamhain, H.J. (2014), *Managing Technology-Based Projects: Tools, Techniques, People and Business Processes*, John Wiley & Sons, Hoboken, NJ.

Tiwary, A. Collaborative intelligence. Alinement Network, 10 May 2010 http://alinement.net/component/content/article/50?Itemid=34.

Tiwary, A. and Unhelkar, B. (2011), Extending and applying business intelligence and customer strategies for green ICT, pp. 83. Chapter 6 in B. Unhelkar (Ed.), *Handbook of Research in Green ICT: Technical, Business and Social Perspectives*, IGI Global, Hershey, PA.

Unhelkar, B. and Tiwary, A. (2010), Business intelligence 2010: Delivering the goods or standing us up?, *Collaborative Intelligence, Cutter IT Journal*, 23(6). Page 13–21

Unhelkar, B., Tiwary, A. and Ghanbary, A. (2009), Transitioning business processes to a collaborative business environment with mobility: An action research based on a service organization. Chapter 7 in B. Unhelkar (Ed.), *Handbook of Research in Mobile Business: Technical, Methodological, and Social Perspectives*, 2nd Edition. IGI Global, Hershey, PA.

Usability of metrics collection system on November 97 at Australian Software Metrics Association's, "Better Business Through Metrics" Conference in Canberra.

Van Solingen, R. and Berghout, E. (1999), *Goal/Question/Metric Method*, McGraw-Hill, New York.

Verzuh, E. (2013), *The Portable MBA in Project Management*, John Wiley & Sons, Hoboken, NJ.

White, A. and Logan, D. (2015), *Governing the Information Governance*, Gartner Inc., Stamford, CT.

Chapter 5

Analytics

Antonio Giusti, Gunter Ritter (2012), *Classification and Data Mining* (Studies in Classification, Data Analysis, and Knowledge Organization), Springer, Heidelberg, NY.

Antti Syvajarvi, Jari Stenvall (2010), *Data Mining in Public and Private Sectors: Organizational and Government Applications* (Premier Reference Source), Information Science Publishing, Hershey PA.

Gutierrez S (2014), *Data Scientists at Work*, Apress, New York.

Davy Cielen, Arno D.B. Meysman, Mohamed Ali (2016), *Introducing Data Science: Big Data, Machine Learning, and More, Using Python Tools*, Manning Publications, Shelter Island, NY.

Dean Abbott (2014), *Applied Predictive Analytics: Principles and Techniques for the Professional Data Analyst*, John Wiley & Sons, Hoboken, NJ.

Ian Gorton, Deborah K. Gracio (2012), *Data-Intensive Computing: Architectures, Algorithms, and Applications*, Cambridge University Press, Cambridge.

Michael Manoochehri (2013), *Data Just Right: Introduction to Large-Scale Data & Analytics*, (Addison-Wesley Data & Analytics Series), Wesley Addison Wesley, Upper Saddle River, NJ.

Miriah Meyer, Danyel Fisher (2016), *Making Sense of Data: Designing Effective Visualizations*, O'Reilly, Sebastopol, CA.

Pascale Zaraté (2013), *Tools for Collaborative Decision-Making* (Focus Series in Computer Engineering and IT), John Wiley & Sons, Hoboken, NJ.

Vincenzo Morabito (2015), *Big Data and Analytics: Strategic and Organizational Impacts*, Springer, New York.

Collaborative working

Bob Familiar (2015), *Microservices, IoT and Azure: Leveraging DevOps and Microservice Architecture to Deliver SaaS Solutions*, Apress, New York.

Dan Sanker (2012), *Collaborate: The Art of We*, Jossey-Bass A Wiley, San Francisco, CA.

David Archer, Alex Cameron (2009), *Collaborative Leadership: How to Succeed in an Interconnected World*, Routledge, New York.

Fatos Xhafa, Nik Bessis (Eds.) (2013), *Inter-cooperative Collective Intelligence: Techniques and Applications* (Studies in Computational Intelligence), Springer-Verlag, Berlin, Heidelberg.

G. David Garson, Mehdi Khosrow-Pour (2008), *Handbook of Research on Public Information Technology*, Information Science Publishing, Hershey PA.

Honbo Zhou (2012), *The Internet of Things in the Cloud: A Middleware Perspective*, CRC Press, Boca Raton, FL.

Kathleen M. Immordino (2009), *Organizational Assessment and Improvement in the Public Sector*, CRC Press, Boca Raton, FL.

Luis M. Camarinha-Matos, Willy Picard (2008), *Pervasive Collaborative Networks: IFIP TC 5 WG 5.5 Ninth Working Conference on Virtual Enterprises*, Springer-Verlag, Berlin, Heidelberg.

Mei Cao, Qingyu Zhang (2012), *Supply Chain Collaboration: Roles of Interorganizational Systems, Trust, and Collaborative Culture*, Springer-Verlag, Berlin, Heidelberg.

Ned Kock (2007), *E-collaboration in Modern Organizations: Initiating and Managing Distributed Projects* (Premier Reference Source), Information Science Publishing, Hershey, PA.

Patrick Van Bommel (2004), *Transformation of Knowledge, Information and Data: Theory and Applications*, Information Science Publishing, Hershey, PA.

Stefan Bente, Uwe Bombosch (2012), *Collaborative Enterprise Architecture: Enriching EA with Lean, Agile, and Enterprise 2.0 Practices*, Morgan Kaufmann Waltham, MA.

William Bratton, Zachary Tumin (2012), *Collaborate or Perish!: Reaching across Boundaries in a Networked World*, Crown, Danvers, MA.

William Y. Chang, Hosame Abu-Amara, Jessica Sanford (2010), *Transforming Enterprise Cloud Services*, Springer-Verlag, Berlin, Heidelberg.

Disruptive technology

Andrea Resmini, Luca Rosati (2011), *Pervasive Information Architecture: Designing Cross-Channel User Experiences*, Morgan and Claypool Publishers, Burlington, MA.

Jan Vom Brocke, Michael Rosemann (2014), *Handbook on Business Process Management 2: Strategic Alignment, Governance, People and Culture* (International Handbooks on Information Systems), Springer-Verlag, Berlin, Heidelberg.

Johyn Jeston, Johan Nelis (2008), *Business Process Management*, Elsevier, Burlington, MA.

Michael J. Kavis (2012), *Architecting the Cloud: Design Decisions for Cloud Computing Service Models (SaaS, PaaS, and IaaS)*, John Wiley & Sons, Hoboken, NJ.

Michael Mirabito, Barbara Morgenstern (2004), *The New Communications Technologies: Applications, Policy, and Impact*, 5th Edition, Focal Press, Burlington, MA.

Niall Cook (2008), *Enterprise 2.0*, Gower Publishing Limited, Burlington, VT.

Rodney Heisterberg, Alakh Verma (2014), *Creating Business Agility: How Convergence of Cloud, Social, Mobile, Video, and Big Data Enables Competitive Advantage*, John Wiley & Sons, Hoboken, NJ.

Chapter 6

Bakker G., Hirdes F. (1995), Recent industrial experiences with software product metrics, *Objective Software Quality: Second Symposium on Software Quality Techniques and Acquisition Criteria*, Florence, Italy, May 1995, Springer-Verlag, Berlin, pp. 16–30.

Basil V. (1995), Applying the Goal/Question/Metrics paradigm in the experience factory, in *Software Quality Assurance and Measurement*, International Thomson Publishing, Stamford, CT, pp. 23–44.

Bazzana G. (1995), Software management by metrics: practical experiences in Italy, in *Software Quality Assurance and Measurement*, International Thomson Publishing, Stamford, CT, pp. 185–193.

Bohem B. (1992), Improving software productivity, *Tutorial Software Engineering Project Management*, IEEE Computer Science Press, pp. 93–107.

Brooks F. (1979), *The Mythical Man-Month*, Addison Wesley, Upper Saddle River, NJ.

Covey S. (1989), *The 7 Habits of Highly Effective People*, Simon and Schuster, New York.

Fairley R. (1992), Risk management or software projects, *IEEE Software*, May 1995, pp. 57–67.

Fenton N., Whitty R., Yoshinori I. (1995) *Software Quality Assurance and Measurement*, International Thomson Publishing, Stamford, CT.

Ferrentino B. (1992), Making software development estimates good, in *Tutorial Software Engineering Project Management*, IEEE Computer Science Press, pp. 236–238.

Goldstein A., Hefner R. (1996), *Lessons Learned Applying Amadeus in an Industrial Environment*, TRW Report.

Grady R. (1992), *Practical Software Metrics for Project Management and Process Improvements*, Prentice Hall, Upper Saddle River, NJ.

Grady R. (1993), Practical results from measuring software quality, *Communication of the ACM* 36(11).

Hetzel B. (1993), *Making Software Measurement Work*, John Wiley & Sons, Hoboken, NJ.

Humpharies W. (1989), *Managing the Software Process*, Addison-Wesley, Boston, MA.

Ishikawa K. (1985), *What Is Total Quality Control?* Prentice Hall, Upper Saddle River, NJ.

Jones C. (1991), *Applied Software Measurements Assuring*, McGraw Hill, New York.

Jones C., Rubin H. (1996), Software assessment and bechmarks, *Software Productivity Research Publication* 6(2).

Kuntzmann-Combelle A. (1995), Quantitative approach to software process improvement, *Objective Software Quality: Second Symposium on Software Quality Techniques and Acquisition Criteria*, Florence, Italy, May 1995, Springer-Verlag, Berlin, pp. 16–30.

Kuvaja P. (1995) BOOTSTRAP: A software process assessment and improvement methodology, *Objective Software Quality: Second Symposium on Software Quality Techniques and Acquisition Criteria*, Florence, Italy, May 1995, Springer-Verlag, Berlin, pp. 31–48.

Neumann P. (1995), *Computer Related Risks*, Addison Wesley, Upper Saddle River, NJ.

Nielsen J. (1993), *Usability Engineering*, Acedemic Press.

Preece J., Sharp H., Benyon D., Holland S., Cary T. (1994), *Human Computer Interaction*, Addison Wesley, Upper Saddle River, NJ.

Ramamoorthy, P. A., Tsai W., Usuda Y. (1992), Software engineering: problems and perspective, in *Tutorial Software Engineering Project Management*, IEEE Computer Science Press, pp. 57–74.

Rubin J. (1994), *Handbook of Usability Testing*, Wiley Technical Communication.

Shepperd M., Ince D. (1993), *Derivation and Validation of Software Metrics*, Clarendon Press, Oxford.

Thayer R. (1992), Controlling a software engineering project, *Tutorial Software Engineering Project Management*, IEEE Computer Science Press, pp. 389–391.

Yourdon E. (1992), *Decline and Fall of the American Programmer*, Prentice Hall, Upper Saddle River, NJ.

Chapter 7

Alexander Borek, Ajith Kumar Parlikad, Jela Webb, Philip Woodall (2013), *Total Information Risk Management: Maximizing the Value of Data and Information Assets*, Morgan Kaufmann, Waltham, MA.

Amit Tiwary, Bhuvan Unhelkar (2010), Business intelligence 2010: Delivering the goods or standing us up?, *Collaborative Intelligence, Cutter IT Journal*, 23(6):13–21.

Amit Tiwary, Bhuvan Unhelkar (2011), Extending and applying business intelligence and customer strategies for green ICT, pp. 83, Chapter 6 in *Handbook of Research in Green ICT: Technical, Business and Social Perspectives*, Bhuvan Unhelkar (Ed.), IGI Global, Hershey, PA.

Andrew White, Debra Logan (2015), Governing the Information Governance, Gartner Inc. Stamford, CT 06902-7700 publication.

Bhuvan Unhelkar, Amit Tiwary, Abbass Ghanbary (2009), Transitioning business processes to a collaborative business environment with mobility: An action research based on a service organization, Chapter 7 in *Handbook of Research in Mobile Business: Technical, Methodological, and Social Perspectives*, 2nd Edition, Bhuvan Unhelkar (Ed.), IGI Global, Hershey, PA.

Craig S. Fleisher, Babette E. Bensoussan (2007), *Business and Competitive Analysis: Effective Application of New and Classic Methods*, FT Press, Upper Saddle River, NJ.

Evan Wheeler (2011), *Security Risk Management: Building an Information Security Risk Management Program from the Ground Up*, Syngress Publishing, Maryland Heights, MO.

Frank Buytendijk, Thomas W. Oestreich (2015), *Organizing for Big Data through Process and Governance*, Gartner Inc., Stamford, CT.

James J. DeLuccia (2008), *IT Compliance and Controls: Best Practices for Implementation*, John Wiley & Sons, Hoboken, NJ.

James Lam (2014), *Enterprise Risk Management: From Incentives to Controls*, John Wiley & Sons, Hoboken, NJ.

James Manyika, Michael Chui, Brad Brown, Jacques Bughin, Richard Dobbs, Charles Roxburgh, and Angela Hung Byers (2011): Big data—The next frontier for innovation, competition and productivity, McKinsey Report, June 2011, Retrieved August 2015.

Jie Lu, Lakhmi C. Jain, Guangquan Zhang (2012), *Handbook on Decision Making: Vol 2: Risk Management in Decision Making* (Intelligent Systems Reference Library), Springer-Verlag, Berlin, Heidelberg.

Laura P. Taylor (2013), *FISMA Compliance Handbook*, 2nd Edition, Spon Press, London.

Maria Manuela Cruz-Cunha (2010), *Social, Managerial, and Organizational Dimensions of Enterprise Information Systems, Business Science Reference*.

Martin Kleppmann (2014), *Designing Data-Intensive Applications, Early Release*, O'Reilly, Sebastopol, CA.

Michael Blyth (2009), *Business Continuity Management: Building an Effective Incident Management Plan*, John Wiley & Sons, Hoboken, NJ.

Omar K. Hussain, Tharam S. Dillon, Farookh K. Hussain, Elizabeth J. Chang (2012), *Risk Assessment and Management in the Networked Economy* (Studies in Computational Intelligence), Springer-Verlag, Berlin, Heidelberg.

P. Balasubramanian, Nalin Kulatilaka, John Storck (1998), *Managing Information Technology Investments Using a Real-Options Approach*, School of Management, Boston University, 24 June 1998.

Reuvid Jonathan (2010), *Managing Business Risk: A Practical Guide to Protecting Your Business*, Kogan Page, London.

Susan Snedaker (2013), *Business Continuity and Disaster Recovery Planning for IT Professionals*, 2nd Edition, Syngress Publishing, Maryland Heights, MO.

Terje Aven (2010), *Misconceptions of Risk*, John Wiley & Sons, Hoboken, NJ.

Tom Kendrick PMP (2015), *Identifying and Managing Project Risk: Essential Tools for Failure-Proofing Your Project*, Amacom, Nashville, TN.

Yen Yee Chong (2004), *Investment Risk Management* (The Wiley Finance Series), John Wiley & Sons, Hoboken, NJ.

Chapter 8

Alexander Osterwalder, Yves Pigneur, 2010, *Business Model Generation: A Handbook for Visionaries, Game Changers, and Challengers*, John Wiley & Sons, Hoboken, NJ.

Annabelle Gawer (Ed.), 2010, *Platforms, Markets and Innovation*, Edward Elgar Publishing, Cheltenham.

Ash Maurya, 2012, *Running Lean: Iterate from Plan A to a Plan That Works* (Lean Series), O'Reilly, Sebastopol, CA.

Bernard Burnes, 2004, *Managing Change* (4th Edition), Prentice Hall, Upper Saddle River, NJ.

Bill George, 2009, *Seven Lessons for Leading in Crisis*, Jossey-Bass.

Brad Federman, 2009, *Employee Engagement: A Roadmap for Creating Profits, Optimizing Performance, and Increasing Loyalty*, Jossey-Bass.

Carla Zilka, 2009, *Business Restructuring: An Action Template for Reducing Cost and Growing Profit*, John Wiley & Sons, Hoboken, NJ.

Christian Schuh, Alenka Triplat, Wayne Brown, Wim Plaizier, AT Kearney, Laurent Chevreux, 2014, *Corporate Plasticity: How to Change, Adapt, and Excel*, Apress, New York.

Clark A. Campbell, Mike Collins, 2010, *The One-Page Project Manager for Execution: Drive Strategy and Solve Problems with a Single Sheet of Paper*, John Wiley & Sons, Hoboken, NJ.

Dave Gray, Thomas Vander Wal, 2012, *The Connected Company*, O'Reilly, Sebastopol, CA.

David Cannon, 2011, *ITIL Service Strategy* (2011 Edition), The Stationery Office.

David Williams, Tim Parr, 2004, *Enterprise Programme Management: Delivering Value*, Palgrave Macmillan.

Fred R. David, 2010, *Strategic Management* (13th Edition), Prentice Hall, Upper Saddle River, NJ.

Indi Young, 2008, *Mental Models: Aligning Design Strategy with Human Behavior*, Rosenfeld Media.

J. Rodney Turner, 2008, *The Handbook of Project-Based Management: Leading Strategic Change in Organizations*, McGraw-Hill, New York.

James Mangraviti, Steven Babitsky, 2012, *The Street Smart MBA: 10 Proven Strategies for Driving Business Success*, Apress, New York.

Jason Wingard, 2015, *Learning to Succeed: Rethinking Corporate Education in a World of Unrelenting Change*, Amacom, Nashville, TN.

Jeff Szymanski, 2011, *The Perfectionist's Handbook: Take Risks, Invite Criticism, and Make the Most of Your Mistakes*, John Wiley & Sons, Hoboken, NJ.

Jim Collins, 2001, *Good to Great: Why Some Companies Make the Leap... and Others Don't*, Harper Perennial.

Michael Armstrong, 2006, *A Handbook of Management Techniques: A Comprehensive Guide to Achieving Managerial Excellence and Improved Decision Making*, Kogan Page, London

Milan Guenther, 2012, *Intersection: How Enterprise Design Bridges the Gap between Business, Technology, and People*, Morgan Kaufmann, Waltham, MA.

Nolberto Munier, 2011, *A Strategy for Using Multicriteria Analysis in Decision-Making: A Guide for Simple and Complex Environmental Projects*, Springer.

Paul R. Thie, Gerard E. Keough, 2008, *An Introduction to Linear Programming and Game Theory*, John Wiley & Sons, Hoboken, NJ.

Ramnath Ganesan, 2014, *The ProfiTable Supply Chain: A Practitioner's Guide*, Apress, New York.

Reuvid Jonathan, 2009, *Managing Business Risk: A Practical Guide to Protecting Your Business*, Kogan Page, London.

Roger Harri, Tom Short (Eds.), 2013, *Workforce Development: Perspectives and Issues*, Springer-Verlag, Berlin, Heidelberg.

Steven W. Michaelson, 2007, *Sun Tzu For Execution: How to Use the Art of War to Get Results*, Adams Media.

Thomas L. Wheelen, J. David Hunger, 2011, *Strategic Management and Business Policy: Toward Global Sustainability* (13th Edition), Prentice Hall, Upper Saddle River, NJ.

Thomas Pyzdek, Paul Keller, 2009, *The Six Sigma Handbook* (3rd Edition), McGraw-Hill, New York.

Timothy G. Habbershon, Maria Minniti, Mark P. Rice, Stephen Spinelli Jr., Andrew Zacharakis (Eds.), 2006, *Entrepreneurship Three Volumes: The Engine of Growth* (Praeger Perspectives) (v. 1–3), Praeger Publishers.

Tom Kendrick PMP, 2015, *Identifying and Managing Project Risk: Essential Tools for Failure-Proofing Your Project*, Amacom, Nashville, TN.

Chapter 9

Philippe Kruchten, *An Ontology of Architectural Design Decisions in Software-Intensive Systems*, University of British Columbia 2004.

Analysis Patterns: Reusable Object Models (Object-Oriented Software Engineering Series), Martin Fowler (Addison-Wesley Professional 1996).

Tom Fuller and Shawn Morgan, Data replication as an enterprise SOA antipattern, *The Architecture Journal* 8 (Microsoft Corporation 2006).

Joseph M. Juran and A. Blanton Godfrey, *Juran's Quality Handbook*, 5th Edition, McGraw-Hill, New York.

Index